Damas

Given in Memory
of

James Graham

by
Gail G. Stickley

Wayfaring STRANGERS

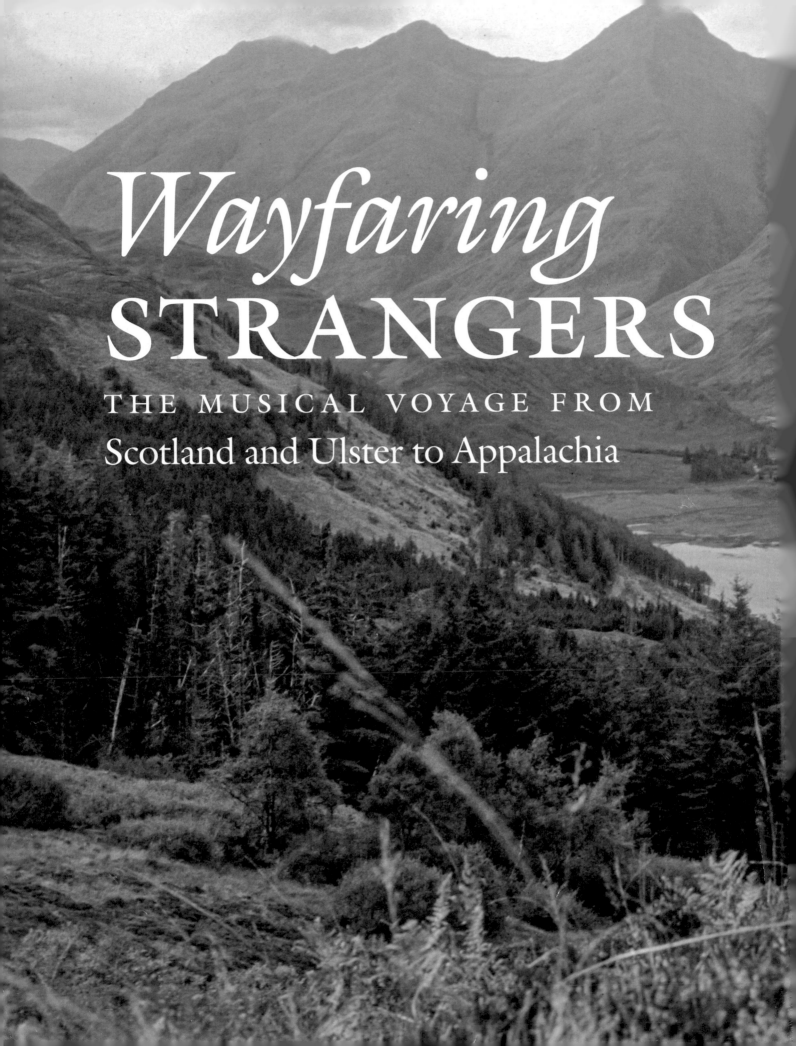

Wayfaring STRANGERS

THE MUSICAL VOYAGE FROM

Scotland and Ulster to Appalachia

Fiona Ritchie & Doug Orr

With the assistance of DARCY ORR

Foreword by DOLLY PARTON

THE UNIVERSITY OF NORTH CAROLINA PRESS   CHAPEL HILL

This book was published with the assistance of the Blythe Family Fund of the University of North Carolina Press.

Additional assistance was provided by generous gifts from:

Joel and Marla Adams
John and Annie Ager
Agua Fund
Thomas S. Kenan III
Jack and Cissie Stevens

We also wish to thank the following, who donated through power2give.org—with matching funds provided by the North Carolina Arts Council—in support of the production and inclusion of the CD:

Anonymous
Bell Family Foundation
William and Martha
  Terrell Burruss III
Bob and Sally Cone
Tom Cox
Pam Curry
Rebecca Evans
Neal and Katherine
  Forney
Estelle B. Freedman
Carole Harris
Elizabeth Harris
Joanna and Norman
  Harris
Penny Hodgson

Mary Holmes *in honor of*
  Robert G. Ray
Howard Holsenbeck
Bea Hoverstock
John and Joy Kasson
Betty Kenan
John and Missy Kuykendall
Madeline Levine
Joan Lorden
Tom and Joanna Ruth
  Marsland
D. G. and Harriet Martin
William P. Massey
William and Anne
  McLendon
Mary Beth Norton

Aidan and Joyce O'Hara
Jane McAlister Pope
Lew and Dannye Powell
James Dennis Rash
Carole Reid
John and Talia Sherer
Kevin Spall *for Thomson Shore*
Ann F. Stanford
Karl and Hollis Stauber
Richard and Jere Stevens
Suzanne Taichert
Rollie Tillman
Allen and Kate Douglas Torrey
Andrew Willard
Ed and Marylyn Williams
Jim and Martha Woodward

All interview excerpts © Fiona Ritchie Productions/ The Thistle & Shamrock®, as heard on NPR®, with the exception of Mike Seeger, "African American and European Roots of Old-Time Music" and "Impact of Radio and the Recording Industry," and Joe Thompson, "African American String Bands," which were recorded in conversation with Banning Eyre for BBC Radio 3's *World Routes*, produced by Peter Meanwell. "An Appalachian Road Trip" was first broadcast on October 17, 2009. The interviews with Doc Watson and Rhiannon Giddens/Dom Flemons were by Doug Orr.

Manufactured in Canada
The paper in this book meets the guidelines for permanence and durability of the Committee on Production Guidelines for Book Longevity of the Council on Library Resources. The University of North Carolina Press has been a member of the Green Press Initiative since 2003.

Library of Congress Cataloging-in-Publication Data
Ritchie, Fiona, 1960– author.
Wayfaring strangers : the musical voyage from Scotland and Ulster to Appalachia / Fiona Ritchie and Doug Orr with the assistance of Darcy Orr ; foreword by Dolly Parton.
  pages cm
Includes bibliographical references and index.
ISBN 978-1-4696-1822-7 (cloth : alk. paper)
ISBN 978-1-4696-1823-4 (ebook)
1. Folk music—Appalachian Region, Southern—History and criticism. 2. Folk music—Appalachian Region, Southern—Scottish influences. 3. Folk music—Appalachian Region, Southern—Irish influences. I. Orr, Doug, 1938– author. II. Parton, Dolly, writer of supplementary textual content. III. Title.
ML3551.7.A57R57 2014
781.62'13075–dc23   2014012347

18 17 16 15 14 5 4 3 2 1

Jacket illustrations: *Travelling Fiddler*, photo by Gordon Shennan, courtesy of Highland Photo Archive, Inverness Museum and Art Gallery, High Life Highland, Scotland; photo of Appalachian Mountains courtesy of Al Petteway; photo of Halaman Bay, island of Barra, Outer Hebrides, Scotland, by Jem Wilcox/LGPL/Alamy.

For

Douglas and Charlotte Orr,

Robert and Anne Ritchie, and Maurice and Sarah Williams,

who kindled the spark,

and

Colin MacGregor Abernathy, Eliza Campbell Abernathy, Quincy Scavron Orr,

Eilidh Ritchie Hodgson, and Finley Charles Ritchie Hodgson,

who will carry the flame.

Contents

Beginnings, 7

Voyage, 63

Singing a New Song, 153

Foreword

Fiona Ritchie has spent over thirty years telling the stories of Celtic music on her show broadcast over National Public Radio, *The Thistle & Shamrock*®. Rightfully, she has received numerous awards and recognition for her contributions to this music. The Smithsonian Institution Center for Folklife and Cultural Heritage has even honored her as a musical ambassador for helping listeners understand the importance of this beautiful and essential music.

This music is close to my heart and part of my DNA. My ancestors, the Partons, came from the Gloucester area of England. It also seems that other Partons may have gone to Scotland. There are various spellings, such as Partan, Parten, Partin, Partyn, and, of course, Parton. There is even an area in Kirkcudbrightshire, Scotland, called Parton. Make no mistake: the music of that area of the Old World is in my blood.

This is why Fiona's new book, *Wayfaring Strangers*, coauthored with Doug Orr, is so important to me and to anyone who loves this music. They have done an outstanding job in researching the origins of the troubadours and balladeers that created this music and spread it throughout the lands, including the United States.

I grew up in the Smoky Mountains listening to these ancient ballads that had crossed oceans and valleys to become an important basis for American folk, bluegrass, and country music.

In *Wayfaring Strangers*, Fiona and Doug have captured the stories of the people, the times, and the songs. They describe the transition in the music as it made its way across the Atlantic and through the valleys of the Appalachian Mountains. They even go into detail about the songcatchers who helped preserve these treasures of songs for future generations.

In 1994 I recorded a live album entitled *Heartsongs: Live from Home*. My coproducer, Steve Buckingham, and I wanted to show the close connection of Celtic music from Scotland, Ireland, England, and Wales with what became bluegrass, country, and old-timey mountain music. We used the finest bluegrass and acoustic musicians from the United States and combined them with one of the greatest traditional Irish groups, Altan. It was a match made in Heaven as the fiddles, guitars, and dobros interacted with the Irish "squeezebox," uilleann pipes, whistles, and bouzouki. We often found that a song known by the Irish musicians under one title would be familiar to the bluegrass musicians under another title.

One of the songs we recorded was the ancient ballad "Barbara Allen." While I sang the lyrics in English, Mairéad Ní Mhaonaigh of Altan sang the Gaelic translation (CD track 1). The combination was unbelievable.

Fiona Ritchie and Doug Orr have captured this magic in their beautiful book, *Wayfaring Strangers*—a song which, by the way, we also recorded on my live album. It just goes to show that the impact and connection of this timeless and classic music will live forever.

Well done!

Dolly Parton
NASHVILLE, TENNESSEE

Letters from Home

Dear Doug,

The fireside chats, pub planning sessions, and transatlantic trips are behind us. Now at last we are ready to embark upon our voyage through *Wayfaring Strangers*. We do not travel light: our old, vintage-leather steamer trunks are chock-full of tales, verses, illustrations, maps, and memories. Years of precious encounters with musicians and raconteurs, all sharing what they have carried in their hearts, urge us onward. The wind is in our sails. Anchors aweigh!

When we began researching this book, I found myself thinking how explorers and wayfarers have, step by muddy step, charted our march through history. Odyssey and pilgrimage have propelled us, fired our imaginations. Yet travel, especially the transatlantic crossing, has surely lost its lustre. The golden age of flight, sixty years on, has given way to today's "bus in the sky." Intercontinental airlines, so recently the glamorous preserve of an elite few, now vacuumpack their 747s with hordes of frequent flyers. What was once a great and fearsome frontier is now a high-traffic international corridor. We take off and land within six or seven hours, bridging a vast ocean we nickname "the pond."[1] Sealed away, we're blissfully blinded to the dark, unfathomed sea 30,000 feet below us. We feel neither relief nor amazement upon safe arrival where the waves meet the shore. When this journey, just a few generations on, has become a grinding routine, how can we begin to grasp the dread of an Atlantic crossing to the unknown?

Early in our research phase, we traveled together to the Ulster American Folk Park near Omagh, Northern Ireland. The outdoor "living history" museum tells the story of eighteenth- and nineteenth-century emigration to America. It was easier in that setting to disregard thoughts of today's humdrum transatlantic crossings. Standing dockside with my tickets clipped and marked "one-way," I could imagine tears clouding the moment I scanned my homeland's horizon one final time and battened down the hatches against what lay ahead.

When I was born, waves from the last emigration ships still washed the shores of my hometown. I know you have visited Greenock, the "Tail o' the Bank," where the River Clyde cuts wide and flows out into the estuary. And you will fondly remember the late Tony Cuffe singing about his fellow Greenockian, Johnny Todd: "He's ta'en a notion for to sail across the sea, / And he's left his ain dear Jeannie, weepin' on the Greenock quay." The verses remind us that, to generations of emigrants, the town's anchorage was their departure scene as they set sail for Ireland or North America. Gourock sits a little further west, at the river's coastal point, and the town was the backdrop to my childhood's dreamy setting. The Clyde was the West Coast's thoroughfare with its flotilla of "Cally Mac" ferryboats, "Clyde puffers," and paddle steamers. Like many Scottish seaside towns, Gourock's pierhead groaned under a throng of day trippers, sailing "doon the watter" from Glasgow for a summer's afternoon of sea bathing, ice cream, and variety shows. For thirty Cold War years, the Clyde resort town of Dunoon, across from us on the Cowal peninsula, provided the shore facilities for U.S. Navy Submarine Squadron 14, Atlantic Fleet. Off-duty American sailors crossed the river daily—disembarking at Gourock pier, clutching their white "Dixie cup" caps to their heads, running to catch the Glasgow train and spend their shore leave amid the city's noise and energy. Tracing the wake of their motor launches, then scanning the horizon to the

hills of Argyll, our youthful counterintelligence was one step ahead of them: we were convinced we could see directly across to the coast of America.

Majestic mountains rise from the waterfront, as the Firth of Clyde grows wider still toward the ocean and the far Hebrides. Ten miles off the Ayrshire coast sits the rounded profile of Ailsa Craig, the granite plug of an extinct volcano. Granite is harvested periodically from the islet, nicknamed "Paddy's Milestone," to craft the world's finest curling stones, but it is primarily a seabird sanctuary.[2] From Scotland, we have crossed these notoriously rough seas together, where Rathlin Island and the Northern Irish coastline are but a curling stone's throw away. Across the water, one of the world's great shoreline journeys hems the Ulster seaboard. Lapped by the North Channel waves, the Antrim Coast Road peaks at the Giant's Causeway. Tell your grandchildren this great legend surrounding its origin: the Irish giant Fionn mac Cumhaill constructed a causeway between Ireland and Scotland to meet his challenger, the Scottish giant Benandonner. Show them a photograph, and they'll ask you: "Why is there no magical bridge across the North Channel today?" You can tell them Benandonner destroyed it in fear, tricked

into believing Fionn to be the mightier giant. The tale spinners of old clearly thought of Scotland and Ireland as connected, if only in legend. For centuries, people on both sides of this stretch of open water shared legends but also, in the physical world, coastlines and climate. They harvested the same sea and land; a scant twelve miles separates Scotland's Mull of Kintyre and Ulster's Country Antrim. My ancestors would have steered their bows toward these horizons, moving freely between their rugged, wave-battered landscapes. For the coastal folk on both sides of the channel, the sea was more bridge than barrier. The invisible borders and boundaries of our modern world would be meaningless to them.

You and I have often reminisced about my first Atlantic crossing in 1980. I embarked upon a study semester in North Carolina at UNC Charlotte, where you were a vice chancellor. I don't recall our paths crossing then; my new friends were mostly students, who loved concocting and sending novel experiences my way, mostly food and drink based. They took me to all-night diners and drive-in movies, ball games and beach parties. But when several people suggested I take in the spectacle and carnival of the Grandfather Mountain Highland Games in the High Country to the northwest, I was lukewarm. Why would a Scot go to a Highland Gathering on one of her final precious weekends overseas? Give me more swimming holes and tailgate parties! That said, I went, mostly to see North Carolina's celebrated Great Smoky Mountains, and to take in the Highland Games too. I remember MacRae Meadows bursting into life the second weekend in July with the world's largest gathering of Scottish clans. The pageantry of a traditional Highland Games, the athletic events and marching pipe bands, were faithfully observed. Like the "Tartan Army," fans of the Scottish national football team, ticket holders at the games were wearing kilts of every color combination. Other adopted Highlanders bestowed American panache upon our national dress. I particularly remember some tartan trews that rightfully would have attracted a ban under the Dress Act of 1746.[3] In contrast, there I stood in a UNC Charlotte "49ers" t-shirt and cutoff jeans, thousands of miles away from home and in the sort of heat and humidity that would have caused mass panic at the Braemar Gathering in Aberdeenshire, upon which the Grandfather Mountain Games was originally based.

It was all good fun, culturally confusing I must say, and a little overwhelming. Taking a break from the crowds, I climbed a wooded hillside to perch among the mountain laurel and view the scene below. The skirl of the bagpipes drifted up from the meadow as my attention switched to a family group, sitting in the shade of the trees. They were all dressed quite poorly; the lavish costumes on parade in the field below were clearly far beyond their means. The father hushed his four young children as he operated a battered cassette tape recorder, outstretched his arm and pointed a microphone toward the pipe bands. Tears filled his eyes, and his passion moved me over and above anything on display among the costumed pageantry in the field below. With his wife and four children, he had crossed the mountains from eastern Tennessee and clambered down the hillside to take a front-row seat amid the dogwoods and the critters. This was a family of "pilgrims," the father proclaiming their heritage with great pride: "We're Scotch-Irish." It was one of the first times I had heard anyone claim this identity, except perhaps the odd student grappling with my accent and how it might relate to the distant ambiguities of his or her heritage.

So my travel year wound down, and I returned to Scotland to finish my studies. My many encounters had planted a seed, however, and it all began to affect my ear for music. I quickly became a forager (a trait we share), gathering albums from old-school record shops in Glasgow and Edinburgh to add to a growing eclectic vinyl collection. At the back of a second-hand album bin, the cover of *Earthspan* (Elektra)

by the Incredible String Band jumped out at me. Visionary music, a heralded set at the 1969 Woodstock Festival, and a famously counterculture lifestyle were hallmarks of these legendary psychedelic folkies. Here were the pioneers of World Music before such a genre had even been conceived. The standout track from *Earthspan* had the Incredible String Band romping through a hoedown arrangement of "Black Jack Davey." I remember cranking up the volume in my dorm room. It seemed to capture the spirit of some of the places I'd recently visited in my American travels, but for all I knew then, it was simply an American song; I'd heard it sung by Bob Dylan after all.

As a scholar and modern-day troubadour, Scottish multi-instrumentalist Robin Williamson knew exactly what he was doing with his Incredible String Band collaborator Mike Heron, taking a ballad that had started in Scotland and having fun with its American cousin. When we met years later in Charlotte for a radio interview, Robin told me he had played fiddle for Tom Paley of the New Lost City Ramblers on a 1963 tour across the northeastern United States. This was where he learned the "jug band and old-timey numbers" he brought into his repertoire. It was a while yet before I would appreciate the lineage of "Black Jack Davey" myself (CD tracks 7 and 8), but my ear was now attuned and my curiosity piqued during those seminal months in North Carolina.

After graduation in Scotland, I returned to live in the United States. Early on, in the summer of 1982, I embarked on a coast-to-coast camping expedition. Have I ever told you this story? On the meandering return leg eastward, with North Carolina and home a day's drive away through the Smokies, I stopped with my fellow wayfarers to pitch our well-worn tent just outside of Nashville, Tennessee. The timbre of a fiddle, drifting on the breeze to the campground, lured us to an open-air stage in a meadow nearby. We sat on the grass to hear a duo, Bashful Brother Oswald and Cousin Charlie. The crowd had thrown blankets onto the ground, relaxing in the humid air, but the tunes had such a ring of familiarity to me that I felt more inclined to dance. With Oswald's guitar, banjo, and dobro and the fiddle-mandolin mix of Charlie, the easy rhythms and pacing were the perfect accompaniment as the sun set on a warm southern evening. The melodies, however, recalled the Scottish country dance band sets that had jigged and reeled from an old valve radio in my mum's kitchen. In the United States for over a year now and a little homesick, this authentic, joyful music went directly to my heart. As you well know, Doug, Scots abroad like to sing of home or at least exchange memories and uncover any connections. As their set drew to a close, I had to find out more and approached the pair as they packed away their instruments. I wanted to tell them that I "knew" their tunes, find out where they had learned them, and maybe reminisce over some trip they must have taken to Scotland. "Honey, this is old-timey music," Brother Oswald told me warmly, "it's from right around here although maybe some of these tunes did come from your country way back." As we chatted on, something clicked into place for me that evening. Deep within me a switch was thrown, lighting up circuits of curiosity that burn brightly to this day. I've since learned that when one feels the impulse to run with an idea like this, there is no "off" switch.

By now, you will have worked out that Brother Oswald turned out to be Beecher Ray Kirby (1911–2002), a Tennessee native who grew up in the Great Smoky Mountains with his fiddle- and banjo-playing father. Kirby took up guitar and banjo, singing gospel music and playing for square dances. He popularized the resonator guitar and dobro in country music and played with Roy Acuff's Smoky Mountain Boys, along with Charlie Collins (1934–2012), whom I had also met on that warm Tennessee evening. In the months following my summer awakening to the Appalachian sound, I realized I was living in a musical heartland, surrounded by songs and tunes that had traveled many a mile, covering much the same ground as I had. But where my journey had unfolded over the past year or so, this musical migration saga spoke of centuries of displacement and detour. The more I looked, the more I found. I loved discovering later that the 1972 Nitty Gritty Dirt Band album *Will the Circle Be Unbroken* featured Kirby as a session musician on the title track, popularized by the Carter Family.

And so my appetite for authentic American music grew—rediscovering Doc Watson (already seen in Edinburgh), immersing myself in Charlotte's lively local folk music scene, getting to know Jean Ritchie on her trips to the city, playing guitar and singing in the back-porch music sessions we both enjoyed. We were fortunate: old-time fiddle and banjo, Appalachian ballads, bluegrass, and early country music were always so plentiful in the city, a musical community for generations. Before Nashville rose to prominence as the home of country music, Charlotte had been an important center for the budding genre. By the late 1930s, the city was operating as a country recording hub, and WBT, one of the oldest radio stations in the South, transmitted hours of live country music every week. Public radio came to the airwaves much later, just as I returned to live over there in 1981, and that was how our paths first crossed. I was naturally drawn to the sound of WFAE-FM, the new NPR® affiliate you helped instigate. Starting there as a volunteer, I was soon hired to promote and raise funds for the fledgling station. I introduced *The Thistle & Shamrock*® on the local airwaves in 1981 and, with the enthusiastic support of you and the station manager, debuted to an unsuspecting national audience less than two years later on June 4, 1983. From that date, I was officially in the business of sharing music from what we loosely called "Celtic" roots to public radio audiences across the United States via Public Radio International (PRI) until 1990, and since then in partnership with NPR®. A desire to get great music out there infused the show with energy, while my youthful enthusiasm disguised the inelegance of someone who was learning on the job. Along the way, I greedily fed my own appetite for all the roots music surrounding me in the South. I quickly learned, despite the historical links, that people now understood little about the music of Scotland, the rest of the British Isles, and Ireland. Listeners often wrote to say it "struck a chord within them," but the sense of how it may have contributed to an enduring cultural legacy in the United States seemed unheeded by most.

And yet what I found most tantalizing, coming from over here, was that very sense of connection. When we first heard Jean Ritchie singing "Shady Grove" at an early Charlotte Folk Society concert, she told us it was derived from the British Isles ballad "Little Matty Groves" or "Little Musgrave." So some people who were involved with this music, like you and Jean, clearly did know a great deal about its lineage (which she always cheerily validated by calling me "cousin"). Through tradition bearers like Jean and many more who swung through Charlotte on their travels, my interest grew apace. As you remember, I often arranged concerts for the radio station to feed both the public radio fund-raising coffers and my own insatiable appetite for the music, a benefit in both senses. From Charlotte, I was well placed to visit other musical landscapes and communities and met some remarkable people, key tradition bearers who linked back to an era already fading in the collective memory. They included North Carolina fiddler Tommy Jarrell (1901–85) and Kentucky coalminer balladeer Nimrod Workman (1895–1994). Before I could fully appreciate their renown, I was privileged to work with many legendary performers, both on radio and stage, and watch them enthrall their audiences. The more I heard, the more I came to feel the power of that Atlantic bridge, carrying a growing sense of the infinite richness of it all and the vibrancy of a living tradition.

Our friendship was surely forged in the realization that we were each exploring parallel pathways. Yours pulled you perennially in the opposite direction to mine, back to your ancestral home and the roots of the music you have always loved. It strikes me how much we have each maintained an immersion in this topic over many years, finding complementary ways to explore its possibilities. Notwithstanding my more recent infatuation for playing clawhammer banjo, my enduring outlet has been to create radio, both in the United States and back here in the United Kingdom. You devised and nurtured the Swannanoa Gathering. Participants from all over the world annually meet in the heart of the Appalachian summer, forging lifelong friendships in the sharing of their music. With Darcy, your wife and our *Wayfaring Strangers* art editor, you have shared a love of song making with an international cast of musicians and scholars who visit your North Carolina mountains each summer. Between the three of us, it was only a matter of time before a book began to materialize from our shared passion for the music that connects both our worlds.

"Connection": how often we use this word. It holds the promise of tangled textures below the surface, of stories to be told, of discoveries to be made. As words go, none can better clarify my motivation for collaborating on this book. For as long as I can remember, I have felt an innate attachment to homegrown music from my own Scottish corner of the world. Making my personal discovery of how it must once have traveled, and how long ago, only strengthens my connection with the United States. So with me "over here" and you "over there," it has been a pleasure to work together on *Wayfaring Strangers*. Sometimes, we seemed to have stumbled upon a half-forgotten old pathway, overgrown through the years yet needing just a little pruning to reveal its timeworn stepping-stones. Thank you, Doug, for helping to clear the trail and for trekking with me across these cherished ancestral landscapes.

Fiona Ritchie
PERTHSHIRE, SCOTLAND

Dear Fiona,

Well, our wayfarer's tale at last comes to life throughout the following pages of narrative, voices of tradition, and images. It has been a long, winding journey, for them and for us. I have often felt as if we were their fellow sojourners over past centuries and far-flung places—their seventeenth-century North Channel voyage from Scotland to Ulster; settling into a new agrarian existence across the Ulster landscape; a perilous Atlantic crossing to the port of Philadelphia and other landfalls; pushing into the Pennsylvania frontier and then down the Great Wagon Road through the Shenandoah valley and into the southern Appalachians. At each step of the way, their roving ways were sustained by music's refrains—the resinging of old ballads, the fiddle tunes that fired up the dance, and the retelling of endless stories. It has been exhilarating to be in their midst.

The seeds for our chronicle of the wayfarer's musical migration were planted long ago throughout our respective journeys. Their music legacy especially springs to life for me during each summer's Swannanoa Gathering, the traditional music workshops on the Warren Wilson College campus. It is a gathering you know well, having served often as an instructor and concert emcee during Traditional Song Week. The images are so implanted in my memory bank that they reappear throughout the year, especially when I stroll past those mountain campus settings where the summer music magic unfolds. The gathering reoccurs day and night for five music theme weeks but never grows old: a cacophony of music floats through the soft mountain air; a July moon silhouettes the surrounding mountains and provides a glow to the tightly bunched circles of musicians as they share fiddle tunes and give living voice to the ghost of old ballads, interspersed with a banter of conversation. It reminds me of a favorite quote from Irish poet and novelist Brendan Kenneally: "All songs are living ghosts that long for a living voice."[1] Meanwhile, a dance band plays in the nearby

hall as dancers glide over the floor in contra, ceili, or square-dance configurations, while the caller oversees the colorful flow. The evening music sessions carry on your Scottish tradition of the ceilidh, the "coming together" of friends and musical kindred spirits to share music, dance, conversation, and stories. I imagine that such music gatherings likely began in the recesses of ancient history. And it reminds me that our *Wayfaring Strangers* story extends back to the cottage hearth and the ceilidh sessions of Scotland, Ulster in the north of Ireland, and subsequently the log cabin firesides and front porches of the Appalachian coves. As told in the pages that follow, there was a tradition of inclusiveness for all comers in a spirit of community transcending social, economic, and cultural divides.

As I absorb the images before me through the Swannanoa Gathering's nightfall, sometimes joining one of the little groups of instrumental jam sessions or song circles, I often reflect upon my early vision for this gathering over two decades before and the fond hope for the perpetuation of the traditional music in our corner of the southern Appalachians. I'm sure you have observed a certain magic in the air as folks pull up scattered chairs or perch on the winding stone walls and form or reform the music circles. Some simply lean forward to listen. Over the years, I began to realize that there was much more going on than initially meets the eye; participants from all over the world have slipped away from the unceasing demands of their professional lives for full immersion in the workshops, concerts, and music sessions extending into these moonlit nights. Many are reconnecting with a musical soul gone dormant for years, buttressed by a spirit of egalitarianism too often lacking in other walks of life, and in the end connecting to something beyond themselves. As the great Spanish cellist Pablo Casals once said, "Music must serve a purpose, it must be a part of something larger than itself, a part of humanity."[2] In witnessing the scenes unfold over the five summer weeks,

Jam session at the Swannanoa Gathering.
(Courtesy of R. L. Geyer)

I am gratified to be a part of it all. It is an old and cherished tradition that never gets old, as gathering around the music feeds the soul. A bard of 400 years ago said as much: "If music be the food of love, play on, give me the excess of it."[3] This gift of music is especially relevant today, as we are relentlessly within arm's reach of some form of electronic gadget that short-circuits face-to-face contact and community. I hear this concern repeatedly from participants, with a wistful longing that if only the week's experience could be their "real world."

As you well know by now, the Swannanoa Gathering is one of the musical ingredients that stirred my interest in telling the story of this musical family tree. But for me, the musical journey goes back a lifetime: to a mother who placed in my hands a mail-order Sears and Roebuck Silvertone guitar; to a father who loved to express his Scottish ancestry by singing the songs of Robert Burns as well as the old Appalachian ballads. Like many others, I was profoundly impacted by the music of the 1960s, witnessing firsthand the role music played in the cause of social justice through its many musical forms and performers. An indelible childhood experience was seeing a nineteen-year-old unknown named Elvis Presley perform a revolutionary blend of music that transcended ethnic boundaries—black gospel, spirituals, country, and rhythm and blues. It was a reminder of the age-old message of the ceilidh and jam session: music can rise above the walls of prejudice. (I learned from you years later that Elvis's ancestry goes back to the cradle of Scottish balladry—Aberdeenshire and the hamlet of Lonmay—and that ancestor Andrew Presley immigrated to America in 1745.) Finally, here was a music that we teenagers could relate to with its tapestry of influences and that would impact the civil rights movement during its embryonic days.

In absorbing and playing the folk music of the 1960s, I grew curious as to the music's roots, of what old-timers in the Appalachians would describe as "way back yonder music." Well, where exactly was

way back yonder? And over what migration path? What was meant by those Child Ballads from song mistresses Joan Baez and Judy Collins? And where did those fiddle tunes with eclectic names come from? These questions lingered through college and graduate school. As you know, I wound up as a university professor and administrator at the University of North Carolina at Charlotte. In 1981 I had the opportunity to make my first crossing to Scotland to attend an international professional meeting with a faculty colleague. I eagerly anticipated the visit to my ancestral land. While we attended conferences and meetings by day, I dragged my friend to every traditional music venue, concert, and pub we could find to soak in the music of my family tree. It was like uncovering musical buried treasure. Plus, the entire ambience of Scotland filled my senses: the iconic profile of old Edinburgh; the bloomin' heather that graced the highlands and glens; the special quality of light and maritime air; the soft blending of land, sea, sky, and wind; and yes, the glow and conviviality of the music pubs. Through a dozen return visits the same sensations engulf me at my home away from home.

Little did I know at the time that you made your initial crossing the year prior but from the opposite direction, and by coincidence landed at my university as a visiting student. Then you returned the following year as a volunteer at WFAE-FM, the new university public radio station I helped launch, and in short order were elevated to the position of director of development. You requested and we encouraged your production of a local program of Celtic music titled *The Thistle & Shamrock*®. (I smile in recalling one supportive staff member who nevertheless commented, "Good luck Fiona, but with that accent you'll never make it in public radio!") Despite a lack of radio experience, you were a natural from the outset with a graceful on-the-air presence, lilting Scottish accent and impeccable ear for the music. That Scottish lilt led some listeners later to write, "Fiona, why don't you just talk for an hour, we love your voice." Two years later, we launched the program's first national broadcast and the listenership steadily expanded over the next thirty years. Many of us are proud that *The Thistle & Shamrock*® has been a resounding success story as one of the longest-running and most popular music programs in public radio history, recipient of numerous awards and accolades. I believe you would agree that the timing of the program's beginning was fortuitous, as the Celtic music renaissance was under way with a plethora of talented groups from Scotland and Ireland: Battlefield Band, the Tannahill Weavers, the Chieftains, the Bothy Band, Planxty, Boys of the Lough, and many others. Public radio was in its infancy in those euphoric days, and we were learning as we went, but it was expanding rapidly through affiliate stations and listenership. There also was a renewed interest in exploring family and ethnic roots of whatever background, a universal sentiment that persists. Folk clubs and festivals were growing on both sides of the Atlantic.

While I had a professional stake in the birth and success of your *Thistle & Shamrock*®, it was of personal interest as well. Through your efforts, I was gaining a deeper understanding of the music from the Celtic lands and the ties that bind to our Appalachians Mountains. You remember that it led several of us to begin attending a weekly folk music jam class at the local community college, and we became involved with the recently launched Charlotte Folk Music Society. It was a helpful entry into the local folk music scene and the many kindred musical spirits. A number of bands evolved out of those weekly sessions. One of our early musical forays together was a band we humorously called Highland Brew, a name we judiciously chose to revise when performing in elementary schools. Later I helped launch the band Maggie's Fancy, which featured a repertoire connecting the music of the Appalachians to Scotland and Ireland. Our eventual CD, *Glen to Grove*, emphasized the relationship with songs of shady groves and glenside tunes, and our band would sometimes travel to the mountains of southwestern Virginia to rehearse at a rustic old mountain cabin owned by my family. The legacy of the place was appropriate for our music. It was built in the early nineteenth century by the MacGrady family, Scots-Irish who had immigrated to the area. The single-room cabin and loft were home to a family of twelve, and the tombstones in a small family cemetery plot nearby gave testament to their rugged and often abbreviated lives.

Significantly, Darcy, a dulcimer-playing fellow band member, would become my wife. Once again, the music was weaving its magic in unforeseen ways. The year of our marriage, we journeyed to Nova Scotia, where the Celtic music thrives, and made an autumn 1987 visit to Scotland as part of your Thistle & Shamrock Tour. Although this was Darcy's first Scotland journey, she experienced a sensation that I also had felt during my initial visit six years earlier: "Somehow, I have been here before." I have heard others express feeling similarly.

Fiona, as we reflect upon those who preceded us and through their migrations "brought us here," there is a shared sense of getting in touch with our ancestral underpinnings. Perhaps that is one reason why traditional folk music is called the root of all our music. There is an abiding authenticity that resonates. As folklorist and musician Ron Pen is quoted later in our book: "It is the music that America comes home to."[4] It is the taproot to our family tree of songs, stories, and people. It encompasses several qualities that sustain our lives and are significant elements in weaving our *Wayfaring Strangers* tale: the music's capacity for expressing deep feelings of community, healing, sense of place, and wanderlust.

Each of these interweaving strands has been at work within traditional music's long journey from earliest origins, through Scotland and Ulster, into the southern Appalachians, and to the current day. And your and my individual journeys coalesced with the vision of this book that would chronicle the carrying stream of the music's migration. You had moved back to Scotland. There, you produced *The Thistle & Shamrock*® from a studio above the little shops in a Perthshire village on the banks of the River Tay and presented BBC programs on American roots music. Yet we continued to communicate, and there were periodic visitations across the water as the book idea persisted. I recall that the project began to crystallize during the summer of 2003 at the annual Smithsonian Folklife Festival on the National Mall in Washington, D.C. Each year, musical traditions of several regions or nations of the world are featured. That summer included Scotland and the Appalachians. Your consultancy with the Smithsonian Folklife Festival involved emceeing several of the Scottish performances, which were recorded by NPR®. Darcy and I represented the Swannanoa Gathering and some of its instructors who would be performing. Perhaps it was that combination of music traditions, highlighted in the nation's capital, that inspired our book conversations to move forward. Under the shade trees of the National Mall on a very warm summer's day, we began in earnest

to discuss our vision for a book that would relate the music's migration journey. Voices of tradition from both sides of the Atlantic, some of whom were performing that day on the National Mall, would tell the story. Much work lay ahead in the way of research, collecting, travel, interviews, transatlantic communications, and writing. It was to be a long and circuitous winding road to our final destination—this book we now hold—but sharing the story of the meandering path that transported these musical traditions, and of voices that steadily recede from our presence, has been worth all the effort. And thank goodness our indomitable, wayfaring ancestors never ceased in their roving ways, as our mutual friend and Scottish balladeer Brian McNeill expresses in the "Rovin' Dies Hard":

> I've tuned up my fiddle and I've rosined my bow
> And I've sung of the clans and the clear crystal
>   fountains
> I can tell you the road and the miles frae Dundee
> To the back of Appalachia's wild mountains.
> And when my traveling days they are over
> And the next of the rovers has come
> He'll take all my songs and he'll sing them again
> To the beat of a different drum.
> And if ever I'm asked why the Scots are beguiled
> I'll lift up my glass in a health, and I'll smile.
> And I'll tell them that fortune's dealt Scotland the
>   wildest of cards
> For the rovin' dies hard.[5]

We would be a much poorer culture had those wayfarers not persisted in gazing beyond the next horizon. So here's to their rovin' and their abiding tale, carried along the wings of a song and a tune. It has been a privilege for us to be able to share in their unfolding story.

Doug Orr
BLACK MOUNTAIN, NORTH CAROLINA

Pete Seeger with authors Fiona Ritchie and Doug Orr.
(Courtesy of Darcy Orr)

Letters from Home

Wayfaring STRANGERS

I'm just a poor wayfaring stranger,

Traveling through this world of woe.

Yet there's no sickness, toil, nor danger,

In that bright land to which I go.

—"The Wayfaring Stranger" (traditional)

> The old songs were in our heads and hearts, like breathing, and were handed
> down through the generations in a living tradition, as if they had been carried
> along in a migration stream from across the sea.
>
> —Jean Ritchie, *Singing Family of the Cumberlands*, 254

Prologue

THE CARRYING STREAM

The clamor of worldwide music media and the identity-blurring effects of globalization—each dazzles our senses in the kaleidoscope of contemporary life. It becomes harder to hear clearly the notes ringing from Jean Ritchie's "old songs," more difficult to see the light they beam into her "living tradition." We must listen and look more carefully today for her family's song stream, part of a remarkable diaspora: the great musical migration from Scotland, through Ulster, to Appalachia.

The story of our central characters unfolds over successive generations and journeys. As Scots in Ulster, then Ulster Scots in colonial America, they became known as the Scots-Irish, settling in and often moving on through Pennsylvania. Some then headed west, but many more followed the Great Wagon Road that started in Philadelphia and led them on through the Shenandoah valley of Virginia into the Carolina Piedmont and the Appalachian Mountains. Each stage of their pathway represented a life-changing and sometimes harrowing episode for the migrants.

This journey is vividly expressed in their songs: laments and emigration ballads for leaving; lively dance tunes for traveling; homesick and hopeful songs upon arrival; and finally, new songs and sounds that emerged as cherished ballads adapted to new lifestyles in an adopted land. Though these songs and the traditions that birthed them reveal many stories, here we chart their imprint along a particular route. Marking the verse and fiddle footfalls, we explore the influences they embraced and consider the lasting impact of it all on contemporary music.

In the eighteenth and nineteenth centuries, Robert Burns, Sir Walter Scott, and Francis James Child had already demonstrated the worth of collecting and cataloging music from folk traditions, preserving hundreds of ballads and songs for posterity. The musical legacy of the Scots-Irish may have been reshaped in the New World, but its heart and soul was captured by nineteenth-century collectors—the "songcatchers"—working in the more-isolated settlement areas of the southern Appalachians. At times, they followed an idealized agenda to be sure. Convinced that the remoteness of some communities had preserved a cultural purity, they took steps in their collecting to guarantee they found just that, often sidelining young, "impressionable" singers in favor of older "source" balladeers and largely overlooking any African influences on the music they uncovered. Still, their work was pioneering in its day and offers something of a guiding light to this book. The "Minstrel of the Mountains," Bascom Lamar Lunsford of Madison and Buncombe Counties in western North Carolina, was an accomplished musician who collected and preserved over 3,000 songs, tunes, square-dance calls, and stories that might otherwise have been lost to history. He held a romanticized reverence for the ancestry of the music and those who came before him, as he expressed on May 22, 1948, in the *Asheville Citizen*:

> "Yes sir," he would say, after a fiddle tune had been
> finished. "Your great-great-great-grandpappy
> might have played the same tune in the court of
> Queen Elizabeth." Then he would tell them how
> the songs and square dances came straight from
> the jigs, reels and hornpipes of Scotland, Ireland
> and England, trying to show that though the
> words had changed from country to country and

(*opposite*)
Giants' Causeway, Northern Ireland. (Courtesy of Ian MacRae Young, www.photographsofscotland.com)

I

An Appalachian farm. (Courtesy of Amy White/Al Petteway)

generation to generation, even from valley to valley in the same range of hills, the essence of the music changed not at all. It formed a link, unbroken, back through time, tying them to the past.[1]

Rooted mostly in the rolling hills of Scotland and Ireland, this music spread along the boughs and branches of a family tree of songs, reaching into the shady wooded groves of the southern Appalachians. It had flowed into the New World along what Scottish poet, songwriter, and folklorist Hamish Henderson so memorably called a "carrying stream." This current was prone to meander along its winding course, and as song collector and scholar John Moulden observed, a song might settle in a mountain hollow as "the end result of an unknown series of passages and re-passages of the Atlantic, the North Channel or the Irish Sea . . . and some versions could have started in Scotland, some in Ireland, and some could have been lurking in New England since being imported on ballad sheets."[2]

Along the way, the Scots-Irish brought their fiddles and jaw harps, adopting the lap dulcimer and, of course, carrying their cache of beloved songs. Old ballads and fiddle tunes were adapted to their new landscape. For those hardy settlers moving into the mountains, the isolated coves were a natural habitat for their evolving customs, vernacular, and music. Old World oral tradition ensured these were conscientiously handed down; New World encounters enlivened the repertoire with fresh ideas and influences. Stories and songs reflected another inheritance running through the Scots-Irish temperament: a deep longing for an old country far away across a half-forgotten sea, balanced all the while by devotion to their adopted home place in the deep recesses of the Appalachian mountain valleys. Music, as ever, provided the social fabric, creating a sense of community amid isolation and reinforcing identity. That said, while the Scots-Irish origin is clearly the dominant one, it is the braiding and weaving of European, African, and indigenous American influences that creates the unique tapestry of Appalachian music.

Extract any one of the essential threads—Scots-Irish, English, German, French, African American, Cherokee—and the pattern is lost.

> They were a man's words, a ballad of an old time
> Sung among green blades, whistled atop a hill.
> They were words lost to any page, tender and
>   fierce,
> And quiet and final, and quartered in a rhyme.
>
> This was a man's song, a ballad of ridge and
>   hound,
> Of love and loss. The words blossomed in the
>   throat.
> This was a man's singing along behind his plow
> With a bird's excellence, a man's shagbark sound.
> —*James Still, "Ballad"*[3]

Over time, details may blur and voices fade in the stories we hold and share. When our own tales pass from individual living anecdotes into collective memory, the characters, places, and distinctive voices become hazier still. Perhaps then, for some, books are primarily a place where traditions can be recorded and preserved, a repository for things "as they were." For us, however, the musical migrations described in *Wayfaring Strangers* live and breathe. They are best experienced through today's tradition bearers and the music they share. This is why it was fundamental to our book that their voices speak through its pages. They have a story to tell that illuminates the gray journals of history with a warm, living flame. You will not hear them claim that their forebears alone laid the foundation stones of country music or rock and roll, as if such clear-cut lineage can ever be established; they are simply immersed in Hamish Henderson's "carrying stream." Today's performers and raconteurs are included to highlight the sheer vibrancy, the "living tradition" of this musical culture. For this is the key to its irresistible appeal and the enduring curiosity about its history.

So *Wayfaring Strangers* features the words of revered tradition bearers who have personal stories to tell and professional insight to share. These include Appalachian singer and dulcimer player Jean Ritchie, who as a young woman visited Scotland and Ireland on a Fulbright Scholarship to trace the roots of her family's songs; Ron Pen, University of Kentucky folklorist and shape-note singer; Alan Jabbour, retired head of the Folk Life Division of the Library of Congress and a longtime fiddle player and scholar of the music; and

Sheila Kay Adams, seventh-generation Appalachian ballad singer, musician, and storyteller from North Carolina who in 2013 was recognized as a National Heritage Fellow. Members of the Seeger family share their wisdom, including Pete, the legendary folk songwriter and grassroots campaigner, and Mike, folklorist and traditional roots-music preservationist. For many years, Grammy Award–winning multi-instrumentalist and song collector David Holt partnered with Doc Watson, North Carolina's flat-picking guitar master; both add their perspectives on the music. A host of their Scottish and Irish counterparts share the view from the other shore, including Archie Fisher, Jean Redpath, John Purser, Jack Beck, Brian McNeill, Cara Dillon, John Doyle, and Len Graham.

Many of the world's cultures share the concept of diaspora as part of their national identity. By choice or coercion, their pioneering forebears endured life-changing relocations, carrying songs, dances, stories, and other priceless traditional arts to the far corners of the globe. And on it goes up to the present day. *Wayfaring Strangers* provides a metaphor, in this respect, for other musical migrations. At some point in life's journey, each of us longs to find our way back "home," and as such, this book may be a welcome companion for many a wayfarer. In this role, the following pages do not seek to offer a new angle on the historic backstory. Indeed, the Scots-Irish migration narrative has been revisited many times as a core tale of American history and culture. How it has usually been told, however, is in itself quite curious. Generations of texts on the story of the Scots-Irish begin in the early seventeenth century, yet movements of people between Scotland and Ireland can be traced back to 8000 B.C. So there really is no starting point; this is a story joined in progress. Likewise, Scots-Irish settlement in the United States is heavily chronicled as an eighteenth-century event, petering out after the American Revolution. If pinpointing a start constrains the story, setting an end point is just as unrealistic. Far from fading out in the mists of time, this narrative

Basket. (Collection of Darcy and Doug Orr; photograph courtesy of Karen Holbert)

flows on as part of an epic migration saga that saw 50 million souls cross the ocean from Europe in the nineteenth century. Emigration is a perpetual chain, each migrant adding a unique link to its infinite length. So the Scots-Irish story is, above all, part of a wider American and even human experience, and that underpins what we seek to chronicle.

To grasp the full scope of this exodus and the effects on its living musical soundtrack, we will follow a twisting trail through discrete stages of our migration story. The first stage, "Beginnings," traces the antiquity of musical traditions to troubadour and minstrel balladry and through people and regions of extraordinary musical influence in Scotland. "Voyage," the next stage, considers millennia of seafaring exchanges between Scotland and Ulster that are concentrated into a planned resettlement scheme, a catalyst for the evolving music traditions of Ulster Scots, leading to yet another epic farewell with songs of parting and emigration. Our story then follows a long and traumatic crossing of the Atlantic "Sea of Green Darkness" in the age of sail, during which the music persisted in their daily lives. Near the end of their transatlantic journey, these wayfarers must reinvent themselves and bring their music to yet another shore, a new horizon of the promised "Canaan's Land." Finally, in "Singing a New Song," we consider how these wayfarers, now at least twice transplanted, express a deep-rooted migratory nature and move on once again to meet and mingle with other cultures, shaping and enriching their music.

After you emerge from this book, resolve to lay aside the words and meet the music in person. Then you will truly grasp its timeless essence and understand very plainly that, just as there is no true starting point, this is also a story to be continued.

The lovely past was not gone, it had just been shut up inside of a song, inside of a hundred songs. I knew that no matter how far apart we might settle the world over, that we'd still be the Ritchie Family as long as we lived and sang the same old songs, and that the songs would live as long as there was a family.[4]

—*Jean Ritchie*

The ballad stories and tunes gathered up everything that came in their path—chanted recitative, dance rhythms and melodies, popular tunes circulated by broadside writers, composed tunes from the theaters, and some which have drifted in from other countries. But whatever their provenience, their treatment by oral tradition over a sufficient period of time established certain traits which gave them their peculiar flavor and that soundness which has led to their long life.

—Evelyn Kendrick Wells, *The Ballad Tree*, 275

Beginnings

The urge to tell stories, make music, and dance is woven into the very fabric of human nature. So it follows that story songs emerged many centuries ago, evolving from disparate people, across scattered communities, through historic happenings and forgotten events. Narratives and melodies may have sprung from individuals, but they certainly passed through the minds, hearts, and voices of many, reshaped and reimagined from the originals, "gathering up everything that came in their path." This act of collective creativity gave birth to new lyrics and tunes as sung stories shifted and changed, often attracting dances along the way. Rarely can we credit any one individual with the creation of what we would now term a "ballad"; indeed the vagaries of when and where they were born are part of their timeless appeal. Word-of-mouth sharing and learning was enough to drive ballads from one generation to the next before the printed word fixed their fluidity. Family, community elders, and traveling tradesfolk all fed free-flowing underground song streams, twisting and deviating along courses that were never linear nor even completely knowable. In more recent times, ballad scholars diverged on whether songs began as community efforts that were crafted collectively when groups gathered to sing and dance (the "communalists"), or whether, in their earliest versions, the songs emerged from single originators, as more scholars believe (the "individualists"). These differences apart, everyone certainly agrees that traditions of balladry have been communicated over a very long time and worked upon by a myriad of forces.

So what did they sing about, those storytelling, news-carrying, dancing music makers? Why does their art still speak to us from across the ages? All human experience found its way into songs: medieval romance, momentous events, supernatural phenomena, comedy, tragedy, criminal acts, the exploits of renegades and outlaws, the lives and times of royal families and their courts, as well as the daily trials of the common folk. The news-making stories of the day were all grist for the ballad mill, especially in the minstrel and broadside ballad tradition, but these were no daily newspaper equivalents; events that barely endured in living memory could also inspire story songs. In a disparate and largely illiterate song-making community, it seems inevitable that most ballads have anonymous creators and forgotten origins (except, perhaps, for a few early ballads written by monks or minstrels who could transcribe their works).

Where lyrics were subject to variation, as songs were passed on through the word-of-mouth learning process known as "the oral tradition," the accompanying melodies could be equally varied. To the present day, hearing the same ballad verses sung to different tunes or catching one tune associated with several ballad stories is fairly common. Balladeers of old might borrow or invent a melody that happened to fit the mood or meter of their lyrics. In time, though, many ballads did settle around the most desirable fit of lyric and tune, which doubtless contributed to their durability and popularity; people could learn, remember, sing, and share their verses. By the time ballad scholars of the eighteenth and nineteenth centuries were approaching the material, however, many of them treated ballads purely as poetry, ignoring their musical dimension and printing them in collections devoid of any tune settings. Scotland's song-collecting bard Robert Burns (1759–96) was an early exception to this standard scholarly approach in the volumes of *The Scots Musical Museum* (1787–1803), which preserved tunes and songs in equal measure. A century later, from his standpoint as a professor of English literature, the great American ballad scholar Francis James Child (1825–96) viewed ballads as poetry in his seminal work, *The English and Scottish Popular Ballads* (1882–98). It was not until the twentieth century that the approach naturally favored by Burns became the

standard one, and composers Ralph Vaughan Williams (1872–1958) and Percy Grainger (1882–1961) viewed the folk songs they collected as lyrical verses to be arranged with tunes. Between 1959 and 1972, ballad-tune scholar Bertrand Harris Bronson picked up where Child had left off: in *Traditional Tunes of the Child Ballads*, he paired each ballad with all of its known tunes, relating their history and describing the development of melody strands or "tune families."

We can easily imagine traditions of narrative songs thriving around the crackling fires of hunter-gatherers and in the smoky shelters of nomadic herders; however, the ballad genre as we know it today is really only traceable to medieval times. Francis Child's monumental collection records the oldest known ballad text as "Judas" (Child 23), dating from the thirteenth century.[1] Thereafter, many roots nourished the ballad family tree; its boughs diverged and reached up to feed a spreading canopy of branches. There were individual poet song carriers, local bards and villagers known for their singing. Courtly poets flourished among the aristocratic set of medieval Europe. Monks drew upon Latin hymns to create ballad stanzas, and their collaboration with minstrels of the day was the likely origin of the "Judas" text and song. Other songs may have been born in the chants and rhythmic patterns of dances; some could have sprung from "singing and dancing throngs." There are tantalizing echoes of this theory to be found today in corners of rural Europe, including Slovakia and the Faroe Islands, where ballads are still simultaneously danced and sung. Whatever the roots, singers most likely fused ballads from disparate origins through time, germinating new shoots from the ballad family tree.[2]

THE AGE OF THE TROUBADOURS

Trawling for ballad beginnings takes us to medieval Occitania, or the *País d' Òc* (the Oc Country). In the twelfth and thirteenth centuries, this southern region of France (largely corresponding to "le Midi" of today)

Early Music

Dr. John Purser, Scottish composer, musicologist, and music historian; interviewed in Dunkeld, Scotland, June 2011, by Fiona Ritchie as he was en route to the National Museum of Scotland after the discovery of ancient musical artifacts at High Pasture Cave on the Isle of Skye confirmed very early musical activity among western Celts.

It's absolutely astonishing. If you can imagine an underwater stream going through limestone, so it's beautifully shaped, and that people have been going down there for over 1,000 years and leaving deposits in it. And of course for a musician going down there, the acoustic is amazing. I've gone down there with Bronze Age horns, and you listen to the stream going along, and it's making all those different sounds as it's going over the smooth stone with water running over it. . . . You go down there with a Bronze Age horn and the sounds there are just wonderful.

I never guessed that there really had been musicians around there, and the proof of that came up more near the surface. They'd built a staircase down to this place, so they were going down there regularly, but they were also having regular feasts up above and big fires. Well, at the bottom of one of these fires—you can tell where it is through all the charcoal, its easily seen—at the bottom of one of these layers of charcoal, what did they find but a bridge for a stringed instrument. There's just no mistaking it; it can't be used for anything else. It's a bridge shape: it's got two legs on it, and they're flat at the base, and there are notches for the strings to sit in. It's a flat bridge, and that means it has to have been a plucked instrument. Now the exciting thing about this (exciting enough even if it had been medieval): this is two to three thousand years B.C. Two carbon dates they've got out of it now, which makes it the oldest such surviving artifact in western Europe. When you start thinking about plucked stringed instruments, you think of the Greek lyre for instance; we've got images older than this in Greece, of course, and also in Brittany, but we don't have material evidence. This is the first bit of really, really early material evidence. And these would be high-status instruments. You'd be playing your lyre or whatever it was (it's only these fragments, so we can't tell you what the shape of the instrument was, but my guess is a lyre type of instrument), this would be being played in the equivalent of a royal court and accompanied by song; a quiet instrument and very intimate.

So people would have to be listening attentively to it. You wouldn't play it outdoors. So that's a very thrilling find. There was a skull there. Whether that was being used as a sound box or was a skull of the man or woman who played it we don't know.

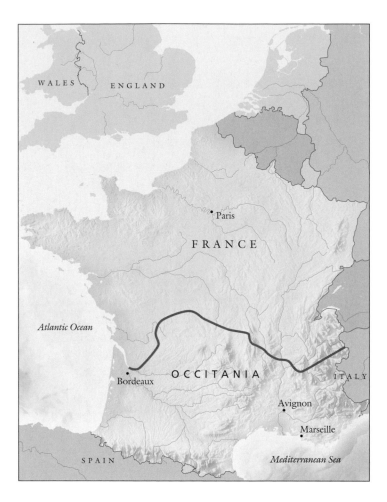

heralded a golden age of composers and performers known as "trobadors," or troubadours. These lyric poets were originally traveling musicians, emerging from the older tradition of minstrelsy as they traveled from village to village, to fairs and festivals, and to major cities and even distant destinations such as the Holy Land. In time, they began to play for royalty in the courts of lords and nobles. Some made a full-time living from composing and performing and were well educated; others were part-time amateurs. Those without independent means would try to win the patronage of the powerful and the wealthy. This elevated their status in society and ushered in a period of flowering creativity. Troubadours sang of courtly love, chivalry, and news of the day, of epoch events

and stories of far-off places. Oxford theologian C. S. Lewis is one of many scholars to credit the troubadours for being first to express fully the deepest human passions, pioneering the poetry of romantic love. They were legendary improvisers, tailoring their topics to suit each venue and audience. They reflected a spirit of high ideals, virtue, and equality and represented diverse backgrounds from a broad spectrum of society—higher and lower nobility, knights, clergy, and even landless classes. Significantly, this was not an artistic realm reserved for men; a woman could also pursue a career as a troubadour, known as a "trobairitz."[3]

Three contributors were invested in a troubadour's ballad: the composer, the scribe, and the performer. Depending on the circumstances, a single individual might be responsible for one or more of these song elements, although anonymity prevailed and author-

The Lute Player, from *Illustrated British Ballads* (1881). (Collection of Darcy and Doug Orr)

ship was usually unassigned. Troubadours operated as part of a network, enriching and expanding the treasure trove of lyric songs and stories that entered the troubadour tradition. It was not uncommon for the melody of a troubadour's composition to be sourced from elsewhere, a formula followed by the musical poet laureates of other eras and settings, from Robert Burns to Woody Guthrie and Bob Dylan.

Troubadour songs were often unaccompanied, though a variety of medieval musical instruments from European, Middle Eastern, and Asian origins also brought texture into the musical mix of the times: the lute, cittern, harp, vielle (similar to the fiddle), psaltry, hurdy-gurdy, rebec (ancestor of the violin), portative organ, tambourine, and cornemuse (a forerunner of the Scottish bagpipe).[4] How instruments featured in troubadour music is a matter of scholarly debate. Mu-

sical instruments must surely have come out to play at feasts, fairs, and festivals; stricter tempo and more volume would have been called for as social dancing grew in popularity. In any event, many of the instruments from the troubadour repertoire migrated, often in adapted forms, to far-off places. The nomadic travels of the folk-instrument family continue to this day.

The Occitanian setting for the medieval troubadour era in southern France embraced the regions of Aquitaine, Auvergne, Languedoc, Perigord, Limousin, Gascony, and Provence, even extending into the Aran valley of northeastern Spain, the northern Italian Occitan valleys, and into Monaco. The troubadours wrote and performed their verses in the romance *langue d'oc* (tongue of Oc), which emerged in Occitania after the fall of the Roman Empire. A sister language, the *langue d'oil*, became established in northern France. However

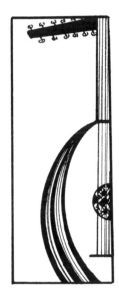

the langue d'oc, also called Old Provencal and today known as the Old Occitan language, was considered more beautiful and lyrical and, as an expressive troubadour vernacular, was favored in poetry and music throughout many parts of western Europe.[5] Troubadours also found their way into Italy, Spain, Greece, and Germany, as well as northern France, where they were known as *trouvère* and produced substantial ballad collections.

The kings of France had ruled benignly during the troubadour era, the artists of Occitania enjoying the patronage of the local nobility and a free, creative existence. Beginning in the thirteenth century, however, dark storms of change gathered over the once-tranquil landscapes of southern France. As the French monarchy strengthened its powers, along with the Roman Catholic Church, Occitania came under siege. Troubadours and their patrons were persecuted for their beliefs, terror swept through the region, and thousands were imprisoned and executed. The glorious era of the troubadour faced a traumatic end.

During the Dark Ages, when famine, crusade, and inquisition were fearful certainties, the artistic spirit of the troubadours still shone brightly, radiating through the Middle Ages. Trade and commerce no doubt facilitated the dispersal of troubadour songs and instruments to lands far from old Occitania. Just as the age of the troubadour had evolved from a minstrelsy culture, so did minstrels subsequently carry on in the custom of the troubadours. Through the ebb and flow of time, the song stream was constantly replenished and refreshed.

While much of their work was lost to the excesses of inquisition, hundreds of troubadour melodies did survive, along with over 2,000 poems. So the troubadour legacy endured and helped give birth to the ballad tradition. Ballads spread as troubadour repertoires once had done: they took their place among the nobility in their castles, palaces, and grand houses while working their way into many layers of medieval society. Elizabeth Aubrey notes that of the surviving manuscripts, some "essence" of the melodic intent of the troubadour composers can still be detected.[6] Modern-day artists perform in the troubadour tradition, while academics research and peruse ancient music manuscripts known as chansonniers (songbooks) containing troubadour lyrics, poems, and songs. These days, even the Old Occitan language is experiencing a revival.

THE MINSTRELS

Minstrelsy existed before and persisted after the troubadours. It included many forms of entertainment in addition to the music—dancing, juggling, miming, wrestling, peddling, and, most memorably in our contemporary impressions of the era, the repertoires of jesters. Not so refined and educated as the troubadours, minstrels were often all-rounders. They did, however, perpetuate the long lineage of the professional singer and performer, reciting in the narrative ballad tradition. They were drawn to audiences wherever they could be found and mingled freely with people from all walks of life—in the marketplace and the village square, along the roadside or in the castle. Sometimes they composed their own ballads and often would memorize and recite lengthy verses recounting myths and legends set in far-off lands and interwoven with tales of chivalry and heroism. Minstrels shared repertoires, harvesting material from the musical family tree, exchanging stories, and revising their settings. In terms of legacy, their most important contribution may well have been to serve as tradition bearers. They set in place a spirit of generosity that persists to this day, wherein the story is preeminent and its carriers serve primarily as vessels for its power as conveyed in a song.

Skilled minstrels were masters of improvisation. Their lyrics were memorized and the mood of the moment might color their delivery. As ballads were learned and in turn shared by oral transmission, each performance was a unique combination of the overarching ballad story or theme and the underlying ballad text. As such, innumerable ballad verses might end up servicing the "big picture" story line.[7] A creative minstrel could draw upon an array of elements to interpret the ballad story in various ways, depending on audience or circumstance. Selecting from a palette of colors to shade a musical canvas was a troubadour technique handed down over the centuries of balladeers and story makers. There is no doubt that minstrels refined this art. Commonly referred to as the "folk process" nowadays, the act of repeating and relaying by oral transmission ensured that songs remained fresh and endured through time, developing organically, free from the confines of the printed page. "A ballad in print is already dying," asserts historian Evelyn Kendrick Wells. "[I]t is no more the living organism than is a sheet of music the sound of that music. The ballad you sing from your memory and your heart is subtly changed as it passes your lips, and, paradoxically, becomes your own as it leaves you."[8]

Ballad melodies were even more prone to variations than the lyrics. There was no great resolve to fix tunes to verses, even with the advent of printing, so new melody and lyric pairings were always cropping up.[9]

The image of a minstrel as festive entertainer, adorned in bright, multicolored costume, lute slung

across the shoulder, has endured for centuries. In reality, many portable instruments were put to good use in addition to the oft-depicted lute. They included fiddle, recorder, harp, bagpipe, and all manner of percussion props. We need only pass buskers and street musicians of today—not always so brightly costumed, perhaps, but confidently ensconced on sidewalks, on pavement street corners, and in rail and subway stations—to hear echoes of the enduring traditions of minstrelsy.

Over the years, wandering minstrels took to the road and spread their song and show throughout much of Europe. They traveled well beyond the troubadour territory of southern France, extending into adjacent lands: Greece, Italy, Portugal, Denmark, England, and Scotland, where they were welcomed into royal courts.

Minstrel performances had reached their peak by the fifteenth century. As the Middle Ages drew to an end and social change followed, their vagabond existence was curtailed. Their freelancing lifestyles, deemed disorderly, were brought under the control of guilds created in fourteenth-century Paris and fifteenth-century England. All minstrels were required to register and join the guild or give up their craft. There followed a steady decline in minstrelsy, and the practice was legislated out of official existence in England during the reign of Elizabeth I. A gradual decline followed throughout Europe, and they had generally disappeared by 1700, although a few did persevere here and there.[10] Nevertheless, as we will see, the legacy of the ballad-sharing and storytelling lifestyle became indelibly imprinted in our imaginations, transcending time and territory.

The epoch of the minstrels was over. Its principal characters had served in royal courts; all too soon they were relegated to leading roles in the woodcut illustrations of history books.

THE BROADSIDE BALLAD ERA

Within the "carrying stream" of balladry, the broadside ballad stands as a direct descendant of the minstrel tradition. Broadsides flourished from about the mid-sixteenth century to the early eighteenth century.[11] Minstrels had been known, on occasion, to post handwritten ballads or news; however, as printing became accessible and affordable, the work of composers, tavern poets, and news couriers could be more effectively distributed on printed sheets. When broadside writers came along, they were actively interested in the news of the day, as well as in storytelling. Their broadsides, also known as broadsheets, broadslips, stall ballads, roadsheets, and even "come all ye ballads," were sold for as little as a penny on city streets, in villages, or at fairs. Sometimes, the sheets would be folded lengthwise to make what were called chapbooks. The term "chapmen," once a general name for hawkers and itinerant dealers, came to refer to chapbook sellers, mentioned in the opening scene of the Robert Burns

narrative poem "Tam o' Shanter": "When chapman billies leave the street." Their wares were most widely distributed in England, Scotland, Ireland, Holland, Germany, France, Italy, Spain, and subsequently in the American colonies.

Broadsides were hugely popular. Politics, religion, public events, stories of romance and adventure, and even drinking songs were all on the agenda. Broadsheet sellers had inherited the dramatic flair of the earlier minstrels. They blended truth with rumor, used biting satire and often sang the message to a suitable melody from their woodcut-illustrated sheets. The broadside writer-balladeer "might report a shooting match in Yorkshire, or a murder in Wiltshire, or a sea serpent off Dungeness, or an attempt to poison the boy King James VI in Scotland, or a 'daungerous shooting of the gunne' at Elizabeth's court."[12] With their emphasis on news and gossip, the broadsides did not have the epic and artistic qualities of their forerunners, the traditional ballads created by troubadours and minstrels, which conveyed greater mystery, drama, and suspense and included more tales from antiquity. The lyrical qualities of refrain and repetition were largely absent from broadsides. These were commercial efforts. Where ballad composers and performers were downplayed in the troubadour and minstrel eras, the author and audience were now paramount.[13]

Broadside ballads thus became some of the most printed material of their day; huge quantities were produced, several hundred thousand annually in England alone. Although broadsides were most commonly created and circulated in the towns and villages, posted on walls or in stalls (hence "stall ballads"), they did travel considerably. Broadside peddlers would roam through the rural landscape, singing from their broadsheets and bringing news and stories to more-isolated communities. By early 1700, further advances in printing technology allowed for the production of news books rather than one-sheet broadsides. They nevertheless remained popular throughout the eighteenth century in Ireland, where spontaneous and expressive public

BALLAD TYPES

A ballad is a narrative poem that tells a story meant to be sung. The word comes from the Italian and old Latin word *ballare* ("to dance"), as medieval ballads often provided musical accompaniment to dancing. Its form varies, but the four-line stanza, or quatrain, was most common. First popularized by the minstrels and troubadours of the Middle Ages, balladry over the centuries evolved into three general types with a limitless range of subjects.

Traditional Folk Ballads. These were the earliest ballad forms. The author was usually anonymous, and the ballads were passed on in an oral tradition from generation to generation and region to region. They evolved in an illiterate or semiliterate society and consequently changed greatly from singer to singer over time and place. The folk ballads usually told a dramatic story in a straightforward manner with an economy of words. The preservation of old ballads was enhanced with the advent of collectors. One of the earliest was England's Samuel Pepys (1633–1703), and thereafter came Scotland's Anna Gordon ("Mrs. Brown"), Robert Burns, and Sir Walter Scott. Harvard University professor Francis James Child compiled his famous collection of 305 numbered folk ballads, published as *The English and Scottish Popular Ballads* between 1882 and 1898.

Broadside Ballads. These were the newspapers of the day, an early product of the printing press. Also known as broadsheets, street ballads, stall ballads, and slip songs, they were printed on sheets the size of handbills and often included a rough woodcut illustration. The lyric sheets seldom included music notation, so the "balladmonger" (seller) would sing the lyrics to a familiar melody. The broadsides were adapted from folk balladry and minstrelsy to sensationalize public events, from births to battles and scandals. They were popular from the sixteenth century into the nineteenth century, when they were supplanted by advanced printing technology that produced the modern newspaper.

Literary Ballads. Intellectuals and a growing upper class fostered interest in the literary, or lyrical, ballad beginning in the latter part of the eighteenth century. Closely aligned with poetic forms, the literary ballad covered the breadth of societal and economic classes but brought forth highly literate figures, such as Scotland's Robert Burns and Sir Walter Scott and England's William Wordsworth and Samuel Coleridge, as composers as well as collectors. An example is the Coleridge lyrical ballad *The Rime of the Ancient Mariner*.

Within the three ballad categories, the whole range of human activity was fertile ballad subject matter: romance, death, religion, humor, historic events, occupations, disasters, outlaws, nautical lifestyles, and the supernatural. Other ballad categories included the Robin Hood ballads about the legendary English hero of Sherwood Forest, the Border Raid Ballads of the Scottish Border reivers, and the Bothy ballads depicting farm life, usually in the North East of Scotland. North American ballad traditions not only drew heavily on those from Europe but also added their own themes of regional relevance: cowboys, Native Americans, frontier lawlessness, and blues.

singing was always encouraged, and in the American colonies, where broadsides might bring the latest news from the Revolutionary War.[14]

Few of the more flimsy and newsy broadsheets have survived the passage of time; the ones more crafted around the character of traditional ballads have endured. A number of ballads in the Francis Child collection, compiled in the nineteenth century, including most of the Robin Hood ballads, originated as broadsides.[15] Other collections also had a broadside input, including *The Scots Musical Museum, 1787–1803,* compiled by Robert Burns, and Sir Walter Scott's *Minstrelsy of the Scottish Border, 1802–1803.* Many broadsides were sold in the numerous small poet box shops in Scottish cities and towns. As a result, Scottish university and city libraries, including Edinburgh's National Library of Scotland, have sizeable broadside collections. So in spite of their tabloid nature, the ubiquitous broadsides provide an intimate and personal insight into the cultural concerns of their time. Although sometimes sensational, they helped to sustain the historic ballad tradition, including preserving versions of older ballads that may otherwise have been forgotten.

BALLADRY TRAVELS

Carried by troubadours, minstrels, and broadside peddlers, ballads meandered along back roads and navigated nautical miles. The oral tradition—sharing and learning by word of mouth—meant that many songs, stories, and melodies drifted away on the winds of time. Some did survive, however, often as fragments; others were occasionally preserved in history's recesses in what musicologist John Purser, quoting Bertrand Bronson, called "a whisper of the Middle Ages."[16] It has been estimated that over 300 Scottish and English folk ballads dating from the twelfth century to the sixteenth century still survive, at least in some form.[17]

The surviving material had staying power. Quite simply, they were great stories: long-form narratives

with archetypes, moral messages, and psychological drama. Tied to the reins of tradition, they were braided, through time, with the strands of new voices and new settings. Ballads were pulled this way and that by local customs and localities, so their pathways were crooked and undulating, exploring side roads and detours along the journey. The best traveled may be the Scottish ballad "Barbara Allen" (Child 84), which has shape-shifted through 198 versions, accompanied by melodies belonging to three tune families.[18] It tells the story of a pair of doomed lovers, Fair Margaret and Sweet William. From their graves a briar and a rose grew, entangling and twisting together for all time. Samuel Pepys speaks of the ballad in his diary entry of January 2, 1665, where he refers to the "little Scotch song of Barbary Allen."[19] No ballad illustrates more clearly the song journey through centuries. It crossed the Atlantic with the earliest emigrants and was first printed in the United States in 1836. It was long established and thus best placed for wider renown from the dawn of the recording age. Bob Dylan recorded it on *Live at the Gaslight* (1962) when he was still mostly unknown outside Greenwich Village, performing the ballad in the early days of his "Never Ending Tour." "Barbara Allen" traveled from her homeland over four centuries ago and has been singing her way into hearts and memories ever since. Who could be immune to the pathos of the opening stanzas, and the unfolding tragedy of two lovers, apparently doomed by a misunderstanding?

> All in the merry month of May
> When flowers they were bloomin',
> Young William on his death-bed lay
> For the love of Barbara Allen.
>
> Slowly, slowly she got up,
> And slowly she went nigh him,
> And all she said when she got there,
> "Young man, I think you're dying."

"O yes, I'm sick and very low,
  And death is on me dwellin',
  No better shall I ever be
  If I don't get Barbara Allen."

"Don't you remember the other day
  When you were in the tavern,
  You toasted all the ladies there
  And slighted Barbara Allen?"

Hurt feelings unresolved, their broken hearts prove fatal:

"O mother, mother make my bed,
  O make it long and narrow,
  Sweet William died for me today,
  I'll die for him tomorrow."

They buried Willie in the old church yard,
And Barbara there anigh him,
And out of his grave grew a red, red rose,
And out of hers, a briar.

They grew and grew in the old churchyard,
Till they couldn't grow no higher,
They lapped and tied in a true lover's knot.
The rose ran 'round the briar. (CD TRACK I)

Discovering Ballads

Jean Redpath, Scottish singer and educator; interviewed in Elie, Scotland, November 2011, by Fiona Ritchie at the singer's home.

Hamish Henderson, who was friend and mentor for many years, came to the Literary Society when I was a student and did a talk on traditional song. He played a tape of Jeannie Robertson singing "The Overgate." And there was epiphany for me because I had a song very like it in a different tune, from my mother, and bubbled up to him saying, "Oh, I know that." And I teased him for years and never forgave him; his response was, "My that's an interesting variant." You know, I had just made this world shaking, life-changing discovery, and what did he call it? "An interesting variant." Anyway, it didn't put me off my stride, and that was the beginning of it, and since then I have become a slightly more organized (not terribly) and a good deal further traveled and gone full circle back to Artist in Residence at the School of Scottish Studies. Some people manage to graduate in four years; it's taken me fifty.

CELTS, PICTS, GAELS, BRITONS, AND VIKINGS

Somewhere between 800 and 600 B.C., in the European mainland north of the Alps, tribal groups emerged whom the Greeks called "Keltoi."[1] The earliest known use of the word "Celts" was by the Greek geographer Hecataeus of Miletus in 517 B.C., and at one time, much of Europe was home to these tribal societies. The Roman Empire and other invaders eventually overwhelmed much of the continental Celtic world, pushing its tribes through waves of migration into the western extremities of Europe, where their influence remains. Today, there are seven areas often referred to as the so-called Celtic nations.: Ireland, Scotland, and the Isle of Man (the Gaels); Wales, Cornwall, and Brittany (the Brythonic Celts); and Galicia in northwestern Spain. Not surprisingly, the idea of a Celtic legacy is strongest in the windswept western outposts of these regions, and each has its distinct language, dialect, and customs, including songs and musical instruments. Ancient Celtic art was also distinctive, characterized by interlacing spirals, intricate patterns, and vivid colors. The Celtic cross and tree of life designs reflected a particular spirituality that was absorbed into early Celtic Christianity. Storytellers, singers, and bards were highly valued, with music being fundamental to community and society. Yet for all these apparently unifying characteristics, the idea that Celts were a race seems to have been a Roman idea, and being "Celtic" was probably more a cultural rather than ethnic identity. In the British Isles and Ireland, it was only after 1700 that anyone referred to himself or herself as "Celtic."[2] Any Highlander tending his croft or fishing around the coast of Scotland in the fifteenth century would have been bewildered if someone had called him a "Celt."[3] Indeed, archae-ologists today challenge the orthodox identity of Celts in Britain and Ireland in light of their research into early Atlantic peoples.[4] The early indigenous peoples of the British and Irish archipelago were largely of local Bronze Age origins. It is now generally accepted, contrary to the modern construct of mass Celtic migration, that Britain had been receiving Celtic peoples in small tribal bands for centuries.[5] They imported crop rotation and land-management techniques and introduced precision instruments. Julius Caesar certainly wrote that British groups he encountered from his first attempted landings in 55 B.C. considered themselves indigenous people.[6] It all has interesting implications for any presumptions about ancient underpinnings for the present-day notion of "Celtic music."

As the last Ice Age receded about 10,000 years ago, sea levels rose, and island Britain emerged separated from mainland Europe and Ireland. It is thought that hunter-gatherers migrated from the land we now recognize as Scotland to the island of Ireland some 8,000 years ago. The "Scots" of antiquity were born in coastal migrations in later millennia; sea-trading Gaels crossed from modern-day Ulster to the west coast of modern Scotland around 350 A.D., and Gaelic settlements began in earnest within a century (the Romans called them "Scotti," or "raiders"). They began to control western coasts and pushed inland to seize lands from the Picts. These indigenous tribes of eastern and northern Scotland, whose Celtic language appears to have been akin to old Welsh, were already conducting guerrilla warfare against the Roman conquerors of the lands to the south, the territory of the Britons.

By the middle of the eighth century, the Picts were

the dominant kingdom in modern-day Scotland, with the Gaels establishing their western stronghold around an emerging seat of power and influence: the spiritual center of the Celtic church at Iona. Gaels had been converting to Christianity for generations and were slowly spreading their religion to the pagan Picts. Then, from across the northern seas, came an abrupt and deadly threat to Picts, Gaels, and Britons alike. The Vikings were putting entire communities to the sword, and when they killed the Pictish king in 839, a Gael with Pictish royal blood stepped up and attempted to unite and rule the kingdoms. It was not until Kenneth MacAlpin's grandson ascended as King Constantine that the Brythonic Pictish language was consciously sidelined and Gaelic became the dominant tongue of the united nation. The Picts were remarkable and accomplished artists who have left beautiful and mysterious carved stones across their kingdom. The earliest image of a small harp was hewn into stone by an eighth-century Pictish artist. But writing was the magical craft practiced in the missions of the monks and scribes of the early Celtic church, and the Gaels wielded the power of the written record. So Gaelic ways—language, religion, poetry, and music—found permanence. Eventually, even the marauding Vikings were repelled, and the country we know as Scotland was forged in the struggle of those early migrations. This national birth also marks a cultural point of origin as the very deepest root of the music we will follow back through Ireland and beyond to the New World.

The political and economic domination of the English language through the centuries, along with emigration from the so-called Celtic heartlands, caused the ancient tongues to fade in use. However, in recent decades there has been a resurgence of interest in the Celtic languages, including efforts by the Scottish, Irish, and Welsh governments to embed linguistic and cultural programs in state education. Six living Celtic languages remain today, and a solid population of native speakers sustains four of these: the Goidelic tongues of Irish and Scottish Gaelic and the Brythonic tongues of Welsh and Breton. (Cornish and Manx, with no native-born speakers today, are each experiencing a contemporary cultural revival.) A traditional arts renaissance has been building momentum since the 1970s. Contemporary Scottish, Irish, Breton, and Welsh singers and instrumentalists, often broadly labeled "Celtic," reaffirm their reverence for the past standard bearers—fiddlers, pipers, harpers, flutists, singers, and storytellers. It is a musical resurgence also at work in Europe and North America, challenged all the while by the unrelenting forces of a technological age.

1. Simon James, *The Atlantic Celts: Ancient People or Modern Invention?* (London: British Museum Press, 1999), 26.

2. Ibid., 17.

3. Ibid.

4. Stuart McHardy, *A New History of the Picts* (Edinburgh: Luath Press, 2010), 21.

5. James, *The Atlantic Celts*, 40.

6. Fiona Ritchie, *The NPR Curious Listener's Guide to Celtic Music* (New York: Berkley Publishing Group, 2004), 12.

The enduring power of this tragic tale lies in its sad tenderness, and the image of the graveyard lover's knot. Ballad traditions like this traveled through the continent of Europe, from Russia to Spain. Many versions took root as they crossed the waters around Scotland, England and Ireland. As Scottish musician, scholar and broadcaster Jack Beck has noted, they often spread "via the lips and ears of sailors and merchants."[20]

Archaeologists and geographers continue to uncover evidence dating transoceanic links between lands and their peoples further back into history than had previously been imagined, let alone documented. Irish author and filmmaker Bob Quinn suggests in *The Atlantean Irish: Ireland's Oriental and Maritime Heritage* that far from being a remote outpost at the northwestern edge of Europe, Ireland experienced frequent early contact by sea with Spain, other Atlantic seaboard countries, North Africa, and even east across the Mediterranean Sea to the near Orient. He observed that, despite distance and linguistic and religious differences, Catholic Ireland and Spain have long been firm allies, and their mutual relationship to the sea was common ground for cross-cultural exchange. It is an alliance marked by the Spanish arch in Galway celebrating the long commercial trade between the two countries. The ancient "sean-nós" (old-style) singing tradition practiced in Connemara and elsewhere on the maritime western flank of Ireland is an unaccompanied solo singing style with subtle vocal decorations and extended story lines. It is very different from the drawing-room singing style of Ireland's grand noble houses, or indeed the street songs of Dublin. Quinn maintains that these ancient songs and singing styles employ complex phrasing and grace notes, which recall the Arabic singing of Bedouins. The similarities in narrative epics and endless stanzas are, according to Quinn, "uncanny." In 1588 the Spanish Armada fleet met with catastrophe along the western Irish coastline when between seventeen and twenty-four galleons in all were shipwrecked. Many survivors were

put to death, while others fled to Scotland. Around a hundred sailors are thought to have remained in Ireland. Could the traditional Connemara dance form of "battering," closely resembling Spanish flamenco, be a legacy of such events?[21]

Quinn's ideas are not without controversy, and, as most early contacts between disconnected cultures are difficult to prove, they are by nature speculative. He does remind us, however, that Ireland's perceived remoteness to the modern map reader's eye is probably misconstrued. Seafaring lanes positioned it well within the flow of vessels from the Baltic Sea, along Atlantic coasts, and extending to the Straits of Gibraltar and the ancient ports of the Mediterranean. The contacts between the European mainland and the Atlantic archipelago of Ireland and the British Isles, such as the early Celtic arrivals from 300 B.C., layered deep influences on Irish customs and music, described by Quinn as a "tightly knitted garment of Irish culture that has loose threads." According to Quinn, he has "spent many years tugging at these loose threads, with the usual consequences: the garment when unraveled is less a seamless jersey of pure 'Celtic' weave than a more interesting coat of many colors."[22] This is perhaps the key message to take from the theories of the Atlantean Irish and one to bear in mind when examining the multifaceted music of Ireland and Scotland.

BALLADRY AND THE SCOTTISH COURT

How do the ballad trails lead to Scotland, at the far northwestern fringes of Europe? During the Middle Ages, the music of the troubadours had an influence in other lands, especially in the royal courts of Europe. Their old Occitan language, with its beautiful and melodic cadences, was the courtly language of many European palaces and one of the languages at the royal court of Scotland. Indeed, Scotland always had strong connections with the European mainland, and especially with France. In 1295–96 the two countries signed a treaty, "The Auld Alliance," to curtail the po-

THE MOTHER TONGUE

Scotland has three native languages: English; Gaelic, a Celtic language related to Irish; and Scots, a dialect blending expressions from Old English, French, Gaelic, and Norse with indigenous words.

Like Irish, Scottish Gaelic is a Goidelic, or Q-Celtic, language, and its speakers suffered tremendous intolerance for centuries. Until recent decades, the use of Gaelic in schools was not encouraged even among native speakers in the Highlands and Islands. As a result, Gaelic is the mother tongue of less than 2 percent of Scots today.[1] Thankfully, the urge to save Gaelic is now tangible across the country, and a large majority of nonspeakers strongly believe the language should be preserved and promoted as a matter of urgency. Immersion courses in the language are being taught, even at the preschool level. Most native Gaelic speakers live in the western Highlands and especially in the islands of the inner and Outer Hebrides, scattered in the Atlantic off the northwestern Scottish mainland.

Many people believe that Scots, which emerged almost a thousand years ago, is such a rich mode of expression that it should be considered a distinct language rather than a dialect of English. Whether the "lallans" of the Lowlands or the "doric" of the North East, Scots is alive and well in many parts of the country. Its lack of status meant it never suffered the legislated persecution endured by Gaelic, yet neither has it enjoyed much in the way of formal support, as Gaelic now does. Nevertheless, many new songs and poetry written in Scots contribute to this living language and build upon a heritage dating back to medieval times.

Speakers of broad Scots have often been disparaged in a way later experienced by Appalachian people, whose dialect reveals many connections with old Scots. Words like "pooch" for pouch; "cloot" for cloth or clothing; "ingerns" (Appalachian) or "inguns" (Scots) for onions; and "fornenst," meaning "next to," have all traveled from Scotland to hide in the hollers (hollows) of the southern Mountains.

1. Scotland's Census 2001, Gaelic Report, General Register Office.

litical and military influence of England. The two royal courts were closely connected and the benefits were more than purely diplomatic, with the French awarding honors and power to Scottish nobility. Between 1419 and 1424, 15,000 Scots traveled to France to unite with their French allies against the English, and they supported Joan of Arc in her campaign to break the English siege of Orleans in 1428.[23] Many formed the "Garde d'Ecossais" bodyguard of the French kings and enjoyed influence and power at the heart of French politics. There is no evidence that "The Auld Alliance" was ever formally dissolved, and, according to histo-rian Dr. Siobhan Talbott, this would make it the most enduring international treaty in the world today.[24]

King James IV (1473–1513) and his son James V (1512–42) of Scotland were enthusiastic patrons of music and the arts, including the literary figures of their time. During their reigns, they ushered in the Renaissance in Scotland. Their courts marked high points in cultural patronage, including elevation of "Makars," or court bards and poets, such as William Dunbar. James V would certainly have been familiar with the troubadour ballads in the original Occitan language, which he spoke along with Scots, Latin, French, and Danish.

He was the last Scottish monarch also to speak Gaelic, the language of the Scots Gaels. James was nicknamed "King of the Commons" and was fond of wandering the back roads of Scotland disguised as a jocular commoner, the "Gudeman of Ballangeich" (husband or master of Ballengeich, which is still a road at the foot of Stirling Castle rock, seat of the royal Stewart court). In disguise among the peasantry, he chatted by their hearths, studied their ways, and passed himself off as a "gaberlunzie man," or wandering minstrel. James V was a poet of rare ability, writing in Occitan and Scots and composing a heroic poem on the rural dances of Falkirk, although no written copies survive today. According to tradition, his ballads include "The Jolly Beggar" (also known as "The Beggarman" and the "Gaberlunzie Man," a variant of Child 279). The story, perhaps autobiographical, tells of a noble lord disguised as a commoner and quickly sets the scene for the unfolding amorous adventure. (James fathered a number of illegitimate children before making two royal marriages.)

There was a jolly beggar, and a-begging he was
    bound
And he took up his quarters into a land'art town,
And we'll gang nae mair a roving
Sae late into the night,
And we'll gang nae mair a roving,
Let the moon shine ne'er sae bright,
And we'll gang nae mair a roving.

He wad neither ly in barn, nor yet wad he in byre,
But in ahint the ha' door, or else afore the fire.

Up raise the goodman's dochter, and for to bar
    the door,
And there she saw the beggar standin' i' the floor.

He took the lassie in his arms, and to the bed he
    ran,
"O hooly, hooly wi' me Sir, ye'll waken our
    goodman."

King James V also played the lute and loved to sing, populating his royal Renaissance court at Stirling Castle with bands of musicians, poets, and artists. In 1538 he took Mary of Guise, widow of the French Duke of Longueville, as his queen. Their daughter and only surviving heir, also Mary, was born in 1542. Crowned Queen of Scots as a baby, she was shipped to safety in France at age four, King Henry of France having sent his own royal galley for her secure passage. Once there and at home with the French royal family, she was betrothed to Francis, the dauphin, and ascended to the French throne by his side in 1559 at the age of sixteen. King Francis II died in 1560, and the young widow returned to Scotland the following year. In the first years of her life in Scotland, Queen Mary attempted to recreate some of the aspects of the French court at Holyrood Palace in Edinburgh. She played the lute, was a fine singer and dancer, and her inner circle of valets were each chosen for their musical ability. In 1561 she employed five viola players and three players of the lute, along with bedchamber valets who could also sing.[25] Her doomed personal secretary, David Rizzio (1533–66), was a talented musician from the Italian/French border country. Before Rizzio's murder at the hands of Mary's husband, Lord Darnley, and Darnley's friends, he would surely have regaled the queen with songs and stories of the old troubadours.

Scotland was a thriving center for the arts in the days of the Stewart kings and even during the turbulent and tragic reign of Mary, Queen of Scots, for whom music was a lifeline during her long years of imprisonment. Mary's story still features significantly in folk song. Her prophetic words of farewell as she set sail for Scotland, uttered over and over from the deck of her galley in 1561, have inspired four centuries' worth of poetry and song: "*Adieu France! Adieu donc ma chère France. . . . Je pense ne vous revoir jamais plus*" ("Farewell my dear France, I think I will never see you again").[26] Elizabeth I of England signed a warrant for Mary's execution in 1587, but her death did not impede the birthright she had fought to fulfill: Mary's son, James VI of Scotland, became King James I of England and Ireland upon the death of Elizabeth in 1603. This Union of Crowns was reinforced a century later in 1707, when formal acts of parliamentary union were signed and the Kingdom of Great Britain was born. The succession of James VI and I marks, as we will see, the most critical era in our musical migration story: during his long reign, James oversaw the beginning of the Plantation of Ulster and British colonization of the Americas.

ABERDEENSHIRE
Cradle of Scottish Balladry

> The first time I heard folk music that really made the hairs on the back of my neck stand up, I remember that feeling. It's a kind of Scottish ballad and a sensibility of grieving, mourning. I know what that is. That's in my bones. We make an emotional, spiritual connection and it means something to us.
> —*Annie Lennox, singer, songwriter, political activist, and philanthropist, born in Aberdeen, 1954*[27]

Any traveler to the British Isles and Ireland cannot fail to notice, but can easily fail to comprehend, the rich variety of spoken languages, dialects, and accents—a verbal embroidery spread across the rural and urban landscapes. Scottish and English balladry likewise has many regional traditions; the English West Country and Northumbria; the Scottish Border Country and the Lowlands, including the cities of Glasgow and Edinburgh; and the Scottish Highlands and Islands

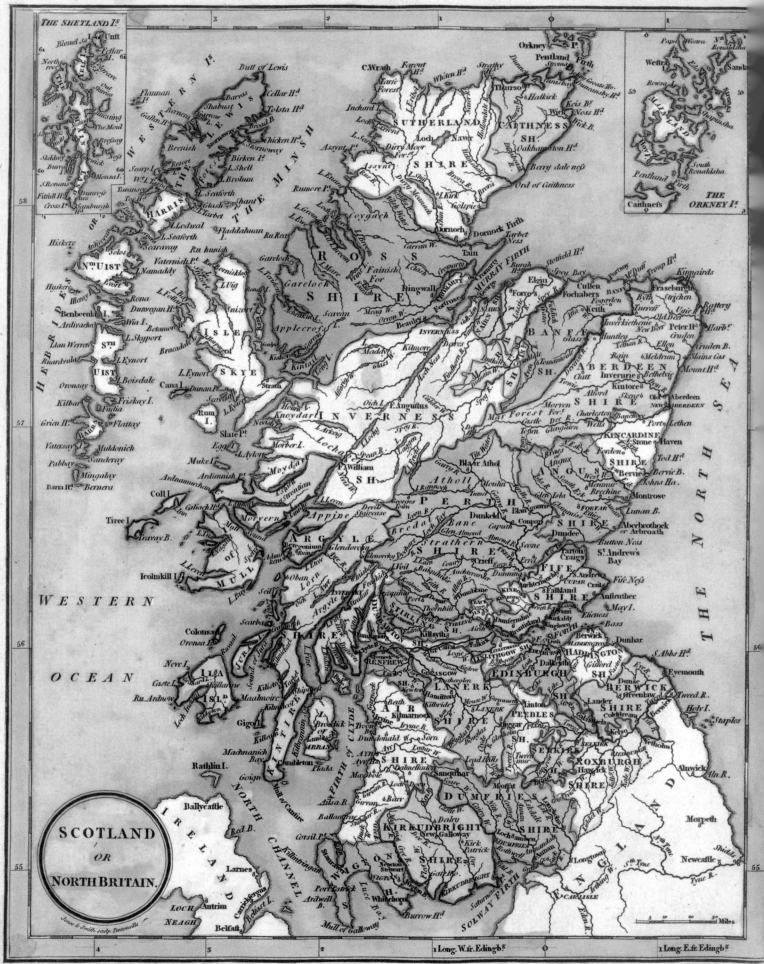

THE SHETLAND Is.

THE ORKNEY Is.

SCOTLAND OR NORTH BRITAIN.

THE NORTH SEA

WESTERN OCEAN

IRELAND

ENGLAND

Published 1st October 1801 by Robt. Laurie & Jas. Whittle 53 Fleet Street London.

each have their song traditions. Among them all, the most fertile ground in the early development of Scottish ballads was undoubtedly the North East region of Aberdeenshire. Today, this corner of Scotland, with the North Sea port of Aberdeen at its center, is especially known for its historic university and the North Sea oil and gas industry; the "Granite City," once primarily a fishing, trading, and shipbuilding port, is now held to be the "Energy Capital of Europe."[28] Settled at least 8,000 years ago, the rich farm country of Aberdeenshire is as singular as its native idiom of "Doric." David Buchan, the renowned Scottish ballad scholar, emphasized that the unique geographic features of his home region made it the ideal setting for an evolving Scottish balladry tradition. Almost two-thirds of the Anglo-Scottish ballad stories in the Child collection are related, directly or indirectly, to the North East.[29]

At first glance, Aberdeenshire, situated on the distant North Sea coastline 125 miles north of the Scottish capital of Edinburgh, may appear an unlikely location for the cradle of Scottish balladry. Bounded by Britain's highest landmass, the colossal granite plateau of the Cairngorms, to the west, by the Grampian Mountains to the south, and by the sea to the north and east, Aberdeenshire could seem isolated from the major cultural and economic currents of much of Scotland. The surrounding mountains, the so-called Alps of Scotland, were almost impassable by horseman or wagon on the rough and rutted dirt roads leading to the rest of the country, or to England far beyond. Yet Aberdeenshire was no backwater. Its inaccessibility allowed the development of distinctive language, customs, and folklore, while its extensive coastline and seaward face was a window to the European mainland. An incoming stream of cultural influences, exemplified by the flow of ballad traditions, avoided the foreboding overland routes, migrating instead by sea.

The Scandinavian, Nordic, and Germanic connections with the North East of Scotland are well established. From the twelfth century, the port town of Aberdeen was a significant commercial center for the North Sea, trading with continental Europe more

Scottish Highlands. (Photograph by Doug Orr)

abundantly than other east coast British ports. The Scandinavian and Norse influence is imprinted across Britain's geography and history but has been especially marked in North East Scotland, with its long coastline physically reaching toward Nordic countries. The 1266 Treaty of Perth between Scotland and Norway advanced a flourishing trade between the two, underscored by the fact that Aberdeen and the southwestern Norwegian port of Stavanger are separated by only 368 nautical miles. (London is over sixty miles further by sea.) Shared traditions are a natural consequence of such long-standing links.

Ballads flowed freely between Sweden, Denmark, and Norway and crossed from Scandinavia to Aberdeenshire. The cultural connections are easily located. One of the most popular ballads collected by Francis Child, "The Twa Sisters" (Child 10), has many Norse and Swedish variants with Aberdeenshire revisions.

It is a murderous, mysterious story of a girl drowning her younger sister, her rival for the attention of the same man.

> There were twa sisters in a bowr,
> [Refrain] Binnorie, O Binnorie
> There were twa sisters in a bowr,
> [Refrain] Binnorie, O Binnorie
> There came a knight to be their wooer,
> By the bonny mill-dams of Binnorie.
>
> He courted the eldest wi glove an ring,
> But he loved the youngest abune a' thing.
> The eldest she was vexed sair,
> And much envi'd her sister fair. [Refrain]
>
> Upon a morning fair and clear,
> She cried upon her sister dear:
> "O Sister, come to yon sea stran',
> An see our father's ships come to lan'."
>
> She's taen her by the milk-white han',
> And led her down to yon sea stran'.
> The youngest stood upon a stane,
> The eldest came and threw her in.

The drowned girl's body floats downstream to a miller's dam to be discovered by a miller's son; a passing harper uses the dead woman's bones and hair to construct a harp, which then plays eerie music.

> He's made a harp of her breast bane,
> Who's sound wad melt a heart of stane.
> He's ta'en three locks o her yellow hair,
> And wi' them strung his harp sae rare.

"The Twa Sisters" has many more verses and versions and is known also as "The Cruel Sister," "The Bonny Swans," "Binnorie," "The Miller and the King's Daughter," and a variant popular in the Appalachians, "The Wind and the Rain." Supernatural themes, common in the Scandinavian ballad lineage, transcended different languages and localities, crossed the North Sea to Aberdeenshire, and migrated onward from there.[30] A strong Scandinavian flavor also permeates the fiddle music of Scotland's North East and the Northern Isles of Orkney. Ten miles north of Caithness on the Scottish mainland, Orkney is an archipelago of seventy islands, twenty of which are inhabited. People have lived on Orkney for 8,500 years, the Picts having been long established there when Norway invaded and annexed Orkney in 875. Although the islands reverted to Scottish rule in 1472, Orcadian spoken dialect remains as unmistakably Nordic in character as the vibrant fiddle style.

Fifty miles northeast of Orkney, the windswept archipelago of Shetland is rugged and rolling, almost equidistant (about 180 miles) between the northern Scottish mainland and the west of Norway. With a current population of 22,000 inhabitants and 110 islands, of which fifteen are inhabited, Shetlanders have lived by the sea and imbibed a seafaring culture for thousands of years. Fishing and sheep farming (there are ten sheep for every person in Shetland) were the predominant economic pillars for centuries. The 1970 discovery of North Sea oil transformed the economy and changed Shetland forever.

The islands became part of the Scottish kingdom in the fifteenth century. Sea trade was robust with the Low Countries, Germany, and the Hanseatic League, a trading alliance centered around the Baltic seaports. Music was always a by-product of this busy North Sea crisscrossing, and so the fiddle found its way to Shetland. Social music and dancing, usually to fiddle accompaniment, became a staple for the islanders at weddings, funerals, festivals, and hearthside gatherings on the long winter nights of the north. Today, a proud tradition of fiddle playing thrives and speaks to the joint Nordic-Scottish heritage, with the hardanger fiddle introduced from Norway at the end of the sixteenth century. The standard fiddle was more commonplace

THE SCOTTISH FIDDLE

Throughout the long history of migrations from Scottish Lowlands and Highlands, the fiddle was the ideal traveling companion, whether for sailors, journeymen, merchants, or emigrants. It was portable, adaptable to new playing styles, the instrument of choice for dances, and perfect both for soloists and playing partners. So it is not surprising that the fiddle eventually followed the Scottish emigration trail all the way to the southern Appalachians. Beginning in the seventeenth century, it took its place as the most popular dance instrument on both sides of the Atlantic. Hanover County, Virginia, hosted the first fiddling contest of colonial times in 1736, held on November 30 in honor of the holiday of St. Andrew, patron saint of Scotland.

The fiddle in its present form came to Scotland from Italy, most likely arriving in the second half of the sixteenth century, and the Italian Amati family made the original violins. Its predecessor in Scotland was the viol, favored in the Scottish court. The fiddle quickly became popular, and soon Scottish luthiers were crafting replicas of the Italian originals. While the music of the classical violin was the initial attraction, folk-style fiddle playing soon followed. These adaptations of the instrument were no doubt related to the widespread interest in dancing at community gatherings, weddings, funerals, and local festivals and fairs, as well as in the ballrooms and drawing rooms of the landed gentry. By the eighteenth century, aspiring musicians from all levels of society were buying fiddles. This was the so-called golden age of Scottish fiddling that saw more than 1,500 tunes being composed on the instrument; Perthshire, in the heart of the country, was considered the main hub of Scottish fiddle music. The reformed kirk (church) did not look kindly upon the fiddle or the bagpipe, and playing music on them was sometimes associated with witchcraft—a wariness expressed much later by Baptists in the southern Appalachians, who referred to the fiddle as "the devil's instrument." There was no stopping the appeal of the fiddle, however, as it drew people together around the hearth, set the rhythm of the dance, and was a centerpiece of many public performances and events.

Distinctive regional fiddle styles developed throughout Scotland: Shetland fiddling, with its fast reels embellished by ornamented triplets and its lovely slow airs reflecting Scandinavian influences; the North East style, with classical underpinnings, including the slower dance strains of the strathspey (drawing its name from the Spey Valley in Inverness-shire); and the West Coast and Highland fiddle styles, using open lower strings to mimic the drone of the bagpipe. Like the pipes, Highland fiddling also imitated the intonation and rhythms of the Gaelic language through ornamentation and grace notes. When the playing of pipes waned in the aftermath of the 1745 Jacobite Rising, the fiddle served as a worthy stand-in. Cape Breton, Nova Scotia, populated by Scots Gaels in the nineteenth century, has a fiddle style similar to the Scottish Highlands and Islands, emphasizing a "driven bow" where equal efforts are invested in the upward and downward strokes. The slower hornpipe cadences were popular in the Borders area, along with a variety of other rhythms and influences. In the increasingly populated central belt of Scotland between Glasgow and Edinburgh, diverse fiddle styles coalesced, as immigrants from rural areas and Ireland arrived and shared their customs. The strongest Irish connection was between Scotland and Donegal, with its proximity by sea to the southwest Scottish coastline. They shared a style closely related to the bagpipes, featuring a straight-ahead, short bow stroke. It was a technique that would find its way across the Atlantic and into the Appalachian Mountains.

Whatever their region, a pantheon of renowned Scottish fiddlers grew over the years. Two in particular have had a lasting impact: Perthshire's Niel Gow (1727–1807) and James Scott Skinner of Aberdeenshire (1843–1927). Both men became celebrated players and characters in their respective eras. Gow gained the patronage and friendship of the nearby Duke of Atholl and became a favorite at balls held by the aristocracy and at dances throughout the countryside. Often accompanied by his brother on cello, he was adroit with the signature "Scots snap," a quick up-bow stroke characteristic of the strathspey rhythm, and his heart-melting slow airs were especially admired. Gow and his five sons were involved in collecting a great amount of Scots fiddle music, publishing ten volumes in addition to their own compositions, and they had an enduring influence on Scottish instrumental music. In 1787 Robert Burns, who also played fiddle, visited the ancient village of Dunkeld on his tour of the Highlands. Gow was summoned from his nearby home, and Burns sat enthralled as the great fiddler played one tune after another. Burns enjoyed Gow's playing so much that he asked for a copy of the tune "Loch Erroch Side," and he used it for his "Address to the Woodlark," one of several Niel Gow melodies for which he wrote lyrics. He also commemorated their encounter in verse, conveying the affection Burns felt for Gow: "Who doesna joy to hear the ring, O' ilika bonny lilt and spring, that ye frae recollection bring, and wheedle through your fiddle." Today, this very fiddle is mounted and displayed in the ballroom at Blair Castle, seat of the Dukes of Atholl, where present-day fiddlers, with appropriate credentials, can apply to play it.

The self-styled "Strathspey King" James Scott Skinner (1843–1927) of Aberdeenshire was so prolific that at least 600 of his compositions are played widely today. In his Victorian age, Scottish music became more gentrified, and classical influences infiltrated the indigenous styles. Skinner would perform in full formal Highland dress (kilt, jacket, and plaid) before huge audiences in Britain and the United States, and, at the dawn of the recording era, he was recorded on a Stroh violin. This instrument was specially devised to allow the bowed notes to record directly onto wax cylinders, but it did nothing to capture the tone and resonance of Scott Skinner's fiddle.

Niel Gow, James Scott Skinner, and their countless compatriots and descendants have bestowed upon the world an impressive Scottish fiddle tradition. Their tunes and bowing styles have crossed borders and oceans, bringing dancers to their feet right up to the present day.

by the seventeenth century, but the influence of the resonant, ringing hardanger fiddle endures in Shetland dance music. Modern communication links and mass media have brought the Shetland style to the Scottish mainland and, indeed, the world. Since the dawn of the recording era, great Shetland fiddlers such as Tom Anderson (1910–91) and Aly Bain have ensured that the broad accent of Shetland fiddle has a lasting impact in Scotland and beyond.

The famed fiddle tradition for which Shetland is now rightly recognized internationally has possibly overshadowed the fact that its unique old "Norn" dialect is repository to some of Scotland's most interesting songs. The flavor of this Scots-Nordic fusion tongue is most richly delivered in the ballad refrain of "King Orfeo" (Child 19), a medieval resetting of the classic Orpheus and Eurydice tale. Francis Child collected it from a printed version appearing in a Shetland newspaper in 1880, and it was all but forgotten until 1952, when it was rediscovered on the Shetland Island of Unst. According to ballad scholar Bertrand Bronson, "that a tune should in the midst of the twentieth century be recovered for this whisper from the Middle Ages, was as little to be expected as that we should hear a horn from elfin-land blowing."[31] This abridged version of the twenty verses reveals the antiquity of both the language and the setting:

There lived a lady in yon ha'
Scowan erla grae [Refrain]
Her name was Lady Lisa Bell
Far yorten han grun orla [Refrain]

The king, he has a-huntin' gane
An' left his lady all alane

The Elfin King wi' his dairt
Pierced his lady tae the hert

When the king cam hame at noon
He spiered for Lady Lisa Bell

His nobles untae him did say
"My lady was wounded, noo she's deid"

Noo they've taen her life frae me
But her corpse they'll never hae.

There were other aspects of the North East that allowed it to become a seedbed for music and balladry. It was a highly communal, agricultural culture, operating as a "clannit society" rather than a feudal system; its primary forces stemmed from bonds of kinship rather than feudal landowning arrangements. Tenant farmers and local chieftains generally lived together peaceably. Music traditions were cultivated in a rather tightly

DANCE MUSIC

The social dance music of Scotland and Ireland varies in style and tempo from region to region, but the tunes have one thing in common: they are accessible, repetitive, and cyclical, and they exert an incontestable invitation to take to the floor. Although formal dance forms draw audiences who will sit and watch a performance or a competition, most of the dance activities practiced in all the Celtic countries and regions are highly social occasions.

Jigs and reels are particularly common in both Scottish and Irish country-dance and set-dance music. The jig was popularized in the sixteenth century, although fiddlers and pipers composed most of the jigs we know today in the eighteenth and nineteenth centuries. Jigs are sprightly in character and are played in four time signatures: a single jig in 6/8 time, a double also in 6/8 but with an eighth note voiced, a slip jig in 9/8, and a straight jig in 2/4. The reel originated in Scotland in the middle of the seventeenth century and is the most popular social-dance rhythm. Danced in 4/4 time, the music consists of four or eight measures, repeated over and over.

Slower than a reel, the hornpipe is thought to have originated in England in the sixteenth century and is now a fixture throughout the British Isles and Ireland. The word "hornpipe" derives from an early double-reed wind instrument made from animal horn. Early versions of this dance are in 3/2 time, but today the hornpipe is usually played in 2/4 and 4/4 meter.

Scotland's dances feature the indigenous rhythm of the "strathspey." This is like a slow reel in 4/4 time but is played with a distinctive restrained skip, or "Scots snap," that is reflected in the steps on the dance floor. The simple strong rhythms of marches in 2/4 time, usually danced in couples, are also popular in Scotland.

Strathspeys have found a home in the north of Ireland, especially Donegal, where musical traditions have been traded with Scotland for centuries. Donegal tunes called "highlands" are derived from Scottish strathspeys and are played in 4/4 time. Slip jigs, in 9/8 time, are also abundant in Donegal, and the county has a tradition of mazurkas, dances of Polish lineage that were possibly imported by soldiers returning from foreign campaigns. Some waltzes in Scotland are likely to have been absorbed by the same process, although Scotland and Cape Breton in Nova Scotia have robust indigenous traditions of this dance type.

Ceilidh is a Gaelic word meaning "a visiting" and was originally used to define an informal gathering in someone's home where music and storytelling might be shared. Now the word is more commonly used to describe a community dance and style of group dancing. Whether dancing in couples or in sets of six, eight, or more dancers, ceilidh (or "ceili") gatherings, country dances, and set dancing are more popular than ever throughout Scotland and Ireland.

Ballad Melodies: "King Orfeo"

Dr. John Purser, Scottish composer, musicologist, and music historian; interviewed in Dunkeld, Scotland, June 2011, by Fiona Ritchie en route to the National Museum of Scotland.

The great thing about all the ballads is that they tell stories and they tell 'em straight. And they very frequently repeat information, you know, so that the performer makes certain that the audience actually are following the action. And that's just a very basic technique of storytelling: you repeat things. Compare it with poets reading their own poetry, complex, intellectual poetry, which they garble. And nobody can follow it, not even themselves I hasten to add, you know, I'm never so indecent as to ask them actually what any of it meant because you're lost, you're completely lost. And, you know, I've got a Ph.D. in English literature, I'm not stupid, I'm nae blate when it comes to understanding these things! But I listen to 90 percent of the poets reciting—I cannot follow what they are telling me. But a good ballad tells a good story, and that will transport anywhere, good stories will transport anywhere where the language is shared.

Then, of course, you have to have the melody that carries it. These melodies are sometimes very simple, but the important thing is that they carry the story. And sometimes the way they carry it is that they don't end on a final note, you know, they leave it in air so you've got to go on to the next verse, because you haven't heard the keynote. It's like going [singing a scale] "da, da, da, da, da, da, dee" and you stop there. That's how they got Mozart out of bed, so they say. Daddy would stop on "dee," and the wee lad would come screaming down the stairs, "ding!" Whether that's true or not, it's certainly psychologically true, and a number of ballad tunes do that.

I think there's also a great deal of chance, you know, because you have an absolutely amazing survival of the ballad tune for "King Orfeo," and that's the one—I love this wee story—this is [Bertrand Harris] Bronson, the great American, he wasn't so much a collector, as the man who assembled all the Child Ballad tunes, every version of them, four volumes. Should be a statue to the man somewhere, you know? Just stunning work, and you get people criticizing his methodology now and they never did a tenth, not a hundredth of the work that man did—absolutely terrific. Well anyway, it's very scholarly and very careful, you know: this is the A group of tunes, this is the B group of tunes, these are the various recordings, this is mixolydian with a touch of, you know. . . . And then he comes to "King Orfeo," which was collected up in Unst in 1951 or something like this. And he can't contain himself—in print—he puts: "That this whisper from the Middle Ages should have survived into the latter half of the twentieth century is as likely as we should hear the horns of Elfland faintly blowing." He was just so thrilled and that's the only version—at all—and it was gotten from an old man at the northernmost island of Scotland, survived by a thread, by a thread. And it's wonderful, and it's a wonderful, wonderful tune. So survival or otherwise is not necessarily dependent upon quality, it's also dependent upon luck.

Ballad Emotions

Jean Redpath, Scottish singer and educator; interviewed in Elie, Scotland, November 2011, by Fiona Ritchie at the singer's home.

Everybody likes a story, and these particular stories were designed to be told in this fashion, which means they're very, very easy to remember—they're repetitive, they're formulaic. You know, things like "The Twa Brothers," once you settle into one verse, the singer knows, immediately, what the next six are going to be like because you're repeating a formula. More importantly, I think, especially with the classic ballads, which you're dealing with, is something that does not change with age, with culture, with country, with geographic location, with economic situation—it's human emotion, and particularly, the emotion of loss, of tragedy. Everybody, no matter what language, feels the same way about losing, and it's—particularly, I think, with the Scottish propensity for pretending we were born without tear ducts—I think it's a case of singing what cannot be expressed any other way. One of the reasons we have this incredibly powerful sung tradition is because, if for whatever reason you can't say it, then you sing it. It also gives you the out, doesn't it? If I sing something and somebody is obviously moved—used to be true, I would find people now coming up with tears in their eyes admitting that they were moved, but—they would come up and say, "Oh, I didn't know you felt that way." "Oh no, not me, it's a good song, it's a good song." One step removed from a personal statement. It's a fascinating thing, it never ceases to intrigue me, what and how an audience will respond to something quite serious and intended to have them reach for Kleenex, whether they can actually cope with that or not. One of the reasons I like the lights up in a hall is so that I can watch faces.

knit agrarian culture, with Scandinavian-style egalitarianism. In this context, balladry developed largely communally, through a nonliterate society, with a special affinity for improvisation and impromptu adaptation.[32]

David Buchan observed that his Scottish North East ancestors were not a demonstrative people. Grounded by connections to the land and its farming culture, his "dour and canny folk" were stoic and reserved. Shared music was their emotional outlet. A major hallmark of the old ballads of the North East was their sense of drama, "with the best integrating lyric emotion and narrative event within powerful dramatic wholes."[33] These were the same contradictory traits that would, in time, characterize another rural, isolated, and musical

people across space and time: the Southern Highlanders of the Appalachians.

The Scots of the North East were exposed to an additional cultural influence: Highland Gaels, who clashed with the predominantly Anglo-Saxon Lowlanders. Aberdeenshire was a mix of the two, primarily Lowland in the larger coastal area, with Gaelic Highland social and political influences at its western reaches. So the North East itself was something of a "Border Area" in David Buchan's words.[34] This cultural interface further enriched the area's history and personality, including its balladry.

In the Middle Ages, Aberdeenshire played host to a series of battles between the barons of the North East and chieftains from the West. The Battle of Harlaw

was contested in 1411 between the Lord of the Isles and the Earl of Mar. The ferocious struggle produced no outright winner, and its bloody battlefield was commemorated as "Reid (Red) Harlaw." An ancient melody named "Battel Harloe," pipe tunes, and a classic North East ballad all date from that time. Another twenty-verse epic, "The Battle of Harlaw" (Child 163), is as good a glimpse as any into the battle-hardened fifteenth century right from the start:

> As I cam in by Denniedeer
> An' doon by Netherha'
> There was fifty thousand Hielandmen
> A-marchin' to Harlaw.
> Wi' my dirrum doo dirrum doo daddie
>   dirrum dey.

> As I cam on and further on
> And doon by Balquhain
> It's ther I met Sir James the Rose
> And wi' him, Sir John the Graham.

> "Oh came ye frae the Highlands man,
> Oh cam ye a' the wey?
> Saw ye McDonald and his men
> As they cam in frae Skye?"

> "Yes we cam frae the Highlands man
> An we cam a' the wey
> And we saw McDonald and his men
> As they cam in frae Skye."

> "Oh was ye near McDonald's men?
> Did ye their numbers see?
> Come tell me Johnnie Hielandman
> What micht their numbers be?"

> "Yes we was near and near eneuch
> And we their numbers saw
> There was fifty thousand hielandmen
> A-marchin' to Harlaw."

The "piobaireachd" ("theme-and-variations-style" music of the Highland bagpipes) and the "call to battle," both dating from Harlaw, suggest that North East tune melodies may have been Gaelic in origin, while ballad texts were homegrown or Scandinavian influenced. Such cross-fertilization from the Highland west and the coastal east provided a rare combination: a kind of interweaving of musical sources that would characterize subsequent ballad traditions migrating onward to other lands.

Over time, the character of rural Aberdeenshire began to change, and with it the region's oral ballad tradition. The 1707 union of parliaments between Scotland and England was a transformational time in Scottish history. While the Scots relinquished a prized autonomy, the union did help facilitate the Scottish enlightenment, with its educational, economic, and scientific achievements, and prompt increased commerce with England and the emerging American colonies. With Shetland now part of this United Kingdom of Great Britain, its trade with northern Europe decreased, and more of its ships' prows turned toward the south. From the mid-eighteenth century, Aberdeenshire society became more literate and its towns more industrialized. Although the era of oral ballad transmission was in decline, the North East of Scotland retained its reputation as a repository of "big ballads" or "muckle sangs" and as home to many powerful singers. The lighter "bothy ballads," meanwhile, vividly recounted the realities of farm life. Single men would gather at "feeing fairs" or hiring markets and contract their labor for the coming season. Using ripe language and bawdy humor, they described their experiences, even including warnings against particularly harsh conditions on some farms. Living in small huts, or "bothies," laborers gathered to share company and songs in the evenings. The bothy ballads of the North East are greatly popular today with many Scots singers.

THE BAGPIPES

Its plaintive, rousing cry stirs deep human sentiments of sadness, celebration, and pride. The bagpipe is mentioned in the Bible, and its history spans three continents. Connecting hollow bones and sticks to an animal bag, primitive versions were most likely developed in agrarian cultures, possibly originating in Sumaria and traced to ancient Hungary, Russia, the Czech Republic, Egypt, and India. Shepherds and herdsmen had ready access to the basic constructive materials: sheep and goatskin for the bellows (bags) and bones, reeds, and sticks for the pipes. The migration of the Celts brought the bagpipe to Greece and Rome, where the emperor Nero (37–68 A.D.) famously played a bagpipe as well as the fiddle (one or the other according to legend) while Rome burned. The troubadours of France and the minstrels of the Middle Ages included the bagpipe in their musical repertoires.

Over the years and in various regions, there have been many bagpipe designs, although the two significant distinctions are the mouth-blown and bellows-blown versions; the latter generates sound by directing air to the instrument via a set of bellows pumped below the player's elbow. In either case, the sound is produced when the bag is inflated and squeezed, supplying a constant flow of air to the pipes, while the melody is fingered on the chanter. Bagpipe sounds vary depending on the reeds used, the number of drones, the pitch tuning, the vibration of the wood, and the nature of the bellows. The great Highland pipes of world renown, the loudest and grandest of bagpipe instruments, best represent the mouth–blown version.

There were several possible routes for the bagpipe to enter Scotland, but many scholars believe that the Romans were the most likely source, although it could have reached Ireland and the British Isles from much earlier Mediterranean migrations; the indigenous people of the Atlantic archipelago never adopted the Roman-style, two-chanter instruments. Pipers are depicted on carved stones in Ireland between the ninth and eleventh centuries; the Irish today consequently like to claim they introduced the bagpipe to their Scottish cousins, who in turn made it a national instrument. Early bagpipes grew in popularity among the clans of the Scottish Highlands, becoming associated with particular families. By the fifteenth century, the bagpipe had displaced the harp as the instrument of choice, especially in its role as a call to battle. According to legend, the pipes were played at the Battle of Bannockburn in 1314 when King Robert the Bruce led the Scots army to victory against the English. Pipe music associated with the Battle of Harlaw (1411) is still played today.

King James I of Scotland (1394–1437) and Henry VIII of England (1491–1547) brought the bagpipe into the royal courts. Both had collections of bagpipes, although the extent to which either played the instrument, if at all, is not clear. Over the years, bagpipes became popular among the general public and especially in the Scottish Borders, where in many towns the pipes would be played for the official beginning and closing of each day. The Border pipes are bellows blown and produce a softer sound than the mouth-blown great Highland pipes or the Scottish small pipes. Sometimes known as the cauld-wind pipes, other bellows-blown variations are the Northumberland pipes across the border in northeast England and the Irish uilleann (Irish for "elbow") pipes. Although the great Highland pipes have long been a mainstay in Scottish regiments, the other varieties of bagpipe have enjoyed a robust revival within the ranks of Celtic folk ensembles and as solo instruments.

The bagpipe in Scotland fell on hard times after the 1745 Jacobite Rising and defeat of the clans under Prince Charles Edward Stuart ("Bonnie Prince Charlie") at the Battle of Culloden. The subsequent breakup of the clan system and the 1746 parliamentary "Act of Proscription" reiterated an earlier "Disarming Act" and extended to a "Dress Act" prohibiting the wearing of tartan and the kilt. As the clan chiefs lost their powers of patronage, so the bagpipe fell into decline, suffering, too, as the Highlands experienced the depopulation of widespread migration. Its warlike image, however, eventually enabled the great Highland pipes to experience a rebirth when the British Empire needed to raise Scottish regiments for foreign campaigns through the eighteenth to twentieth centuries. Pipe bands remain an important part of regimental life to the present day, and the pipes still provide their age-old rallying call on active service throughout the world. Outside the regimental setting, the Highland bagpipe is most familiar internationally because of its role, along with drums, as a marching-band instrument. Scottish pipe bands in full regalia are a dramatic sight and sound at many Highland Games and civic gatherings throughout the world.

Although the bagpipe did not accompany the first eighteenth-century wave of Scots from Ulster to America and therefore did not migrate into the southern Appalachians, it did begin to appear in the American colonies during the Revolutionary and French and Indian Wars. Today, bagpipes are heard throughout the world in massed bands, in folk groups, and as solitary instruments. Perhaps no instrument in any musical genre can deliver a lament or slow air with quite the emotional authority of the pipes, and so the bagpipe is often the preferred solo tribute in mourning. Apart from the laments, marches, and "piobaireachd" (the "theme and variations" classical music of the pipes), the rhythms of the dance floor—marches, reels, jigs, and strathspeys—are now common in any piper's repertoire. Today, bagpipes of all descriptions are more popular than ever. Glasgow's international "Piping Live!" Festival incorporates the World Pipe Band Championships and annually welcomes well over 50,000 spectators and 8,000 musicians.

TRAVELLER TRADITIONS

Aberdeen was also home to one of the twentieth century's greatest ballad singers, Jeannie Robertson (1908–75), whom American folklorist and ethnomusicologist Alan Lomax called "a monumental figure of world folksong."[35] Her ancestors belonged to two of the long-established families of Travellers, the Robertsons and the Stewarts, itinerant workers who roamed the North East and beyond. The Travellers' role as guardians of song and story became more widely appreciated after the poet, songwriter, and collector Hamish Henderson (1919–2002) discovered Jeannie Robertson and other remarkable tradition bearers. His work in documenting their songs and raising public awareness of a remarkable heritage secured his reputation as the catalyst of the Scottish folk revival. (Indeed, it was Henderson who, in the 1950s, served as a guide for both Alan Lomax and Jean Ritchie when they each traveled to Scotland making field recordings of traditional singers.) Jeannie Robertson's prowess as an interpreter of the great ballads was legendary; she was

Collecting: Going to the Source

Sara Grey, American traditional singer, banjo player, and song collector; interviewed in Perth, Scotland, March 2010, by Fiona Ritchie at the singer's home.

I would like to see a lot of the younger people ground songs more. I would also like to see more people listening to old singers, to source singers and not just trying to learn things in a modern sort of way. I don't mean to sound like an old stuffed shirt, but it really—and I know my son Kieron (Means) feels strongly about that. He's a great example, because he and people like Siobhan Miller have grown up with the music . . . so the nurturing of these songs and the passing them on is very, very important to both of them. And that's a great thing, but I don't always see that, and I've had instances where young singers have come up to me and said, "Oh, I would like you to give me all your songs." And at first I thought, why am I feeling reluctant, this is silly because nobody possesses old songs. But when I really began to question why I was feeling the way I was, I realized it was because these people need to experience, if they can, in this last generation that's coming along, they've got to be able to experience some of this for themselves. And if you're lucky, you might still have a few [source singers] who are still left who will be able to remember some of these songs, and that will make it so much more memorable for you because you'll be able to exchange a song for a song. That's the way you're going to get the most satisfaction out of it.

I know when Jeannie Robertson had her stroke, then some of the people who'd collected from her didn't want to know her anymore. And I was enraged by that, how can you separate the two out? You know, there is no separation between the person and the song, and what you put into a song, or what you interpret when you're singing a ballad or a song, you are so intrinsically bound up in this story, of getting that story across. I would rather hear somebody who's just totally immersed and totally focused on that—getting that story out. Because those are the great tellers, you are the bearer of those songs, and it's your responsibility to get that out there.

GUARDIANS OF TRADITION: THE TRAVELLERS

The community of itinerant traditional Travellers in Scotland, England, and Ireland—sometimes known as gypsies and "tinkers" (now usually considered pejorative)—is an important source of traditional music, especially ballads and stories. Travellers have suffered centuries of marginalization and discrimination. Yet their very position on the fringes of society allowed them to keep song and story traditions alive, while other such traditions all but died out in more-settled communities. A simple, materially poor lifestyle in bow tents (similar to dome tents) and horse-drawn caravans, then later motor caravans, trailers, and permanent homes, ensured that their ancient oral culture thrived in their close communities. Most significant, an itinerant lifestyle following the seasons and working to the rhythm of the agricultural calendar meant they gathered and sowed the seeds of tradition as they went. For example, they would travel between Scotland and Northern Ireland for such pursuits as pearl fishing, gathering in the evenings with Irish Travellers to exchange songs and stories.

The Traveller repertoire was remarkably rich; traditional ballads; broadside ballads; songs about love, work, and death; supernatural songs; bawdy verses; humorous ditties; songs for "diddling" babies on the knee; and rhythmic vocals for dancing were all part of the song tradition they upheld. Pipers in the Travelling community were especially revered, often being patronized by gentry. These included Jock Stewart, piper to the seventh Duke of Atholl at Blair Castle in Perthshire, Scotland, reputedly the character celebrated in the eponymous drinking song.

Beginning in the 1950s, the rich seam of balladry drew academics and collectors to the Travelling communities. Hamish Henderson, Ewan MacColl, and Peggy Seeger headed to the berry-growing fields in the fertile Carse of Gowrie to the east of Scotland. In Blairgowrie, Perthshire, heart of berry country, collectors found "the Stewarts of Blair" family of well-known ballad singers and pipers. They still sang songs dating back as far as the twelfth century that had been learned around campfires and passed from generation to generation. In 1953 poet, songwriter, and collector Hamish Henderson, cofounder of the School of Scottish Studies at the University of Edinburgh, encouraged the family to sing their traditional songs at folk clubs. He also investigated their dialect, "Perthshire Cant," tracing many of its words to Gaelic and old Scots. Today, the last known speaker of Perthshire Cant is the unaccompanied traditional ballad singer, storyteller, and author Sheila Stewart. She is the daughter of Belle Stewart (1906–97), herself a songwriter and the matriarch of the Stewarts of Blair. Sheila spent her childhood traveling all over Scotland, working with her family on farms, and, starting in 1954, she sang in concerts with her parents and her sister Cathie. Fewer families travel now, and many who grew up in Travelling communities have moved into permanent housing or static caravans, diluting the strong culture. Eastern European migrant workers now pick the Perthshire berry crop, which was still largely the work of Travellers until the 1980s.

Repertoire apart, singers like Sheila Stewart are still noted for their astonishingly passionate and affecting singing style. Few singers occupy the position of "singing legend" more completely than Jeannie Robertson (1908–75). Her reputation as the twentieth century's greatest interpreter of ballads is secure. Robertson grew up among the Travelling community and absorbed a large repertoire of ballads and love songs. Recorded in 1953, her album *What a Voice* was produced shortly after Hamish Henderson discovered her. It dates from the time when Robertson was just embarking on her relationship with the international community of folklorists and ethnomusicologists, and so it marks the earliest record of her talking about her life and childhood. What makes this album compulsory listening, however, is Robertson's delivery of ballads. They include "My Son David" (also known as "Edward"; Child 13), "Andrew Lammie" (Child 223), and "Lord Bateman" (Child 53).

Sheila Stewart sang as part of the U.S. bicentennial celebrations and has lectured on Travellers' culture at Princeton and Harvard Universities. In spite of the reverence shown for Traveller culture by academics, it has taken the settled society in Scotland a long time to appreciate fully their contribution to cultural history, especially in the realms of song and story preservation. Best-selling books in recent decades, however, have included autobiographies and family stories by women who grew up among these communities: Betsy White, Jess Smith, and Sheila Stewart, who was honored by Queen Elizabeth II for services to the oral tradition of Scotland's folk music and her advocacy for Travelling People.

"Tinker" once referred to skilled craftsmen, makers of tin pots, pans, plates, and cups. Although the term was often used to insult them, some members of the Travelling community now reclaim it with pride, believing it properly identifies them and confers status.

Travelling Fiddler. (Photograph by Gordon Shennan; courtesy of Highland Photo Archive, Inverness Museum and Art Gallery, High Life Highland, Scotland)

Travellers. (Watercolor; courtesy of Madeleine Hand)

held to be a spellbinding performer. Like other Travellers, she had memorized a treasure trove of ancient songs and stories passed to her through what is now recognized as one of the oldest oral cultures in Europe. Travellers revere their finest singers for their ability to deliver a song in a manner that vents emotion in the listener, a quality they call "the conyach." It conveys passion, a connection to the past, and an ability to let the song speak through the singer. This is a special gift among the traditional Travelling communities of Scotland and Ireland, who were a conduit for song and story traditions between the two countries as they followed the agricultural seasons living in tents and caravans. The reputation of the Travellers as tradition bearers who, as Lomax said, "kept the tradition alive and burning across all time" continues undiminished today. Furthermore, their concentration in the North East of Scotland consolidated the region's estimation as a cradle for the evolution of balladry, influencing other regions, including the Scottish Borders.

Traveller Treasure

Brian McNeill, Scottish songwriter, singer, multi-instrumentalist, and novelist; interviewed in Swannanoa, North Carolina, July 2013, by Fiona Ritchie during Traditional Song Week at the Swannanoa Gathering folk arts workshops.

I was always fascinated by the contribution that the gypsy [Travellers] made to the preservation of our traditional music. And there was a wonderful singer called Betsy White. And Betsy, she never made a penny from music in her life. She sang for her own edification and her family's, and she was one of these people: if she'd been from a nice, comfortable middle-class family, she'd probably have been an opera star. But she wasn't, she was a gypsy [Traveller], she lived in a bow tent up in the glens. Betsy's first job was to sit on the banks of the fast-flowing rivers in the east of Scotland—the Tay or the Isla or the Earn—and keep watch while her father was in the river fishing for pearls. The rivers on the east coast are shallow, and very fast and very clean. And there were mussel beds and oyster beds. They had a great way of doing this: they would go out in the middle of the stream, and they would have either a bucket or a box with the bottom cut out of it, and they would have a pane of glass in it. And they would put that down on the surface of the water to take out the reflection of the sun on the surface of the water, and that let them look forward and locate the oyster beds. Ecological fishers: they never took too much; they never took anything that was unripe. But of course, all of these stretches of water were owned by big sporting estates, by aristocrats, by fishing syndicates, by powerful people. And inevitably, somebody always told that there was a gypsy in the river fishing for pearls, and many of these big estates had what was essentially their own police force. They were called the water baillies (water bailiffs that's just short for) they would come, and they would patrol the banks of the rivers to make sure there was nothing untoward going on. And Betsy's job was to sit there on the banks, and when the water baillies came, she had to make the noise of an owl to warn off her father. And her father was a rare gypsy indeed, because he knew how to swim. So when he heard the sound of an owl, he would abandon his gear and head for the other bank.

The real pearl was the traditional music that these people saved for us.

BORDERS BALLADRY
AND SIR WALTER SCOTT

The English folklorist Cecil Sharp left his home in Stratford-on-Avon in 1916 to spend some of the next two years collecting ballads in the coves and hollows of the southern Appalachians. There, he found what he believed were "time capsules" for the old ballads, which he connected to the Border area overlapping Scotland and England. Cecil wrote: "From an analysis of their traditional songs, ballads, dances singing-games, etc. . . . they came from a part of England where the civilization was least developed—probably the north of England, or the Border country between Scotland and England."[36]

Like many ballad scholars before and since, Sharp was completely vague on the whereabouts and significance of the Scottish-English border. He also overlooked the fundamental Aberdeenshire contribution to ballad history, such as the peerless collection by Mrs. Brown of Falkland. Sharp had formed the notion that culturally, Lowland Scotland and northern England were one and the same, at least in terms of folk song. At best, it was an approach lacking subtlety and accuracy. He did call attention to the Borders, however, as that other rich seam of Scottish balladry. The rolling hills

and moorlands of the Borders nourished an abundance of ballads. This was a landscape of strange and forbidding beauty, with undulating hillsides and narrow valleys. The American writer Washington Irving would provide a vivid Borders portrait of "great waving hills, monotonous in their aspect, and so destitute of trees that one could see a stout fly walking along the profile."[37] Once forested, the hills and valleys provided a display of soft greens in the spring and early summer that turned to autumn's purple heather and then shades of winter browns. The Border country, historically known as the "Scottish Marches," includes areas known today as Dumfries and Galloway and the Scottish Borders, and on the English side, parts of Cumbria, County Durham, and Northumberland.

From the Middle Ages, this was a turbulent land of legend, described as "the soul of romance and the bane of good government."[38] Wild and lawless, there was constant feuding, robbery, and cattle theft by "reivers," or raiders among the family groups of the area, both north and south of the Anglo-Scottish border. With an economy based on cattle and sheep, retaliatory raids were the norm. Blood relationships were paramount, with the families of the sixteenth and seventeenth centuries organized around a series of strongholds that followed river courses of the Teviot and the Tweed,

Collectors' Confusion

Jack Beck, Scottish traditional singer and broadcaster; interviewed in Dunkeld, Scotland, June 2012, by Fiona Ritchie as he led a group of American ballad scholars on tour in Scotland.

What's interesting is Cecil Sharp described them as English ballads in the title of his famous collection. I guess he probably meant English Language rather than English, you know. But that's the way these things go. And of course, Child also titled his grand collection English and Scottish, putting English before Scottish—so he did make the distinction. But, again, it would probably have been more accurate to describe them as Scottish and English, but [laughing] that's the way these things go. It is interesting—strong Scottish connections.

together with the Ettrick, Yarrow, and Liddel Waters. Loyalty to extended family was absolute, well above any allegiance to the crown. Additionally, considerable hostility was directed from Border clans toward the societies to the south and north—England and the Scottish Highlands—no doubt compounded by the fact that for over 700 years, possession of the Border lands had been a source of conflict between England and Scotland. Highlanders were a relentless threat as sometime predatory reivers themselves, plundering Lowland farms and towns. To complicate matters, the people were of mixed ancestry, social status, and religion—a combination of Scottish Celts and Picts, with influences of ancient Britons, Anglo-Saxons, and Irish all contributing to their identity.[39] Exposed to the crosscurrents of history, a borderland setting like this is sometimes called a "shatter belt" by geographers. It is a fitting name for a region exposed to constant fracturing through raids and retribution.

Border shepherd and ballad singer Willie Scott

(1897–1989) came from a long line of singers, and his repertoire of old Border ballads seem to echo from another time, including "The Shepherd's Song," "The Kielder Hunt," and "The Dowie Dens of Yarrow" (Child 214). Published as a broadside in 1880–1900, the ancient melody of "The Dowie Dens of Yarrow" is held to be the source spring of a tune stream that flows through the early nineteenth-century spiritual "The Wayfaring Stranger" (CD track 19). There are also familiar magical allusions in the tragic tale of "The Dowie Dens of Yarrow," typical of other so-called big ballads. The feuding culture of reiving families is established even in these opening verses:

> Thair lived a lady in the north
> I ne'er could fin her marrow
> She wis courtit by nine gentlemen
> An a ploughboy lad fae Yarrow
>
> Late at e'en, drinkin the wine
> An e'er thae paid the lawin
> Thae hae made a pact amang thaim aa
> Tae fecht for her at the dawin
>
> She's washed his face, she's kaimed his hair
> As aft she's dune afore-o
> She's made him like a knight sae braw
> Tae fecht for her on Yarrow
>
> As he gaed owre yon high, high hill
> An doun by the holms o Yarrow
> It's thair he spied nine armed men
> Come tae fecht wi him on Yarrow
>
> "Thair's nine o you an ane o me
> That's a gey unequal marrow
> But A'll fecht ye aa, ane by ane
> On the dowie dens o Yarrow"

Although the debatable lands of the Borders meant that the inhabitants were resigned to restlessness and instability, it did result in a treasure trove of raw mate-rial for legend, story, and song. Evelyn Wells described the area as a place where "[s]tories, like thistledown before the wind, fly everywhere and attach themselves to any bush or twig; and no place more than the Scottish Border has had winds of legend blow across it."[40] The reiving and plundering lifestyles of some powerful Borders families created a prolific breeding ground for ballads. The ones that emerged often identified local individuals and place names with stories that were, at times, quite clearly exaggerated. These were the "Border Raid Ballads," echoing earlier Robin Hood Ballads that likewise highlighted tales of adventure and daring against neighboring adversaries. The Border Raid Ballad "Jamie Telfer" is set around the harvest, at the November 11 feast day of Saint Martin (Martinmas time) and moves swiftly to the main event: reiving (raiding).

> It fell about the Martinmas
> When the steads were fed wi corn and hay,
> The Captain of Bewcastle said to his lads,
> We'll into Tivotdale and seek a prey.

Revenge always simmered just below the surface. Real or perceived wrongs would not be forgiven, even over generations, as the Border Raid Ballad "Johnny Armstrong" avows:

> Oh then he bespoke his little son,
> As he was set upon his nurse's knee:
> If ever I live to be a man,
> My father's blood revenged shall be.

Generations later, this hard and fast grudge bearing, indifferent to the passage of time, was to become a trait of the Appalachian mountaineers, reflected in the expression: "They never learn and they never forget." To whatever extent such traditions may have migrated across the seas, the Border Raid Ballads themselves, with their emphasis on specific times, places, and indi-

Ballad Versions

Jean Redpath, Scottish singer and educator; interviewed in Elie, Scotland, November 2011, by Fiona Ritchie at the singer's home.

Over the years I've sort of incorporated, for one reason or another, the fact that a Scottish song will start out in one shape and finish up moving from the mountains in the east to, perhaps, Texas, and be transformed entirely by the time it gets there. Mostly not so much as an ethnomusicological (there's a word for you), not so much as any kind of formal study, but because it's good for a giggle—you can get a laugh out of an audience at the same time as you are imparting some information. And finding versions of Border ballads sung where the River Yarrow meant nothing, so it comes out as Ero—it's an oral reading and, in that case, of course, it's equally powerful.

What's the one that I'm fond of? I guess it's the little tag on, is it "Lord Gregory"? [singing:] "Wha will shoe your bonnie wee feet? And wha will glove your hand? And wha will bind my middle jimp, With the long linen band?" And I think I probably learned that from Joe Gordon in the fifties. I think he sang a version of that. Now it's a very appealing little question-and-answer thing, but when it hits the states, it picked up some wonderful tunes. I have no idea where this melody came from . . . I've forgotten where I heard it, I just thought it was a cracker. And, Lord knows, at this hour of the day, whether you are going to get anything, but let's see [singing:] "Oh who will shoe your foot, my love and who will glove your hand? And who'll kiss your red rosy cheek when I'm in a far off land?" Now if you'd never heard of "Lord Gregory," that melody tells you that you're still dealing with somebody sad, it's a very serious [song]. . . . And then you get to Texas, you know—and I'm sure it's covering all sorts of places in between—but you get [singing:] *"Who's a gonna shoe your pretty little feet? Who's a gonna glove your hand?"* And, you know, and we're off on a different tack entirely. Which I find fascinating, and again it's something that I can use to make people find that Scottish music isn't out there in a tartan haze somewhere and has nothing at all to do with them. In fact, I've been quoted many times as saying, "All of the best American melodies started out in Scotland." And I find if you deliver a nonsensical statement like that with enough confidence, somebody will believe you.

viduals, did not for the most part relocate to America. The cowboy songs of the Wild West are a logical descendent of the genre, however, with their themes of frontier lawlessness and retribution not unlike the Border ballads or indeed the English and Irish highwaymen ballads.[41]

Like the subsequent Appalachian and cowboy cultures of America, Borderers could find festivity and levity in the midst of violence and an often brutal exis-

tence. Country life was not always so grim, however. Fairs were popular, where farmers could legitimately market cattle, horses, and wool. Craft merchants would set up stalls to peddle their wares. Drambooths sold whisky, and taverns thrived. And whether at the fair or the hearth, many communities were enriched by their local ballad singers, harpers, pipers, fiddlers, and storytellers. Dances and games were ever popular, and special holidays were celebrated.[42] Traditional piping tunes were kept alive by the traveling "toun pipers," who commuted between towns and villages performing on Lowland pipes. They were professional pipers, paid for their performances just as the itinerant harpers enjoyed the patronage of the landed gentry in Ireland and Scotland.

Minstrelsy of the Scottish Border, the song collection of Sir Walter Scott (1771–1832), cast a wider net in assembling material from many sources. One of Scotland's most celebrated writers, the author of *Waverley*, *Ivanhoe*, and *Rob Roy*, Scott had an unending curiosity, an ability to connect ballad stories to all walks of life, and a remarkable capacity to commit to memory lengthy stories and poems. His appetite for storytelling began at an early age. Born in Edinburgh in 1771, he was sent to live with his grandparents in the Borders to recover from the polio that left him lame. There, he absorbed the speech patterns in the tales and legends of the Scottish Borders. Scott was a precocious reader of history, poetry, myths, and fairy tales who began his study of classics at the University of Edinburgh when he was a mere twelve years of age. He loved the rolling hills of the Borders and developed his passion for the region's oral traditions, obsessively collecting stories. His love of the landscape of his ancestors ensures that he is remembered not only as a prolific and influential writer but also as a Borderer through and through.

Scott began collecting ballads during excursions through the Borders in 1792 and developed the idea of publishing his collection when he reconnected with an old school chum, publisher James Ballentine. His initial plan was to focus on the colorful historic events of the Borders, essentially highlighting the Border Raid Ballads, but he soon broadened his reach to include historic and romantic pieces from further afield. Scott's appointment as deputy sheriff of Selkirkshire in 1799, which took him into many corners of the county, opened a rich seam of material for him. It also was a much-needed supplement to his income, particularly when the printing and publishing house of James Ballentine failed, creating financial difficulties

for Scott. The building and interminable upkeep of his Baronial-style home, Abbotsford, stunningly situated on banks of the River Tweed, was also a drain on finances. (Open to the public, Abbotsford has been completely restored since Scott's last descendant to reside there died in 2004).

Scott was able to enlist the assistance of a number of other ballad collectors to join him in the laborious work of tracking down fragments of the old ballads throughout the area. No collector was more influential in his collecting than Anna Gordon, better known as Mrs. Brown of Falkland. Born in Aberdeen in 1747, her collection is considered one of the most significant and oldest in Anglo-Scottish balladry.[43] She learned most of her songs as a child from a family nurse and her mother's relatives. Anna Gordon was middle-aged when she married the Reverend Andrew Brown, a former chaplain based in Falkland, Fife. When she died in Old Aberdeen in 1810, she left a rare collection that captured the essence, context, and content of orally transmitted balladry. In years to come, Francis Child would draw heavily on Mrs. Brown's collection of ballads. "Willie's Lady" (Child 6), for example, has all the hallmarks of a North East ballad with its echoes of enchantment and dark Scandinavian plot lines.

> Willie has taen him o'er the fame,
> He's woo'd a wife and brought her hame.
> He's woo'd her for her yellow hair,
> But his mother wrought her mickle care.
> And mickle dolour gard her dree,
> For lighter she can never be.
> But in her bower she sits wi' pain,
> And Willie mourns o'er her in vain.
> So to his mother he has gone
> That vile rank witch of the vilest kind
> He says: "My ladie has a cup,
> Wi' gowd and silver set about.
> This goodlie gift shall be your ain,
> And let her be lighter o' her young bairn."
> "Of her young bairn she'll ne'er be lighter,
> Nor in her bower to shine the brighter.
> But she shall die and turn to clay,
> And you shall wed another may." (CD TRACK 18)

As for Scott, Mrs. Brown's collection was his single most-important source and underscored the significant influence of the Aberdeen ballad tradition upon Border balladry. In fact, the oft-cited archetypal Border ballad "Thomas the Rhymer" is just as often located in Aberdeenshire.[44] Like the ballad traditions of both areas, elements of the supernatural were commonplace, and long story lines lacked choruses. "Thomas the Rhymer" is the story of a wandering singer, his journey to fairyland, and his ability to prophesize

events. His tryst with a fairy queen sets the scene in the opening verses:

> True Thomas lay on Huntlie bank;
> A ferlie he spied wi' his ee;
> And there he saw a lady bright
> Come riding down by the Eildon tree.
>
> True Thomas he pull'd aff his cap,
> And louted low down to his knee,
> "All hail thou mighty Queen of Heaven!
> For thy peer on earth I never did see."
>
> "O no, O no, True Thomas" she said,
> "That name does not belang to me;
> I am but the Queen of fair Elfland,
> That am hither come to visit thee."

Scott published *Minstrelsy of the Scottish Border* in 1802 and documented ballads on a wide variety of themes and from many sources. Like Robert Burns (1759–96) before him, he loved to reflect the whole range of Scottish society—the ordinary rural folk, the middle class, the professions, and the landed nobility—and had a keen ear for expressions from individuals across the spectrum of society. Although he accepted Scotland's 1707 political union with England, he lamented the accompanying decline in Scottish identity and traditions, another sentiment he shared with Burns.

Neither man was overly concerned with specific origins of song fragments, which are difficult to ascertain anyway, but Scott was fond of the term "minstrel," which he used to represent any kind of authorship or origin.[45] As he gathered the ballad strands and variants, Scott assumed considerable editorial license in authenticating and arranging material in a way he felt best represented the ballad's travels and meaning up to that point. It was not unusual for him to amend words, rhymes and rhythms to create a better fit. He considered this approach to be consistent

Treading Carefully into Tradition

Sara Grey, American traditional singer, banjo player, and song collector; interviewed in Perth, Scotland, March 2010, by Fiona Ritchie at the singer's home.

I knew in my heart the way to collect songs is not to exploit, and I just felt there was a lot of exploiting going on by some of the folklorists. Some who had come over here in particular, and I knew that to be a singer of old songs: that's the best way to collect. So it was this communal feeling of—and I probably never even expressed it as a young person—I just knew intrinsically that this was what I loved and what was important to me.

So when I came over in 1969 and heard a lot of the psalm singing in the islands, I thought to myself: that has got to be the link between the sacred harp tradition. And very few people were even articulating that until much, much later. But I just quietly thought to myself, that has got to be, and all these ideas kept springing into my mind every time I kept hearing a Scottish song; I kept hearing all the links of songs that I knew from home. And I know it does sound very naïve in a way, but back then, people weren't really connecting songs up that much. Jean Ritchie was, and I was doing it around that time as well, and thinking, I really want to be over in the U.K. I mean, in the 1970s, this was a time when it was just cooking over here. There were so many venues in Scotland and England and Wales that you could go into one area and sing and sing and sing and you know, you could carry on for weeks at a time in some areas. There were thousands of venues, and everybody—it was fresh, it was something new—well new in that forming folk clubs within a pub where you had a function room and there was a sort of reciprocal arrangement with the pub owner. And it was very much appreciated, you know, putting bums on seats when you could bring people in and they would in turn buy beer and you would give them a free room.

And they were amazingly vibrant times, they were, everywhere all over the British Isles, and I was just so lucky to be a part of that. And when I first arrived, I found that people didn't know quite what to make of me. I was terrified to say or do anything that might brand me as an ugly American. And I know it sounds silly, but I was very aware, you know, other singers and musicians, a few people had come before me and had not . . . had been a little bit . . . had been branded a little bit with that title. So I wanted to be very sure. So I treaded very carefully, and it's taken me years . . . to just gradually show people—because a lot of people thought songs dropped into the Atlantic. They thought when they were on this side, the U.K. side, they thought, yeah, you're a good American singer, but we're British and you're American and you couldn't possibly have anything that would be of value. And I couldn't seem to quietly get across to these people that the link was there, that these songs were your songs, a lot of them. And it's taken years, and now, of course, everybody's running around linking up songs, but back in those days, maybe it wasn't a fashionable idea.

with the fluid nature of an oral tradition that needed an experienced collector as editor. This process was not without criticism and provoked a verbal rebuke from a longtime practitioner of the oral ballad tradition, Margaret Laidlaw, the indomitable mother of Scott's contemporary, writer James Hogg, the "Ettrick Shepherd." Mrs. Hogg, on seeing Scott's printed versions of songs she had actually sung to him, stated in agitated fashion: "Ther never ane o' ma sangs prentit till you prentit them yoursel' and ye hae spoilt them a' thegither. They were made for singing and no for reading, but ye hae broken the charm now and they'll never be sung mair. And the warst thing o' a', they're nouther right spell'd nor right setten down."[46] Mrs. Hogg's sentiments would echo through subsequent years of tension between traditional singers and collectors, from Scotland to Ulster and eventually to the songcatchers of the southern Appalachians.

Scott's success as a writer placed his name before an international audience and led to the publication in 1805 of a full-length narrative poem, "The Lay of the Last Minstrel." He published an additional volume of ballads in his *Minstrelsy* collection and second editions of both works, augmented with more ballads. Three more editions appeared in 1812, presenting some ballads in print for the first time. His romantic spirit and vivid imagery of the Scottish landscape next found an outlet in "Marmion" and "The Lady of the Lake." When his storytelling impulse took full flight, Scott invented the historic novel genre. This luminous legacy stands alongside his extensive ballad collections, which (notwithstanding Mrs. Hogg's criticisms) preserved much that might otherwise have been lost. Several editions of Scott's *Minstrelsy* chronicled about a quarter of Scottish ballads known at that time.

With his historical novels, Scott was consolidating and popularizing a Scottish story and sense of nationhood that had been stimulated by Robert Burns.

Woody Guthrie

Pete Seeger (1919–2014), singer, songwriter, campaigner, and activist; interviewed in Beacon, New York, November 2008, by Fiona Ritchie and Doug Orr at the artist's home.

Woody Guthrie, like Robert Burns, was a genius who came from a small town, and he could have been very famous if he'd wanted to, taking jobs in the city, but like Robert Burns, he turned them down. He was very ornery. He came to New York in the winter, February of 1940, and Alan Lomax and I both came up from New York to hear him sing. It was a benefit concert for California Agricultural Workers who didn't get paid very much money. And so onstage, they called them Oakies. Texies came from Texas, Arkies came from Arkansas, Kanzies came from Kansas, Woody was an Oakie. He stood there with his cowboy hat pushed on the back of his head telling short stories. He said, you know, Oklahoma is a very rich state. If you want some oil, just go down a hole in the ground, get you some oil. We got lead mines in Oklahoma. You want some lead, go down the hole, get you some lead. If you want food, clothes, or groceries, just go down the hole and stay there. And he'd sing another song.

ROBERT BURNS AND WOODY GUTHRIE

In 2009 Scottish Television conducted a poll on who should be "The Greatest Scot." The announcement was made on St. Andrews Day (November 30) that Robert Burns had been voted the greatest Scot of all time, narrowly beating Scottish patriot and independence campaigner William Wallace. Few artists have imprinted a more lasting impression on the hearts and minds of his country folk.

Despite an all-too-brief life (1759–96), Robert Burns had a prodigious literary output, producing over 500 poems. He spent his last eight years especially concentrating on preserving Scottish traditional song. With his health steadily declining, Burns collected, arranged, and composed 368 songs. Many appeared in coeditor James Johnson's *Scots Musical Museum, 1787–1803* and later in George Thomson's *Select Scottish Airs*.

> Ev'n then a wish (I mind its power)
> A wish, that to my latest hour
> Shall strongly heave my breast;
> That I for poor auld Scotland's sake
> Some useful plan, or book could make,
> Or sing a sang at least.
> —From "The Answer, to the Guidwife of
> Wauchope-House," 1787

When American folk song laureate Woody Guthrie was in the merchant marine, he visited Scotland and sought to connect with the work and spirit of Robert Burns. Like many American artists and poets, including Maya Angelou, Guthrie closely identified with the ploughman poet who had shared Guthrie's commitment to equality and humanitarian causes. In Woody's famous poem "To That Man Burns," he wrote:

> Dear Robert Burns, Your words turned into songs and floated upstream and then turned into rains and drifted down and lodged and clung to drifts of driftwood to warm, heat and fertilize new seeds. Your words were of the upheath and the down, more from the heather than from the town. . . . I bought your little four-inch square book while I was in Glasgow as a torpedoed seaman walking over your clods and sods of Glasgow and the little book says on the outer cover, "Fifty Songs of Burns," the price 4d, and I read from page to page and found a woman on every page. I thought as I picked the book up here at home that maybe the book ought to have some kind of new name. Like, "Fifty Pages Fifty Women, Enlarged Upon by Robert Burns."

Guthrie's interest in Robert Burns inspired, in turn, a young Bob Dylan to reach through Guthrie and toward Burns's legacy to "fertilize new seeds" of song. Dylan's pilgrimage to the British Isles in the early 1960s, and his musical journey ever since, are links in a song chain connecting through Guthrie and Burns to the treasure trove of traditional balladry that "floated upstream and then turned into rains and drifted down" again.

There is a portrait hanging in Abottsford that captures the scene of the two writers' only encounter in 1786, when Walter Scott was a lad of fifteen.[47] Scott was profoundly affected by the easy charm of the bard, by his rustic dignity and poet's temperament. Much later, in his journal entry for February 10, 1826, Scott wrote: "We have however many men of high poetical talent, but none of that ever gushing, and perennial fountain of natural water." Scott's passion for song collecting must surely have been fueled by his lifelong admiration for Burns. For where Scott is remembered today more for his Waverley Novels than his ballad collections, the romantic image of Burns often overshadows what is arguably his chief legacy. Original poetry and songs apart, Burns was the foremost collector and arranger of traditional Scottish songs. The product of this labor of love was *The Scots Musical Museum, 1787–1803*, compiled by Burns for his coeditor, James Johnson (later George Thomson). In collecting and extending fragments of traditional verse for these five volumes and by preserving old melodies he chose for the songs, Burns, through an obsession in life and bequest in death, has had an immeasurable impact on Scottish heritage and culture. As singer Jean Redpath often says in her performances of Burns songs: "He was a walking encyclopedia of Scottish music. If you're looking for a ballad, a drawing-room song, or a dance tune with four sets of lyrics, you'll find it in Robert Burns."

We seek, in this book, to trace the migration of songs the long way, mile by mile across land and sea and on down through the generations. As we follow the trail, it is sobering to bear in mind a heartfelt song of friendship, penned in words that many only vaguely understand, sung universally at the dawn of each New Year. Robert Burns collected the fragment around which he composed "Auld Lang Syne" from an anonymous ballad emerging from the Middle Ages, "Auld Kyndnes Foryett," and possibly another scrap gleaned from a courtly poet of James VI. The anthem's ceaseless spread to the far corners of the earth makes

the most compelling case for the universal appeal, and the power, of an honest song; it is now even taught in Chinese schools as "You Yi Di Jiu Tian Chang" ("Friendship Forever and Ever"). In his life's work, Burns changed the course of folk song in the British Isles and beyond, making it enduringly popular in all the territories through which our ballad stream will flow.

> Should auld acquaintance be forgot
> And never brought to mind?
> Should auld acquaintance be forgot
> And auld lang syne!

Dylan Influences

Jean Redpath, Scottish singer and educator; interviewed in Elie, Scotland, November 2011, by Fiona Ritchie at the singer's home.

Miki Isaacson, whose apartment I stayed in on and off for several years, that was serendipitous, because Miki, who loved traditional music, did not sing herself. So what she could do was provide crash space for all the itinerant musicians around: I being one of the fortunate beneficiaries, and Bobby Dylan being another; and he landed in New York City, of course, at exactly the same time. So I, through no fault of or credit to myself, landed smack in the middle of the action, as it were, in Greenwich Village, and it was a very exciting time, and one needed to be twenty-three to survive it, I think. I do remember something that makes me vaguely uncomfortable at this point because it was so totally unconscious. I do remember one evening, Bob and I were on the same bill at Gerdes Folk City, and he had done his set, and I got up and sang whatever it was I was singing at the time, including "The Patriot Game." And when I came off, somebody said to me, "Well, that was pretty gutsy!" And I said, "What?" He said, "Were you making the point that Bob's song ("With God on Our Side") was a traditional tune ("The Merry Month of May") that had another set of words to it ("The Patriot Game")? I said, "No, it was totally unconscious." Obviously, I heard him sing and it pushed a button in this global search that goes on in the head. That's the song that it spat up.

BOB DYLAN AND BALLADS

Throughout his long career, Bob Dylan has populated his own songwriting with references to the folk songs of Britain and Ireland. In 2004 the influential American musician traveled to Scotland to be awarded a doctor of music degree by the University of St. Andrews. Previously, Dylan had only accepted an honorary degree from Princeton University in 1970. Professor Neil Corcoran of the University of St. Andrews's School of English said at the ceremony: "It seems appropriate that his second such degree should come from Scotland's oldest university, since Scottish Border Ballads and folk songs have been the inspiration for some of his melodies, and his great song 'Highlands' is an elaborate riff, or descant, on Robert Burns."[1]

Like Burns, Dylan has specialized in writing new lyrics to old tunes. He acknowledged a debt to Irish singer Liam Clancy in his performance of the Scottish folksong "Lang A-Growing" at his first major New York concert in 1961. Bob had met Clancy and the Scottish singer Jean Redpath, with whom he shared an apartment in New York's Greenwich Village in the early 1960s. In addition to her performances of the songs of Robert Burns, Jean is renowned for her vast repertoire of British Isles ballads. Redpath and Dylan had shared a bill at Gerdes Folk City on at least one occasion.

In 1962 Bob Dylan made a trip to the United Kingdom that was to be the catalyst for change in his music. He became friendly with the great English folksinger and guitarist Martin Carthy, who introduced Dylan to a number of English folk songs. Upon his return to the United States, Dylan produced two albums, *The Freewheelin' Bob Dylan* in 1963 and *The Times They Are A-Changin'* in 1964, in which he began to express the music, rhythms, and bold language of traditional ballads in his own songwriting.

Dylan acknowledged that the roots of his "Girl from the North Country" reach back to the popular ballad "Scarborough Fair," taught to him by Carthy. "Lord Franklin" is a forerunner to "Bob Dylan's Dream," "Farewell to Tarwathie" was echoed in his "Farewell Angelina," and "The Bonnie Lass o' Fyvie" inspired Dylan's "Pretty Peggy-O." There are many more examples.[2] Although always acknowledging the influence of folk song on his own imagination, Dylan has been famously vague about which specific songs inspired him. Controversy surrounded Dylan's crafting of "With God on Our Side," in which the theme and melody closely resembles "The Patriot Game" by Irish writer Dominic Behan (1928–89). However, Behan's song had connections to an older American song, "The Nightingale," which in turn had its roots in an even older English ballad. For Dylan, the relationship between his own songs and the authentic originals was never important. Like the early minstrels, he used ideas from songs that captured his imagination, transplanting them into new settings to engage the audience of the day.

In 1987, during a London concert series, Dylan attended the Islington Folk Club. There, he heard the Ian Campbell Folk Group, one of the most respected ballad-performing bands in the British folk scene of the 1950s and 1960s. Campbell's parents, from North East Scotland, were also performing at the club, and Dylan met them too. This gave him the opportunity to hear more traditional material directly from source singers.[3] "Tramps and Hawkers," a nineteenth-century song from the North East, is a clear influence on Dylan's "I Pity the Poor Immigrant." For their part, the Ian Campbell Folk Group enjoyed a U.K. top-fifty chart success with a version of Dylan's "The Times They Are A-Changin'" in 1965. This is one of Dylan's celebrated and most covered songs. In the liner notes for *Biograph* (Columbia Records), a 1985 box set tracing his career to that point, Dylan said of the song: "It was influenced of course by the Irish and Scottish ballads . . . 'Come All Ye Bold Highway Men,' 'Come All Ye Tender Hearted Maidens.' I wanted to write a big song, with short concise verses that piled up on each other in a hypnotic way."[4] As is often the case, it is left to the commentators to determine what song(s) may have been most inspirational in this creative process. Hamish Henderson's "51st Farewell to Sicily" is now widely accepted as the most seminal source influencing Dylan's "The Times They Are A-Changin'." Henderson had written his verses while on active service with the 51st Highland Division in Sicily in 1943.

A great collector himself, he then set them to the pipe tune "Farewell to the Creeks," composed during World War 1 by Pipe Major James Robertson.[5]

It all goes to show how Dylan's songs lie along a far-reaching line—from the ancient tradition of ballads in the British Isles and Ireland through singers like Jean Redpath, collectors such as Hamish Henderson, and the traveling twentieth-century bard Woody Guthrie, then on to Dylan. He has styled himself as another link in the chain connecting Burns and Guthrie, both of whom he greatly admired. His link is an important one: he is a collaborative songwriter who actually met the carriers, now mostly gone, of traditions that fired his imagination. The impact of Bob Dylan's songs on contemporary music demonstrates how echoes of the old ballads, passed through the oral tradition and onward into popular culture, still speak to us.

1. University of St. Andrews press release, June 23, 2004.
2. "Bob's Ballad Bases," BBC Radio 2, May 24, 2011.
3. Ibid.
4. Bob Dylan, *Biograph*, liner notes, Columbia Records 1985.
5. "Bob's Ballad Bases."

A Highland cottage. (Photograph by Doug Orr)

View out over the sea to Ailsa Craig from the road back from
Mull of Kintyre. (Courtesy of Matthew Hart/Alamy)

THE SEEDS OF ULSTER EMIGRATION

Well before Sir Walter Scott collected and published songs and poems and Raid Ballads of the Scottish Borders, seeds were sown for inhabitants of the area to emigrate across the sea to Ulster. For thousands of years, people had been crossing the North Channel of the Irish Sea, back and forth from both directions. Armies crossed the sea during the Middle Ages, and Highland mercenaries, the "Galloglaich," served in the Irish infantry. Barely twelve miles separates the Mull of Kintyre in Scotland and Fair Head in Northern Ireland, and clear weather allows each coastline a view of the other on the horizon. Over the years, the emigrants to Ulster came from all over Scotland and England, although the majority originated in the Borders.

In the sixteenth century, powerful political and religious forces were brewing that would permanently transform the Borders as well as the rest of Scotland, more than the reiving lifestyle could ever have done. Revolutionary teachings of the Protestant reformer John Calvin took root in Scotland and changed society for the Lowland Scots. John Knox (1505–72), a Scot who had studied under Calvin in Geneva, returned to Scotland and led the populace to embrace the Reformation in 1560. The emerging Presbyterian movement and its church, the Church of Scotland, challenged Roman Catholicism and introduced dramatic cultural changes: equality, individual conscience, material austerity, education, and a resistance to authority in religious practice, with a particular rejection of the old religious ways. This had a profound impact on life in the Borders, along with another radical change of circumstances: Scotland's James VI—now James I of England and Ireland, too—began a process of suppressing warring factions along either side of the Anglo-Scottish border. A brutal "pacification" of the bloody region was intended to subdue the lawless reivers. Public hangings and drownings were commonplace. In a drive to break up the tribal cul-

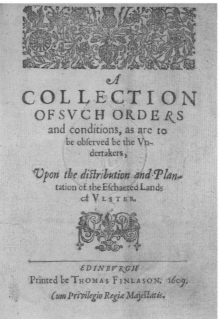

ture, entire families were outlawed. The heyday of the old Border warlords was ending, as they were denied power, income, and property. A cruel system of escalating payments from tenants called "rent racking" was implemented, and many were subsequently evicted from their homes. (This was a practice to be repeated with subsequent generations of Scots who emigrated to Ulster, especially during the Scottish famine years of the 1690s.) There also were road riots throughout the Border area, and these were brutally suppressed.

King James was determined to pacify his kingdom in Ireland and believed that the "barbaric," Gaelic-speaking Catholic Irish could be brought under control by "planting" English-speaking Presbyterians from the Borders. He decreed that private plantations would be created in Ulster in the counties closest to the Scottish mainland. Border Scots and northern English who had been trying to scrape a living from depleted lands would be offered arable farming property. This was a lengthy consolidation process, beginning in 1603 and extending through 1707, when the Acts of Union united the parliaments of Scotland and England. The policy created a new, substantial Scottish presence in Ulster, especially along its northeast coastal counties. So the first dramatic episode of "leavings" in the long chronicle of Scottish emigration was under way, a farewell that would be recited in Scottish story, song, and legend over many generations from Scotland to Ulster and onward to America.

Are you not weary in your distant places,
Far, far from Scotland of the mist and storm,
In drowsy airs, the sun-smite on your faces,
The days so long and warm?
When all around you lie the strange fields
    sleeping,
The dreary woods where no fond memories roam,
Do not your sad hearts over seas come leaping
To the highlands and the lowlands of your Home?
—*Neil Munro (1864–1930), "To Exiles"*[48]

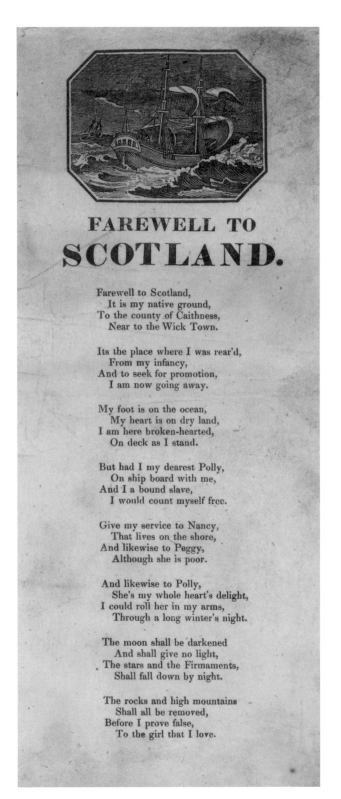

FAREWELL TO SCOTLAND.

Farewell to Scotland,
    It is my native ground,
To the county of Caithness,
    Near to the Wick Town.

Its the place where I was rear'd,
    From my infancy,
And to seek for promotion,
    I am now going away.

My foot is on the ocean,
    My heart is on dry land,
I am here broken-hearted,
    On deck as I stand.

But had I my dearest Polly,
    On ship board with me,
And I a bound slave,
    I would count myself free.

Give my service to Nancy,
    That lives on the shore,
And likewise to Peggy,
    Although she is poor.

And likewise to Polly,
    She's my whole heart's delight,
I could roll her in my arms,
    Through a long winter's night.

The moon shall be darkened
    And shall give no light,
The stars and the Firmaments,
    Shall fall down by night.

The rocks and high mountains
    Shall all be removed,
Before I prove false,
    To the girl that I love.

It was a' for our rightfu' king

We left fair Scotland's strand

It was a' for our rightfu' king

That we e'er saw Irish land my dear

That we e'er saw Irish land.

—Robert Burns, "It Was a' for Our Rightfu' King"

(CD TRACK 2)

Voyage

Farewell

With an eye on the next destination and a wayfaring tendency seemingly encoded in their DNA, Scots had been in a collective state of perpetual motion since the Middle Ages. In Britain and Europe, the prospect of adventure and opportunity sat eternally across the next horizon. By the seventeenth century, their gaze had turned westward across the North Channel to Ulster, where together they would write another chapter into their growing story of diffusion and diaspora. Their pattern of leave-taking may have had deep roots, yet there was a persistent tension between wanderlust and homesickness, retold in song and story over the generations from Scotland to Ulster to America. Robert Burns conveys the anguish of departure in "Farewell":

Adieu! A heart-warm fond adieu;
Dear brothers of the mystic tie!
Ye favoured, enlightened few,
Companions of my social joy;
Tho' I to foreign lands must hie,
Pursing fortune's slidd'ry ba';
With melting heart, and brimful eye,
I'll mind you still, tho far awa'.

OVER THE SEA TO ULSTER

For the ancient maritime communities around the North Channel of the Irish Sea, the water was more a thoroughfare than a barrier. Land was impenetrable and, in places, densely wooded, so the sea was the way. Coastal migrations were the essence of life, and the North Channel was actively navigated in both directions throughout time: the first post–Ice Age crossings by Stone Age people from Scotland to Ireland over 8,000 years ago; Saint Ninian's fifth-century outposts and early mission work to convert the Picts;[1] Saint Columba's epic voyage in the sixth century, crossing from Antrim to Galloway in a flimsy leather currach and succeeding with Christianity where Rome's military conquest had failed;[2] seafaring raiders ("Scotti" or "Scoti" as the Romans named them) colonizing western Scotland from Ireland; the Galloglaigh and the Redshanks, mercenary soldiers of the Middle Ages recruited from the Scottish Highlands and the Hebrides to fight for Irish chieftains. Foremost among these warriors were the MacDonnells of the Scottish Isles and Antrim. They were part of the branch of the Dàl Riata (Dalriada), a dynasty that established itself in modern-day Argyll and the Inner Hebrides, perhaps driven to spread from Ireland to Scotland as a result of successional tensions. Indeed, while Lowland Scots have always been linked with Ulster migrations, innumerable Highland Scots moved to Ulster's Glens of Antrim between 1400 and 1700. Their settlement, along with Lowland Scots' influence, helped shape Ulster's language, music, and folkways.

The MacDonnells managed to create and command a sphere of influence that spanned the North Channel, drawing in eastern Ulster and parts of western Scotland under a single rule.[3] By 1530 they oversaw the territory as a cross-channel cultural domain. The ancient Scots Gaelic lullaby "Bidh Clann Ulaidh," (The Children of Ulster) emphasizes the connection. As well as the king's family, the mother sings her guest list of Scottish clansfolk that will attend her baby daughter's future wedding: the MacDonalds, the MacAulays, the MacKenzies will all be there. Pride of place, named first, are the guests who will sail across the North Channel to come to the festivities.

Bidh Clann Ulaidh, luaidh's a lurain
(The Clans of Ulster, my darling, my treasure)
Bidh Clann Ulaidh air do bhanais
(The Clans of Ulster will be at your wedding)
Bidh Clann Ulaidh, luaidh's a lurain
(The Clans of Ulster, my darling, my treasure)
Dèanamh an danns air do bhanais
(Will be dancing at your wedding)
—"Bidh Clann Ulaidh"

The sea separation is so narrow that there are numerous places on the Ulster coast where the southwest of Scotland is easily visible on the horizon. Coastal villages on either side were connected by route ways well known to the seafarers of the day, who worked their way toward their destinations by relying on visual memories of rocky islets, coastal inlets, and a keen sense of direction. Mediterranean mariners had access to detailed harbor books of their ports of call, coastal maps, and travel time between ports; it was a body of information developed and shared between Venetian, Genoese, and Catalonian draftsmen. Setting sail across the North Channel was never so straightforward, and points of embarkation had to be picked very carefully. The Irish Sea can whip up a squall in a matter of minutes, and small vessels would have been easily endangered, as they are today.[4] The small harbor town of Portpatrick on the Rhinns of Galloway Peninsula in Scotland has a natural harbor and a name that proclaims its historical role as a port of transportation to and from Donaghadee in Ulster. This crossing is a distance of only twenty-one miles—in fair weather a relatively easy voyage in either direction. Depending on the wind, weather, and sturdiness of craft, travel time could range widely from three to twelve hours. As emigration and trade from Scotland grew through the centuries, a whole assortment of materials might accompany the voyage, including grains, cattle, textiles, and mail. In time, it became feasible for friends to pay each other visits by crossing such channel routes.[5]

View from Scotland over the sea to Ulster.
(Photograph by Doug Orr)

Ancient Seafarers and Channel Crossers

Dr. John Purser, Scottish composer, musicologist, and music historian; interviewed in Dunkeld, Scotland, June 2011, by Fiona Ritchie en route to the National Museum of Scotland.

Take things like, of course, the Sea Shanties. Ah, now, here's a wonderful example in Wedderburn's "The Complaynt of Scotland," which is in 1549 that he writes this. And, poor devil, he'd had his house burnt down in Dundee by the English, and he'd moved down into Fife, and he's grumbling away, "The Complaynt of Scotland," you know, you can just see him, dipping his pen into the ink well of his thoughts, brutal, bitter thoughts, you know, writing down. And then he thinks, "But Scotland is so wonderful, and we have this wonderful music and all of these tunes," and then he gives this huge list of tunes and dances. And then later he goes on, and he describes coming down towards a port, and the sailors are getting ready to sail in a big sailing ship and he has all their cries. And there's about half a dozen different languages in there in 1547, and it's just this extraordinary macaronic kind of splurge of sounds, almost half of it is very hard to make out what is meant because, you know, "Sarabossa! Sarabossa!" What the hell does that mean? I haven't a clue. It's some Portuguese or Spanish thing that they're shouting. It will be a little group of sailors on the ship that handle one particular capstan or something like that. But this has ended up in a Scottish manuscript in 1547.

Well, if you're taken right back to the Stone Age, you can see right up the western seaboard of Europe—from Brittany, Cornwall, Wales, Ireland, parts of England, Scotland, Scandinavia—these huge henges: monolithic structures and burial graves, burial mounds, and so on. Now there are big regional variations, but they are clearly part of the same culture, overall it is a western European seaboard culture, and these guys are moving around. And then when you get to the Bronze Age, you've got the Phoenicians coming out, the Flying Tin Men as they were called, coming to Cornwall, which had a big supply of tin. But they're also looking for copper, you know, after Santorini [the volcanic Greek island] blew up, you see, that suddenly screwed up copper supplies. Now these skills in handling rock and turning it into metal are these styles, and technologies are spreading right up and, indeed, possibly down the west coast.

Take the Bronze Age horns in Ireland—well, mostly in Ireland, one found in Scotland, one down in England—but the manner of working bronze from the bronze smiths of that period in Ireland is the same as the bronze smiths in Orkney and Shetland at the same time. So these boys, you know, the experts are running up and down the coast, and so yes, these influences can be very widespread. People were more mobile than you might imagine, or at least the people with technological skills were certainly mobile, and you could say the upwardly mobile people—musicians tend to be mobile, a long, long tradition of traveling musicians, and I mean, *plus ça change, plus c'est la même chose*, you know? If you want to be a Scottish musician, why not just go to America or Germany, where they might even pay you?

Possession of a boat and the ability to handle it across the North Channel, you know, you can't just be anybody to be able to do that. The saints that came over from Ireland, and anybody who was remotely holy was a saint, these were all upper-class people, you know, Saint Columba and his followers, they all came from aristocratic families, which is how they were able, to a degree, to take over, when Dál Riata [Dalriada] became a kingdom across the North Channel, in fact, the Scottish end of it became bigger than the Irish side of it eventually. And, yes, at the same time, there would be people that scarcely ever moved. Just as there still are, I mean, my neighbor, Katy Mary, had never been out of Scotland until her son got married in New York, and she's never been on the European Continent, and she's very rarely left [the Isle of] Skye. She started off on Harris [in the Outer Hebrides], and coming to Skye was quite enough [laughing].

And if you look particularly at the clarsach [harp], the Scottish clarsairs [harpers] were always going over to Ireland and getting an education there as often as not, sometimes getting their harps made from there, sometimes they were made in Scotland. The so-called "Brian Boru" harp was almost certainly made in Scotland. That went right on into the nineteenth century, there's a photograph of one of them [Patrick Byrne], a Hill and Adamson photograph, wonderful one. And he's in a sort of Bardic robe with his harp and his Bardic pose—it's a great picture. But he would be one of the last examples of a traveling harper.

Map of the Province of Ulster, 1676. (Mapmaker, John Speed; courtesy © Antiquarian Images/Mary Evans Picture Library)

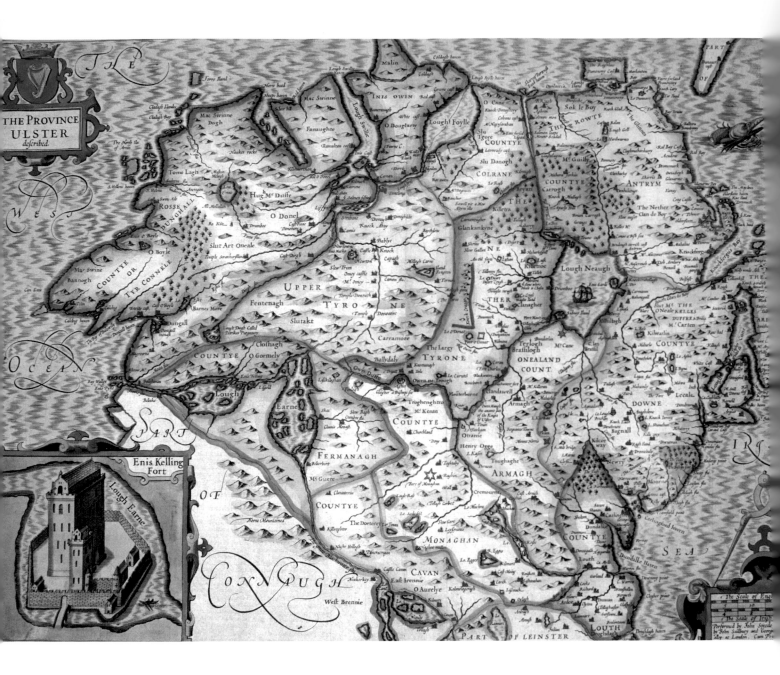

The connections between Scotland and Ireland were forever altered by the Plantation scheme of King James VI and I. The idea was not new; the Glens of Antrim, with their close proximity to Scotland and long history of clan intermarriage, were the setting in 1380 for Clan Donald establishing a strong foothold of Scots. In that year, John Mor MacDonnell of Islay in the Hebrides became the first of the MacDonnells of Antrim to build castles at Battlecastle, Red Bay, and Glenarm in Ulster. Their headquarters was the fortress of Dunluce Castle, sitting atop a rocky outcrop and surrounded by sea on three sides. Today, the farmland around the rock is littered with lumps and bumps, remnants of a lost settlement. When archaeologists lifted the sod in 2011, they exposed a well-preserved seventeenth-century Scottish townscape with cobbled streets and merchants' houses laid out on a grid—all indications of the significant trading post built there by Randall MacDonnell, the first earl of Antrim. Dunluce was attacked and set ablaze during an Irish rebellion in 1641, after which many settlers returned home to Scotland and the town was abandoned. Archaeologists continue to unearth many artifacts, and, as the remaining 95 percent of the town is carefully excavated, they will uncover the material story of the early Scottish settlements of Ulster.

The principle of "planting" peoples on Irish land started with Henry VIII in 1541. In 1556 Queen Mary authorized a similar scheme in southern parts of Ireland, and her policy of land grants to English land-

Ulster and Scotland: An Ancient Link

Len Graham, Irish traditional singer and song collector; interviewed in Swannanoa, North Carolina, July 2013, by Fiona Ritchie and Doug Orr during Traditional Song Week at the Swannanoa Gathering folk arts workshops.

Common language, common culture, the whole fiddle tradition and the whole music tradition is all very, very similar and connected. The history and the geography have all played a part in it. You know the shamrock, the rose, and the thistle, meaning the three—England, Scotland, and Ireland—all contribute to what we now call the Ulster song tradition, or Ulster music tradition for that matter. And you know, you've got the bagpipes, which are common to both Ireland and Scotland. It became popular with the British regiment, you know, Scottish and Irish regiments, in the nineteenth century, but it was a common instrument in both countries. The harp, of course, is common to both Ireland and Scotland. The fiddle is most popular by far in Scotland and Ireland [with] traditional musicians. And then the songs reflect that as well. You've got songs that have got definite Scottish origins but with very much an Ulster or a northern dialect or accent. And you find that goes two ways. One of the early songs that I would have heard from my grandmother, and it also turns up in Kintyre [Scotland] about a shipwreck, the *Enterprise*, that went down in 1834. So that song turns up and was collected by Hamish Henderson in Campbeltown in that area of Argyllshire, and also I got the same song because that distance is so close—twelve miles—and the ship had gone down between the two. So the song turns up in both camps. There's those connections, but there's much more than that: the history, the language, the Irish language, the Gaelic language, as you call it in Scotland, was spoken. So there's a long association between the two countries.

The success of the 1606 Hamilton and Montgomery settlement secured the foothold that facilitated the Plantation of Ulster, launched by King James in 1610. It also emboldened James with his Virginia colony, and in 1607 the first English settlers arrived in Jamestown. With the "Dawn of the Ulster Scots," the Ulster Scots–American connection was also born.

The Scots were "a people on the move." As the seventeenth century began, their population was increasing, and there was a surplus of young men seeking employment and adventure overseas, not only in Ulster. In fact, during the early part of the seventeenth century, Scots were more likely to emigrate to Scandinavia and Poland than to Ireland. The period was, nevertheless, marked by periodic waves of Scottish emigration over the sea to Ulster, especially through the ports of Carrickfergus and Derry-Londonderry. The Scottish famine years of the 1690s unleashed an exodus of tens of thousands, at which time the Scots became a majority community in the province of Ulster.

THE ULSTER SCOTS

The rose of all the world is not for me.
I want for my part
Only the little white rose of Scotland
That smells sharp and sweet—and breaks the heart.
—*Hugh MacDiarmid, "The Little White Rose"*[6]

Scots in Ulster began settling into life in their new land, but the memories were still fresh of a home across the sea. The old life may have been tough and trying, but their urge to explore beyond the next horizon was tempered, as ever, with nostalgia for the place left behind. For some, the connections were restored by occasional return visits to see family and friends. The majority never again set foot on their ancestral land, however, which gradually receded into folk memory. Some who left were missed eternally by those they left behind. In the Hebridean song "Dh'fhalbh Mo

lords persisted under Elizabeth I, with limited success. James Hamilton and Hugh Montgomery, two entrepreneurial Scots from Ayrshire, founded private Ulster enterprises in 1606. The focus of their settlement projects were Antrim and Down, the two counties closest to Scotland. Both allies of King James I, Hamilton and Montgomery offered cheap rents to attract new tenants across the water. In May 1606 the first boatloads of Lowland Scottish (almost entirely Presbyterian) settlers arrived to take up tenancy on the Hamilton and Montgomery estates. There, they established the first permanent settlement of "Ulster Scots"; today's descendants of Sir James Hamilton (the Rowan-Hamilton family) and Sir Hugh Montgomery (the Montgomeries of Greyabbey) still live in the area.

Nighean Chruinn Donn" (My Lovely Brown-Haired Girl Has Gone), a man sings in Scots Gaelic of his lost love, gone to live in Newry, near the Mountains of Mourne.

> Dh'fhalbh mo nighean chruinn donn (My lovely brown-haired girl)
> Bhuam do'n Iùraidh (Has gone from me to Newry)
> Dh'fhalbh mo nighean chruinn donn (My lovely brown-haired girl)
> Cneas mar eal' air bhàrr thonn (Her breast as white as the swan on the waves)
> Och 's och, mo nighean chruinn donn (Oh, my brown-haired girl)
> A dh'fhàg mi-shunnd orm (You have left me unhappy)

She may have married for better prospects in Ulster, but sorrow lingers on both shores.

> Ged tha thusa an drasd' (Although you are now)
> Ann an Gleann Iùraidh (In a glen in Newry)
> Ged that thus' ann an tàmh (Although you are dwelling there)
> Tha t'aigne fo phràmh (Your mind is sorrowful)
> Agus mise gun stàth (And I am without purpose)
> Le do gràdh ciùrrte (With the pain of your love)
> (CD TRACK 3)

As the Plantation plan proceeded into the seventeenth century, many more families began making the journey toward resettlement in Ulster. The majority of the Scottish emigrants entered this new colony as landless tenants. They would rent from a class of principal landowners called "undertakers." These English and Scots settlers received up to 2,000 acres and were required at their own expense to settle ten Scottish or English families for each 1,000 acres. Other designated landowners were the "servitors," administrative and military men who were granted Ulster estates from the government in London.

Belfast to London was over 460 miles by land and sea, and the region was undeveloped, underpopulated and noncompliant to English rule. So the Ulster Plantation, Ireland's largest, was a high priority for colonization. During much of the seventeenth century, rents were low and land abundant, fostering a steady stream of immigration into the colony. The year after the King James Plantation era was launched, approximately 8,000 new families had settled into the six official Plantation counties: Armagh, Cavan, Donegal, Fermanagh, Londonderry, and Tyrone. Antrim and Down, the coastal stretches of East Ulster with closest proximity to Scotland, had been part of the original private Plantation plan, and they continued to absorb the largest number of Scottish settlers.

Scots settlers were more accustomed to difficult living conditions and humble means than their English Plantation neighbors. More restless by nature, too, they were prone to relocate in search of better farmland. The largely rural culture best supported the small individual agricultural settlement called a "clachan," which housed a cluster of cottages whose tenants worked together on the surrounding land. Much smaller than the organized agricultural villages elsewhere in Europe, the clachan communities were less regulated, more self-sufficient, and only semipermanent. Yet there was a sense of neighborhood, ties

THE PROVINCE OF ULSTER

The Province of Ulster is of special historic significance to both Northern Ireland and the Republic of Ireland, although today it has no official administrative or political status. Its name is derived from the Irish "Cuige Uladh," which translated means "Fifth of the Ulaidh." The Ulaidh were a collection of prehistoric tribes in the area, and the "fifth" refers to the five ancient regions of Ireland. Ulster evolved as one of Ireland's four provinces, along with Leinster, Munster, and Connacht. Meath, originally the fifth province, was absorbed into Leinster, with smaller parts included in Ulster. The late Irish musician Tommy Makem composed the iconic ballad "Four Green Fields" to represent the shared essence of the four provinces, notwithstanding contemporary national boundaries and political divisions.

Historic Ulster comprised nine counties: Antrim, Armagh, Cavan, Donegal, Down, Fermanagh, Derry-Londonderry, Monaghan, and Tyrone. The 1920 Government of Ireland Act oversaw the partition of the island, with the Republic of Ireland established in the south and Northern Ireland created out of six Ulster counties (both sections remained part of the United Kingdom). Counties Donegal, Cavan, and Monaghan were assigned to the newly independent Irish Free State, known today as the Republic of Ireland, with its capital in Dublin. Northern Ireland's capital is Belfast, home of the Northern Ireland Assembly. This was established in 1998 by agreement of political parties in Northern Ireland and the British and Irish governments and is the devolved legislature of Northern Ireland. The assembly is responsible for making laws regarding certain matters in Northern Ireland, with the United Kingdom of Great Britain and Northern Ireland's Parliament in London assuming designated government functions on behalf of all the constituent parts of the United Kingdom.

The partition of Ireland was calculated to place the Unionist counties (which had safe Protestant majorities) in Northern Ireland and the Roman Catholic counties in the Republic of Ireland. Today, however, Tyrone and Fermanagh have Catholic majorities, and slightly more than half of Northern Ireland's 2 million people are Catholic. To this day, Antrim and Down, the two private Plantation counties that were resettled by Scottish landowners and are closest to Scotland, are the Irish counties with the largest percentage of Protestant citizens.

The ethnonationalistic conflict in Northern Ireland began with intensity in the 1960s but has deep roots in the area going back to King James's seventeenth-century Plantation colonization. The 1998 Good Friday Agreement largely ended three decades of sectarian violence between Nationalist (Catholic) and Unionist (Protestant) paramilitaries. Political tensions between the once-bitter rivals have eased considerably, although the official peace has failed to eliminate conflict from the troubled housing estates of the Province, and sectarian rioting still erupts periodically. The two communities, separated in some parts of Belfast by "peace walls," work on jointly run programs to help children integrate across the historic divisions. The Good Friday Agreement also saw the establishment of the Ulster-Scots Agency (Tha Boord o Ulstèr-Scotch). Funded by government departments from north and south of the border, the agency supports the use of Ulster Scots or "Ullans" as a living language and promotes understanding of Ulster Scots history and culture.

The landscapes of Ulster are beautiful, from northwest coastal Donegal on the windswept shores of the Atlantic and the volcanic formations of the Giant's Causeway on the northern coast to the scenic villages that rim the North Channel looking toward Scotland and Lough Neagh, the largest lake anywhere in Ireland or the United Kingdom. The capital of Northern Ireland, Belfast, is the country's largest city, with a population of around half a million people. The university town is a historic center for shipbuilding, including the ill-fated RMS *Titanic*, constructed at the Harland and Wolff shipyard. The second-largest city in Northern Ireland is Derry, or Londonderry. Founded in the sixth century by Saint Colmcille (Columba), Derry was renamed Londonderry in 1613 upon receipt of its royal charter for King James I. The city's name has always been contentious; today's Catholic and Protestant com-

munities have settled on a new name for the city, symbolized by its famous Peace Bridge across the River Foyle: Derry-Londonderry.

Lough Foyle was the most important embarkation port for eighteenth-century Ulster Scots' emigration to America. Along with the familiar names of well-loved villages and counties, Northern Ireland's two main cities are celebrated in many a traditional Ulster song—from the legacy of the early Scots to heart-rending love ballads, American Wake songs, and the storytelling ballads that recorded personal tales of emigration across the Atlantic foam.

of kinship and church, music gatherings (including songs from their Scottish background and Presbyterian Church hymns), and fairs and markets to bind the district together. These were key elements of a society that their descendants would later replicate in their southern Appalachian homesteads.[7]

The Presbyterian faith of the Ulster Scots was a significant element of their lives and communities. The Plantation schematic was a complex cultural environment of three contrasting yet intermingling groups: Scottish Presbyterians, Irish Catholics, and English Anglicans. The original Plantation blueprint had been designed to deliver a controversial outcome: the displacement of the native Irish. The undertakers, which included land-owning Scots, were thus forbidden to lease land to Irish tenants. However, the reality of Plantation life caused theory and practice to differ; workers were needed on the farms, and the Scots leased land to Irish tenants from the outset, with the promise that they would not be deposed. There had, understandably, been considerable resentment by the Irish, who feared not just the loss of land to the settlers but also the depreciation of the old Gaelic order. Yet in the harsh reality of their existence, Scots and Irish lived amicably and worked side by side, and the government had to accept that it could not force the landowning undertakers to evict their Irish tenants. Consequently, a 1628 accord permitted the leasing of up to one-fourth of Plantation lands to the native Irish. Cordial and close interrelationships between the Scots and Irish were settled and accepted from then, transcending linguistic and religious differences. Seventeenth-century plantation life found its balance.[8]

I ONCE LOVED A LASS
Intermingling and Intermarriage

I once loved a lass and I loved her sae weel,
That I hated all others that spoke o' her ill;
But noo she's rewarded me weel for my love,
She has gone tae be wed tae another.

"I Once Loved a Lass," an old song of unrequited love with roots in Scottish and Irish balladry, embodies the melancholy sense of loss running through the heart of many a song and story: love lost through cultural, religious, and economic divides; family intervention; departures to foreign fields of work and war. The close-at-hand clachan communities of the Ulster Scots and their Irish neighbors must have presented opportunities for romance across the boundaries of class or church.

So this begs the question: with intermingling of the two cultures established, to what extent was there intermarriage? And in view of that, are the Scots-Irish in the United States of mixed Scots and Irish blood? Scholars have debated these questions and differ sharply. James Leyburn, in his landmark book, *The Scotch-Irish: A Social History*, addressed the issue from both sides, while admitting that no documentary evidence is available to settle the matter firmly.[9]

Only an examination of Ulster marriage records of the time could provide clear proof of intermarriage, but such documents do not exist. Circumstantial evidence of intermarriage is, however, quite significant. The communities shared bonds of language (a good percentage of early Presbyterian settlers were Gaelic speaking), work, and hardship, and—tellingly—they also shared family names. In the close-knit clachans, there is no doubt that some young people would have been moved more by romantic impulse than by religious loyalty. Surely, marriage and, as a consequence, religious conversion must occasionally have taken place.[10]

Leyburn is more persuaded that religion and pride of culture were significant deterrents to intermarriage. Irish Catholics and Scottish Presbyterians living their faith could each be zealous in their religious fervor. It was a passion that ran deep in the veins of Irish patriots in the long struggle for freedom from the English.[11] Crossing the religious line beyond routine socializing was taboo and met with strong parental disapproval. In the tragic County Down ballad "Johnny Doyle," parents intervene between Catholic Johnny and his Protestant lover, and the girl's family forces her to marry a boy of her own faith.

> There's one thing that grieves me and I must confess,
> I go to meeting and my true love goes to mass,
> But for to go to mass with him, I would count it no toil,
> For to kneel at the altar, with young Johnny Doyle.
>
> A horse and side-saddle, my father did provide,
> With four and twenty horsemen to ride by my side,
> Five hundred bright guineas, my father did provide,
> The day that I was to be Sammy Moore's bride.
>
> Folding down the clothes, he found she was dead,
> And Johnny Doyle's handkerchief tied round her head,
> Folding down the clothes, he found she was dead,
> And a fountain of tears over her he did shed.

Over and above the religious boundaries, Leyburn contends that the depth of cultural pride, especially on the side of the Irish, was profound. If a marriage was made, Leyburn adds, it usually involved the Irish partner coming into the colonizing Scottish or English family.[12] Others, such as Ulster scholar and musician Len Graham, take a broader view, citing the dynamics of substantial intermingling already mentioned and the evidence of merged Irish and Scottish surnames in America.[13] Time may well have obscured any clear answer, but it is commonly accepted that there was a great deal of contact between the Ulster Scots and the Irish, whether at work or at social gatherings. The irrepressible nature of folk traditions suggests, at the very least, that some shared musical culture would surely have been woven among the communities.

An assortment of threads and textures would have

colored the musical fabric as smaller ethnic groups also came to Ulster, attracted by the linen industry—Welsh, French Huguenots, and English Plantation settlers among them, foreshadowing the later melting-pot scenario of the United States. Through the ages, traditional musicians have exhibited openness and a strong democratic streak, inviting a diversity of people and their music into the circle. No one person, or indeed any community, has ever been able to constrain the power of a song or a tune as a force for mutual understanding and shared joy.

ULSTER SONG
The Hearth and the Ceili

> I am a rambling Irishman, in Ulster I was born in,
> Many's a happy hour I spent on the banks of sweet Lough Erne.
> —*The Rambling Irishman* (CD TRACK 5)

Although the music of Ulster Scots bore an indelible imprint of the original Scottish immigrants, it

Scottish-Irish Connections

Nuala Kennedy, Irish singer, songwriter, and flute and whistle player; interviewed in Dunkeld, Scotland, June 2013, by Fiona Ritchie during Kennedy's concert tour playing Irish and Appalachian music with A. J. Roach.

There is a good connection historically between the east coast of Ireland and Scotland because it is so close. Gerry O'Connor, a friend of mine and a fiddle player from Dundalk, he did some research into a manuscript: "The Donnellan Collection." And we looked through that together, through all the tunes, and I recognized a lot of them (from living over here in Scotland) as Scottish pipe tunes. So there was obviously a lot of interchange musically between the east coast of Ireland and Scotland through the years.

You're probably aware of a great record that was made a few years ago by Colum Sands and Maggie MacInnes, "Báta an tSìl" [CD track 3], about Newry in the north of Ireland, and how there were people coming from the Western Isles of Scotland and traveling down to the east coast of Ireland to the Newry area for marriage and for trade, so it seems like there's a pretty strong connection.

I play in a band with Gerry called Oriela that plays the music of that area, which is the old Kingdom of Oriel (Airgíalla), which is an old division of Ireland around about the seventh century, and so the repertoire that we're playing is local to that area. So it's satisfying to me to have grown up in that area and come away and lived in Scotland and lived in America, but now to come back and explore my own native music again.

I came to Scotland to go to Edinburgh College of Art and came across some sessions and loved the atmosphere and the people that were playing. The music was very vibrant; the whole city was alive with it. I discovered all the pipe music and really got into that. I'd see the titles of tunes written in Gaelic, and I, having grown up with Irish, I'd recognise names; it's very similar to Irish. And that sparked a deep interest in Gaelic, so I ended up studying a bit of Scots Gaelic in Inverness. It was great to find that connection over here. It really made me feel at home in Scotland in a very connected way with the culture here.

steadily evolved beyond simply Scottish music now played in Ulster. Geography dictated the most obvious influences. Ulster place names, from Belfast and Derry-Londonderry to the River Foyle, appeared in the lyrics of many an Ulster refrain, and plenty of songs and instruments crossed back over the North Channel to Scotland. Other elements of Ulster Scots' music bore the hallmark of the native Irish, and new compositions stemmed from the hybrid culture of thistle and shamrock. Wherever people gathered to sing or dance to a fiddle tune, the stage was set for the spark of something new. This might happen around the cottage hearth, at "ceili" gatherings (in Scotland, "ceilidh"), in music halls, and even at rural crossroads, where young people from a scattered community would unite at a midpoint on their country roads, a fiddle or accordion in hand to play for open air dancing. Since the church at the time frowned

upon dancing, crossroads marked a safe haven for the musical fun. From Ulster to the Outer Hebrides, such scenes can be witnessed in paintings and old photographs; a single flute, an accordion, a fiddle, or a set of pipes is invariably in the frame, with the dancers evidently making the most of the experience. (Heavier road traffic, even in rural areas, brought the days of crossroad dancing to a close in the modern era.)

Most of all, however, family gatherings by the hearth with friends and neighbors were the primary social outlet, especially during the long winter nights. In an era lacking electric power or easy transport, ceilis or ceilidhs were inclusive, regardless of social status and ethnic background. In these circumstances, it is easy to imagine a free flow of oral song and story traditions as described by Len Graham in his biography of legendary Irish musician Joe Holmes:

This sort of ceilidh with song, story, and dance was common to many houses in County Antrim and other parts of Ulster irrespective of religious affiliation and background. The sub-culture of the ceili-house which was the scene of fireside philosophers, rustic bards, storytellers, balladeers, traditional musicians and dancers was that of ordinary people with extraordinary skills and imaginations. The Holmes hearth and homestead was a welcome oasis bringing together neighbors, tailors, tinkers, itinerant musicians and singers

THE CEILI, OR CEILIDH

Stemming from an old Gaelic root word meaning "companion," the spellings have diverged into the Scottish "ceilidh" and the Irish "ceili"; however, the essence of the tradition is the same. A later definition was "a visit," and the ceilidh culture retains its drop-in, social spirit. Other tags may capture the idea just as well: "spree," "song swap," "kitchen time," "kitchen racket," "bottle night," and "big night." In the rural areas of Scotland and Ireland prior to modern transportation and entertainment, it was the major social activity throughout the eighteenth and nineteenth centuries. A warm welcome was guaranteed to all, especially those known to bring stories, songs, instrumental tunes, and dances.

In days gone by, the get-togethers were a forum for sharing the news or gossip of the day. This is not such a central part of the gatherings today, but what has endured is the egalitarian spirit, allowing a social mix of revelers from different backgrounds and places. Poteen (illegal whiskey) was common—and one reason for the clergy to stay away (though this is not necessarily the case any more). Whether the beverage was legal or not, glasses were filled and refilled from the flask, explaining the origin of the name "bottle night." Within the modest family cottage, the activity centered around the hearth or in the kitchen, which in many cases was the same room. In larger dwellings, one room might host the songs and stories, impromptu and in seamless transition, while dancing was held in another room and sometimes in a barn or outbuilding. This dancing custom gave name to the varieties of ceili and ceilidh dances that are still extremely popular at parties, weddings, and concerts. At the end of the evening, a parting glass was shared, along with songs for the road from the vast pool of parting songs in the Scottish and Irish repertoire. In some ways, the evening shared elements with the American Wakes; however, there was jollity in the air because the partings were not permanent.

> Of all the money that e'er I had, I spent it in
>   good company.
> And of all the harm that e'er I've done, alas it was
>   to none but me.
> And all I've done for want of wit, to memory
>   now I can't recall.
> So fill to me the parting glass. Goodnight and
>   joy be with you all.
> —*The Parting Glass* (CD TRACK 20)

While the home remained a place for a ceili or ceilidh, over time the ceilidh house—"taigh ceilidh"—became a more common site for gatherings, along with public houses and hotels in recent decades. It is a tradition very much alive and well, with music sessions hosted in many a home, hall, or pub in Ireland and Scotland. The spirit of music making and revelry has followed the Scottish and Irish diaspora to Australia, New Zealand, Canada, and the United States. The southern Appalachians would carry on the tradition, in essence if not in name, through jam sessions and song circles from the front porch to the crossroads store.

which was the "university" of Joe's learning and experience.[14]

Music author Aidan O'Hara refers to this coming together of various musicians and their music as a "shared fusing," unconcerned by the background of the participant—Catholic or Protestant, Irish or Scot, farmer or tradesman.[15] As such, the "playlists" for a ceili, usually spontaneous, might include a lively fiddle tune that set the visitors dancing, or a song—sad or humorous—from any origin or era. Nonsense choruses were always enthusiastically shared.

Here I am amongst you and I'm here because
  I'm here,
And I'm only twelve months older, than I was
  this time last year, righ-ah,
With me to-righ-ah, with me to-righ-oor-i-ah,
Righ de dom with me to-righ-ah, with me
  to-righ-oor-i-ah.
Oh, the more a man has, the more a man wants,
  the same I don't think true,
For I never met a man with one black eye, that
  wished that he had two, righ-ah.
With me to-righ-ah, with me tour I oor I ah, etc.[16]

A well-traveled song that originated in Scotland, was sung at ceilis in Ulster, and eventually found its way to the Appalachians was the "Dark-Eyed Gypsy." Its many variants go by as many names, all of which reflect the constant enduring themes of love and class. Tracing roots to Scotland as "The Earl o' Cassillis Lady" or "The Gypsy Laddie," it sailed onward to Ulster to be reborn as "The Raggle Taggle Gypsy." In the United States, Woody Guthrie learned the song from his mother as "Gypsy Davy." The popular Appalachian version is "Black Jack Davy." This is the oral tradition at its busiest—lyrics and titles are changed with careless abandon, but the essence of the story remains constant: the lady of the castle always runs off with the "dark-eyed gypsy o."

The Scottish version sets the ballad among the characters and countryside of Ayrshire in the southwest:

The gypsies they came to my Lord Cassillis' yett,
And O but they sang bonny;
They sang sae sweet and sae complete
That down came our fair Ladie.

She came tripping down the stairs
And all her maids before her,
As soon as they saw her weel-far'd face,
They coost their glamourie o'er her.

She gave to them the good wheat bread,
And they gave her the ginger,
But she gave them a far better thing,
The gold ring off her finger.

Will ye go with me, my hinny and my heart,
Will ye go with me, my dearie?
And I shall swear by the staff of my spear
That your Lord shall ne'er come near thee.

Gae tak' from me my silk manteel,
And bring to me a plaidie;
For I will travel the world o'er
Along with the Gypsie Laddie. (CD TRACK 7)

In "coosting their glamour" or casting a spell over her, the Scots ballad retains a magic and mystery that is missing from the American "Gypsy Davy," which cuts, literally, to the chase:

It was late last night when the squire came home
  and he's asking for his lady
Only answer that he got, "she's gone with the
  Gypsy Davy"
[Refrain] Rattle to my Gypsum, Gypsum, Rattle
  to my Gypsum Davy-O

"Go saddle me up my milk white steed, the black
  one he ain't so speedy
I'll ride all night I'll ride all day til I bring home
  my lady"

Well he rode all night until broad daylight til he
   comes to a river raging,
There he spied his darling bride in the arms of
   Blackjack Davy

"Come home my true love, come home my honey
I'll put you in a tower so high where the gypsies
   can't come around you"

"Well I won't come home my true love, I won't
   come home my honey
I wouldn't give a kiss from the gypsy's lips for all
   your lands and money"

"Would you forsake your house and home would
   you forsake your baby?
Would you forsake your husband dear for the love
   of Gypsy Davy?"

"Yes, I'll forsake my house and home, I'll forsake
   my baby
And I'll forsake my husband dear, for the love of
   Gypsy Davy" (CD TRACK 8)

Songs like this, heard throughout the British Isles,
Ireland, and the United States, are the footprints of
a traditional culture on the move. In their earliest
homes, they were usually sung unaccompanied (a capella) and solo in the revered "sean-nós" ("old-style")
tradition. The most riveting sean-nós singers rarely
made eye contact, standing quite still and letting the
song take center stage. Shared in this way, songs belonged to an entire community, enduring across time
and place. Although some came to be associated with
great singers in different eras, they belonged to a living
communal song pool.[17] Over time, people embraced
other forms of singing, including two or more a capella singers joined in unison (without harmony)—a
particular Ulster style—as well as voices accompanied
by different musical instruments.

An Ulster tradition and song style evolved. It resonated with an unmistakable Scottish influence through
songs with roots in Aberdeenshire and the Borders of
Scotland, in the Highlands and Islands, and in towns.
Although Robert Burns never made it to Ulster in his
travels, his songs certainly did become popular there.
"A Man's a' Man for a' That," Burns's stirring anthem
for equality and justice, was first published anony-
mously in *The Glasgow Magazine* in August 1795 and
then two months later in Belfast's *Northern Star*, a
radical newspaper of the United Irishmen. Considered
somewhat provocative at the time, it appeared the next
year in the *London Oracle* with authorship attributed to
Burns. This caused him concern, as the sedition laws
were in force and he was working for the government
at the time. His "Address to the Toothache" was first
printed in the *Belfast Newsletter* in September 1797.[18]
Burns's larger body of work crossed the North Channel as well, including "Song Composed in August"
("Westlin' Winds"), "Afton Water," "Highland Mary,"
"The Banks o' Doon," "A Red, Red Rose," and "Ae
Fond Kiss." All were popular in the different communities of Ulster, his love songs easily covering ground
throughout Ireland. The Burns family even fit the
profile of Ulster Scots, some migrating from Ayrshire
in the southwest of Scotland across the sea. His sister
Agnes is buried in St. Nicholas Churchyard, Dundalk,
County Louth, and granddaughter Eliza Everitt lived
in Belfast's York Street area. Her daughter entrusted
Eliza's private Robert Burns collection to the Linen
Hall Library in Belfast. Another substantial Burns collection belonged to Andrew Gibson, who, like Burns,
was a native of Ayrshire. He became governor of the
Linen Hall Library, to which he bestowed his internationally significant collection of Burnsiana.

Religious psalms and hymns formed the basis
of another song legacy that made the journey from
Scotland to Ulster and then to America. When entire
Presbyterian congregations followed their ministers
on the promise of greater religious and economic
freedom, their religious music made the crossing with
them. "Singing schools" were common among the
Presbyterian congregations in Ulster. These gatherings convened at the meeting house, or at members'

Burns and Ulster

Len Graham, Irish traditional singer and song collector; interviewed in Swannanoa, North Carolina, July 2013, by Fiona Ritchie and Doug Orr during Traditional Song Week at the Swannanoa Gathering folk arts workshops.

Robert Burns, the national poet of Scotland, is very much loved and admired and recited [in Ulster]. My earliest recollection is hearing songs of his being sung, and versions actually of melodies and interpretations that are very different to what you would find in Scotland, so he was very much revered and still is revered in Ulster. His older sister Agnes married a man [William] Galt from Stephenstown, and she's actually buried in St. Nicholas's churchyard in Dundalk in County Louth. His granddaughter, Elizabeth, married a local doctor, Everett, and she lived in Belfast for quite a while. And he had also a nephew, Valentine Rainey, who taught harp in the harp academy in Belfast in the early years of the nineteenth century. See, what you have to remember: there was only one university in Ireland, an Anglican university in Dublin, up until 1840's, when Queen Victoria built the colleges, the Queen's colleges they were known [Queen's University]. Prior to that, the Northern Irish Presbyterians sent their people for third-level education to Scotland. So they were all going over to Edinburgh and St. Andrews, Aberdeen and Glasgow, and coming back and forth, to the extent that Burns, [though] he never came over to Ireland personally, his poetry came over and appeared in the Kilmarnock edition here before the Belfast edition was printed. The ports would be Portpatrick in Galloway and Donegal Bay: those two ports would be in-flowing with people bringing their songs, traditions, poetry, all those cultures were coming back and forth constantly, right, for a long time.

homes, to sing psalms paired with one of the twelve melodies, the "auld twelve" used by the Covenanters of old.[19] Group singing was eased along by the old Scottish custom of "lining out" the lyrics, whereby the minister or song leader would "give out the line" one at a time. This practice later proved popular in the southern Appalachians, where hymnbooks were often scarce and illiteracy common. Today, leading by vocal lining out is still used in the Gaelic psalm singing on Lewis in Outer Hebrides and in a few rural churches in the American South, including some African American congregations. Over time, the Ulster Presbyterians introduced hymns and instrumental accompaniment to their services, but not without some resistance.

Tunes were played at rites of passage—weddings, christenings, and wakes. Dances would be held at fairs and ceilis, where a fiddler would be called upon to bring the dancers to the floor. By the seventeenth century, the sound was enriched by an array of instruments entering Ireland from other lands, including wooden flutes, tin whistles, accordions, and concertinas. With the arrival of the Boehm system keyed metal flute in the early half of the nineteenth century, classical musicians began to discard their old wooden flutes. Irish musicians also acquired the metal flutes and found them ideally suited to Irish traditional music. When Englishman Charles Wheatstone invented the concertina in 1829, these, along with the melodeons and accordions from continental Europe, soon brought the sound of free reed instruments into the music and had enough volume to hold the floor in dance halls. Percussion drove the tempo; simple tambourines,

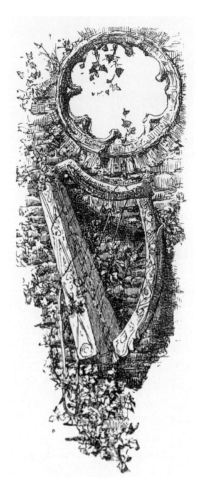

homemade frame drums constructed with willow branches and leather, and bones or spoons all were used. The jaw harp was common in Scotland, Ireland, and England dating back to the early seventeenth century. This modest instrument had many names across Asia and Europe and was known as the "trump" in Scotland and northern England. It could easily be used in combination with vocal "lilting" of mouth music to provide rhythm for dancing in the absence of pipes or fiddle. The jaw harp (often called the "Jew's harp") became a popular companion of the Scots-Irish settlers on the trail southward along the Great Wagon Road into the southern Appalachians.

The long historical sagas of Ireland and Scotland, if set to music, would surely be played on the small harp

and bagpipe. A ninth-century woodcarving in Ireland depicts a piper, and mouth-blown bagpipes were established in Ireland and Scotland from ancient times; there are many tales of bagpipes and music being passed down by minstrels and their oral traditions. In 1396 bagpipes, or "warpipes," were carried into the Battle of the North Inch at Perth, and there has been a long tradition of Highland pipes being played at battles up into the twentieth century, when the 51st Highland Division used them at El Alamein during World War II. On the Highland bagpipes, "piobaireachd," or "ceol mor" (big music), the so-called classical music of the "piob mor" (big pipes), dates back to the 1500s, when it was conceived by the MacCrimmon family, hereditary pipers to the Clan MacLeod on the Isle of Skye. However, most instrumental pipe music—reels, jigs, hornpipes, and strathspeys—is dance music dating back little more than three centuries.

It is often claimed that the bagpipes were banned in Scotland under the Act of Proscription, created to weaken the clan system after the defeat of Jacobite Highland clans at the Battle of Culloden in 1746. While wearing tartan and kilts was formally outlawed under the "Dress Act," no records exist documenting prosecutions for owning or playing pipes. Certainly, the fact that clan chiefs were stripped of their powers would have ended the system of patronage that had supported generations of pipers and harpers. The decline of Highland society and widespread emigration were more contributory to the instrument's decline. Regiments were raised in the Highlands in the late eighteenth century, and eventually Highland bagpipes were integrated into nineteenth-century regimental life, initially as a rallying instrument to bolster the ranks. The bagpipes have been associated with military bands and Scottish and Irish regiments ever since. In the eighteenth century, bellows-blown bagpipes entered England, Scotland, and Ireland via Europe. Various types of bellows pipes thrive today in Northumberland in England (Northumbrian pipes) and as "cauld-wind pipes" in Lowland Scotland. The most sophisticated

THE HARP

The primitive harp, still found in Africa, was once widespread throughout the world. Did the harp find its way into the hands of the Atlantic Celts from the ancient European continent? It may be the case that harp instruments were independently born among the ancient people of the British Isles and Ireland, evolving there independently. Certainly, in Ireland and Scotland, the harp has been established since ancient times, as several different stringed instruments were being played in both countries by the eighth and ninth centuries. Images of triangular-framed harps were carved onto Pictish stones on the east coast of Scotland in the eighth century.[1] Irish carvings show lyres from this era, and the first triangular framed harp appears on a carved stone in Ireland in the twelfth century. So we know that harp-like instruments have been played in Scotland and Ireland for more than 1,200 years. The earliest ancient specimen, the Brian Boru harp, dates from the thirteenth century and is housed in Trinity College, Dublin.

The small harp, or "clarsach" (Scotland) and "clairseach" (Ireland), played an important role in the ancient culture and identity of both countries. This was the instrument of the aristocracy, who held their professional harpers in high regard. Traditionally, harpers would accompany epic poetry of great heroic and tragic tales. Their patrons expected them to be able to summon tears, laughter, and sleep. They played laments, lullabies, and formal listening music that, in Scotland, may have provided inspiration for the highly stylized theme and variations "ceol mor" ("big music") or "piobaireachd" of the bagpipe repertoire. Harpers were performing the art music of their day, and, like many song tradition bearers, they considered it a point of pride that their music was not written down. They carried their tunes, poetry, and tales in memory, passing them orally from teacher to pupil and from player to player. It may be that much of the older music composed for the harp was picked up on bagpipe and fiddle as the harp waned in popularity with the fading of the traditional clan-based society, often termed the "old Gaelic order."

The 1790s saw the beginnings of modern Irish nationalism, accompanied by a cultural revival that injected momentum into efforts to document traditions in music and language. This awareness of an endangered cultural heritage coincided with a sharp decline in harp playing. In response, Belfast citizen Dr. James MacDonnell organized a gathering of harpers in the city, intending to witness and record the ancient music of the Irish harpers before it disappeared. He engaged the services of organist Edward Bunting to transcribe their music. Ten harpers, six of whom were blind, attended the festival and played their tunes over a three-day period, including ninety-seven-year-old Donnchadh Ó hAmhsaigh (Denis Hempson, 1696–1807). The melodies set down by Bunting for his *General Collection of the Ancient Music of Ireland* (1796) — the riches of an era of orally transmitted music reaching back centuries — were captured just in time. Bunting then traveled throughout Ulster to complete his first volume of tunes and followed with two more in 1809 and 1840, including dances and pipe airs, some of which would have been adopted as song melodies. The music contained in Bunting's collections offers a glimpse of a passing age in rural Ireland, when music, like song, existed only as an oral tradition.

1. Keith Sanger and Alison Kinnaird, *Tree of Strings* (Temple, Midlothian, Scotland: Kinmor Music, 1992), 20.

of these instruments evolved in Ireland as the "union pipes"; in the twentieth century, these became known as the "uilleann" (meaning "elbow") pipes.

The small harp has been made and played in Scotland and Ireland since at least the eighth century, when its image was hewn onto Pictish stones from that era in Scotland's North East. Both countries supported a system, over a period of centuries, where clan chiefs and other gentry patronized hereditary resident pipers and other itinerant musicians. Many of these were harpers who would visit their patrons' homes in an extended grand tour. Much traditional Highland music was composed under this system of patronage by legendary harpers, such as Rory Dall Morison ("blind Rory," 1656–1713). After English colonization began in Ireland under Henry VIII, harpers, pipers, and other wandering musicians were often routed out. By 1640, Oliver Cromwell's troops would ruthlessly track and kill pipers and destroy their instruments, as the army of Elizabeth I had done sixty years earlier. Although no

longer outlawed, the status of harpers was very much diminished by the end of the seventeenth century. The blind harper Turlough O'Carolan (1670–1738) was born during a relatively peaceful time when the ancient harp was staging a brief comeback among the landed gentry. Smallpox had robbed him of his sight, so he studied harp to make his living playing in the big houses of the few remaining wealthy landowners. He would be expected to recite, sing, and compose for his patrons, the remnants of a ruling class for whom the harp was a beloved bond to a more-glorious past. Carolan composed more than 200 melodies and became known as the "last of the Irish Bards." Many compositions, some of which he called "planxtys," were named for his patrons and are still popularly played today.

In Ulster, however, the voice of one instrument rose above all others at dances and music sessions. The fiddle had migrated to the western reaches of Europe from the Continent, and so did some of its dance-tune repertoire. In his book *Folk Music and Dances of Ireland*, Brendan Breathnach maintains that the reel, schottische, and strathspey come from Scotland; hornpipes come from England; most of Europe had some variation of the jig; and polkas and mazurkas have origins in eastern Europe.[20] It was all stirred into the cultural broth of the Ulster Scots and Irish, seasoned and served up as their own.

In Ulster halls and homes, fiddlers gave their tunes a Scottish or Irish definition. Many are familiar today in the Appalachians: "Blackberry Blossom," "Miss McLeod's Reel," "Soldier's Joy," and "Flowers of Edinburgh." In fiddle music, an atavistic return to roots running deeper than memory gave voice to the old Celtic reverence for beauty, passion, and romance, as Len Graham captured in "The Fiddler":

The fiddler with ancient art,
Fingering and bowing, heard and unheard
    melody,
The sensitive lug, the inherent part,
No man can drum into you.

Ulster's Unique Sound

Sara Grey, American traditional singer, banjo player, and song collector; interviewed in Perth, Scotland, March 2010, by Fiona Ritchie at the singer's home.

I've heard a lot of songs from the North of Ireland . . . because my husband's family to-ed and fro-ed a lot between that part of Dumfries and Galloway and Northern Ireland, where the crossing is short. But when it comes to songs, when you listen to the style in Northern Irish singing, it's quite different from the Scots style of singing. Every area: the big ballad areas of the North East of Scotland, the midland area—the Lowlands Scots, the Border Scots, and the Western Isles, they don't sound like Northern Irish singers. There's a cadence that the Northern Irish singers have that's quite different from the sean-nós style of singing certainly, and I think it's very different than the lyrical Border ballads style that you get and the lyrical style that you get in the North East of the big ballads.

And somewhere along the line, I don't know if you've found this, but Ireland got bypassed when it came to a lot of the big ballads. You know, I don't think England gets enough credit for the ballads because the big ballads were primarily Scotland and England. Some of them dropped from Ireland, but most of them went from England and Scotland and then to Ireland and then across the pond. And sometimes they bypassed Ireland all together, and I've sung with so many different Irish people who know very few of the big ballads, you know. And it's something that's puzzled me, I've never known quite why that is so. I mean, when you listen to the Ulster people sing, it's just almost like a spoken word, it's almost like the Ozark region. 'Cause I've done a lot of listening to old singers around Mountain View and Timbo, Arkansas, and you get that almost extended lines where they're wonderful, they're a little bit—what's the word they use for it? Oh, "crooked": you get slightly crooked songs.

Rhythm and time; notes with "ghost,"
Pass over inept ears.
But to those who know—no mighty host,
A few unsung peers.[21]

People, goods, and languages were all intermingled in the historic comings and goings between Scotland and Ulster, especially its three most northerly centers of Antrim, Derry-Londonderry, and Donegal. The rocky reaches of the Atlantic shores became home to an extended musical society that would eventually make its way to America. Fair Head on the Antrim coast is the closest point to Scotland, with the Mull of Kintyre in Argyll only twelve miles away. The ancient kingdom of Dalriada encompassed a large swathe of present-day County Antrim and Scotland's Argyll and Bute, including the Scottish Western Isles. The kingdom's independence ended by the end of the eighth century with the arrival of the Vikings, who marked the area with a Norse imprint. However, Donegal's deeply rooted ties with Scotland extend back more than 1,500 years. It is often said that the people of Donegal historically looked toward Scotland and Spain more than Dublin and London for their commerce and culture. Donegal is one of nine counties within the ancient boundaries of Ulster, although today it is one of three, along with Cavan and Monaghan, that are now part of the Republic of Ireland. A simple scan

UISGE BEATHA: THE WATER OF LIFE

The ethnonationalistic conflict, known colloquially in Northern Ireland as "The Troubles," is a tragic demonstration of the consequences of imposed change. There are many other legacies of the Ulster Plantation era of King James VI and I, some more benign than others. One of the more permanent—and welcomed—legacies was the license to distill granted by King James to Sir Thomas Phillips, landowner and governor of County Antrim. This allowed him to found the Bushmill's Distillery near the Giant's Causeway in 1608, almost within sight of his sovereign's motherland. Not only the first distillery in the British Isles, Bushmill's is now the oldest licensed whiskey distillery in the world. Subtle and distinct differences mark the shared heritage of this legendary beverage. First, it is spelled slightly differently: "uisge beath" or "whisky" in Scotland and "uisce beatha" or "whiskey" in Ireland, both meaning "lively water" or "the water of life." Irish whiskey must be distilled three times and stored in casks for a minimum of five years before it can officially be labeled as whiskey. For Scotch whisky, the requirement is twice distilled and then aged for a minimum of three years. The triple-distillation Irish whiskey can be the smoother beverage and has considerable potency. While the Irish usually blend their whiskey, however, the Scots maintain their distinguishing tradition of distilling Single Malts as well as blends. Both are made from fermented grain mash and from different grains—barley, malted barley, wheat, rye, and corn—and are typically aged in oak casks. Bourbon, sherry, and port barrels are recycled from other drink manufacturers, and this gives the different labels their special taste characteristics.

Distillation is an ancient art, possibly tracing back to the Babylonians in Mesopotamia and subsequently to the Greeks in the third century A.D. Thirteenth-century Italian monasteries were the first places to record the distillation of alcohol from wine. The practice came to Scotland and Ireland in the early fifteenth century, and King James IV of Scotland, in addition to his taste for music, had a liking for the early Scotch whiskies. From the fifteenth century, whisky was heavily taxed in Scotland, and most of the spirit was illegally produced. The English Malt Tax of 1725 essentially drove Scotland's whisky manufacturers underground, launching a tradition of illegal distilling that eventually spread to America and the Appalachian Mountains. Scottish distillers came up with creative subterfuges, operating homemade stills out of sight of the government excise men (the infamous "revenuers" in America) and under the cover of darkness—hence the name "moonshine." In 1823 Parliament finally passed an act that penalized unlicensed distilling and made commercial distilleries profitable in Scotland.

From the very beginning, the colorful stories of making and imbibing the "sacred juice" were tailor-made for poets and song makers; "Whiskey You're the Devil," "Nancy Whisky," "Fare Ye Weel Whisky," "The Moonshiner," "Gie the Fiddler a Dram," "Whiskey in the Jar," and "A Bottle o' the Best" are but a few examples. Scottish writer Robert Louis Stevenson hinted at the illicit nature of the refreshment shared by three friends "while the mune was shinin' clearly," while Robert Burns made it clear that the bravado of his everyman hero Tam o' Shanter was very much bottle sourced: "Wi' tippenny, we fear nae

evil; Wi' usquebae we'll face the devil!" Len Graham collected "Flowing Bowl," an old Glens of Antrim song in praise of Irish whiskey:

> Oh the whiskey me boys keeps my mind alert
>   and free,
> 'Tis the whiskey that makes life's cares lie light
>   on me,
> Each bold rustic bard it is hard that he should
>   be denied,
> Of his darlin' reward that his pipes well with oil
>   be supplied.
>
> It cures all diseases that seizes the human frame,
> The heart-ache it eases, the toothache, the gout
>   and the spleen,
> The coughing, stuffing, water-stopping, the stone
>   and the small-pox,
> By it buying and supplying you would close up
>   Pandora's box.

Whisky Still in the Moonlight; McIan postcard. (Courtesy of
Photo Archives, Inverness Museum and Art Gallery, High Life
Highland, Scotland)

Whisky barrels at a distillery. (Watercolor; courtesy of
Madeleine Hand)

of the map, forgetting present-day borders, makes sense of the Scottish-Donegal connection. Inishowen Peninsula protrudes into the North Channel in clear sight of Kintyre and the Scottish Hebridean islands of Jura and Islay. Early people managed to navigate that twenty-mile-plus crossing in the first post–Ice Age migrations from Britain to Ireland. Centuries later, seasonal migrations of Irish farm laborers traveled in the opposite direction, following many routes to Scottish farms. Today it is all very routine, with a daily ferry/bus service between Inishowen and Glasgow. Locals joke that "Scotland is the northernmost county of Ulster."[22]

Inishowen had a notorious reputation for distilling illicit "poitín" (poteen, or Irish moonshine), and Scottish influences are significant on the legal distillery business. Intermarriage was more commonplace here than elsewhere in Ulster, and tunes were traded as commonly as drams of whiskey. The short staccato bow strokes of the Donegal fiddle style set it apart from the rest of Ireland. This freer and less-ornamented style would one day crop up in the southern Appalachians. Donegal voices amalgamated phrasing from Irish sean-nós singing with Hebridean pitch and tempo and Scots wording. Eventually, the "high lonesome sound" of the Appalachian and American bluegrass styles harked back to the sound of early Donegal voices.

SENSE OF PLACE

This is my country,
The land that begat me.
These windy spaces
Are surely my own.
And those who toil here
In the sweat of their faces
Are flesh of my flesh,
And bone of my bone.
—*Sir Alexander Gray, "Scotland"*[23]

Many cultures celebrate the idea of home in their music, stories, and literature but few people have their sense of place etched as plainly on their hearts as the Scots and Irish. Irish scholar Linde Lunney described the feeling of belonging to Ulster.

It has been said that if you know where you are you know who you are . . . and in the north of Ireland you still occasionally hear someone say something like "Johnny Archibald belonged to Ballymoney" or "Sammy Taggert belonged to Ballyportery." The concept that an individual in some sense is owned, presumably in perpetuity, by the place where he is born is a wonderfully strong and poetic way of describing the merging of self and background. Even if you willfully tear up your roots, you still belong to that place, and cannot not belong there.[24]

It is an eternal feeling, this longing for home and nostalgia for the old familiar place. As ever, poets and song makers are best placed to capture the sentiments. The word "nostalgia" stems from the Greek word for a return home. Home is an eternal compass, guiding life's journey, an abiding memory or a real destination for the return trip. A village, hillside, stream, road, or waterside, named for a setting in a far-off land, will trigger deep emotions. For Irish Nobel Laureate Seamus

Heaney, the poet's sense of place ideally rose above physical landscape and "picturesqueness," becoming "a country of the mind."

Tory Island, Knocknarea, Slieve Patrick, all of them deeply steeped in associations from an older culture, will not stir us beyond a visual pleasure unless that culture means something to us, unless features of the landscape are a mode of communication with something other than ourselves, something to which we ourselves still feel we might belong. . . . As we pass along the coast from Tory to Knocknarea, we go through the village of Drumcliff and under Ben Bulben, we skirt Lissadell and Innisfree. All of these places now live in the imagination, all of them stir us to responses other than the merely visual, all of them are instinct with the spirit of the poet and his poetry . . . our imaginations assent to the stimulus of the names, our sense of the place is enhanced, our sense of ourselves as inhabitants not just of a geographical country but a country of the mind.
—*Seamus Heaney, "The Sense of Place,"* Preoccupations[25]

This depth of connection to the "country of the mind" surely explains why the Irish and Scots have managed to engrave their place names on features of the physical landscape in every continent. It follows that the towns and landscapes of Scotland and Ireland are among the most heavily cited of any of the world's song traditions. In Scotland, "The Gallowa' Hills," "The Road to Dundee," "The Loch Tay Boat Song," "Bonnie Glenshee," and "The Dowie Dens of Yarrow" barely scratch the surface of the inventory. From Robert Burns, "The Birks of Aberfeldy," "The Banks o' Doon," and "Sweet Afton" are but three compositions that demonstrate the bard's unfettered urge to publicize his fond feelings for the landscapes of home. On the Ulster side, "Star of the County Down," "Slieve Galleon Braes," "Carrickfergus," "The Banks of

Claudy," "Boys from the County Armagh," and "Fare Thee Well to Enniskillen" are, again, just a few from a long list of titles. The Republic of Ireland would show a good many more. Beyond the titles, lyrics of traditional songs are a directory of town and country from Belfast to Glasgow, between and beyond.

> I wish I was in Belfast town and my true love
> along with me,
> I would get sweethearts plenty, to keep me in
> good company,
> With money in my pocket and a flowing bowl
> on every side,
> Hard fortune ne'r would daunt me, while I'd be
> young in this world wide.
> — *The Rambling Boys of Pleasure*

> My name is Jamie Raeburn, frae Glasgow toon
> I came;
> My place and habitation I'm forced to tae leave
> wi' shame;
> From my place and habitation I now maun gang
> awa',
> Far frae the bonnie hills and dales o' Caledonia.
> —*Jamie Raeburn*

As Ulster Scots made ready to sail onward again, they sang from the heart in their native dialect of homelands past and present. Their artistic descriptions were cultural archives and personal directions, all memories to treasure and transport.

TO CANAAN'S LAND
The Promise of America

> To Canaan's land I'm on my way where the soul
> of man never dies,
> And all my nights will turn to day where the soul
> of man never dies.
> —*To Canaan's Land* (American spiritual)

> But Moses being a holy man got orders from God,
> And from the house of bondage set his children
> free.
> And led them to fair Canaan's land,
> Where they have cause to weep no more,
> Yet after all he brought them to the land of liberty.
> And perhaps we'll meet again in time where milk
> and honey flows.
> —*Campbell's Farewell to Ireland*

The biblical land of Canaan has been held as a timeless symbol of the Promised Land for history's emigrants and refugees. The lyrics of the spiritual join together the hopes of enslaved Israelites in Egypt with the destitute and the desperate seeking passage to America's land of liberty, as well as the "Hereafter" destination of American hymn singing. "Canaan" also was a code word for the slaves of the American South pursuing the Underground Railroad route to the North and Canada. "Campbell's Farewell" likely traces its roots to the eighteenth-century Presbyterian emigration from Ulster, the Campbells being a prominent and staunchly Protestant clan in the west of Scotland. Like the spirituals of the South, it makes the universal plea: a cry for a better chance over the horizon.

Whether from countryside to city or across national boundaries and oceans, factors that drive people onward are universal. "Push" forces come into play as life becomes unbearable owing to political, economic, or cultural challenges. The "pull" of another place offering greater opportunity and the promise of freedom from oppression, including religious persecution, completes the cycle. The Ulster Scots began to feel the pull of Canaan's land of milk and honey, which they imagined flowing across the American soil, as they became disillusioned in their still relatively new homeland. The Scottish settlers that had left their ancestral homes and crossed the sea to Ulster held high expectations for their new lives and prosperity. Initially, their lives were improved. The eighteenth-century Plantation system in Ulster was governed and controlled by a small landowning elite. In London, the Guilds that were expected to fund the plantation project diverted their attention to New World plantations around Jamestown, Virginia, and many British Protestant settlers emigrated there or to New England. More than that, it was mounting economic and religious discrimination that combined to alienate the discouraged Ulster Scots. Parliament in London decreed that Anglican Protestantism, the Church of England, be the official denomination for the Ulster Scots. They established severe penalties for dissenters who refused to fall in line, a practice already firmly in place for the native Irish Catholics. Having been pioneers for their new faith, Ulster Presbyterians were now a persecuted people. The Church of Scotland, Presbyterian, was officially recognized in 1690, and so it became commonplace for Ulster Presbyterian ministers to journey to Scotland for sermons. Presbyterians living close to the east coast of Ulster might even cross the North Channel to have their children christened. Jaded Ulster Presbyterian ministers began to fan the vapors of discontent among their parishioners, promoting emigration.

The economy was even more forceful in the push Ulster Scots felt toward America. A rent escalation practice known as "rent racking" and a decrease in the length of land leases made it increasingly difficult for the settlers to sustain a living. The population had grown, and land was scarcer. Paying more for less made no sense. Recurring crop failures and poor prices for meager harvests sealed the argument. They could also see that in Scotland, where Presbyterian Calvinist values were by now embedded, an egalitarian and democratic spirit was spreading. As David Fischer writes in *Albion's Seed*, "They were increasingly exploited by rent-racking landlords, bullied by county oligarchies and taxed by a church to which they did not belong."[26] They seemed hopelessly trapped in an oppressive economic and political vice: "Betwixt landlord and rector, the very marrow is squeezed out of our bones."[27] The traditional Ulster ballad "Slieve Gallion Braes" makes the case clear:

My name is James McGarvey, as you may
    understand,
I come from Derrygennard where I owned a
    farm of land.
But the rents were getting higher and I could
    no longer stay,
So farewell unto you bonny, bonny, Slieve
    Gallion Braes.

It was not the lack of employment alone,
That caused the poor sons of old Erin to roam.
But it was the cruel landlords who drove us
    all away,
So farewell unto you bonny, bonny Slieve
    Gallion Braes.

Ireland, and particularly Ulster, did experience intermittent waves of prosperity during the eighteenth century; a booming domestic linen trade, the only industry fully supported by the British government, was a case in point. Ulster settlers had a long tradition of weaving linen for their own use. Rural landlords encouraged tenants to grow flax, as opposed to other less-reliable crops, and to spin and weave linen cloth, which literally paid the rent. Throughout the eighteenth century, approximately half of Ireland's exports were linen. Overdependence on a single commodity was precarious, as the market for linen was prone to repeated boom-and-bust cycles and farming families were highly vulnerable. The linen industry had a much bigger appetite for flaxseed than Ireland could generate. Huge quantities were imported from American ports on the Delaware River, especially Philadelphia, thereby establishing regular Atlantic shipping lanes between Ulster and America. In addition to flaxseed, the ships imported news from Pennsylvania. Quakers had heavily settled the colony, many from Wales, and their reputation for religious tolerance was appealing to the long-suffering Ulster Presbyterians. A ship's

hold, freshly relieved of its heavy flaxseed cargo, had no prospect of a stable return across the Atlantic. Owners and ships' captains actively recruited prospective emigrants from Ulster for the return voyage to Philadelphia, occupying the hold as living ballast before the next shipment of flaxseed was hauled in.

Ulster Scots were well and truly fed up at home. Advertisements began appearing in newspapers from Belfast to Derry-Londonderry promoting sailing toward a new, more-promising life in America. Agents circulated testimonials and letters of enticement, often highly exaggerated, as they promoted emigration at fairs and markets. A lack of funds was not a hindrance; passengers with inadequate funds were signed to indentured servitude, usually for three to four years,

in return for their passage. These "redemptioneers" signed contracts with the ships' captains, who sold them into labor upon arrival in Philadelphia and other ports. Shipping company posters painted a flattering picture of the New World, boasting of an abundance of cheap land, opportunity, religious freedom, and a better lifestyle. To increase their chances of closing the deal, they would contrast the best of America and the worst of Ulster.

> They tell me America's the place where everything
>   is free;
> Well if that's the case I said to meself then that's
>   the place for me.
> —*"The Boat That Took Me Over"*

The Bridal Boat

Brian McNeill, Scottish singer, songwriter, multi-instrumentalist, and novelist; from liner notes for Back o' the North Wind *(Greentrax Recordings, 1991).*

The further Scots are blown from home, the more that home seems to exert its pull on them—and that's a paradox which has become part of our national character; anyone who wants to understand Scotland today must look at the lives of Scots abroad, past and present. And nowhere have these lives had more impact than across the Atlantic.

Shortly before my great uncle Jim left Scotland, he went to visit his sister in Glasgow, and saw a liner sailing off down the Clyde for America; it was the ship known as "the bridal boat," because so many girls, fiancées, and brides left on it to join men folk who had gone ahead to find work.

There had been a modest flow of emigration from Ulster to America before 1718; in that year, it began in earnest. The figures correlate with the undulating economy of the colonies throughout the eighteenth century. An estimated 250,000 people departed Ulster for America between 1718 and 1800, with a pause during the Revolutionary War. The majority—85 percent—were Ulster Scots, and the remainder were made up of both Anglo and Gaelic Irish, together with transit passengers emigrating directly from the Scottish Highlands and Lowlands. Ulster Scots continued to leave into the nineteenth century before gradually easing their hankering for emigration to Philadelphia and the Delaware valley destinations (the primary eighteenth-century funnel through which the emigrants would make their way to the southern Appalachians). The huge mid-nineteenth century emigration from Ireland due to the catastrophic potato famine sailed more in the direction of northeastern cities and Canada's St. Lawrence region.

So for the second time in just a few generations, the Ulster Scots were on the move. Just as their recent ancestors left Scotland with high hopes for a better life in Ulster, they looked farther still for the promise of Canaan's Land.

For to live poor I could not endure,
Like others of my station.
To Amerikay I sailed away,
And left this Irish nation.
—*"The Rambling Irishman"* (CD TRACK 5)

AMERICAN WAKES AND PARTING RITUALS

The night before they are leaving, all the
    neighbors in the house do throng,
To take a farewell glass and likewise for to sing
    a verse of a song,
Well they danced all night 'til it was morning,
    lads and lasses danced 'round the floor,
The mother came in she was a-wailing, saying,
    "See our children to the door."
The very next morning as we went a-walking,
    down the road we chanced to go,
We saw a crowd to us approaching it surely set
    our hearts a-woe,
To see the carts and carriages moving, onward,
    forward to the quay,
The handkerchiefs were all a-waving, saying,
    "Fare-thee-well old Granuaile."
—*"Yankee Land"*

Leaving rituals, practiced through time to mark passages and departures, are heartfelt and harrowing in equal measure. Many European cultures expected their young people to leave the parental home for marriage, employment, adventure, or pilgrimage. Fairy tales are populated with sons jauntily striding toward the horizon to seek their fortunes. In reality, perilous migrations by land or sea and struggles on distant shores were reason enough for tense and tearful farewells, let alone the knowledge that, in all likelihood, the parting was permanent. The "American Wake" was much in the Irish tradition, also described as the "Parting Spree," "Feast of Departure," or "Farewell Supper." It was also called a "Living Wake" because, while the gathering had many upbeat features, many of the rituals paralleled remembrances for the recently deceased.

Such parting customs were certainly practiced by Ulster Presbyterians as well.[28] They were meant to unite community feelings and vent emotions surrounding the departure and to give tight-knit neighborhoods a chance for farewell. Sadness was ever present, especially for the parents and elderly family members left behind. Like some timeworn funeral rituals, the older women set about mourning in the form of "keening"—long, wailing cries anticipating the impending separation from loved ones. Customs might be devised to soften the wrench of parting. As they left the family home, some emigrants would remove a burning ember from the hearth and place it in the fireplace of a neighbor. They were leaving behind a spark of hope that one day, upon return, they might be able to restore the warmth of a glowing ember to the family cottage.

THE AMERICAN WAKE: A STORY

I remember still with emotion the emigration of young people of the neighborhood to America. In those days the farmer's children were raised for export. There were times of the year, in spring or fall, when there would be sort of a group emigration, that is, a dozen or so would start off together once or twice a week for a few weeks to take the train or boat at Queenstown or Derry. Generally each group was bound for the same town in America where they had friends or relatives who had paid their passage money beforehand or sent them their tickets. The night before their departure there would be a farewell gathering called an American Wake in one of the houses of the emigrating boys or girls. There would be singing and dancing interlarded with tears and lamentations until the early hours of the morning, when, without sleep, the young people started for the train, the mothers keening as at a funeral or a wake for the dead, for the parting would often be forever and the parents might never see again the boy or girl who was crossing the ocean. There was, I remember, a steep hill on the road near our house, and when the emigrating party reached the bottom of it, it was their habit to descend from the sidecars and carts to ease the horses, and they would climb the height on foot. As they reached the top from which they could see the whole countryside, they would turn and weepingly bid farewell to the green fields, the little white houses, the sea, and the rambling roads they knew so well. The hill was called the Hill of Weeping in Gaelic, because of all those who had wept their farewells from the top of it.

—*Mary Colum,* Life and the Dream

Amid all the grief, the sentiments of American Wakes could be mixed and complex; depending on the circumstances, there might be a buzz of excitement around those anticipating a new life and the opportunities it might offer. For most emigrants, the rituals of leave-taking would veer between sorrow and hope, uncertainty and excitement. As the American Wake tradition grew through the latter years of the eighteenth century, they had more of a party atmosphere, especially in the more urban settings. Barney Mulligan, the father-in-law of Irish American fiddler Eileen Ivers, recalled his mid-twentieth-century leaving in "Parting of Friends."[29]

No they didn't think I had died,
That night in '48,
When the villagers gathered in my home,
For my American Wake.

They came to wish me happiness
In the new world so far away,
The house was full, so much fun,
That I wished that I could stay.

But the time had come to say goodbye
To everything so dear to me,
My aging mother and my family,
My friends and country.

Box Player outside Cottage. (Woodcut; courtesy of Declan Forde)

Ulster Emigrant Embarkation Ports

The dark and stormy Atlantic was a fearful place. In an era of minimal long-distance communication, travel beyond the western horizon was akin to severing all earthly ties or a descent into the grave. Superstition held that westward travelers from rural farm families who added west rooms to their cottages were destined to disappear into the sea-shrouded mists, fated for early demise.[30] Younger emigrants put on a brave face, declaring their intentions to return home after achieving "fame and fortune in America." The sense of obligation and guilt placed on the shoulders of departing voyagers was heavy: never forget the old home place, write frequently, send back regular remittances, and eventually come back to your own dear native land.

Parting rituals would begin with a week of touring around nearby friends and relations to bid fond farewells and extend invitations to attend the parting wake evening. The priest or minister usually avoided the wake itself, with its abundance of the demon drink and the prospect of uncouth dancing. So he might be paid a visit on the farewell tour. In some poorer, more rural areas, the food and drink offerings could be modest, with a collection taken for the drinks. Either way, there was a great deal of preparation, baking, cooking and cleaning, and stocking up on the supplies of whiskey, beer, and stout. At the heart of the gathering, music and stories were shared, and fiddles, flutes, pipes, and accordions—whatever instruments were at hand—might set the company dancing. Favorite songs and stories were called for—folk compositions, broadside ballads, and, into the nineteenth century, ballads in popular songbooks. As John Moulden points out, the songs were not necessarily gloomy but carried the hopes and aspirations for a new land, even contributing a cautiously optimistic tone.[31] As tall tales and memories were shared, drink and tears flowed freely. Spirits might run high, but the veneer of merriment was fragile. Author Kirby Miller tells the story of a father at an American Wake who turned to his son and said: "Get up here son and face me in a step for likely

it will be the last step ever we'll dance." There was not a dry eye in the house.[32]

At daybreak, feelings were more subdued, but final parting rituals still had to be observed. Family and friends would gather at the front door of the family home, forming a convoy to accompany the voyager to the edge of the community. Its resemblance to a funeral procession was poignant and deliberate. At first, transportation was by foot or cart (in later years, perhaps carriage or train) to the port of embarkation. As the home place and neighborhood receded from view, probably forever, the emigrant would take in a "last look," imprinting its topography on a heart that would beat for home through the uncertain years ahead.

I'll never forget the cheers and tears
That nearly broke my heart that night,
But the saddest moment came next day
Watching Ireland going out of sight.

Standing on the rolling deck
And through a tearful view,
I Said "God Bless and keep you,
My beloved Roisin Dubh."
—*Barney Mulligan, "Parting of Friends"*[33]

The outward bound of Ulster and Ireland did not always participate in such ritualistic leave-taking, especially in more urbanized and Anglicized areas. For communities that experienced successive generations of emigration, however, the rituals eased what was one of life's most traumatic events. In this way, leaving home is a universal human experience; the notions of the "exile" and the "prospect of return" were interlocked in people's minds as soon as they first conceived of "home." John Doyle is a contemporary singer, songwriter, and guitar player who left his native Ireland in the early 1990s for New York City and now resides in Asheville, North Carolina. John confirms that traces of the American Wake remain, if not the all-night rituals.

There were stories, music, and emotional good-byes at the time of his departure. Today, communication and transportation have alleviated much of the despair felt by his grandmother when she said on parting, "John, we'll never see you again." She did see him on a return visit, but his initial leaving was the last time John was in the presence of his grandfather.[34]

The hearth is hard to leave this long night,
As we face a long and treacherous road.
But hard times must be faced undaunted,
Our loved ones lighten up our load.

And though we bid farewell in sorrow,
We may meet again in distant lands.
And drink a health in joy for parting,
For the exile will return again.
—*John Doyle, "Exile's Return"*

THE PARTING GLASS
Songs of Emigration

Our ship at the present lies in Derry harbor,
To bear us away across the wide swelling sea.
May heaven be her companion and grant her fair
    breezes,
Till we reach the green fields of Amerikay.
—*"The Emigrant's Farewell"*

The Scots and Irish have made an art of the farewell song: "The Scottish Emigrant's Farewell," "My Last Farewell to Stirling," "Jamie Raeburn's Farewell," "The Emigrant's Farewell to Donside," "Campbell's Farewell to Ireland," "McKee's Farewell to Ireland," "Fare Thee Well Enniskillen," and "The Parting Glass." There is the fisherman's ballad of leaving, "Farewell to Tarwathie," and a Scot's invitation to return, "Will Ye No Come Back Again?" " MacPherson's Farewell" is a defiant song of final departure on the way to the gallows, and a pledge to renounce strong drink is commemorated in

THE COLLECTORS

Principal Scottish song collectors such as Anna Gordon ("Mrs. Brown of Falkland"), Robert Burns, Sir Walter Scott, and Hamish Henderson, through his work with the Scottish Travellers, were united in preserving a significant body of verse from the treasure trove of traditional music (see chapter 1). Their works contributed to a long tradition of Scottish song and tune anthologies, including Allan Ramsay's *The Tea-Table Miscellany* (1724); James Oswald's *The Caledonian Pocket Companion* (1751); Robert Ford's *Vagabond Songs and Ballads*, volumes 1 and 2 (1899 and 1901); and John Ord's *The Bothy Songs & Ballads of Aberdeen, Banff & Moray, Angus and the Mearns*, published posthumously in 1930. Captain Simon Fraser's 1816 collection *The Airs and Melodies Peculiar to the Highlands of Scotland and the Isles* harvested 240 tunes. Some of these were instrumental settings of Gaelic songs he had heard sung by his father, grandfather, and their acquaintances, while others were traditional and newly composed dance tunes from the period. One splendidly titled Scottish volume by David Herd deserves special mention, as its title sums up the collectors' diligence and dedication: *The ancient and Modern Scots Songs, Heroic Ballads, &c. Now first Collected into one Body, from the various Miscellanies wherin they formerly lay dispersed. Containing Likewise, A great Number of Original Songs, from Manuscripts, never before Published* (1769).

The *Greig-Duncan Folk Song Collection* is an important compendium from the Scottish North East. Schoolmaster and musician Gavin Greig (1856–1914) and his collaborator, minister James Bruce Duncan (1848–1917), began their project in 1902, and it was completed around the onset of World War I. A further selection of Greig's collected songs was published in 1925 as *Last Leaves of Traditional Ballads and Ballad Airs*, collected in Aberdeenshire. More-recent Scottish song collections include Norman Buchan's *101 Scottish Songs* (1962), affectionately nicknamed the "wee red book" during the years of the Scottish folk revival in the 1960s and 1970s.

Throughout Ireland, song collectors have worked meticulously across more than two centuries. Many songs and tunes would not have survived without dedicated efforts to protect a heritage buffeted by music migrations. Even so, many bearers of oral traditions have challenged the collectors' ways, such as the indomitable Mrs. Hogg, who admonished Sir Walter Scott, scolding that old ballads "were made for singing and no for reading." This is a sentiment also expressed in the Appalachians, where the "song-catchers" would one day scour the remote mountain hollows, gathering the old songs.

Systematic and scholarly Irish song collecting can be dated to the work of Edward Bunting (1773–1843). His transcriptions of tunes played at the Belfast Harp Festival in 1792 were published in several collections, including *The Ancient Music of Ireland*, consisting of 151 tunes. The seminal Irish traditional music group the Chieftains dedicated their album *The Celtic Harp* to Bunting as a tribute to his pioneering work. A close friend of Bunting was Dubliner George Petrie (1790–1866), a Victorian-era musician, painter, and archaeologist whose father was from Aberdeen, Scotland. One noteworthy tune in Petrie's 1855 collection was collected from Jane Ross of Limavady in Ulster, who had heard the tune played locally. "The Londonderry Air" appeared in Petrie's collection, and English barrister and opera librettist Fred Weatherly later set words to the tune, creating the vaudeville tenor's favorite "Danny Boy."

Thomas Moore (1779–1852) was an earlier lyricist who often set his verses to traditional harp airs collected by Bunting. The Irish poet, musician, and singer was Ireland's first internationally celebrated man of letters who, along with Sir Walter Scott and Lord Byron, soared to heights of fame as a pillar of British romanticism. This was, however, the main reason Moore became unfashionable even by the end of his own lifetime. Living in England during a turbulent time in Anglo-Irish history, Moore's music was viewed with suspicion as having been crafted for eighteenth-century drawing rooms. Nonetheless, he is credited with writing one of the most popular songs ever written. During the nineteenth century, one and a half million copies of the sheet music for "The Last Rose of Summer" were sold in the United States alone.

The greatest repository of Irish jigs, reels, hornpipes, marches, and dance tunes is *O'Neill's Music of Ireland*, a nine-volume collection. It was the lifework of Chicago police captain Francis O'Neill (1848–1936). Born in Ireland, O'Neill became a merchant seaman at age sixteen and later settled in the United States, where he joined the Chicago police force. He quickly rose through the ranks to become chief, during which time the amateur musician recruited many traditional musicians to the force and would seek out tunes whenever he heard of a recent arrival from the Old Country. One of his significant sources was fellow policeman James O'Neill (1862–1949), who had emigrated from County Down in Ulster and also played the fiddle. Many tunes in Francis O'Neill's collection came directly from this Ulster source.

Sam Henry (1870–1952), a customs and excise officer from Coleraine, assembled by far the most comprehensive collection of Ulster material in *Songs of the People*. Although Henry's collecting took place primarily around his home base in Counties Derry-Londonderry and Antrim, he embraced a great diversity of songs from other areas, including Scotland, England, and North America. *Songs of the People* grew from Henry's long-running Coleraine newspaper column, and among his 836 articles were approximately a thousand songs.

The collecting vocation continues to this day. John Moulden has ranged all over Ireland in search of songs, and he pursues a lifelong quest to sing his discoveries. His "The Printed Ballad in Ireland: A Guide to the Popular Printing of Songs in Ireland, 1760–1920" examines the role of the simple printed sheets gleaned from the oral tradition between 1760 and 1920. He is a scholar of the emigration ballad, and his *Thousands Are Sailing: A Brief Song History of Irish Emigration* includes many ballads from Ulster and Derry-Londonderry. Len Graham of County Antrim is a revered Ulster singer who has been collecting for over fifty years, working with a variety of musicians, poets, and storytellers. Graham's *Joe Holmes: Here I Am Amongst You* is a valuable repository of Ulster song and tune histories as well as a biography of the venerated late musician. Architect Frank Harte (1933–2005) was renowned for his love of singing and collecting. His father was a pub landlord of The Tap in Chapelizod, Dublin, and Harte was immersed in a world of sean-nós songs from an early age. His song collection was immense from both Roman Catholic and Protestant traditions, and he was often heard to say: "Those in power write the history, while those who suffer write the songs, and given our history, we have an awful lot of songs."

The Scotish EMIGRANTS Fareweel.

Fareweel, fareweel, my native hame,
    Thy lonely glens an' heath clad mountain
Fareweel thy fields o' storied fame,
    Thy leafy shaws an' sparklin fountains
Nae mair I'll climb the Pentland's steep,
    Nor wander by the Esk's clear river,
I seek a hame far o'er the deep,
    My native land, fareweel for ever.

Thou land wi' love an' freedom crowned—
    In ilk wee cot and lordly dwellin',
May manly-hearted youths be found,
    And maids in ev'ry grace excellin',
The land where Bruce and Wallace wight,
    For freedom fought in days o' danger,
Ne'er crouch'd to proud usurpin' might,
    But foremost stood, wrong's stern avenger

Tho' far frae thee, my native shore,
    An' toss'd on life's tempestous ocean;
My heart, aye Scottish to the core,
    Shall cling to thee wi' warm devotion.
An' while the wavin' heather grows,
    An' onward rows the windin' river,
The toast be " Scotland's broomy knowes,
Her mountains, rocks, an' glens for ever.

"Fareweel Tae Whisky." They all show that an earnest farewell can be extended in many directions.

The sheer immensity of the emigrant song repertoire practically defined an era, dominating the balladry of the day. Some were dreamy and poetic:

Our ship is ready to bear away
Come comrades o'er the stormy sea
Our snow-white sails they are unfurled
And soon will wave in a watery word.
— *"Farewell and Remember Me"*

Other crudely printed broadsheets featured clumsily worded, unoriginal, and mawkish verses. "The Boat That Took Me Over" started as a dance tune:

I wept and wailed
When the big ship sailed
For the shores of Amerika

Flowery images might illustrate an idealized outcome that rarely matched reality, such as the final verse of "The Rambling Irishman":

Now when we arrived on the other side, we were
    both stout and healthy,
We cast out anchor in the bay, going down
    through Philadelphi-ay;
So let every lass link with her lad, blue jackets and
    white trousers,
Let every lad link with his lass, blue petticoats and
    white flounces. (CD TRACK 5)

It is easy to stereotype the sentiments of the emigrant experience. Certainly, the songs covered a range of human emotions—sadness, pain, regret, anger, resignation, fear, and hopeful anticipation.[35] Each wave of emigrants layered the genre with another raft of ballads until the emigrant song portfolio peaked in the middle to late nineteenth century. In the New World, wistful homesick songs were circulated back to Ulster, Ireland, and Scotland. Songs were composed by emigrants themselves and later by songwriters who felt their plight. The tradition of the exile song flourishes to the present day and still has the power to infuse us with that forlorn ache, feeling the wrench of distance and the call of home.

For the Ulster Scots pioneers, once they had walked down from their glens and boarded the ship for Philadelphia, there was no going back. More recent emigrants have been able to consider returning, even after an extended period out of the country. Their repeated conviction that they will reverse an involuntary exile is now reflected by contemporary songwriters, including Cathy Jordan of the Irish band Dervish in her "All the Way Home":

I know that someday my heart will take me,
To the old ground where my loved ones rest.
And you'll put your arms like a coat around me,
In the one place that I call home.

Maybe it's the mountains above the valley,
Maybe it's the long road that winds on down.
Maybe it's the sunbeams that kiss the water,
Maybe it's you that keeps calling me home.

From then to now, songs traveled on the tide with generations of wayfarers. A pioneering outlook would gradually see the sad songs of exile and homesickness eased from the firesides of the New World and into the songbooks. But the toil of travel and the reality of dispersal were not enough to weaken timeworn tunes and ballads, treasured through generations. Once settled, it was only a matter of time before the music and song would take root, grow, and blossom once again.

At one time, a small craft sailed regularly from the Hebridean island of Barra to trade with the Ulster town of Newry. It was known as Bàta an tSìl, or "the Seedboat," since it transported seed potatoes and grain between the two places. In their own way, the oceangoing passenger vessels of the Atlantic were also destined to serve as "seedboats," whether transporting flaxseed for the linen mills of Ulster or human cargo for propagating a new land with the folkways of an older world. An enduring tie to the beloved past, these ways would be cherished, though in time they would sprout in a vernacular more suited to the contours of an altogether unfamiliar terrain.

Turning a corner, taking a hill in County Down,
    there's the sea
Sidling and settling to the back of a hedge.
    Or else,
A grey bottom with puddles dead-eyed as fish.
Haphazard tidal craters march the corn and the
    grazing.

All around Antrim and westward, two hundred
    miles at Moher,
Basalt stands to. Both ocean and channel
Froth at the black locks on Ireland.
And strands take hissing submissions off Wicklow
    and Mayo.

Take a minute. A tide is rummaging in
At the foot of all fields, all cliffs and shingles.
Listen. Is it the Danes, a black hawk bent on the
    sail?
Or the chinking Normans? Or curraghs hopping
    high.

On to the sand?
Strangford, Arklow, Carrickfergus, Belmullet and
    Ventry
Stay, forgotten like sentries.
—*Seamus Heaney, "Shoreline"*[36]

Crossing

However with all those difficulties with which we encountered, I managed to keep care aloof. We had music and dancing (sometimes however with empty stomachs) every evening that permitted, and tripped it upon the quarter deck, and sang 'till Neptune raised his hoary locks from out the raging ocean, waved his trident in the air, and with ecstasy cried out—encore!

—*From William Campbell, ship's surgeon, to his father, the Reverend Robert Campbell, Templepatrick, County Antrim, October 28, 1832*

Captains of emigrant ships knew well that music and dancing provided a morale boost for passengers, also enticing them out onto the deck for a bit of fresh air and exercise. Some skippers felt this was important enough that they prioritized the position of fiddler second only to the ship's surgeon when they were hiring crew. Before setting sail, some captains were known to scour the ceili halls and pubs in search of a musician for hire. The job was not for the fainthearted fiddler: a difficult and perilous voyage lay ahead, and seafarers' tales had generated abiding fears about venturing westward on the dark and unknown sea.

THE SEA OF GREEN DARKNESS

Long before the Ulster Scots crossed the Atlantic for America, the Sea of Green Darkness fueled their imaginations. This was an ancient name for the vast ocean, whose western horizon had forever tantalized early seafarers and explorers from western Europe, the Mediterranean, and Africa. To them, this seemingly endless sea represented the edge of the known world, populated by terrifying monsters. It had other names:

with which we had to contend, I managed to keep care and sorrow aloof. We had music, and dancing, sometimes however with empty stomacks every evening that permitted, and tripped it upon the quarter deck and sang, till Neptune raised his hoary locks from out the raging ocean, waved his trident in the air, and with extacy cried out Encore.!!!

The reason why I said in the commencement that you probably had heard of the loss of the Billy Booth is that we were driven ashore upon the island of Bic a short way up the St Lawrence. The storm was truly dreadful, our cordage and canvass, was torn to totters, aye to babyrags, the women of course screamed, (that's natural) the Captains countenance looked blue, the sailors behaved like jolly tars, and most of the passengers assisted. There was one however that I could not but remark, when the storm was at the worst. He was upon his knees, with his hands clasped round the mast beating his breast and vociferating with religious fear. "Hail Mary, Sweet Mary, Mother of God save us" I gave him a kick on the posterior and ordered him up to assist, told him there was no time to be lost in praying upon such an occasion, he turned round with a face, "Shade of Hogarth whither art thou fled!! a face that would have made a complete frontispiece to the book of lamentations, and sung out "Sweet Mary save us" at length we came to anchor in a small creek shut out from the view of every other vessell, and lay there repairing our sails for three days. I could not get landing at Quebec but was obliged to forward Mr McLeur's letter to Lieut Pemberton of which I suppose you now know. From thence to Montreal in a Steamer. then by land on foot to Lachine. Cornwall. Prescott Coburgh Peterboro' My travelling companions (indeed the only ones with whom I associated) were a Mr Orr of Mowermore, and his brother in law Mr Thistle "Nemo me impune lacefit" and three more pleasant warm hearted fellows never trod the road before us. I would advise every one in coming out to be particularly careful what ship and Captain the come with, and when arrived at Montreal if the wished to proceed farther to come as I did by land instead of the river St Lawrence. The country from Montreal is entirely woody except now and again you will hear of a farmers house, long before you see it, by a large bell hung round old Glofsy that gives the children their milk. the whole country is in a state of infancy with regard to farming, in comparison of Curl Ireland You could imagine nothing like it. A farmer gets probably two hundred acres at five shillings an acre in the wood builds himself a log house; and in the course of two or four years has got 10 or 20 of it cleared. he pays no rent no tithe no cess, in fact he just manages to eat and drink, and keep himself clothed, they generally live well ―――

Peterboro is a very improving place, four years ago there was not more than four houses in it. Mr Ferguson's was one, now it is larger, and more respectable by 100 to 10 than Bally clare. If I had space I could give you a wonderful history of the manners of the French Canadians, the Yankees the Indians of this country, the canny Scotchman and the Wild Irishman, but I must reserve the next leaf for other matter.

Bloody Foreland, Donegal coast, Ireland.
(Courtesy of Ian MacRae Young,
www.photographsofscotland.com)

the Great Outer Sea and the Ethiopian Ocean (given by Mediterranean-based sailors); the Sea of Perpetual Gloom; the Great West Sea; the Western Ocean (favored by the Irish and Scottish emigrants); and, among the navigators of Columbus's time, the Ocean Sea, an assumed watery pass to the western shores of Asia and its abundant spices.

Before early explorers ventured onto the Sea of Green Darkness, artists, writers, and poets were impressed by the relentless waves and tides of the sea, its mesmerizing far horizons, and the awful beauty of the heaving dark waters. One of the earliest literary reflections on the Atlantic dates from the eighth century. The eight stanzas of "Storm at Sea" were translated from Irish in the 1950s by the novelist and poet Frank O'Connor.

> When the wind is from the west
> All the waves cannot rest
> To the east must thunder on
> Where the bright tree of the sun
> Is rooted in the ocean's breast.[37]

The long-held popular belief that the Columbus expeditions were the first in western oceanic exploration is no longer held as credible. It is now generally believed that a small band of Norsemen were the first nonaboriginal people to set foot on the continent and, in essence, "discover America" in the early eleventh century. The legendary "Vinland" was America's first short-lived European settlement at L'Anse Aux Meadows on the northwestern tip of Newfoundland. This landing was proof that Mediterranean sailors did not have the monopoly on oceanic exploration and innovation. Long after the Phoenicians but well before the Portuguese and Spanish expeditions, northern explorers launched their boats into the colder, stormier waters of the North Atlantic. Their motives were somewhat different from those of the Mediterranean explorers: curiosity drove them onward rather than commerce and acculturation of indigenous peoples.

There are other pre-Columbian tales of contact with the New World from various locations on the western fringes of Europe. In 1398 Earl Henry Sinclair sailed from Orkney and is believed by some scholars to have reached Guysborough, Nova Scotia, before traveling southward.[38] The evidence is intriguing: a knight in armor carved into stone by indigenous people of Massachusetts, and then the Sinclair family's master mason chiseling perfect ears of corn onto his intricate and beautiful stone columns at Roslyn Chapel south of Edinburgh.[39] (Corn was not known in Europe until the Spanish brought it back from the New World in the early sixteenth century.)

In the first millennium, there are two groups of seafarers that are worthy of review: the Vikings most notably, but also the Irish, whose feats at sea, dating from an even earlier era, have been half forgotten in the annals of history. The Norse and Irish boat build-

ers could not have constructed more dissimilar vessels. The Vikings sailed forth in their famous longships, resolute on conquest, conducting a violent campaign around the coast of the Atlantic archipelago of Britain and Ireland. Using place names, historians and linguists can trace the spread of their settlements dating from their first incursions in the eighth century, showing increasing concentration the farther north they investigate. The Battle of Largs in 1263 finally settled the centuries-old territorial dispute between Scotland and Norway, driving the longships back from the Ayrshire coast.

Longships, strong and designed for speed, were the embodiment of Norse naval power. The Irish sailed into the churning waters of the Western Ocean in less-robust craft. A currach (sometimes "curragh") was constructed around a wooden ribbed frame over which animal skins were stretched, with tar used to seal the skin joints. *Navigatio sancti Brendani abbatis* is the Latin account of the voyage of Saint Brendan the Abbot (489–583), born in the southwest of Ireland and, according to legend, one of the first to make a sustained voyage through the waters of the North Atlantic. This account describes his monks' construction of an oceangoing vessel covered with hides and cured with oak bark, with a central mast and sail. It must have been a sizeable boat, as Brendan is supposed to have voyaged with as many as sixty brother monks. They set sail from a small estuary on the Dingle Peninsula in southwestern Ireland, heading north to the Scottish Outer Hebrides, on to the Faeroe Islands, westward to Iceland, and finally, it is speculated, to Newfoundland, the promised land of the Irish saints. This route came to be known in the chronicles of North Atlantic exploration as the island "stepping stones."[40] The voyage is principally a wonder tale, and Saint Brendan claimed to have encountered an "Island of Sheep," the "Paradise of Birds," "pillars of crystal," "mountains that hurled rocks at voyagers," and eventually the "Promised Land" as he crossed the Atlantic. British historian and explorer Tim Severin, renowned for his work retracing historical expeditions, decided to test the legend of Saint Brendan's seven-year voyage across the Atlantic. Using traditional tools, he built a handcrafted replica currach on a frame of Irish oak and ash. Severin made landfall in the Faroes, then Iceland, and eventually, after sailing "The Brendan" from May 1976 to June 1977 across 4,500 miles and through violent squalls, he and his crew reached Peckford Island, Newfoundland. The expedition confirmed Severin's conviction that the legend could have been rooted in historical fact—provided that, as a local Irish boat builder stressed to him, "the crew was capable enough." Such a possibility fueled the public imagination, and Severin's account of the expedition, *The Brendan Voyage* (1978), became an international best seller, translated into sixteen languages.

Severin established that Saint Brendan the Abbot could have navigated the North Atlantic; however, he could not prove that such a voyage actually ever took place. Indeed, no evidence of early Irish expeditions across the Atlantic to North America has ever been uncovered. Although written sources do establish the antiquity of the currach, their flimsy construction has ensured that marine archaeologists will never unearth ancient remains of such crafts. Certainly, the nautical technology of the time might well have allowed skilled navigators to reach Iceland or even Greenland, but surviving a crossing to the North American mainland seems less likely. No early Irish artifacts have been found in North America.[41] Nevertheless, in the practiced art of the Irish storyteller, where colorful embellishments are encouraged, the legends of Saint Brendan of Clonfert "the Navigator," "the Voyager," or "the Bold" endure in myth and song, one of the earliest Irish monastic saints to be so remembered. "St. Brendan's Voyage," by Irish singer Christy Moore, takes it all to a new level of fun and fantasy, with the indomitable monk sailing to such far-flung destinations as Long Island, Hawaii, Australia, China, and Japan.

A boat sailed out of Brandon in the year of 501,
'Twas a damp and dirty mornin' Brendan's voyage
   it began.
Tired of thinnin' turnips and cuttin' curly kale,
When he got back from the creamery he hoisted
   up the sail.
He ploughed a lonely furrow to the north, south,
   east and west,
Of all the navigators St. Brendan was the best.
When he ran out of candles he was forced to
   make a stop,
He tied up in Long Island and put America on
   the map.
Did you know that Honolulu was founded by
   a Kerryman,
When he went on to find Australia then China
   and Japan?

When he was touchin' 70, he began to miss the
    craic,
Turnin' to his albatross he sez "I'm headin' back."

Mythology may have merged with reality, but
clearly the intrepid Ulster emigrants of the eighteenth
century had a rich tradition of seafarers, fabled and factual, from which to source their tenacity. They would
in turn write their own episode of this continuing narrative, each chapter opening with a squint at the horizon and a scan of the gray green swell beyond. Their
sea, the "Western Ocean," became a central character
in their stories and songs.

Oh the times were hard and the wages low,
Amelia where you bound for?
That land of promise there you'll see,
Across the Western Ocean.

THE EMIGRANT PASSAGEWAYS

While the earlier exploits of Norse and Irish seafarers
receded into the realms of myth and legend, the fifteenth and sixteenth centuries were the golden age of
Atlantic exploration, and the colonization of America
naturally followed. The 1607 Jamestown Settlement
in the Colony of Virginia, and then Plymouth in New
England in 1620, were early English footholds; other
Europeans, notably the Dutch, also landed and settled
along the New World's eastern seaboard. Ship construction technology and the tools of navigation were
constantly improving, and regular sea routes were
soon established. The eighteenth and early nineteenth
centuries were lived in the age of the sailing ship, however, and anyone taking to the high seas did so at the
mercy of the ocean's prevailing winds and turbulent
conditions.

No Atlantic crossing can have been more fearful and
oppressive than the notorious "Middle Passage" of the
West African slaves, caught in the ruthless and inhu-
man vice of a triangular transatlantic trade connecting
western Europe, Africa, and North America. During
the slave-trading era of the sixteenth century to the
nineteenth century, it is estimated that as many slaves
died en route and upon arrival as survived to live in
bondage. Yet with faith and fortitude, these resilient
souls persevered, and, among a myriad of cultural
legacies, their musical traditions would blend with
the songs and tunes of the Ulster Scots to create, with
other influences, the melodic sounds of Appalachia.

So it was in this environment of transoceanic sailing—often enforced, sometimes embraced—that the
eighteenth-century Ulster Scots launched their emigrations to Canaan's Promised Land of America. Unlike the brutal removal of West Africans, theirs was an
extended pathway, passing across several thresholds,
each tinged with its own emotions and challenges.
The first phase involved the departure from the family
home place, proceeding then by "convoy" to the edge
of the local community. Sites, such as "The Bridge of
Tears" in West Donegal, marked a location of sorrowful passage on the road to the port of embarkation.[42]
Throughout the eighteenth century, the journey was
by foot or cart, regardless of age or physical strength.
By the nineteenth century, cart, carriage, and even train
were all means of transport to the coast. Ireland may
be an island, but for many, this was the first time they
had seen the ocean they were soon to cross. Each phase
of the journey, then, represented a boundary negotiated and a new frontier confronted.

Throughout the eighteenth century, the vast majority of Ulster emigrants departed from one of five ports.
The largest were Belfast, Derry-Londonderry, and
Newry. Smaller ships were also berthed and boarded at
Larne and Portrush. A few would-be voyagers traveled
south to seek passage from Dublin and Sligo. Upon
arrival, they encountered another threshold: the ship
may have been in port, but they still had to secure
their passage. Apprehension must have been magnified
greatly by the indeterminate time spent waiting and

The Bridge of Tears, County Donegal, Northern Ireland.
(Courtesy of CatMac Photography)

Marker at the Bridge of Tears in Gaelic. Translation: "Friends and
family of the person who was emigrating used to accompany
them as far as this spot. This was the place where they parted.
This is the Bridge of Tears." (Courtesy of CatMac Photography)

THE EMIGRATION OF THOMAS MELLON

> Next we pass the ancient town of Strabane, and our little river soon widens at its reception of the tidewater into Loch Foyle. As the train passed down from Victoria Bridge to Derry on the west side of the Strule, I could see the road on the east side that went to Derry on our way to America; and when in sight of Derry I could see the bridge over which we crossed from the east side of the river on that long ago occasion. . . . I sought and mounted the stone steps to the top of the wall, which I again aversed as when a little boy led by the hand of my father, feeling very much the same as then, only my thoughts now were tempered more with sadness.
>
> —*Thomas Mellon, Thomas Mellon and His Times, 1885*

The autobiography of Thomas Mellon tenderly reveals the inner life of the emigrant and exile. In his old age, he returned to visit Ulster and retraced the steps of his boyhood farewell journey from the family farm and cottage. Many emigrants retained equally strong impressions of their beloved Ulster homes, but few achieved the remarkable success of Mellon, an accomplished attorney, judge, entrepreneur, investor, and founder of the Pittsburgh-based banking dynasty. Several presidents of the United States were of Scots-Irish lineage, but Thomas Mellon emigrated directly from Ulster. His descendants would build upon his achievements and, along with the families of Rockefeller, Ford, and Carnegie, became giants of American industry and philanthropy. Mellon's son Andrew served as secretary of the treasury under three presidents, founded a university, and was himself a highly successful banker and industrialist.

Thomas Mellon's humble background gave little indication of the prodigious success that lay in his future. Like so many in his home community, his Presbyterian family had emigrated from Scotland in the seventeenth century. He maintained a lifelong

the ambiguity of their chances of embarking. Upon arrival at the port, they had to find lodging of some kind that was both affordable and convenient to the docks. This was the period of limbo when emigrants and their families were at their most vulnerable, prey to unscrupulous ticket agents, ships' captains, and dockside chancers with their misleading information about departure, quality of vessels, pricing, and lodging.[43] Many could not afford the crossing and were thus susceptible to becoming "redemptioneers" by undertaking a contractual promise to be sold into labor by the ship's captain before they could disembark on the other side. There also were numerous fairs and markets at port towns where aggressive agents signed up potential emigrants for their passage and subsequent indentured servitude. Pamphlets and newspaper advertisements were everywhere, painting a flattering picture of the New World's opportunities: liberty, an abundance of cheap land, an easier existence. If only they would leave the old life behind and sail toward the destination celebrated in John Doyle's chorus:

Sailing to liberty's sweet shore,
Sailing to liberty's sweet shore.
We left all we know, to this new life we'll go,
Sailing to liberty's sweet shore.

link to his Scottish ancestry through a love of the poetry and songs of Robert Burns and formed a close association with industrialist and philanthropist Andrew Carnegie, an emigrant directly from Scotland.

Mellon was born in 1813 in a cottage built by his father and his uncle Archie on the family farm in County Tyrone. His grandparents and many other relatives had already emigrated to the United States, and Thomas's parents had increasingly set their hearts on crossing the Atlantic to join them. When they made the decision to emigrate in 1818, they were given an American Wake, a community parting ritual with family and friends that culminated in the emotional journey to the port of Derry-Londonderry for embarkation to Philadelphia. Settled in Pennsylvania, Thomas grew up on a small farm at Poverty Point, some twenty miles east of Pittsburgh. A walk to the dynamic and flourishing city at the age of ten made a lasting impression upon him with which a life on the farm could never compete. Reading Benjamin Franklin's autobiography steered Mellon in the direction of a career in law, and he resolved to be part of the bustle, wealth, and power of city life. He trained as a lawyer, founded the Mellon Bank, and, when he died in 1908, Judge Thomas Mellon was the patriarch of one of America's most renowned and influential families. Today, the Mellon family cottage is part of the Ulster American Folk Park near Omagh, County Tyrone, a living history museum of eighteenth- and nineteenth-century Ulster life. The park plays host to music festivals, which occasionally feature bluegrass and Appalachian music with ancestral roots in Ulster. The Mellon Centre for Migration Studies stands by the entrance to the Folk Park. A short stroll from the boyhood home of Thomas Mellon, it is a principal archive for the family records of Scots-Irish and Irish families whose descendants are spread far and wide in North America and across the globe.

One emigrant, Thomas Gaffikin, would later describe how "in the emigrant season whole families of country people wandered about the lanes and docks of Belfast, filling lodging houses about Pine Street for several days, until their chosen vessel was ready to sail."[44]

The emigrant vessels of the Ulster Scots sailed for ports along the American seaboard from New York to Charleston, but Philadelphia and the Delaware valley were by far their most common destinations due to the flourishing linen trade between Philadelphia and ports throughout Ireland. American-grown flaxseed was steadily supplying the Irish linen looms, so regular shipping lanes were already established; shipowners and captains were eager to fill their holds with emigrant cargo for the return voyage. It has often been said that, without the linen trade, eighteenth-century emigration to America might not have occurred on anything like the scale recorded by history.

The would-be emigrants existed in a kind of limbo, arriving at the port, waiting to board a ship, and contemplating their voyage and ultimate arrival in America. There was time for anxiety to build: thoughts of loved ones left behind, missing the only place they had ever known, fear of the impending voyage and the looming perils of the Atlantic, qualms about this

so-called promised land, distant and unknown. The disquiet found its way into songs such as "Knox's Farewell."

> I now must cross the raging sea and leave my
>   native shore,
> To seek my fortune in the West with comrades
>   gone before.
> Your daughters fair and all your sons whose praise
>   no tongue can tell,
> Stern fate has issued her decree that I must say
>   "farewell."

Despite optimistic rhetoric about America as a place of opportunity, there were widespread tales of the perils of the crossing, some from recent reports and others rooted in legend. Turbulent storms, colossal waves the size of ships, drownings, disease, shipwrecks, and piracy all haunted the dreams of impending passage between the Old and New Worlds. Hopes and prayers for a reliable vessel and crew seemed to offer barely enough protection, so superstitions were rife, and good-luck tokens were coveted well into the twentieth

century. Charms, sometimes handed out at American Wakes, might be sewn into clothes to safeguard against storms and fevers, treasured as forget-me-not mementos, and even kept as reminders for eventual return to "Paddy's Green Shamrock Shore."[45]

> Our ship she lies at anchor, she's standing by the
>   quay
> May fortune bright shine down each night, as we
>   sail over the sea
> Many ships were lost, many lives it cost on the
>   journey that lies before
> With a tear in my eye I'm bidding good-bye to
>   Paddy's green shamrock shore.
>
> So fare thee well my own true love, I'll think of
>   you night and day
> And a place in my mind you surely will find,
>   although I am so far away
> Though I'll be alone far away from my home,
>   I'll think of the good times once more,
> Until the day I can make my way back to Paddy's
>   green shamrock shore.

Travelers in the seventeenth century and the first half of the eighteenth century made their crossings at the height of the age of sail; it was not until 1838 that the first crossing was made by steam ship. Sailing vessels were fitted to hold up to 100 passengers and weighed less than 150 tons. The 3,000-mile passage was undertaken in approximately fourteen voyages annually, in spring or late summer, sailing from the Ulster ports primarily to Philadelphia and returning full with their flaxseed cargo to fuel the production of Irish linen. The square rigger sailing ship plied her way through the waves at eight to ten knots per hour, and the crossing time ranged from six to ten weeks on average, depending on wind and weather, which in extreme cases could extend the voyage to as much as nineteen weeks. If the vagaries of wind and current were especially unfavorable, the end of a twenty-four-hour period could see them even farther from their destination than they had been at its start. By the close of the eighteenth century, the standard fare was approximately four pounds, with one guinea (one pound and one shilling) required as down payment. For this, emigrants were entitled to bring a single trunk for belongings, and they traveled light since their possessions were meager. Some carried cash from the sale of property leases and other assets that they planned to use to acquire a few goods and household items when they settled into their new homes.[46] In many cases, most earthly belongings were sold or left behind to fund the journey.

> My father sold his second cow and borrowed
>   twenty pounds,
> Being in the merry month of May we sailed from
>   Derry town.
> There were thousands more along the shore,
>   all anxious for to roam,
> And leave the land where they were reared,
>   called Erin's lovely home.
>   — *"Erin's Lovely Home"*

Beginning with the day of boarding to debarkation in Philadelphia, each phase of the crossing was detailed in the verses of emigration songs, such as "The Emigrant's Farewell":

> Our ship at the present lies in Derry harbor,
> To bear us away across the wide swelling sea.
> May heaven be her companion and grant her fair
>   breezes,
> Till we reach the greenfields of America.

The boarding scene at the docks combined sights and sounds of quayside clamor, the barking of orders from the dockmasters to keep the line of departing vessels in order, the scurrying of the late arrivals and shouted last good-byes from the wharf. Each emigrant's step took them deeper into the unknown, leaving behind "their dear native land," an experience they shared with thousands.

> They put their foot on the tender just leaving the
>   strand,
> And gave one look back to their dear native land.

Their hearts are a-breaking for leaving the
    shore,
Good-bye dear old Ireland will I ne'er see you
    more.
   —*"Thousands Are Sailing to America"*

SAILING FROM SHORE

Leaving the home place had demanded a "last look"; now, so did the sail out of harbor and toward the great unknowns of the Western Ocean. At Ireland's most southerly point, there is the small islet of Fastnet Rock. The Norsemen named it "Hvasstann-ey," meaning "sharp-tooth isle," and in Irish it is the "Carraig Aonair," or "Lonely Rock," with its stark lighthouse perched upon a crag. Fastnet was also nicknamed "Ireland's

Teardrop" since this was the emigrants' last sight of home before the open sea. Ulster emigrants took their fond farewells of different landmarks. Boats leaving Belfast harbor would sail past the historic harbor town of Carrickfergus and the commanding Clan Ferguson Castle and on into the North Channel. The crew was always eager to make an efficient exit from these notoriously rough seas. From Derry-Londonderry, ships sailed out of Loch Foyle, and emigrants straining for a last look would take in Malin Head on the Inishowen Peninsula, County Donegal, the most northerly point on the Ireland landmass. Then they would look to the tiny island of Inishtrahull, now uninhabited and crested by a lighthouse (still manned until recent decades). "Rising out of the ocean bed," Inishtrahull was a sight the emigrants held in their hearts as it slowly faded beyond the eastern horizon, a parting sentinel for all emigrants leaving Ulster.

> At twelve o'clock we came in sight of famous
>   Malin head,
> And Inishtrahull, far to the right, rose out of the
>   ocean's bed;
> A grander sight now met my eyes than e'er I saw
>   before,
> The sun going down 'twixt sea and sky far from
>   the Shamrock Shore.
> —*"The Shamrock Shore"*

Homesickness for loved ones left behind must have been all too evident, although songs give the impression of maintaining a brave face as thoughts turned to anticipation of the New World and the strangers that lay "across the ocean blue."

> Farewell to Ballymoney and County Antrim too,
> Likewise lovely Molly, I bid a fond adieu,
> Amerikay lies far away, across the ocean blue,
> And I'm bound for there dear Molly and again
>   I'll ne're see you.
> —*"Farewell Ballymoney"*

From "lovely Molly" to "my brown-eyed girl" to "my Nancy," departing was a sweet sorrow, and there was often a wistful hope to return to the lass left behind.

> Our ship is well-manned love and we are bound
>   for sea,
> Our captain he gave orders and him we must
>   obey,
> "Aloft, aloft my lively lads, without fear or dread,
> There's a south wind rising that will clear us
>   'round the Malin Head."
>
> Sailing down Lough Foyle me boys, Magillian
>   Point we passed,

Irish Coastal Waters (Oil painting; courtesy of Hugh O'Neill, b. Belfast, County Antrim, Northern Ireland, 1959)

> I never will be happy 'til I wed my brown-haired
>   lass,
> And when we reach the other side we'll drink a
>   flowing glass,
> And the toast will be right merrily "here's a health
>   to my brown-eyed lass."
> —*"The Brown-Haired Girl"*

> The very first night I slept on board, I dreamt
>   about my Nancy,
> I dreamt I had her in my arms and well she
>   pleased my fancy;
> But when I woke out of my dreams and found my
>   bosom empty,
> You may be sure and very sure that I lay
>   discontented.
> —*"The Rambling Irishman"* (CD TRACK 5)

Sometimes, the loved ones they left behind shared their sense of emptiness in song, sentiments captured by nineteenth-century Australian writer and poet Henry Lawson in "The Outside Track":

CHARLES DICKENS, ESQ., CROSSES THE ATLANTIC

In the mid-1800s, steamship operators were competing for contracts to carry mail, passengers, and cargo on the most profitable routes. They were now beating sailing ships by offering both cheaper rates and faster crossings. The *Acadia* was the first of four paddle steamer services across the Atlantic Ocean ordered by Samuel Cunard for the British & North American Royal Mail Steam Packet Company. In January 1842 the celebrated English novelist Charles Dickens (1812–70) sailed with his wife, Kate, from Liverpool to Boston aboard the *Acadia*'s sister steamship, the RMS *Britannia*. Mr. and Mrs. Dickens differed from most Atlantic passengers in two crucial ways: they were not emigrating but were crossing instead to tour around the East Coast and Great Lakes areas of the United States and Canada; and they were able to travel in relative comfort, booking a stateroom for "Charles Dickens, Esquire, and Lady," which, though small and snug, would have been luxurious in comparison to the quarters endured by the vast majority of voyagers. The author's travelogue paints vivid pictures of the dockside scenes of departure.

Packing-cases, portmanteaus, carpet-bags, and boxes, are already passed from hand to hand, and hauled on board with breathless rapidity. The officers, smartly dressed, are at the gangway handing the passengers up the side, and hurrying the men. In five minutes' time, the little steamer is utterly deserted, and the packet is beset and over-run by its late freight, who instantly pervade the whole ship, and are to be met with by the dozen in every nook and corner: swarming down below with their own baggage, and stumbling over other people's; disposing themselves comfortably in wrong cabins, and creating a most horrible confusion by having to turn out again; madly bent upon opening locked doors, and on forcing a passage into all kinds of out-of-the-way places where there is no thoroughfare; sending wild stewards, with elfin hair, to and fro upon the breezy decks on unintelligible errands, impossible of execution: and in short, creating the most extraordinary and bewildering tumult.[1]

Weather was the great leveler, and no amount of money could insulate Charles and Kate Dickens from

The port-lights glowed in the morning mist
That rolled from the waters so green;
And over the railing we grasped his fist
As the dark tide came between;
We cheered the captain, we cheered the crew,
And our own mate, times out of mind;
We cheered the land he was going to,
And the land he'd left behind.

TURNING TO THE WEST

When any lingering remnant of the motherland was completely out of sight, the heaving waves of the Western Ocean sounded their steady drumroll over the ship's bow. Anyone who had never cast eyes on the sea until arriving in port must have been gripped, in equal measure, with wonder and dread by the relentless energy of the ocean, the constant creaking of the hull, the rhythmic roar of waves, the flap of linen sailcloth, the Atlantic swell. In his travelogue, he provides a hair-raising account of heavy seas and headwinds, leading inevitably to seasickness, a horrifying experience he claimed was "impossible for the most vivid imagination to conceive."

It is the third morning. I am awakened out of my sleep by a dismal shriek from my wife, who demands to know whether there's any danger. I rouse myself, and look out of bed. The water-jug is plunging and leaping like a lively dolphin; all the smaller articles are afloat, except my shoes, which are stranded on a carpet-bag, high and dry, like a couple of coal-barges. Suddenly I see them spring into the air, and behold the looking-glass, which is nailed to the wall, sticking fast upon the ceiling. At the same time the door entirely disappears, and a new one is opened in the floor. Then I begin to comprehend that the state-room is standing on its head.

A steward passes. "Steward!" "Sir?" "What is the matter? what do you call this?" "Rather a heavy sea on, sir, and a head-wind."

A head-wind! Imagine a human face upon the vessel's prow, with fifteen thousand Samsons in one bent upon driving her back, and hitting her exactly between the eyes whenever she attempts to advance an inch. Imagine the ship herself, with every pulse and artery of her huge body swollen and bursting under this maltreatment, sworn to go on or die. Imagine the wind howling, the sea roaring, the rain beating: all in furious array against her. Picture the sky both dark and wild, and the clouds, in fearful sympathy with the waves, making another ocean in the air. Add to all this, the clattering on deck and down below; the tread of hurried feet; the loud hoarse shouts of seamen; the gurgling in and out of water through the scuppers; with, every now and then, the striking of a heavy sea upon the planks above, with the deep, dead, heavy sound of thunder heard within a vault; —and there is the head-wind of that January morning.[2]

1. Charles Dickens, *American Notes for General Circulation* (London: Chapman & Hall, 1842), 591–92.
2. Ibid., 595–96.

the wind whipping around the rigging. When a squall blew in, the fierce Atlantic gales must have instigated pure terror.

Then lo! A dreadful storm arose; the seas like
   mountains roll;
Blue lightning's flash on every side, and rush from
   pole to pole;
Regardless both of winds and waves and hoarse
   loud thunder's roar,

None of my own to hear me moan, far from the
   Shamrock Shore.
   —"The Shamrock Shore"

Some voyagers kept journals; these provide intimate glimpses of life on board. John Cunningham, a passenger on the ship *America*, recorded the daily incidents of his stormy passage from Belfast on a voyage that spanned from September 27 to December 12, 1795:

Saturday 7th. Last night was tremendous all the night. At 11 o'clock the vessel shipped a sea which washed away the lee quarter boom boards . . . and filled the cabin full of water; which alarmed every soul aboard. We expected every moment would be the last—in short, words cannot relate what we felt on the occasion as its happening at night made it all the more terrible. I believe if the vessel had gone to the bottom I could not have stirred out of my berth. The gale somewhat abated this morning but still a very high sea running and some spray flying over the vessel. . . . Mr. Neil's two youngest children and the sailor before mentioned all bad in the smallpox.[47]

Inevitably, seasickness soon supplanted homesickness among the passengers. Most had no experience on "Paddy's Green Shamrock Shore" of any moving conveyance other than horse and cart. Now they were being relentlessly pitched and tossed as they clung to their belongings below deck.

> We sailed three weeks, we were all seasick, not a
>   man on board was free
> We were all confined unto our bunks and no-one
>   to pity poor me.
> No father kind nor mother dear to lift up my
>   head, which was sore,
> Which made me think more on the lassie I left on
>   Paddy's green shamrock shore.

Conditions on the emigrant ships varied but were generally grim. Shipowners were all about maximizing profit, so they encouraged captains to cram as many passengers on board as possible. Sleeping accommodation was usually a bare straw bed space or

a hammock. Decks were less than five feet apart and dimly lit, with ventilation only by porthole. They had to batten down the hatches during stormy weather, when it would have become very murky on the lower deck. To minimize costs, rations were nominal and monotonous: potatoes, salthorse (salted beef), and occasional stale pork or fish. The "ship's biscuit," an inexpensive and long-lasting staple known in the nineteenth century as hardtack, served as bread. Prepared months before sailing, ship's biscuits were baked hard as a rock from flour, salt, and water and were intended to ease hunger by swelling in the stomach. Since water would not remain fresh for long in barrels, beer was a standard drink, even for the children. Space was not so severely confined as in the notorious slave ships transporting their human cargo from West Africa, but conditions could deteriorate in similar ways. With the crowded, unhygienic conditions and austere diet, infectious diseases were omnipresent—dysentery, typhus, cholera, and smallpox, often collectively known as "ship fever." In one recorded instance, sixty of the ship's ailing passengers died at sea. Not surprisingly, babies, young children, and the elderly were more likely to perish on the voyage. At 2 percent, the mortality rate did not come close to the mid-nineteenth-century coffin ships of the Irish potato-famine era, when as many as one-quarter of the passengers suffered on-board death, or indeed the horrifying mortality of slave ships.[48] However, burial at sea was a terrible trauma for families, as their deceased loved ones were rolled into their bedding, anchored with stones, and, after a few prayers, dropped overboard into the dark ocean, a ritual starkly described by John Doyle and Cathy Peterson:

Well we're bowed down in sickness and hunger,
And pray for the hand of the Maker.
My child was lost to the fever,
A quick prayer then hauled overboard.
—*"Liberty's Sweet Shore"*

THE DANCE AT SEA

The character of the captain and his crew could make a significant difference to the atmosphere of the voyage. Some captains were humane with their fragile passengers; others showed a lack of concern and even brutality. The day-to-day routine was tedious, and boredom might easily have crushed the passengers' spirits. They had already made drastic adjustments: removal from everything familiar, tolerating mind-numbing seabound days for an indeterminate number of weeks, and accepting the harsh realities of the passage, including the threat of mortal danger. All things considered, the endurance of eighteenth-century emigrants was remarkable. Not only was the shipboard mortality rate much lower than those of the mid-nineteenth century, when extreme overcrowding and disease unfortunately were rampant, but also fewer eighteenth-century ships were lost at sea; there were only three such losses recorded, despite the relentlessness of Atlantic gales and tempests.

Passengers' hopes and spirits could be buoyed by a natural inclination deeply embedded within them: the love of music and dance that had played such a

Dancing between Decks. **(Courtesy of Illustrated London News/Mary Evans Picture Library)**

role in their communities at home. This became a mainstay of their lives at sea. In fact, daily dancing was even mandatory on most of the vessels, an important way for the passengers to gain some level of exercise during their confinement. With space on deck so limited, elaborate dance sets were not practical, so dancing on the spot took place instead, amounting to a type of aerobic exercise. As it had been at home, the fiddle was the dance accompaniment of choice for the crossing (CD track 4). Dance tunes at sea tended to be hornpipes; they were already popular with sailors and had a tempo well suited to these on-deck dance workouts. Seafaring dance tunes were often named for various Ulster ports of embarkation: "Derry Hornpipe," "Belfast Hornpipe," "Newry Hornpipe,"

and the old standard "Sailor's Hornpipe."[49] Few other instruments made the nineteenth-century crossing. The flute was portable, and one might occasionally be produced to supplement the fiddle. The accordion and concertina, popular with later sea shanties, were not introduced until the next century. Bagpipes, today such an international symbol of everything remotely Scottish, did not accompany the eighteenth-century Ulster emigrants in any significant way for several reasons: they had reduced in popularity with the decline of clan chiefs' power and patronage; they tended to be more the preserve of the wealthier class of the time; and they were difficult to maintain, and tuning would have been a challenge for a damp, salt-sea crossing. (The pipes came later, beginning with American mili-

The Company of Songs

Nuala Kennedy, Irish singer, songwriter, and flute and whistle player; interviewed in Dunkeld, Scotland, June 2013, by Fiona Ritchie during Kennedy's concert tour playing Irish and Appalachian music with A. J. Roach.

I imagine and try to put myself in the place of people who were leaving home all those years ago and traveling to America, and leaving under painful circumstances very often. If you have the gift of these songs with you and you have the memory of them in your mind, it's like a company for you in your life. They are almost your friends that will mind you on your journey. If things are tough, you can think on the stories they can tell you. And the process of singing and the process of remembering the words; it's a very powerful personal one. Having arrived wherever you are, people who maybe couldn't remember all the words, they would appreciate being able to share them and being able to hear those songs again. So I'm sure that people who could sing and could remember the songs were probably in demand in their new communities perhaps even more than they had been at home, I imagine.

tary regiments during the Revolution and French and Indian War, when skilled pipers were recruited to their ranks from across the sea.)

Singing at sea was a common pastime. Like dancing, songs brought together passengers from all walks of life, origins, and persuasions, harking back to the egalitarian spirit of the ceilis at home that smoothed over cultural differences. With the sharing of lyrics and stories, the wayfarers were upholding something of value that would survive the Atlantic passage with them: traditions to carry down from the decks of the ships and on into a new land and, by future generations of Ulster Scots, into the southern Appalachians.

THE LONG EMIGRANT LINE

On Jordan's stormy banks I stand and cast a
   wishful eye,
To Canaan's fair and happy land where my
   possessions lie.

Oh the transporting rapturous scene that rises
   to my sight.
Sweet fields arrayed in living green and rivers
   of delight.
I am bound for the promised land,
   I am bound for the promised land;
   Oh who will come and go with me?
   I am bound for the promised land.
—From John Rippon's 1787 "Selection of Hymns,"
The Southern Harmony and Musical Companion
(New York: Hastings House, 1835)

An estimated 250,000 emigrants departed Ulster for America in the eighteenth century, beginning in earnest in 1718 and continuing in several waves thereafter. The flow subsided considerably during the American Revolution and picked up again later at a stable but reduced pace. From 1783 to 1799, about 60,000 emigrants came freely from Ulster, not by that time under any indentured servitude. Irish and Scottish emigrations throughout the nineteenth century headed

OTHER LANDFALLS

Immigrants arriving from all around the world first set eyes on American shores from one of a number of East Coast harbors. Boston was New England's foremost seaport, and its merchants had established flourishing trade routes with Britain and other parts of the colonies. In the nineteenth century, Boston was a major destination for Irish immigrants. They contributed an Irish American identity to the city's Charlestown neighborhood on the banks of the Mystic River and to South Boston, where they embedded a lively music scene that is renowned to this day. As the mid-Atlantic colonies rapidly grew, Philadelphia and New York soon surpassed Boston as the primary ports of entry. Charleston, South Carolina, was a popular destination for Scots, Scots-Irish, and Irish, although not on the same scale as the northern ports. In 1726 Scots immigrants established the philanthropic St. Andrew's Society of Charleston, the oldest Scottish society of its type in the world, and a congregation of twelve Scottish families founded Charleston's historic First Scots Presbyterian Church in 1731. Savannah, Georgia, was also a focus of Scottish and Irish immigration, such that today, Savannah holds the second-largest St. Patrick's Day parade and festival in the United States after New York City.

Highland Scots settled North Carolina's Cape Fear area, although Wilmington was not a major port facility. Flora MacDonald, heroine of the 1745 Jacobite Rising, emigrated from Scotland to North Carolina in 1774. She and her husband took the Loyalist side in the American Revolution, and when Allan Macdonald was taken prisoner with Flora in hiding, Patriots ravaged their farm and took all their possessions. She was persuaded to return to the Isle of Skye with her daughter on a merchant ship in 1779, and they survived an attack at sea by privateers. When her husband also returned in 1784, they managed to regain their estate, raising a large family on Skye. The MacDonalds are a rare example of successful eighteenth-century repatriation.

New York City, with its huge natural harbor and emergent metropolis, eventually became the most popular gateway to America. Even before the Ellis Island Immigration Station opened in 1892, 8 million immigrants had already entered New York City by way of the Castle Garden Immigration Center in lower Manhattan. Opening in 1892, Ellis Island was America's first federal immigration center and is now part of the Statue of Liberty National Monument. By the time the center closed in 1954, it had welcomed over 12 million immigrants from all over the world to the Land of Liberty. Today, over 100 million Americans can trace their ancestry via processing at Ellis Island. It was the largest point of entry for late nineteenth-century Irish refugees from the aftermath of the Great Hunger potato famine, as 1.1 million of them sailed from across the Atlantic into New York Harbor. Immigration from Scotland to Ellis Island also was substantial, with a total of about 600,000 Scots coming through the center. Italy, however, provided the largest population of arrivals, as approximately 4 million Italians trod through Ellis Island en route to their new lives in America. Over 1 million Germans and Poles reached Ellis Island,

and on the busiest day recorded, nine ships docked, with a total of 12,668 passengers from Germany, the Netherlands, Italy, Denmark, England, Scotland, and Northern Ireland.

As the human influx proceeded on a sizeable scale into the twentieth century, a robust, nativist anti-immigration sentiment surfaced, crystallized by World War I. Restrictionists in Congress warned of the "dangers of the American melting pot" and succeeded in passing the first Quota Act in 1921, thereby ending America's open-door policy. Monthly and "place-of-origin" quotas were set, and by the end of World War II, Ellis Island was becoming too costly to operate and its functions devolved to centers across the country. Today, the island has been restored as a museum and an impressive monument to an unparalleled immigration stream that helped shape a nation.

In the immigration story of the eighteenth-century Ulster Scots, it is the city of Philadelphia that stands today as a symbol of their life-changing passage to the mid-Atlantic Pennsylvania colony. Reminders abound throughout the Philadelphia area. The Scotch-Irish Society of the United States of America is headquartered there, as are archives of Scots-Irish genealogy. The Presbyterian Church in the United States was essentially born in Philadelphia, and today, Pennsylvania has more Presbyterian churches than any state, as well as more Presbyterian-related colleges. (North Carolina—at the terminus of the Great Philadelphia Wagon Road—registers the second-highest number.) The first successful daily newspaper in the United States, the *Pennsylvania Packet*, was published in Philadelphia, and twenty-six issues dating from 1787–88 feature poems and songs by Robert Burns. As this is likely the first American example of Burns in print, the National Library of Scotland recently acquired the collection.

By the Delaware River waterfront, just a short walk from historic Philadelphia, today's visitors encounter Penn's Landing Park, landfall for so many Ulster immigrants. Two impressive monuments honor the hardy souls who made the long and arduous voyage by sail. The Irish Memorial is a wedged-shaped, bronze sculpture with its higher end facing to the west, depicting a cluster of uncertain but hopeful immigrants. The Monument to Scottish Immigrants depicts a family freshly arrived from Scotland's shores to step into their new land of opportunity. The St. Andrews Society of Philadelphia, founded in 1747 to aid newly arrived Scots, dedicated this monument on October 11, 2012. It is located by Penn's Landing very close to the original site of the Tun Tavern, where glasses were raised, songs were shared, and traditional toasts were offered to wayfarers bound for the frontier.

> May the road rise to meet you,
> May the wind be aye at your back,
> A when you're gaun up the hill of fortune,
> May you ne'er meet a frien' comin' doun!

CAPE BRETON AND CAPE FEAR

The glen that was my father's own
Must be, by his, forsaken;
The house that was my father's home
Is levell'd with the bracken.
Ochon! Ochon! Our glory's o'er,
Stole by a mean deceiver.
—*James Hogg*, The Jacobite Relics of Scotland[1]

At an American Wake, pipes and fiddles were fired up to toast outward-bound people. It may have seemed, for a while thereafter, that music at these gatherings was also playing its own valediction. Ever since the Elizabethan conquest of Ireland, the country's chief export had been people; at least a million had already departed even before the onset of the Irish Potato Famine, known as the Great Hunger or "an Gorta Mór," which extended from 1845 to 1852. The effect of this exodus on the cultural life of communities throughout the island was felt for generations. Francis O'Neill's nine-volume tune collection in the early twentieth century, collectively known as "The Book," became the largest and most important individual effort to preserve Irish music. When his books found their way back to Ireland, they served as an inspiration to a musical community struggling to survive the aftermath of mass emigration.

Scotland, too, saw a waning of interest in music and song traditions as the notorious Highland Clearances took their toll in the nineteenth century. Landlords, many of whom were clan chiefs to whom their tenants had been tied for generations, depopulated their lands to make way for more-profitable tenants: sheep. There followed enforced mass emigrations transporting Gaels to the Carolinas, Nova Scotia, and beyond. In the years to come, the Clearances and their aftermath saw the emptying of a fairly densely populated Highlands and Islands landscape, as thousands followed the evicted communities to the Lowlands, England, Australia, New Zealand, the United States, and Canada.

Cape Breton Island, Nova Scotia, received 30,000 cleared Highlanders in the nineteenth century. They joined a community of some 20,000 Scottish Gaels who had emigrated there several decades earlier, bringing their Gaelic language and songs, their dances, and their fiddle and pipe music. By the beginning of the twentieth century, there were around 80,000 to 90,000 Gaelic speakers in Cape Breton. They were remote, sheltered from the influences of other countries, and they were able to preserve an antiquated fiddle style and much of their Gaelic song. Cape Breton's very isolation, allied with the Gaels' innate pride in their language and culture, allowed the islanders to maintain a continuous tradition of Highland fiddling from a golden age of Scottish music. Gaelic waulking songs, sung by tweed weavers in the Hebrides, were preserved in Cape Breton as milling songs. Step dancing thrived there, even as it all but fell into distant memory in Scotland. Today, Cape Breton Island stands as the only remaining concentration of Scottish Gaelic language and culture in North America and as a confirmation of the tenacity of oral tradition.

Highlanders did not begin their settlement of Nova Scotia until the 1770s.[2] In 1729 Highland Scots settlers arrived in eastern North Carolina and began clearing the longleaf pines, cultivating the flat, sandy area around the Cape Fear River. Their numbers quickly grew, both as a result of the final failure of the Jacobite risings in 1746, when the deported Jacobite prisoners arrived, and the Highland Clearance deportations. In 1760 the North Carolina General Assembly established a permanent community there called Campbelltown, named for the west coast Scottish town near the Mull of Kintyre. John MacRae, who emigrated from Kintail in 1774, wrote the lullaby "Dean Cadalan Sàmhach" (Sleep Peacefully) in the eastern North Carolina settlement. It is thought to be the first Gaelic song written in the Americas.

The area became a hotbed of activist activity during the American Revolution, when loyalties were divided. In 1776, barely thirty years after the carnage of Culloden's battlefield, a division of Loyalist Highland Scots marched to Moore's Creek Bridge, only to be defeated there by a brigade of Patriots.[3] Two years later, 400 citizens suspected of being Loyalists, many of them Highland Scots, were required to take an oath of allegiance to the Provincial government. In 1783 the legislature changed the name of Campbelltown to Fayetteville, a tribute to the French Marquis who had staunchly supported the American Revolution.

By the mid-nineteenth century, the Highlanders in the North Carolina low country had formed the largest Scottish settlement in North America. So where are they now? First, their culture was undermined by the fervor of religious revivals. Then, in an unpublicized twentieth-century clearance, they were dispersed to make way for the establishment of the enormous U.S. Army camp at Fort Bragg in 1918. A small graveyard in the heart of the guarded military complex is one of the few in the country encompassing markers with Gaelic inscriptions. It remains one of the only physical traces of these early settlers. Had the forces of revolution and war bypassed the Gaelic-speaking community of eastern North Carolina, remote in its own way, we might yet have had a Cape Breton–style culture in that area, an interesting cultural counterbalance to the Lowland and Ulster Scots of the southern Highlands. With their charismatic Gaelic psalm-singing style now thought to have influenced African American Baptist music of the South, who knows how else their songs and folkways might have endured and been passed along and adapted across the generations.

1. James Hogg, *The Jacobite Relics of Scotland: Being the Songs, Airs, and Legends of the Adherents to the House of Stuart* (Paisley, Renfrewshire, England: Alex Gardner, 1874), 185–86.

2. Duane Meyer, *The Highland Scots of North Carolina, 1732–1776* (Chapel Hill: University of North Carolina Press, 1961), 67.

3. Ibid., 111.

toward other destinations: the Irish to northeastern cities of the United States and Canada, and the Highland Scots to coastal Carolina, Georgia, and Canada. The substantial and steady stream of Ulster Scots migrating throughout the eighteenth century and a bit beyond, mainly into Philadelphia, was, however, the dramatic unfolding story for generations of families. They had departed an old world, endured a long ocean crossing, and stood ready to scan the horizon of their future lives. The first cry announcing the sighting of land must have been music to their weather-beaten ears. As the memory receded of their last sight of home, their first glimpse of the Promised Land was the next unforgettable image in their lives. As the wake of the voyage ebbed on the waves, a momentous new passageway awaited, while the sailing ship covered its last nautical miles and advanced on the American shore.

> To try my fortune I took notion,
> To cross the ocean where billows roar;
> Our topsails set sweetly, she glided neatly,
> And took me safe to America's shore.
> —*"Clough Water"*

Horizon

> We landed on the other side in three and thirty
>   days;
> And drinking o'er a parting glass, we took our
>   several ways.
> We took each comrade by the hand, perhaps to
>   meet no more;
> And thought on all our absent friends and the
>   lovely Shamrock Shore.
> —*"The Shamrock Shore"*

LANDFALL

In 1682, with the founding of the port of Philadelphia, a beacon of hope was ignited for European emigrants. So it was for the newly arrived Ulster Scots, who had scanned the western horizon for just such a guiding light and now waited for it to shine down upon them at "the other side." Germantown, a part of today's Philadelphia, was the first settlement of non-British Europeans in the English colonies. German and Dutch religious congregations had founded the community, around which developed the attractive "green country town" of Philadelphia, laid out in orderly squares by its Quaker founder, William Penn.[50] Dutch and

Swedish settlers had originally colonized the area. In 1681 Charles II granted a land tract to William Penn to repay a debt owed by the King to Penn's father. Penn founded the colony as a sanctuary for Quakers and named it for his family and the region's dense woods (from the Latin *sylvania*). It proved attractive initially to Welsh Quakers, who settled in the land to the north and west of Philadelphia, giving many towns and features their distinctive Welsh place names.

The colony's reputation for religious tolerance was especially attractive to the Ulster Presbyterians, who had long suffered under the yoke of the English Anglican Church, and it represented one of their only prospects for resettlement. To the immediate south was Maryland, with extensive plantations already established and no space for new arrivals seeking small farming plots. Besides, it had already been established as a territory with religious freedom for Catholics and was growing into one of the few predominantly Catholic regions among the English colonies in North America. The coastal areas of Virginia and the Carolinas were dominated by plantations and slaveholding. From the outset, New York and New England had wanted nothing to do with the "Ulster dissenters." So word traveled quickly back across the Atlantic that Pennsylvania had available fertile farmland and—just

LATER EMIGRANTS AND REFUGEES

The eighteenth-century Ulster Scot diaspora was only the first wave of emigrant crossings from Ireland and Scotland across the Atlantic. The chronicle of succeeding emigrations is often viewed as a single all-encompassing story, each chapter recounting a certain set of circumstances, a time, and a place. As a result, distinctions have blurred between each emigration era. It is worth untangling the knot of confusion.

The exodus of Scots and Irish from Ulster expanded dramatically into the nineteenth century, and an astounding 1.3 million left their homes for North America between 1820 and 1890. Several "push" emigration forces were at work before the 1845 Great Famine: a slump in domestic industry, especially the linen trade; a decline in available arable land for agriculture; population growth; relaxation of shipping regulations; and more-frequent ship departures. The port of Liverpool in England offered larger vessels and increased ocean traffic, and so it usurped the Irish ports as the preferred embarkation center.

When the potato blight descended across Ireland in 1845, the situation grew ripe for a set of catastrophic conditions that included famine, widespread malnutrition, long-standing rural poverty, and callous government neglect in London. They all combined to terrible and tragic effect. From 1845 to 1849, the Great Hunger (in Irish, "An Gorta Mor") caused 1.5 million men, women, and children to die of starvation and related diseases of deprivation. This disaster also triggered a massive demographic hemorrhaging; over a million people left Ireland for North America, although many perished en route in the notorious, disease-ridden "coffin ships." To this day, Irish history is written with a dividing line between the pre– and post–Great Famine eras. Unlike the eighteenth century emigration of Ulster Scots, who were largely rural and Presbyterian, subsequent emigrations involved both Roman Catholics and Protestants, who were directed to northeast cities of the United States, to Canada, and also to Australia. By 1859, up to a quarter of the populations of New York, Boston, Baltimore, Philadelphia, Toronto, and Montreal were Irish. Considerable numbers also headed for London, Liverpool, and Glasgow, all of which have significant Irish communities today. Prior to 1845, the population of Ireland was in excess of 8 million people. Through the famine years, the total population of Ireland, including Ulster, rapidly declined to 4 million, and it currently stands at 6.4 million. Famine refugees found work, usually for basic wages, in North America's cities, down mines, and on railroads. They were targets of relentless discrimination, but they formed strong neighborhoods and managed to make a unique contribution to the American story—particularly through music, literature, and the arts. Many cities in the United States, from New York and Boston to Chicago and Detroit, resonate with a life-affirming legacy from those desolate days through the sounds of Irish traditional music, conveyed by refugees and reinvigorated by the generations who followed them.

An unconnected exodus, meanwhile, saw waves of refugees from the Scottish Highlands coming to North America during the eighteenth and nineteenth centuries. Again, famine played a part in this flight, but it was for the brutality of forced evictions that this particular upheaval became notorious. The Highland Clearances ("Fuadach nan Gàidheal," or the "Expulsion of the Gael") was a program of population removal across much of the Scottish Highlands and Islands authorized by its aristocratic landowners, both Scottish and English. Some of these were clan chiefs to whom their tenants had demonstrated loyalty for generations. This was the first tactic in an agricultural revolution by which the lairds converted their crofts—small tenant farmsteads—to sheep, cattle, and eventually hunting estates. The evictions were immediate, affecting entire families, and in some cases, turf roofs of cottages were set ablaze to compel reluctant tenants to leave. The landlords characterized these methods as necessary "improvements," but their traumatic effect rendered the victims vulnerable to starvation and homelessness. Some were shepherded directly to emigration ships, occasionally by their church ministers, while others were relocated to coastal areas to attempt to forge a living from fishing—despite these crofters being completely unfamiliar with this lifestyle. The first clearance occurred during the last half of the eighteenth century. A second, more-widespread phase began in 1822, compounded by famine from a Highland potato blight and an outbreak of cholera. Highland Clearances drove people to the cities of Scotland, especially Glasgow and the shipbuilding ports along the River Clyde, and also into England. Large numbers chose to emigrate to North America, Australia, and New Zealand, where they named towns, mountain ranges, lakes, and rivers—and where their descendants thrive today. Many of the Presbyterian Highland emigrants settled in the areas of coastal Carolina and Georgia, including North Carolina's Cape Fear and Fayetteville regions, and the port cities of Charleston and Savannah; ironically, all of these are "lowland" settings, although some Scottish Highlanders did find their way into the Carolina Piedmont and mountains to the west.

Other removed Highlanders, including a number of Roman Catholic communities, made the Atlantic crossing to Maritime Canada and Ontario. Their legacy endures, no more so than on Nova Scotia's ("New Scotland's") Cape Breton Island, which echoes Scottish scenery, culture, and music. The Cape Breton cultural scene has produced an abundance of internationally admired musicians, such as fiddlers Buddy MacMaster and his niece Natalie MacMaster; family bands that include the Barra MacNeils and the Rankins; and Cape Breton step dancers, who preserve dance styles closely allied to the rhythms and sequences of the fiddle music. Gaelic singers such as Mary Jane Lamond have ensured that the song traditions they uphold are part of a living culture in Cape Breton. The fiddlers, singers, and dancers all draw upon a strong Scottish influence while suggesting other Canadian flavors and reflecting their own individual styles. Cape Breton musicians are frequent visitors to Scotland, participating in many connections and exchanges. Indeed, Cape Breton step dancers have reseeded this old dance style in Scotland, where it had all but died out in favor of country, ceilidh, and Highland dancing. Cape Breton's annual October Celtic Colors Festival is presented at venues all over the island, from large theaters to small music pubs, drawing Celtic roots musicians from across the globe. In homes, schools, and village halls throughout the year, fiddles and bagpipes drive Cape Breton–style square dances, and the Gaelic language lives on in song.

as important—was both welcoming and tolerant. In addition, the growing colony had a need for labor, indentured or otherwise, and the linen trade had created strong commercial ties with maritime routes to Ulster. Philadelphia had topographical shortcomings as a port: it was 110 miles from the ocean up the shallow Delaware Bay, and its winding river channel would freeze over in the winter. New York's expansive harbor also could be reached by a shorter voyage, as it was 200 miles closer to Europe. But the Pennsylvania backcountry offered enough enticements to the Ulster farmers that their choice was clear: they were Philadelphia bound.

Beginning in the summer of 1717, Quaker and German residents of Philadelphia noticed an increase in the frequency of immigrant vessels moored alongside the dock. By the close of the summer sailing season, the Delaware River estuary and its anchorage were teeming with ships. It would have been a magnificent spectacle from the shoreline, and even more so for the arrivals standing on deck after their after interminable weeks at sea. Relief and excitement must have accompanied their first views of Delaware Bay. As their vessels sailed slowly past Reedy Island at the mouth of the estuary and on into the narrowing Delaware River, they were rewarded with a closer view of their new world. Open fields and swathes of forest flanked both riverbanks, and on the distant horizon was a profile of the Blue Mountains. Some vessels took moorings at smaller Delaware River ports on the west bank, such as New Castle and Chester. However, most docked at William Penn's "City of Brotherly Love," which, with 20,000 people, was the largest town in the American colonies. So many immigrants disembarked at the Philadelphia landfall that Market Street became the most important colonial avenue of the day. It also was the starting point of the Great Philadelphia Wagon Road, which headed west and then turned southward into the Appalachians, the route that would eventually lead many of the immigrants onward to their mountain homes.

STEPPING INTO A NEW WORLD

I know dark clouds will hover o'er me
I know my path is rough and steep
But golden fields lie out before me
Where weary eyes no more will weep.
—*"The Wayfaring Stranger"* (CD TRACK 19)

The business of alighting at the pier and moving onward to the port buildings was not always handled very efficiently. Other European arrivals at New York's Ellis Island more than a century later would encounter a similar bureaucratic maze of inspection and detainment. Before their official entry was realized, relates the exhausted voyager in the song "The Shamrock Shore," "We were taken as passengers by a man and led 'round in six different ways." During the wait, provision of food and water was minimal, and the risk of contagious diseases was reason enough for immigration officers sometimes to impose lengthy quarantines on the travel-weary incomers from "Erin's Lovely Home":

When we had reached America our numbers were
but small,
And fourteen days of quarantine was worse to us
than all.
In this sad state we had to wait, though anxious
for to roam,
In a strange land—a feeble band from Erin's lovely
home.

For some of the new arrivals, there was the prospect of an emotional reunion with family or friends who would help settle their kin into accommodations and perhaps even employment. Indentured passengers were led to meet the merchants or farmers who had purchased their bonds. For others, the transition was fraught with anxiety. The redemptioneers, who had no funds to pay for their passage and had not signed indenture contracts with future employers, were held aboard ship until the captain had redeemed the cost of their passage by selling their labor to the highest bidders.

The custom of securing necessary labor by means of immigrant indenture was a common one during America's colonial era. The indenture period was usually limited to three or four years but could extend to seven years. Some immigrants were certainly exploited and ill-treated. The practice did allow the poorest people to attain their coveted ocean passage, however, while also providing the burgeoning colonies with a much-needed labor force. Immigrants to Pennsylvania were more often than not employed on farms, as well as in households and businesses. In these working environments, they were generally more assured of reasonable management, reinforced by the close regulation of indenture contracts by the Pennsylvania Quaker colonial government. It stipulated that, in return for the immigrant's industrious labor, the owner must promise fair treatment, adequate food and lodging, and a specified reward at the end of the indenture period.[51] The immigrant was free thereafter to find other employment and a place to live. Freedom did not always bring immediate returns, however, as house and land ownership could be a long time in coming. Freeholding was another matter, and a newly released indentured servant would have dreamed of gaining the privileged freeholder status. Use of this term marks the origins of the eighteenth-century ballad "Pretty Saro," collected by early twentieth-century songcatchers in the Appalachian Mountains, including Cecil Sharp. It is still widely sung there to this day.

Down in some lonesome valley, in some lonesome
place,
Where the wild birds do whistle and their notes
do increase,
Farewell pretty Saro I'll bid you adieu,
And I'll dream of pretty Saro wherever I go.

My love she won't have me so I understand,
She wants a freeholder who owns house and land,
I cannot maintain her with silver and gold,
Nor buy all the fine things that a big house can
hold. (CD TRACK 9)

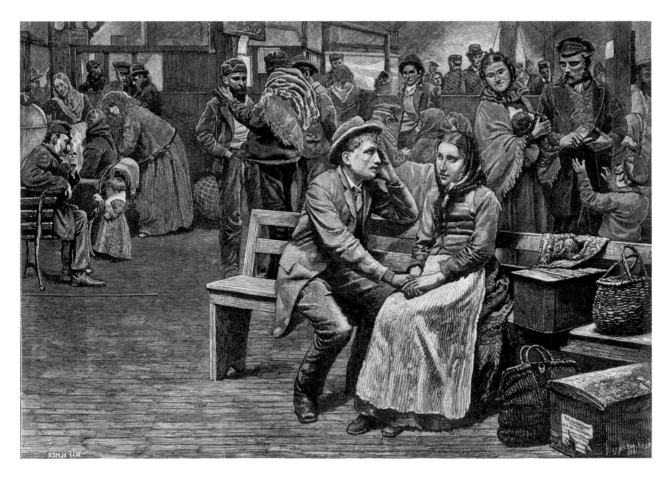

The quaysides leading to Philadelphia's Market Street spilled into an array of shops, inns, and taverns, all ready to supply and serve any new arrivals that had a bit of money to spare. Signs hung from a colorful row of edifices: Blue Anchor, Crooked Billet, Pewter Platter, Seven Stars, Cross Keys, Hornet and Peacock. Shipmates, united by the trials of their ocean adventures, would gather in these hostelries to bid a last goodbye before heading, hither and yon, into the vastness of their newly adopted land. From the harbors of Ulster to the Philadelphia docks, they had shared momentous times. Over a parting glass, they would drink a health to their seaworthy vessel, such as the brig "Eliza," wish the captain and crew "fair winds and following seas," and toast the old homeland, now far behind. Finally, they took their leave of one another.

The Eliza brig you can't defeat, to her no danger
 fearing;
On the twenty-ninth we took our leave, of
 captain, mate and sailor.
We gave three cheers for old Ireland, it being our
 former quarter,
Like a flock of sheep we strayed away, then we
 shook hands and parted.
— *"The Eliza Brig"*

As they went their separate ways into their new lives, one of the many bittersweet songs they exchanged was "The Parting Glass." It was well known long before Robert Burns's farewell anthem "Auld Lang Syne" came into the popular repertoire. Printed as an eighteenth-century broadside, it would have

been easily distributed among the inns and taverns of Philadelphia's Market Street, whose buildings might yet echo with the voices of successive waves of immigrants, raised in heartfelt chorus "to drink a health whate'er befalls" for their final toast of "The Parting Glass."

> Oh of all the money that e'er I had, I spent it in
> good company;
> And of all the harm that e'er I've done, alas it was
> to none but me.
> And all that I've done through want of wit, to
> memory now I can't recall.
> So fill to me a parting glass, good night and joy
> be with you all.
>
> Oh of all the comrades that e'er I had, they are
> sorry for my going away;
> And of all the sweethearts that e'er I've loved, they
> would wish me one more day to stay.
> But since it falls unto my lot, that I should rise
> and you should not;
> I will gently rise and softly call, goodnight and joy
> be with you all. (CD TRACK 20)

After the farewells, new arrivals faced a bewildering array of choices. If indentured, their course was predetermined by their contract of servitude. If not, without much in the way of funds or connections, to whom and where might they turn? The first concern was whether to try to settle in an established township, such as Philadelphia, or to strike out for the backcountry. Some only had strangers to direct them, and there were many possible routes, both physical and figurative, toward that first foothold on life's new path. For those who had limited means, the business of finding a "situation" (employment) was all the more complicated. They may already have been exploited on the crossing, especially through the excesses of redemptioneering, and those who came later in the eighteenth century were plunging into a more densely populated labor market.[52]

In the face of such uncertainty, it was natural to yearn for the old home place. Some immigrants' letters constantly expressed a longing for family and friends, including the earnest promise that "you will see me once more." Others put on a brave face, a facade of reassurance concealing the lasting trauma of the crossing. In August 1801, James Horner wrote to his parents in County Derry-Londonderry after his arrival in Philadelphia:

> Dear father and mother, I have taken this opportunity in letting you know that I am well at present thanks to God for his mercies towards me. I am well and happy since I left you; I was very bad for three weeks at first for we had very rough weather that time but I soon got better and was able to eat some of my sea store; we had nine weeks sailing passage besides two weeks at Innashone and a week at New Castle. We had some tribute to pay . . . for a permit to get our wearing apparel . . . they have annexed a law that says every passenger must pay a dollar for a certificate or pass; they put down our names and age and occupation and where you intend to reside.[53]

For some, lingering homesickness was not just a passing phase. Recent arrivals still held clear images of home in their minds and fond memories of family close to their hearts. Not all of them were able to settle in the New World.

> My name is Edward Connors, and the same I'll
> ne'er disown,
> I used to live in happiness, near in to Portglenone,
> I sold my farm as you will hear which grieves my
> heart full sore,
> I sailed away to Amerikay and left the Shamrock
> shore.

In the ballad "Edward Connors," the emigrant family had lived by the River Bann in County Antrim. Although Canada was their first destination when they sailed from Belfast, the song ends with a universal caution to "all who are intending now strange countries for to roam," suggesting that emigration, by now so commonplace from Ulster, was not best suited to everyone.

> Before that you cross over the main where
> foaming billows roar,
> Think on the happy days you spent, all on the
> Shamrock Shore.

Irish musician and author Mick Moloney has observed that "old songs might well have been one of the few remaining links . . . to the now distant loved ones and homeland."[54] There was a keen recollection of well-loved places and a sense of "auld lang syne" in the wistful homesick songs. "Clough Water," a stream that rises in Ulster's Glens of Antrim, is fondly evoked in one typical song of nostalgia:

> I oft-times think while in Philadelphia, of the
> happy singing and scenes of fun,
> And of the sweet Clough Water, where I oft-times
> wandered with my dog and gun.
> But while the ocean keeps in motion and surges
> on the dark rocky shore,
> I will revere thee with fond emotion, the land of
> my childhood, old Erin's shore.
>
> So farewell, father and farewell mother and
> farewell brothers and sisters too,
> And to my comrades both lads and lasses, I kindly
> send respects to you.
> Should fickle fortune to me prove kindly, I might
> once more in Erin dwell,
> Where I hope to meet with a friendly welcome,
> I'll drop my pen with a word,
> "farewell."

Indeed, a number of Ulster immigrants' songs suggest that some people never let go of the conviction that they would one day return to their old homes. These verses are especially poignant. If they accepted that it would not happen in the physical realm, they might yet hope for it in the spirit world. Until then, they returned in their dreams to well-loved locations, such as this song's setting: a gentle green valley by "The Winding River Roe."

> Benbradagh's crown o'er Dungiven town
> Is still within my view
> And the Benedy Glen I worshipped then
> Still lives in memory too
> The beautiful scene of Cashel Green
> Still haunts where ere I go
> And in all my dreams I see it seems
> The winding river Roe.
>
> If fortune smiles on me a while
> I'll cross the sea again
> And all those years of toil and tears
> Will be forgotten then
> And when at last my life has passed
> Contentedly I'll go
> Across the sea to the Benedy
> And the winding river Roe. (CD TRACK 6)

The dream song was sometimes quite an elegant blend of symbol and sentiment. In "Erin's Green Shore," Ireland is represented by a beautiful maiden who appears to the storyteller and laments the "wrongs of her country," giving an insight into the otherworldly nature of the dreamer's homesick yearnings.

> One evening for pleasure I rambled, on the banks
> of yon clear purling stream,
> I sat down on a bed of primroses and I gently fell
> into a dream.
> I dreamt I beheld a fair female, her equal I ne'er
> saw before,

The Winding River Roe

Cara Dillon, Northern Irish singer and songwriter; interviewed in Pitlochry, Scotland, November 2006, by Fiona Ritchie during the singer's visit to the Perthshire Amber Festival.

There's one song in particular called "The Winding River Roe" which we recorded, and the song's all about a local man in my hometown who emigrated to America. And he was full of promise for the future and excited like most people were, but they didn't realize the harsh reality: that maybe they wouldn't survive the crossing, getting there, and then it wasn't really the American Dream when they got over there because the conditions were so hard. Maybe they only survived, and they never ever returned to see their families again. And the song's basically all about him reminiscing, saying that if he had one last dying wish, it would be that his soul would return to the place that he loved the most. That kind of stuff is priceless. You just don't get that in a modern pop song these days. You don't get something so raw that can appeal to people worldwide. Because even nowadays there's still people leaving home and still emigrating and still finding it hard when they get to the other side to set up and make a living for themselves. So, aye, I think it's all still very relevant today.

The plight of the refugee is a plight that never goes away. With each year that passes, we are focusing on different parts of the world and displaced people experiencing problems, so those songs have timelessness to them and speak to people across generations. They are written by people who really have experienced it and people who really went through it, then the emotion comes right through across the generations. I've got ancestors, and you have, who've been through that before, and I think it's our duty to remember them. They did it for us so that we would have a better life today, so I owe it to them to keep singing these songs.

I think you absorb stuff from the land, I really do. The people there were so passionate about what had happened and the terrible tragedies. And there's a lot of very haunting melodies that have resulted from sadness. I think it's in the blood. It runs through your veins. It makes up the essence of who you are. You have to accept that, when there's been so much loss and so much hardship in the country, there's going to be a certain element of magic in a voice that's putting out the stories and the songs. You are going to capture all that. It's running through the veins of the people and the land.

THE SONG OF THE EMIGRANT.

PRICE ONE PENNY

Copies of this song can always be had at the
Poets Box 190 & 192 Overgate Dundee

I'm lying on a foreign shore,
  An' hear the birdies sing,
They speak to to me o' Auld Langsyne,
  An' sunny memories bring,
Oh, but tae see a weel kent face,
  Or hear a Scottish lay,
As sung in years lang, lang bye-gane,
  They haunt me nicht and day.

My hair aince like the raven's wing,
  Noo mixed wi' silver threeds
Mind me o' ane wha used to sing,
  O Scotia's valiant deeds,
She sung while I stood at her knee
  The dear sang o' Langsyne,
"Auld Robin Gray," an' "Scots Wha Hae
  Or " Myrtle Groves " sae fine.

She sang to me " The White Cockade,
  She sang " The Rowan Tree,"
" There was a lad was born in Kyle,"
  An' ' Bonnie Bessie Lee."
Whaur is the song can melt the heart,
  Or gar the saut tear fa',
Like auld Scotch sangs sae dear to me,
  Noo that I'm far awa'.

I've watched the sun at morning tide,
  Strike o'er the lofty Ben,
I watch him yet wi' greedy e'e,
  To whaur he sets again.
I ken he shines on Scotia's shore,
  Tho' far across the sea,
An' while I being have I'll sing—
  My native land of thee.

And she sighed for the wrongs of her country,
  as she rambled around Erin's green shore.

Transgression of joy I awakened and found it was
  only a dream,
The beautiful maiden had vanished and I longed
  to be slumbering again.
May the heavens above be her guardian, though
  I know I'll ne'r see her no more,
May the goodliest sunbeam shine upon her, as she
  lies sleeping on Ireland's green shore.

The firm resolve to return, no matter how unlikely such a trip might be, was never far away in songs, or indeed in the letters sent home, as James Horner shows in the closing lines to his parents: "Dear mother, do not fret for me being away from you but think that this time will soon be over, that you will see me once more. I believe it was my fortune to come here to a strange land."[55]

Isolated from home—a stranger in a strange land—the immigrant had the sense of being in exile, neither a resident of the new country nor physically connected any more with all he or she held so dear. This feeling of being suspended at a midpoint would subside with each generation, but the melancholy was lasting enough to pass along down the line through song.

The lament of the exile lilts softly through the ages, a timeless cry that rings true for anyone far from home today. Contemporary songwriters, touched by the immigrant's plight, have added to the anthology, such as Scottish singer-songwriter Dougie MacLean in "Garden Valley":

Now I know and feel it well,
Poor immigrants deep sunken feeling,
Standing at the gates of Hell,
There is no peace for me.
Burned out by their master's greed,
Cruel exile transportation,
Robbed of every love and need,
There is no peace for me.

But in the darkness struggle cold,
I think about a garden valley,
Gentle as the leaves unfold,
Singing out across the Tay,
Distant and so far away,
There is no peace for me.

The tradition of the homesick song still flourishes. MacLean's "Caledonia" was written during a period of overseas travel for the singer, who memorably vowed: "Caledonia, you're calling me and now I'm going home." It has become a popular contemporary folk anthem, a love song to Scotland (Caledonia). The Canadian army in the nineteenth century banned bagpipe music because it threatened to overwhelm their Scottish recruits with loneliness and nostalgia.[56] The song of the exile, like the pipes, continues to have a powerful effect on the emotions of the listener.

That sense of place, a deeply ingrained inheritance, brought with it a need eventually to "lay down their bones" in the old country, and there is ample evidence that emigrants from Ireland, including Ulster, were more susceptible to chronic homesickness.[57] That so few managed a return crossing in the eighteenth century is a measure of their enormous outward-bound effort, further weighed down by the complications of their lives since landing. Cost was the obvious constraint, perhaps along with indentured servitude. Repeated relocations deeper into the frontier may have taken them many miles from a seaport. They might also have been burdened by traumatic memories of a first, "never again" voyage. Though a returning exile was not unheard of, the notion of homecoming was never more than a recurring dream for most, living only in story and songs such as "The Exile of Erin":

There came to the shore a poor exile of Erin,
   the dew on his thin robe
was heavy and chill,
For his country he sigh'd when at twilight
   repairing, to wander alone

by the wind beaten hill.
But the day star attracted his eyes and devotion,
   for it shone on his own
native isle of the ocean,
Once in the fire of his youthful emotion.

A "golden stream" of remittances, no matter how meager, became the more common link to home, and immigrants from the poorest families were often the most faithful with these gestures. Along with "a promise to write," sending money fulfilled a vow made to loved ones at the point of departure, often professed among all the emotional turmoil of the American Wake. Enclosing small sums with letters maintained a connecting cord to family and a faint hope, glimmering across the ocean, of a reunion some day.

AN ELUSIVE IDENTITY

With dry land under their feet and their sea legs gradually settling, the new immigrants were ready to sort through their options for future employment and first destination. Those freed from the bonds of servitude were also ready to start an independent life in their new country. Quakers and Germans, already well established in Philadelphia, had their set ways; the Ulster newcomers they encountered seemed a bizarre lot. As the arriving men and women advanced from the wharfs into the streets of Philadelphia and beyond, one Quaker described "these strangers to our laws and customs, and even to our language." With the outsider's eye for detail, he brings a three-dimensional clarity to first impressions of the newly arrived Ulster Scots.

These new immigrants dressed in outlandish ways. The men were tall and lean, with hard, weather beaten faces. They wore felt hats, loose sackcloth shirts close-belted at the waist, baggy trousers, thick yarn stockings and wooden shoes "shod like a horse's feet with iron." The young women startled Quaker Philadelphia by the

THE PEOPLE WITH NO NAME

Gritty, determined, fiercely protective of their individual rights, hardworking, sentimental—these are just some of the qualities, perhaps even clichés, often associated with the people on the move from Scotland to Ulster to America. Neither easily led nor prone to unite around the same cause, they were elusive in the past and are just as difficult to pin down for the historical record. For author Patrick Griffin, these wayfarers were challenging both to locate and to label; they were "The People with No Name."[1] In fact, they went by several names across the generations, though other people designated most of these. Today, they are usually defined in the United States as Scots-Irish or Scotch-Irish, names often used interchangeably.

The Romans called the sixth-century Gaels who raided the northwest coastline of mainland Britain the "Scotti" (or "Scoti"), a name they would eventually give to the northern part of the island. The Scots who later migrated to Ulster as part of the seventeenth-century Plantation scheme were simply "Scottish settlers" and later "Ulstermen." Over time, they preferred the name "Northern Dissenters" to declare their general dissatisfaction with their status in their adopted land.

Some Scots took the straight route across the Atlantic. They immigrated directly into the American colonies from Scotland, did not spend any time in Ulster, and alighted in three areas: Chesapeake, Virginia; eastern North Carolina; and Charleston, South Carolina. For these "Scots," there was no naming issue. They were always Scottish, and so Scottish Americans they eventually became. Ulster Scots arriving from the north of Ireland were usually regarded as "Irish" by their New World neighbors, who were simply making the obvious connection with their most recent island home. The new arrivals did not identify with this label, however, and when the Irish potato crop failed in the mid-nineteenth century, triggering the Great Hunger and mass migration to the United States, they acted to differentiate themselves from the more recent famine refugees. So they adopted their next title: the "Scotch-Irish." As these people on the move settled into the expanse of new pioneer lands, they preferred to call themselves "Frontier Inhabitants," but time erased that name as well.

The Scotch-Irish label seemed to dominate their identity through the years, reflected in the title of the Scotch-Irish Society of the United States of America.

---

sensuous appearance of their full bodices, tight waists, bare legs and skirts as scandalously short as an English undershift. The older women came ashore in long dresses of a curious cut. Some buried their faces in full-sided bonnets; others folded handkerchiefs over their faces in quaint and foreign patterns. The speech of these people was English, but they spoke with a lilting cadence that rang strangely in the ear. Many were desperately poor. But even they carried themselves with a fierce and stubborn pride that warned others to treat them with respect.[58]

The restrained and proprietary Quakers and Germans initially accepted the newcomers, despite their odd appearance and speech. Friction developed, however, as Quakers resented the Scots-Irish participation in Pennsylvania politics and their later dominance

Robert Burns and then Sir Walter Scott had each used the term "Scotch" for their country folk, reflecting the common vernacular of their times. By the late 1800s, however, it became more common in Scotland to replace Scotchman or Scotchwoman with Scotsman, Scotswoman, or simply the neutral label of "Scot"; all are in common usage today. Indeed, in Scotland the term "Scotch" identifies one thing only nowadays, and that comes in a bottle. In the United States, "Scotch plaid," "Scotch Pine," "Scotch Tape," "Scotchgard," and a miscellany of commodities have further confused the terminology, so that the term "Scots-Irish" is now more generally used to describe the people. Interestingly enough, although the terms "Ulster Scots" and "Ulstermen" had occasional use in colonial America, they did not catch on and have only recently been adopted in Northern Ireland.

One thing is clear: if "The People with No Name" were difficult to identify in their migrations and resettlements, they were far from invisible. With each incoming wave, they made an indelible imprint on the living landscapes they encountered and inhabited. The census of 1790 recorded that 12 percent of the fledgling country's population was of "Scots" or "Scotch-Irish" descent.[2] James Monroe, fifth president of the United States, was descended from a Scottish clan chief, and the seventh president, Andrew Jackson, came from a Scots-Irish family. The family trees of more than half of American presidents have had branches leading to Scots or Scots-Irish lineage.[3]

1. Patrick Griffin, *The People with No Name: Ireland, Ulster Scots, America's Scots-Irish, and the Creation of the Atlantic World* (Princeton, N.J.: Princeton University Press, 2001).
2. Alistair Moffat and James F. Wilson, *The Scots: A Genetic Journey* (Edinburgh: Birlinn, 2011), 220.
3. Ibid.

of the Pennsylvania Assembly in 1756. The Germans found the Scots-Irish to be impetuous and hotheaded, and the two groups generally gave each other a wide berth, socially and in their settlements.

There is no doubt that the Ulster immigrants streaming steadily into Pennsylvania were an elusive crowd. With their nomadic history and general wariness, having been marginalized back in Ulster, they defied any easy definition. In fact, they bristled at others' labels for them—"Irish," "Irish Presbyterians," "Northern Irish," or even "Wild Irish." Their ethnic profile was not so clearly defined as the other Pennsylvania settlers— Quakers, Germans, Welsh, and English—and they came to think of themselves simply as "frontier inhabitants." The "Scotch-Irish" label was eventually given to them after the mid-nineteenth century's famine-driven mass exodus from across Ireland to distinguish them from those more-recent Irish "Great Hunger" refu-

gees. They did publicly proclaim their Presbyterianism, asserting individuality and upholding a tradition they had carried from Scotland to Ulster and on to America. They were certainly opposed to any kind of Anglo identity whatsoever.[59] Twice in living memory they had moved, leaving behind one life for another, and their own sense of identity was a work in progress. They had already risen to the challenge of crossing a span of water to forge new lives in Ulster. Across an ocean, the New World they now embraced was itself in a state of profound transformation. As strangers on another shore, they were certainly not alone in having to reinvent themselves. And as people long used to subsisting with little means, they demonstrated a striking adaptability to adjust to new circumstances and places. Already twice transplanted, they had acquired a migratory habit. Once acquired, such habits are liable to persist; the wayfarers moved on.

As they took to the road, they faced a stark choice at the first junction: head toward established communities or out into the backcountry and on to places unknown. In 1783 James Patton emigrated from County Derry-Londonderry, Ulster to Pennsylvania. He eventually settled in Asheville, North Carolina, as one of the town's first residents and later expressed his early doubts and fears in a letter to his children.

> I had boarded for some time with Mr. Shaw, a countryman of mine, and when I left his house, he took two horses and assisted me along the road for some distance. He inquired where was I going? I told him that I was going to Canada, that my mother had told me she had an uncle and brother in that country, who had become rich; and that I would endeavor to find them out. But this was not my real motive, I was really afraid that nothing awaited me but misery and poverty, and that news would reach Ireland that I was in a most destitute situation, and being naturally of proud spirit, I wished to go where I should not be known by any person. My health was at this

Scheitholt. (Darcy Orr)

Reconstructed American log cabin on the Pennsylvania frontier,
Ulster American Folk Park, Omagh, Northern Ireland. (Courtesy
of Ian MacRae Young, www.photographsofscotland.com)

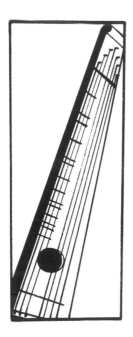

time so bad, that I was unable to do anything for myself; but thanks to the great and mighty God! I had a mind that enabled me to surmount all difficulties. When Mr. Shaw left me, I went off the road into the woods, sat down by an oak tree, and gave vent to a torrent of tears.[60]

In southeastern Pennsylvania, soils were fertile and land initially abundant and cheap. The Scots-Irish headed to the area's Cumberland valley, creating a trail of Ulster place names for their new settlements: Antrim, Derry, Donegal, Coleraine, Londonderry, and Fermanagh. They had attained a certain freedom and acquired land, often government granted, for clearing and cultivating, building modest log cabins. The style of these dwellings already embodied the spirit of New World cross-fertilization: it was a structure borrowed from the Germans, although with a similar floor plan to the thatched stone cottages of their native Ulster. Their adaptability had become an asset. A patchwork

of European ethnic groups had spread across the region in addition to the Germans and Welsh Quakers: French Huguenots, English, and Swedes, as well as the Conestoga and Delaware Native Americans. Having handled tensions with native Irish upon their earlier migrations from Scotland, the Ulster Scots were experienced in intercultural relations. This would prove beneficial as they put down roots in colonial Pennsylvania. When they first settled, uneasy relations existed between the groups in southeastern Pennsylvania, with its rich ethnic diversity and close proximity of settlements. This atmosphere eased when they migrated into the sparse frontier country to the west and south.

Their German-influenced log cabin construction technique was a foretaste of these immigrants' willingness to adapt by borrowing ideas from other cultures and communities. Although they staunchly preserved a stubborn independence and distinctive culture, they eagerly fused this with the new: from the Native Americans, they adopted the deerskin for clothing; in their agricultural pursuits, they shifted from the Ulster tradition of barley, oats, sheep, and cattle to a farming combination of Indian corn, wheat, and pigs; from the Germans, they acquired the long rifle and a stringed musical instrument called the scheitholt. It was to become a defining emblem of their musical culture; as the settlers later moved down the Great Philadelphia Wagon Road and into Virginia, they would modify the scheitholt to their own design and create the gentle song of the mountain dulcimer (from the Latin *dulcis*, or "sweet," and the Greek *melos*, or "song," "sound").

THE MUSIC COMMUNITY ON THE PENNSYLVANIA FRONTIER

Life in the Pennsylvania backcountry was challenging. A lack of basic materials, long and wearisome winters, and a struggle to maintain general family health and well-being could make for a harsh, lonely existence. The communities pulled together, however, and there were regular social gatherings, such as house-raisings, flax pullings, log rollings, corn shuckings, and quilting parties. It all encouraged neighbors to mix and mingle, no matter how scattered they were throughout the backwoods, and this socializing was more marked among the Scots-Irish than the more reserved German and Anglo-American settlers. Music and dance was the social current flowing among the settlers and connecting them with a sense of community, wherein ballads and fiddle tunes could be shared and exchanged. Taverns were well set up for such gatherings in the towns and villages, as they had been in Philadelphia; in the backcountry, neighbors hosted house parties, with visitors always welcome. Food and drink were shared; the children might play games while the older folk exchanged the news of the day and indulged in a jigger or two of whiskey. As it had been in Ulster and Scotland, a "dram" (a small glass of whiskey) was still the drink of choice. With the whiskey flagon on the table, old ballads flowed freely. A fiddler might play, and even the confined space could not restrict a bit of dancing.

The crossroads store also was a popular place to gather. It served as a market for produce, sold a miscellany of goods, and hosted music gatherings—not unlike the later role of the "country store" in the southern Appalachians. The local gristmill might sometimes serve as a social center when the miller would be host by default. Finally, the church provided a similar function, in addition to its services of worship. Families would travel such long distances over rough and rutted roads that they might only be able to manage monthly attendance, so they would make a whole day of it. Church days were eagerly anticipated for the social exchange, shared dinner on the grounds, and the music, including communal psalm and hymn singing as they had practiced in Ulster.[61]

The cultural confidence of the Scots-Irish strengthened with the realization that, whatever the setting, they could still carry on their old Ulster and Scottish tradition of the ceili (what they would call "cayleying") and pass it along to the next generation. When they did gather, the distances that separated them did not matter, and yet sharing the traditions they carried came to matter more and more. The very act of rehearsing the old songs, stories, and dances reinforced their evolving sense of self and bolstered their ethnic identity. Author Peter Gilmore described the culture of cayleying in western Pennsylvania, recalled by a resident:

> The long winter evenings were passed by the humble villagers at each other's homes, with merry tale or song, or in simple games; and the hours of the night sped lightly onward with the unskilled, untiring youth, as they threaded the mazes of the dance, guided by the music of the fiddle, from which some good-humored rustic drew his Orphean sounds. In the jovial time of harvest and hay-making, the sprightly and active participated in the rural labors and hearty pastimes . . . attended by all without any particular deference to rank nor riches.[62]

In Ulster, it had seemed as if any occasion was an excuse for dancing. It was no different in western Pennsylvania. Dances and tunes harkened back to the old country and were just as eagerly shared on the frontier. Social status was unimportant; everyone took part in the jigs, reels, hornpipes, and country dances, mirroring the dance sets across the water. Solo and step dancing, a fixture on the restricted decks of immigration ships, could be more freely enjoyed. This included a variation of the old Scottish sword dance, substituting anything in place of the crossed swords: broomsticks, shovels, spades, sticks, and even a bow laid across a fiddle.[63]

No event on the frontier featured dancing more than weddings, which were full of customs unique to the occasion. Families were invited from miles around to the home of the bride, and everyone made a great effort to attend. Social distinctions were largely meaningless on the frontier, so there was never an issue of marrying "above or below one's station." After marriage vows were exchanged, everyone would kiss the bride, and a bottle or a loving cup would be passed around; everyone took a swig, with the minister first to indulge—a "cup o' kindness for auld lang syne." After feasting on whatever could be offered, toasts were proposed, and then it was time for the fiddler to rise and the dancing to begin. It was common for frontier wedding dances to last all night and bleary-

eyed guests to make their way home the next morning.[64] One wedding party during this period recorded a dance setlist with "ninety two jigs, fifty-two country dances, forty-five minuets and seventeen hornpipes, which at five minutes per dance would add up to more than seventeen hours of dancing."[65] A couple of weeks later, the neighbors would gather for a house-raising for the newlyweds, followed by a housewarming, which could last for several days, propelled by more music and dance. This completed the sequence of wedding activities, other than anticipating the couple's first appearance together at the next church service.[66] Frontier life for newlyweds began in a simple shelter—the log cabins were usually a single room with a loft—yet it was embarked upon in the security of strong social bonds confirmed throughout the marriage festivities, with music at the heart and soul of the community.

The skippers of Ulster's emigration ships were well aware of the value of music for boosting morale, and hiring a fiddler was a priority for a captain's crew. The fiddler's status was every bit as high on the frontier,

in demand from the villages to the backwoods. They certainly needed stamina. Dancers were unflagging in all-night sessions. Following one of the frontier weddings, a marathon dance party began, lasting until morning, "with three- and four-handed reels, or square sets and jigs . . . and no matter how exhausted, the luckless fiddler was ordered to play the tune 'Hang on Till Tomorrow Evening.'"[67]

The legacy of traditional music on the Pennsylvania frontier has been documented in a number of collections, especially in the work of Samuel P. Bayard, who served on the faculty of Pennsylvania State University for many years. In his *Hill Country Tunes* (1944), he located the roots of the area's music to Ireland and Scotland. His voluminous collection *Dance to the Fiddle, March to the Fife* (1982) contains 651 instrumental pieces, many of which are of Irish and/or Scottish origin.[68] "The King's Tune," a Pennsylvania march, is closely connected to the Scots air "Logan Water," as well as to the Irish hornpipe "The Poor Old Woman." The Pennsylvania fiddle tune "Good Lager Beer" is a schottische adaptation of an old Scottish tune that also influenced the famous Irish air "The Wearing of the Green." Bayard also contends that the familiar American old-time fiddle tune "Turkey in the Straw" likely derived from the Scots "The Bonny Black Eagle."[69]

Examples of the borrowing and blending of traditional tunes abound among the Scots-Irish immigrants of the Pennsylvania frontier, and just like the ballads, they were carried through time in the oral tradition. The product was a fusion similar to the long intermingling of Scottish and native Irish music in Ulster. In Pennsylvania, there was also a dash of English and Welsh in a classic British Isles blend, and so the story goes. As ever, music was the great common denominator for people, regardless of their origins, denominations, and vocations and heedless of the politics and religious dynamics of the day. It was an approach to cultural exchange that would eventually reside and root just as well in the southern Appalachians.

Homesick Pioneers

Alan Reid, Scottish songwriter, singer, and keyboard player; interviewed in Torrance, Scotland, March 2013, by Fiona Ritchie on a visit to the artist's home.

I think when we first went over there, especially to the South, you'd hear a song or tune and you'd think: oh, we've got that one. And that kind of really brought it home. It's interesting to think, though, that so much music went over there with the migration of people from the southwest of Scotland through Ulster or directly from the Highlands of Scotland over to parts of North Carolina—particularly the Scots and Ulster-Scots connection that takes us to the Appalachians—and how that fed into their music. Even in very simple terms, seeing place names that are familiar, and I'd think, that's a place back home, and so somebody must have come from that place and obviously people took their music with them and it would be passed orally, you know, from generation to generation.

The first time we went to New Zealand, I got a phone call the night after the concert, and it was from a minister from a Scottish church in Wellington, and he wanted me to come down to the church. And when I went down there, he presented me with this poster, which was a replica of an advert of an immigrant ship leaving from Greenock in 1848. And he told me that it took them about three months or whatever to get there, and when they got there, half of them were so homesick they didn't want to be there, they wanted to go home, but they couldn't because they'd spent all their money and there was nae return ship. And that really hit home to me that in those days when people traveled across the world, that was it; it was a one-way ticket. I think the immigrant, as a rule, clings more to the homeland and to culture and music than the person who's surrounded by it all the time. That would often be the last sight of their homeland, it would be the last sight of their nearest and dearest, and yet, over and above that, they still felt the need to go and try and get a better life, whether it was voluntary or whether they were thrown off their lands or whatever.

Traveling a huge distance over an ocean, going to a strange land, seeing other foreign-looking people, Native Americans, whatever, and thinking, wow, what have I landed myself in here? Then you would quite naturally cling to the familiar, you would quite naturally look out for your own kind, if I can put it that way, for support and reaffirmation of who you were.

Although I think it's really interesting, this has always struck me that the Scots in particular have been much less clannish than, say, the Irish or the Italians in migrating and setting up their own wee areas, their own parts of cities. The Scots, it seems to me, have been actually more independent and kind of disappeared into the woodwork, and maybe in places like Appalachia, it was quite natural to go up the valley, build your cabin and have your family and hardly see anybody else—which could be good and bad. The idea of not having a support, a big support network, that other nationalities seem to have. We have this image of the independent, self-supporting, pioneering Scot that, you know, I guess would build his cabin and set up the fence for the borders of his territory, of his property, and then defend it against all comers. So they would make great pioneers, you know, pushing that frontier forward. I'm not saying it was just them, but they were, I wouldn't say the elite, but willing, desperate, stubborn, aggressive enough.

Although eastern Pennsylvania's land was fertile, careful crop rotation had not been practiced; the Scots-Irish had stuck to their old Ulster traditions of hunting, herding, and moving on whenever soils were depleted. By 1740, meanwhile, Greater Philadelphia and southeastern Pennsylvania saw their populations mushrooming. As more immigrants continued to pour in, the rapid population growth began to affect the availability and price of land. Many of the immigrants were not landowners and were often criticized for being squatters. So before long, with a packhorse or wagon to haul their few household goods, the Scots-Irish were on the move again. They headed steadily westward, across the Susquehanna River and toward the distant mountains. With each footfall, they shaped another verse in the unfolding story. Like their long and timeworn ballads, the tale would encompass many families and meander across many miles. These wayfaring strangers were fixing their gaze on another horizon.

Old-time music is the living history of the American people as told through the continuous oral tradition of their music, dance, and story. It is a living history of a people who migrated from the Old World, primarily Scots-Irish but also other Europeans and African Americans who settled in the new land. It is the living history of a music that people have cherished enough to preserve despite incursions of new lifestyles and technologies. And it is the music that America continues to come home to in order to renew its ties to the earth, the country, and a sense of community.[1]

—Ron Pen, folklorist and musician

Singing
A NEW SONG

Another crook in the road and the indomitable Scots-Irish were on the last leg of their journey. Pennsylvania was their third ancestral home in just a few generations, and some did choose to remain there. A significant number, though, looked to the far horizon, yielded to their perpetual urge to move onward, and headed out to cheaper land and better prospects in the distant west. Their trail from southeastern Pennsylvania took them across the Blue Mountains and the Susquehanna River, the Allegheny Mountains of western Pennsylvania rising beyond them.

The Alleghenies comprise the rugged western center portion of the vast Appalachian Mountain range that extends across the eastern United States and into Canada. Their peaks climb to almost 5,000 feet, with their eastern face dominated by the steep escarpment of the Allegheny Front. The Alleghenies were renowned in story and song as a beckoning destination

"Across the Blue Mountain" in the long trek from the east.

> One morning, one morning, one morning in May,
> I overheard a married man to a young girl did say.
> "Arise you up pretty Katie, and come along with
>   me,
> Across the Blue Mountain to the Allegheny."
>
> We left before daybreak on a buckskin and a roan,
> Past tall shivering pines where the mockingbirds
>   moan,
> Past dark cabin windows where eyes never see,
> Across the Blue Mountain to the Allegheny.

Crossing the Alleghenies into western Pennsylvania and beyond set up likely confrontations with Shawnee and Iroquois bands, hostile to outside settlers and

unwilling to sell their land. At the same time, the governing authorities in the colonies of Pennsylvania and Virginia were looking for settlers to occupy the eastern flank of the Alleghenies into the Shenandoah valley in order to serve as a buffer between the eastern parts of the colonies and the Indians and French to the west. From Ulster to the New World, this was not the first time the Scots-Irish had been recruited as a living barricade. So land was made available for settlement, and they chose to veer away from an Allegheny crossing and follow the route of the Great Philadelphia Wagon Road into the Shenandoah valley. The Wagon Road was an ancient trail, following the course of the old Indian Warrior Path, and a foothold settlement was established around 1750 on the Opequon Creek, near the present city of Winchester, Virginia. This became their gateway into the Shenandoah valley, set amid the long ridgelines of the Appalachian Mountain chain. It

was an unfamiliar vast landscape for the nomadic pioneers. The wilderness, rather than intimidating them, seemed to lure them onward.

THE UNENDING MOUNTAINS

The Cherokee called the Appalachians the "Unending Mountains," and their serpentine course extends northeast from the Flagg Mountains in Alabama to the north end of Belle Isle in the Canadian provinces of Newfoundland and Labrador. This chain of mountains, ridges, and valleys was originally more endless than the Cherokee could ever have imagined. Around 400 million years ago, Europe and North America formed one large continent. Running along its spine was a colossal chain of mountains, connecting North America with what became northern Europe, including Scotland and Ireland. Today, the connection is

Remoteness and Beauty

Dr. John Purser, Scottish composer, musicologist, and music historian; interviewed in Dunkeld, Scotland, June 2011, by Fiona Ritchie.

There's a toughness in a lot of these ballads, and there's a strength in the music and the dance, an athleticism in it. These are mostly mountain people, or hill people—they're fit. They have come from a country [Scotland] which has been defending itself for hundreds of years from a much-more-powerful neighbor, never mind its own infighting. In Northern Ireland, they were in a similar situation, and then they go to America, and they're battling to make a living there.

I was actually going up through North Carolina and western Virginia with Bonnie [Rideout] just a wee while back there, and I'd never been through all these long valleys, sort of the Shenandoah area, and by God, I was thinking, this is great moonshine country. You know there's all of these wee glens going back up into the hills and, I mean, you'd have loads of warning before the Revenue got onto you. But there were also these tight-knit little farming communities—tiny, tiny, and there was actually quite an enclosed sense about it, shut off. And partly, of course, when you're in these relatively remote situations, when you're living in it, you don't think it's remote, but to others it's remote, and it is remote in the sense that the external influences are going to be coming to you a little bit later than elsewhere, and so a tradition has a better chance of survival, quite simply. You know, if you're in radio shadow, or you can't get the telly or whatever, well, what are you going to do of an evening, you know? There's only two things, and one of them is make music and the other . . . we'll leave to the birds and the bees.

I've twice written the history of Scotland's music; that is to say that there was a completely revised second edition and, although it is chronological, it's very rarely linear. I deliberately did not set about

known as the Caledonian-Appalachian mountain chain, "Caledonia" being the Latin name for Scotland. About 50 million years ago, geological movement began to drive the continents apart; the Atlantic Ocean formed to separate, sculpt, and eventually serve as the conduit between Europe and the Americas.

To underscore the symbolism of the Caledonian-Appalachian geologic connection, 2010 saw the official extension of the Appalachian National Scenic Trail, the Georgia-to-Maine hiking track popularly known as the Appalachian Trail, or the A.T. Today, the International A.T. follows a Scottish course stretching from Cape Wrath in the far north of Sutherland to the Mull of Galloway in the southwest, and in 2012 Scotland hosted the annual Conference of the International Appalachian Trail. Compared with the long Appalachian history of the Cherokee, the scope of the Scots-Irish migration narrative unfolds across a relatively short timespan, yet it is intriguing to consider that these ancient mountain ranges, once physically joined in the deep time of Earth's past, eventually witnessed a movement of people from one to the other.

The Appalachians, which formed more than 125 million years before the Rockies, are among the oldest mountains in the world. They have witnessed alternating periods of deposition, upheaval, and erosion

drawing inferences or outlining influences—occasionally I did, I wasn't going to avoid it as a matter of principle—but generally speaking, I didn't. Being a composer, I've suffered, especially when you're a young composer, you can't have an original idea. Your first time your piece comes out, somebody says, "Oh, you can hear the influence of Bartok there and you can hear—," you know, and you're made to feel like you're not you. And it's most unreasonable because you can say exactly the same thing of Beethoven. You know, large chunks of Beethoven sound pretty like Haydn. And Mozart and Haydn, occasionally you would be forgiven for not being quite sure which of them you were listening to unless you had studied it quite closely. . . . This is natural, this is normal—so I've tended to avoid that because then what you miss out on is the beauty of the thing itself. It's fun to follow influences, but one can make too much of them, I think, and sometimes in looking for them, people will find influences that were never, ever there at all, however plausible they may seem.

Well, you know what I think of when you talk about bluegrass and banjos and all the rest—I don't think about influences and people going across the Atlantic and whether they came down in February of '84 or January of '84. And I've heard discussions of this kind, oh, long discussions in North Carolina, down to the day, I mean, real minutia—and this from just ordinary folk, not from the scholars. But what I think of is someone sitting on a porch with the sun streaming down and the smell of the trees and the grass and maybe a fag or a cheroot in the mouth, or even ideally a bit of straw in the teeth and playing away for the fun of it, and the dog asleep. We don't need to . . . well I'm not trying to undermine my trade, almost, of being a scholar, but I think you can make too much of it and lose—lose the here and now and the beauty and the fun.

over hundreds of millions of years. The ridges, slopes, and coves are well watered—there are almost limitless pockets of microclimates—so these mountains are covered with an unparalleled abundance of plant life. The Great Smokies section alone is home to more than 130 tree species, or about forty-five more than exist in all of western Europe. The Fraser Fir, native to the Appalachians, is named after the Scottish botanist John Fraser (1750–1811), who made numerous botanical field trips to the area. The American chestnut was a boon to early Scots-Irish settlers. They would have struggled without its durable wood and substantial nut crop; sadly, these magnificent trees were destroyed by a chestnut blight early in the twentieth century. When Scottish naturalist John Muir made his 1867 "Thousand Mile Walk to the Gulf," he set out from Indianapolis resolving to traverse the Appalachians and "to go by the wildest, leafiest, least trodden way I could find." His description of the Hiawassee River Gorge as "vine draped and flowery as Eden" suggests that Muir fulfilled his quest.

These mountains have beguiled all who enter their province—from indigenous people to eighteenth-century pioneers, John Muir in the nineteenth century, and present-day fall-color connoisseurs. To delve into their deepest groves is to encounter a mysterious

The Southern Appalachian Mountains

(*opposite*)
Mountain hollows with fog rising. (Courtesy of
Joye Ardyn Durham)

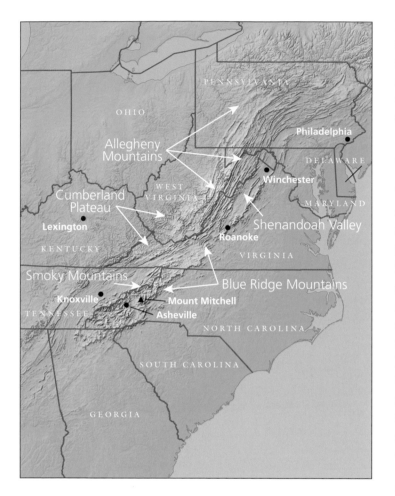

Hell Ridge, Pumpkin Patch Mountain. So on down the Great Philadelphia Wagon Road they headed, into the midst of this wild, ethereal milieu, with its many moods and dramas. In forest canopy clearings, they would transplant, graft, propagate, and plant a ballad and tune heritage on the frontier.

THE GREAT PHILADELPHIA WAGON ROAD

The Wagon Road came to be known as the most significant "highway" in colonial times, with thousands of settlers following its route south. It originated in the bustling colonial port town of Philadelphia. Heading out by the city's inns and taverns, it veered west across the Susquehanna River. The trail followed the meandering Potomac and ferried across to Winchester at the mouth of the "Great Valley of Virginia," the Shenandoah valley. The Wagon Road's course from Philadelphia to its Yadkin valley terminus in North Carolina was a 450-mile journey. In time, it extended further into the south, eventually reaching Augusta, Georgia, on the Savannah River. By then, anyone traveling its length had covered a distance of almost 750 miles.

Just south of Big Lick (Roanoke), at present-day Radford, Virginia, a western fork of the Great Philadelphia Wagon Road opened up in 1762. This stretch snaked its way southwest across the New River and into the remote frontier. Some years later, a Scots-Irish adventurer from Pennsylvania blazed a new trail from that point westward. Daniel Boone had migrated south on the Wagon Road with his family, trapping and hunting along the western fringes of Virginia. In the spring of 1775, Boone, accompanied by thirty axmen, marked and cleared a path through the Cumberland Gap to Boonesboro, Kentucky. Initially, this was little more than a narrow path through the deep forests, negotiable only on foot or horseback. In time, Daniel Boone's "Wilderness Road" was to become one of the historic American settlement routes.

The Wilderness Road took twenty years to become

and unexpected world, an inner sanctum. A labyrinth of steep inclines plunges into remote hollows, sharp ridges rise unexpectedly, and meandering streams wind their way into the distance. Successive waves of hillsides stand in relief, a natural decoupage receding into the mists and far horizons. The grandeur of the highest places is palpable: forty-six peaks rise above 6,000 feet, including North Carolina's Mount Mitchell, at 6,684 feet the highest peak east of the Mississippi, dominating the skyline of the region known as the rooftop of eastern North America. The names of mountain places speak of their inhabitants—Cherokee first, and later Scots-Irish—who made their homes in John Muir's "wildest, leafiest, least trodden" landscape: Unaka, Cheoah, and Wayah; Rough Butt Bald, Parson Bald,

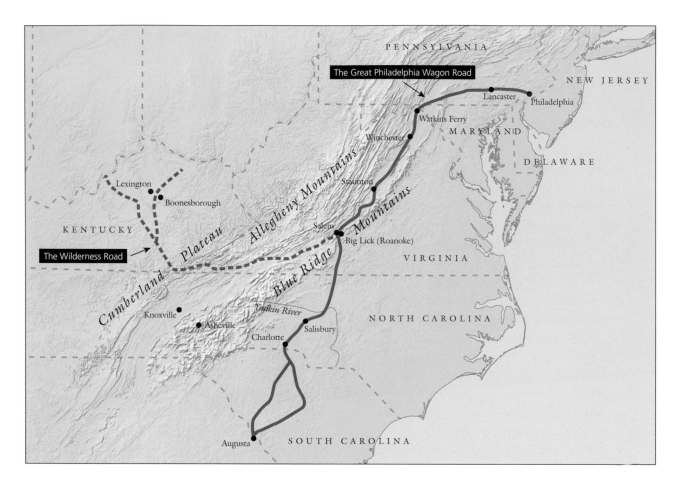

a true wagon trail. The course cleared by Boone and his men developed into a significant trunk route for settlement and commerce. Between 1775 and 1810, an estimated 200,000 to 300,000 pioneers negotiated the Wilderness Road through the Cumberland Gap, where it opened to Kentucky and points west. Much later, the story of the pioneer trail was recalled in the song "Cumberland Gap":

Lay down boys and take a little nap
and we'll all wake up in the Cumberland Gap.

Me and my wife and my wife's pap
Was the first ones through the Cumberland Gap.

Cumberland Gap's such a dry place
Can't get no water for to wash your face.

Daniel Boone's on Pinnacle Rock
He's shootin' at the b'ars with his old flintlock.

Back on the Wagon Road, Presbyterian missionaries in the 1730s made up a first wave of wayfarers. Traders and cattle drivers soon followed, then settlers migrating in the hope of reaching newly available land. How people undertook the arduous journey varied. Many traveled on foot, while others were able to pay their way—by load and mileage—onto wagons named for the Conestoga River in Lancaster County, Pennsylvania, and introduced by German Mennonite settlers to that area. Depending on the load, the fastest Conestoga wagons could cover five miles a day, and a journey down the entire course of the Wagon Road might take two months. Teams of up to eight horses

Locating Appalachian Source Singers

John Cohen, American string-band musician, song collector, photographer, and filmmaker; interviewed in Swannanoa, North Carolina, July 2008, by Fiona Ritchie and Doug Orr during Traditional Song Week at the Swannanoa Gathering folk arts workshops.

So, when I first went to Kentucky to find out more about this kind of music and the life around it, and that was in 1959, and that's when I met Roscoe Holcomb, back in Daisy, Kentucky, and I'd hear these stories about, "Well my cousin so-and-so, who's up that hollar, off that creek, and then he's got a cousin there, and then that was back in the old Civil War and that was back in the old Revolution War" . . . and I'm getting this image of a map, a huge map that's in their heads, locating themselves both in space and in genealogy and, "yeah, well, our family come over in the last century from North Carolina where they did something bad so we had to change our name." You know, you're hearing this incredible web of information that makes a map, and then I went back to New York, and there was my grandmother . . . about eighty-five years old. I said, "Grandma, meeting all these people, and they had this incredible understanding of the world and their past." I said, "You never told me anything about my background." "So why do you want to know?" I said, "Give me a memory from when you were a little girl." "I was a little girl in Russia, and I went out in the street from the house, and there was a horse and carriage coming down the street, and the drivers had their heads cut off, so I screamed and ran back in the house." [pause] Well, no wonder she never told me any stories. So in a strange way, my whole understanding of my past ain't there, unless I went to history books.

But I came to that understanding about myself because I heard the incredible maps that the people in Appalachia had. It was so interesting and moving to me. Now, but back to when I first heard Roscoe Holcomb and the Scots-Irish; I didn't know if I was listening to something that was really archaic or something that was very modern, 'cause the beat of his guitar, the rhythm, dack-a-dack-a-dack. It was just . . . not like a machine gun, but it was very regular, like a weaving pattern. And then with the melody, this long lyrical ornamented voice, against this rat-a-tat regular rhythm. It also reminded me of John Cage, very modern music. I was clearly feeling that at the same time, and that's why it was partly just pulling me apart. I didn't know if I was listening to old, or abstract, or very traditional, and which traditions? I mean it was so . . . energizing.

pulled the wagons, and eventually a draft breed, the Conestoga horse, was raised for the job. In spite of its historical name, however, the road was not passable by wagon all the way south until later colonial times, and it was a tough trial for the migrants; severe mountain weather, river flooding, disabled wagons, and illness and death from disease were some of the ordeals they might have to endure along the way.

THE SONG OF THE ROAD

If ship's captains had been the colorful characters of the ocean-crossing era, wagoners were their dry-land counterparts. Often rowdy and unrefined, the wagon drivers had to handle their heavy loads through harsh weather, dangerous situations, and endless days. Yet the intense conditions of life on the road generated their own camaraderie, and the wagoner was at the heart of it all.[2] The wagoner would greet other convoys on the Wagon Road and, if circumstances warranted, pull over to let them pass by—cattle and pig drovers, families in their smaller wagons, teams of packhorses, carts and the many foot travelers. Such encounters were also an opportunity to exchange news, share weather reports, and warn of road hazards.

Wagoners were often natural storytellers, and some emerged as minstrels of the Wagon Road, especially those who carried a fiddle or banjo. The pocket-sized jaw harp was an especially popular musical accessory, so much so that stores along the route, beginning in Philadelphia, sold them in large quantities along with other provisions for the expedition. Colonial governors were even known to supply jaw harps as gifts to pioneers who benefited the colonies by carving out new settlements.[3]

The wagoner had a wide-ranging song repertoire to call upon and would have alleviated the drudgery of the miles by singing. He also became a character in songs; in "The Wagoner's Lad," he proved that the road held more sway over his heart than the ladies he might court along his way.

Oh I am a poor girl my fortune is sad,
I've always been courted by the wagoner's lad.
He's courted me daily by night and by day,
And now he is loaded and going away.

Your parents don't like me because I am poor,
They say I'm not worthy of entering your door.
But I work for a living my money's my own,
And if they don't like it they can leave me alone.

Your horses are hungry go feed them some hay,
Come sit down beside me as long as you stay.
My horses ain't hungry they won't eat your hay,
So fare thee well darlin' I'll be on my way.

Your wagon needs greasing your whip is to mend,
Come sit here beside me as long as you can.
My wagon is greasy my whips in my hand,
So fare thee well darlin' I'll no longer stand.

I'll go to yon mountain the mountain so high,
Where the wild birds can see me as they pass me
    by.
Where the wild birds can see me and hear my sad
    song,
For I am a poor girl and my lover has gone.

Old ballads and hymns were especially popular among the travelers. And if the party was fortunate enough to have a fiddler along, dancing might be enjoyed within the cluster of parked wagons. Such gatherings were a break from the rigors of the road; music was a social stream flowing along the Great Wagon and Wilderness Roads, filtering into the surrounding hamlets and hills. Over time, songs and fiddle tunes took up permanent residence in the inns and taverns that eventually sprung up along parts of the meandering trail.

A new instrument was born along the furlongs and footfalls of the Great Philadelphia Wagon Road: the Appalachian, or mountain, dulcimer. Its predecessor—a stringed, zither-like sound box called the scheitholt (or scheitholz)—had come to America with German immigrants. Similar instruments were played in France, the Low Countries, and Scandinavia, with antecedents in the Persian Gulf area (home of the unrelated hammered dulcimer) and Turkey. Rectangular in shape, the scheitholt had two or three strings and lay horizontally across the player's lap or on a table. The melodic strings could be played with a bar or individual fingers, with the lower string and its tuning generating its distinctive drone sound. The Pennsylvania Germans had tended to play their scheitholt music rather slowly, often bowing their instruments. So at what place and time did the German instrument transform into the Appalachian dulcimer? According to Ralph Lee Smith and Madeline MacNeil, "Exactly what happened, when and where is beyond recall . . . but the keys to this mystery are along the Great Philadelphia Wagon Road and the Wilderness Road."[4] If there were main developers of this instrumental lineage, time has long since erased their identities, but it is known that only the scheitholt was played in Pennsylvania; in the Shenandoah valley of Virginia, there were predominantly scheitholts but also a few modified and transitional artifacts, and after turning west from the Wagon Road to the Wilderness Road, the early dulcimers came onto the scene.

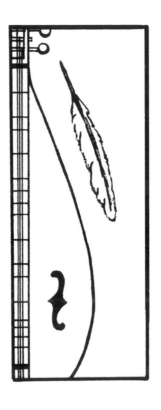

The earliest modifications of scheitholt to dulcimer had lengthy rectangular sound boxes, and frets were placed under selected strings, creating diatonic (eight-tone) rather than chromatic (thirteen-tone) scale. In Kentucky, the preferred shape was hourglass, whereas Virginia-style dulcimers had a single curved body.[5] Crafted in various styles, the instrument quickly became established throughout the southern Appalachians and was solidly identified with the Scots-Irish settlers regardless of its roots in German Pennsylvania (where the scheitholt gradually died out). It also picked up a few name variants, such as dulcimore or delcymore. Today, it is widely known as the Appalachian or mountain dulcimer, sometimes the fretted or lap dulcimer. When the Scots-Irish settlers adopted this remodeled instrument, they put it to good use accompanying their dances, so it found its voice in the old fiddle tunes. To do this effectively, the player had to generate an up-tempo rhythm, often strumming using a wild turkey feather quill. In time, the dulcimer rep-

Dulcimer: "Just Play, Play, Play"

Jean Ritchie, American traditional singer, Appalachian dulcimer player, songwriter, and author; interviewed in Swannanoa, North Carolina, July 2008, by Fiona Ritchie during Traditional Song Week at the Swannanoa Gathering folk arts workshops.

Almost every house had a dulcimer hanging on the wall or sitting on something or hidden behind something, but so many people belonged to the new churches that were coming in, and they were very much against frivolous things like playing instruments. They wouldn't even sing harmony because that was frivolous. But the way they decorated the songs sometimes, it turned out to be harmony without anybody trying, and that was always pleasing to their ears! But if you saw someone coming, one of the preachers coming over for dinner or something, you sort of put the dulcimer behind the Davenport or something where they wouldn't see it. So Maud Karpeles said when she and Cecil Sharp came collecting, that when I was talking about dulcimers being around us, she said she didn't see any dulcimers. She couldn't figure out what I was talking about! And I said to her, you didn't know where to look, that's all!

Nobody had ever seen a dulcimer in New York that I found. Maybe there were some people there that knew what they were, but I never found them. I would always take my dulcimer wherever I played and tell people in the crowd that came that it's a very easy thing to play. Anyone can play it, come up after the program, and I'll show you all I know about the dulcimer in five minutes. And I could still say that, because I don't know very much about it. I just play the way I play. I play sort of a countermelody to the voice, and that's all I do. I ramble around on the dulcimer. I just use it as a second voice, as an accompaniment. And it was an icebreaker always. I would carry it on the subway, wrapped up in a shawl because I didn't have a box or a case for it. And I'd have it all kind of tied up a little bit to keep it from coming apart. And a lot of people would say, "What is that?" They'd see this end of it sticking out. And I'd say, "Well, it's a dulcimer, from Kentucky." They'd say, "Play it!" I said, "With the subway going? You couldn't hear it if I played it." And they said, "Play it anyway!" So I'd play . . . and they'd say, "Oh!" But you'd have to do it right in their ear, you know. "Oh!," they'd say, as if that was the most gorgeous sound they ever heard! It was a completely new thing to everybody, and I would keep on telling everybody, "Just play, play, play," and some of them did. After a while, a lot of people got to play on them. I won't claim solo credit for getting the dulcimer 'round the country, but I certainly started early and urged a lot of people to play. Did my best.

(*opposite*)
A Farm on the French Broad (North Carolina).
(Courtesy of D'Etta and Neal Leach)

ertoire was extended to slow parlor tunes and ballad accompaniment. Usually built from maple, cherry, or walnut wood, the simplest traditional dulcimers had three strings, one for melody and two as drones. For playing slower tunes, the player would strum all the strings with one hand while sliding a finger or wooden stick along the melody string. Even in these early dulcimer designs, the Scots-Irish crafters retained one important element from the old scheitholts: the drone strings. That sonic quality, along with the absence of a fully chromatic scale, combined in the dulcimer to echo an ancient instrument long left behind in their original homeland and one around which many of the old ballad tunes evolved: the bagpipes.

The dulcimer spread steadily throughout Appalachia, and in the twentieth century, mountain settlement schools and the craft movement widened its exposure. In the 1930s, folksinger, song collector, and composer John Jacob Niles first brought the dulcimer to national awareness in the United States, performing with his own modified instrument. Jean Ritchie deserves credit for taking the Appalachian dulcimer to an even wider audience when she located to New York's Greenwich Village in the late 1940s, bringing her dulcimer to accompany her pure mountain singing voice. She became a vital contributor to the Greenwich Village folk-song scene of the 1950s and 1960s. During this time, she became involved with the historic Cherry Lane Theater in Manhattan and introduced another young Appalachian musician to the world: guitarist and singer Doc Watson. In the late 1960s, Canadian singer-songwriter Joni Mitchell adopted the Appalachian dulcimer, playing it on her album *Blue* (1971) and in concert. The Rolling Stones used an electric dulcimer on several of their 1960s recordings, and its versatility and timeless appeal endures today in Appalachian, Celtic, and classical music, as well as in jazz. Forever in touch with her Appalachian roots, country music star Dolly Parton has played a rhinestone-decorated dulcimer onstage. Shape, material, fretboard, and tone account for the diversity of instruments crafted by skilled luthiers, and playing techniques have developed to include new strumming methods and fingerpicking. As for Appalachian instrumentation, the birth of the dulcimer along the wagon trails signaled the beginning of a steady stream of inbound influences, as it traveled, with fiddles and balladry, up into the hills and among poet Frances Pledger Hulme's "singing trees."

This tree made music for your father's ears,
A dulcimer for spring to tune and strum,
A summer fiddle to bow away their fears,
Autumn's gold horn, and winter's shadow-drum.

Now in your day the music, though diminished,
Spreads still, over the years of sun and storm,
Its leafy ceremony never finished,
Those airs your fathers cherished, chill or warm.

So in the time when you will not be hearing,
Yourself one note in fuller harmony,
May others of your kind come to this clearing
And hear, as you have heard, your fathers' tree:

Old melodies against the sunset bars,
Rooted in rock and whispering to the stars.
—*Frances Pledger Hulme, "Singing Tree"*[6]

LIFE AMID THE MOUNTAINS

The majority of the Wagon Road migrants followed the main route through the Shenandoah valley and into the Piedmont of Virginia and the Carolinas. Some had settled in the broad Shenandoah basin or eastward into the foothills; most kept moving toward the Yadkin valley terminus in North Carolina. The earliest settlers had arrived in 1746 and embedded themselves along the fertile river valleys. A smaller contingent of resilient pioneers followed the more westerly route from Big Lick in southwest Virginia, settling deeper into the frontier wilderness. In 1775 the flow of migrants rose on the tide of rebellion and especially increased as the

PRICKLY AND STUBBORN: APPALACHIAN CLICHÉS

It has often been remarked of the Scottish character, that the stubbornness with which it is moulded shows most to advantage in adversity, when it seems akin to the native sycamore of their hills, which scorns to be biassed in its mode of growth even by the influence of the prevailing wind, but, shooting its branches with equal boldness in every direction, shows no weather-side to the storm, and may be broken, but can never be bended.

—*Walter Scott, Old Mortality (1816)*

"Nemo me impune lacessit" is the Latin motto that has appeared on the royal coat of arms of Scotland since 1707. It means "no one will harm me and go unpunished" and is expressed in Scots as "wha daur meddle wi' me?" This maxim, combined with the thistle, the ancient national emblem of the country, is often presented as illustrative of the Scottish identity.

The cautionary message of the motto and the image of a prickly plant, thriving on even the most rocky and windswept of landscapes, certainly offer salient symbols of courage, tenacity, and independent spirit. It is often said that the people of the southern Appalachians share that prickly character, and that they might substitute the briar for the thistle, another hardy plant, to extend the similarity.

The Scots, Irish, and Appalachian people have been some of the most stereotyped in the American cultural melting pot. Casually attributed character traits often suggest that any of them may, at some point, have a tendency to be hospitable; intensely patriotic; passionate; independent; self-deprecating; thrifty; prone to alcohol abuse and related violence; be good at making things; inclined to sing choruses at the drop of a hat; and nostalgic for lost causes, far-flung places, and old times. As lazy as character clichés can be, they are sometimes traceable to

American War of Independence came to an end in 1783. The state of North Carolina encouraged this westward expansion by granting mountain property to veterans of the Revolutionary War. Others followed them, buying land for five to ten cents an acre, and subsequent treaties with the Cherokee opened up more low-cost land. Wilma Dykeman, in her book *The French Broad*, describes the independent character of the Scots-Irish pioneers who took up the call to head west:

> The Scots-Irish were always roamers and adventurers, and the ones who continued on to middle and upper Carolina were especially strong in wanderlust and sense of individuality, for they left behind the ones in Pennsylvania who were content

with rich farms and full barns and deep roots. The second and third generation who finally reached the valleys and the mountains of the French Broad, could therefore be called the essence of Scots-Irishness. They had pushed on beyond the most forbidding barrier, discovered the most rugged country and settled under most isolated conditions a country where individual liberty was the prize, with loneliness and privation the cost.[7]

This fierce impulse to achieve a new level of freedom, where "individual liberty was the prize," is voiced concisely in the motto of West Virginia, which is also the title of the Pierce Pettis and Tim O'Brien song "A Mountaineer Is Always Free":

specific events or historical eras. Certainly, people who have been required to move and relocate into remote and inhospitable territory, carving out a pioneer life where others have feared to tread, must have possessed (or at least soon developed) courage, defensiveness, and independence. A "waste not, want not" approach would have been critical to survival, especially during the isolation of the winter months. Self-sufficiency would have been essential for families that might make only one or two annual trips to a trading post. The ability to produce many material items with whatever was at hand was a valuable attribute, and the distiller's craft, imported from the Old Country, would have eased isolation and lubricated social occasions. Yet stereotypes are by their nature unreliable and easily outmoded. Similarities can likewise seem clear, but dig a little deeper and the nature and strength of connection may be superficial. For example, Scots and Ulster Scots are likely to feel a strong yearning for the sea. This is, for most Appalachian people, a long-forgotten emotion preserved only through ballads.

By 1900, it was well established that the people in the hills and deep forests of the southern mountains were set apart from the American cultural mainstream, and there were attempts to integrate the rural communities of Appalachia through charitable initiatives. The dialect of the mountains, also noted as "different," was more cruelly viewed as inferior and unsophisticated. By the twentieth century, writers and moviemakers habitually used Appalachian-style speech as a shortcut to designating uneducated characters. In recent years in the United States, as in Scotland, the extraordinary richness of the old manner of speech is now valued, and where the "otherness" of mountain folk was once viewed with suspicion, it is now understood as the very essence of the region's unique musical heritage.

I'm one of the few, proud to be standing,
I walked up the pier from the coffin ship's
   landing.
My clothes were just rags, no use in this weather,
But my back was strong, my hands tough as
   leather.

I climbed these hills where I came to the spot
   where I stand,
I cleared these fields and I pulled up the stumps
   with my hands.
No more wanderer no more refugee,
A mountaineer is always free.

Took a Cherokee bride, she gave me five babies,
I sang at the wakes, I cried at the weddings.

FRONTIER FOOD

To them who must plant
There is no season well-defined,
Only doing and planting and birthing
and burying.
—*Gregory Dykes*[1]

Centuries have passed since pioneer Scots-Irish settlers made their way into the mountain hollows of Appalachia and established their independent lifestyle. When roads and a cash- and credit-based economy eventually followed them up into hills, the need for their self-reliance largely disappeared. Today, people associate old recipes, preserving meats and vegetables, and harvesting wild plants with a childhood visit to granny. The domestic ways of the Scots-Irish pioneers and their neighbors are now found mostly in history books.

Oats were the dietary staple of seventeenth- and eighteenth-century Scots and Irish, and oatcakes, served with greens, were a popular accompaniment to all meals. Oats did not offer such a plentiful yield in the southern Appalachians, however, so the settlers had to adapt their diets and substitute corn as the main crop.[2] Corn cakes or cornbread became stan-dard with meals, supplemented with wild onions and garlic, nettles, dock leaves, sorrel, chickweed, chicory, and many other wild-growing greens.[3] From the Cherokee, they adopted the habit of gathering wild angelica, branch lettuce, poke, ramps, and pigweed to eat with their cornbread, and they also cultivated native squash and sunflowers.[4] The Cherokee also built *v*-shaped fish traps in the rivers, and the settlers used and maintained these into the twentieth century. Cooked salads were served warm or cool, including potato-and-dandelion salad. German settlers introduced sauerkraut and the mountain word "salat."[5] They also introduced the Scots-Irish to liver mush and liver pudding and, along with the English, imported their love of dumplings. Tough and crisp flatbread had long been a staple, not least on the emigration ships, and the mountaineers improved these biscuits with yeast and raising agents to make them soft and more suitable for meals of biscuits and gravy, still popular today.[6] Beans and potatoes were standard fare in mountain communities from all origins.

The early Scots-Irish pioneers had to produce everything themselves or gather it in the Smoky Mountain forests. Hog raising had long been

I taught all my children the songs of my youth,
To dance to the fiddle and practice the truth.

I carried them up on my shoulders to where they
could see,
The whole world before them just so they would
know what it means.
No more wanderer, no more a refugee,
A mountaineer is always free.

No kings and no landlords to treat us like beggars
and thieves,

There's no one but God here to look down
on me.
No more wanderer, no more refugee,
A mountaineer is always free.

Throughout the mountains and the Piedmont, the Scots-Irish established dispersed settlements, with mixed farming of crops and livestock using very basic farm tools. In this way, they were also agricultural pioneers, practicing frontier farming that was faithful to their Ulster traditions. Cheap land was abun-

practiced in Scotland, Ulster, and Pennsylvania. In the mountains, they continued mixed livestock farming, also keeping hens and cattle. A vegetable garden was a cornerstone of their smallholdings. Income might eventually be supplemented by male family members finding work down mines or in sawmills, but families had to be essentially self-reliant, making only rare trips to a general store or a trading post. They had crossed vast distances to clear the dense woods and build homesteads. Yet, like the ballads, some settlers held onto recipes they had carried and passed along since their days in Ulster, such as the following recipe for colcannon.

Colcannon

2 onions, minced

2/3 cup milk

4 large potatoes, boiled

2 parsnips, boiled

Salt and pepper

1 cup cooked shredded cabbage

1 tablespoon butter

1 tablespoon minced parsley

Cook the minced onions in the milk until soft. Mash the boiled potatoes and parsnips together; season with salt and pepper. Slowly add the onions and milk, beating well. Combine with the cooked shredded cabbage. Serve garnished with bits of butter and minced parsley.[7]

1. Marita Garin, ed. *Southern Appalachian Poetry: An Anthology of Works by Thirty-Seven Poets* (Jefferson, N.C.: McFarland, 2008), 61.

2. Patricia B. Mitchell, *Mountain Foodways: Flavors of Old Europe on the Southern Frontier* (Chatham, Va.: Mitchell's Publications, 2000), 12.

3. Ibid., 16.

4. Ibid.

5. Ibid.

6. Ibid., 9.

7. Ibid., 21.

dant, so when soils were depleted, they cleared, broke ground, and cultivated new plots. Since level land in the mountains was limited to river basins and coves, the settlers ended up in isolated locales, soon set apart from any cultural mainstream. The frontiersmen and women in these "mountain hollers" (hollows) prized their privacy, and many a mountaineer resolved it was time to move on when "you could see smoke from a neighbor's house."

As surely as Presbyterianism took root in Virginia's Great Valley and the Piedmont Carolinas, it became equally clear that the structure of the Presbyterian Church, with its emphasis on trained clergy and formal education, was not a good fit for the frontier. Rough mountain living was, by its very nature, far removed from the support of organized church and community. It all served to reinforce and exaggerate the typecast image of Scots-Irish pioneers: wild, godless, and fiercely autonomous. It also fueled a mythology that their creed was one of "drinking, fighting, and dancing." This has been actively reinforced over the years, most recently by James Webb's *Born Fighting: How*

the Scots-Irish Shaped America (2004). The reality is far more complex. While the contributions of the Scots-Irish have been considerable, from education and religion to government, politics and even the White House, the frontier life did have its untamed side. Whiskey making and drinking certainly amplified the stereotype. It was a long-established tradition dating back to Ulster and Scotland (where moonshine got its name), and the backwoods offered many recesses for concealing stills. An instruction manual for productive moonshine distilling is provided in one old song, "The Copper Kettle":

> Get you a copper kettle, get you a copper coil,
> Fill it with new made corn mash and never more
> you'll toil,

You'll just lay there by the juniper, while the
    moon is bright ,
Watch them jugs a-fillin' in the pale moon light.

Build you a fire with hickory, hickory, ash and oak,
Don't use no green or rotten wood, they'll get
    you by the smoke,
You'll just lay there by the juniper, while the
    moon is bright ,
Watch them jugs a-fillin' in the pale moonlight.

My daddy he made whiskey, my grandaddy did
    too,
We ain't paid no whiskey tax since 1792,
You'll just lay there by the juniper, while the
    moon is bright,
Watch them jugs a-fillin' in the pale moonlight.

Discovering Tradition Bearers

David Holt, American multi-instrumentalist, singer, and collector; interviewed in Swannanoa, North Carolina, July 2009, by Fiona Ritchie and Doug Orr at the Swannanoa Gathering folk arts workshops.

It was 1969. I traveled with my friend to the mountains, and that's when I saw this world of traditional musicians still alive that were born in the late 1800s. And I don't know how clearly it dawned on me, but something in me realized these people were like my grandparents, who had been born in the late 1800s. My grandparents were dead, and these people weren't gonna be around much longer, and what they knew was different than what the generation behind them knew. The generation behind them was bluegrass, more modern, Bill Monroe–type stylists. And the older people like Tommy Jarrell and Byard Ray, Aunt Zipporah Rice, Dellie Norton; these were people from almost another world. And luckily, I had the foresight to realize this was it for me. Aunt Zipporah Rice was one of the people I learned from, and she had been collected by Cecil Sharp at forty years old in 1916.

You know, this generation of people that I was lucky enough to learn from, somebody said to me they were born before self-doubt was invented. And I think the media and just our modern world, the pace of it, creates this kind of unease inside of us. You wouldn't have found that in Tommy Jarrell, you wouldn't have found that in Dellie Norton. These people were just as centered as you could possibly get. Now that doesn't mean they were always right, you wouldn't want to over-romanticize how great they were because they were just people. But, nonetheless, not being influenced, not having their life being built around pop culture because that pop culture didn't start till they were old, it was a huge factor in who they are, who they were. And those people don't exist anymore.

Appalachian song collector, songwriter, and musician Bascom Lamar Lunsford penned the well-known comic verses "Mountain Dew" extolling the virtues of moonshine (possibly inspired by an Irish version, "The Old Mountain Dew"); it even gave name to the soft drink widely distributed today.

My brother Bill runs a still on the hill
Where he turns out a gallon or two.
And the buzzards in the sky get so drunk they
   can't fly,
Just for sniffing that good old mountain dew.

My uncle Mort he is sawed off and short,
He measures 'bout four foot two,

But he thinks he's a giant when you give him a
   pint
Of that good old mountain dew.

[Chorus] Well they call it that good old mountain
   dew,
And them that refuse it are few.
I'll shut up my mug if you fill up my jug,
With that good old mountain dew.

Embraced by the surrounding mountains, generations of Scots-Irish developed a special bond with their hills, coves, and hollows. They became keenly attuned to their natural world, from sensing changes in weather systems to understanding nuances and rhythms of the

Moonshine still. (Postcard, North Carolina Collection, University of North Carolina at Chapel Hill)

Porch Scene. (Woodcut by Paul Laune; collection of Darcy and Doug Orr)

seasons. Their Ulster and Scottish forebears, equally acclimatized to their physical environments and ties to home, were preoccupied by an urge to move on. Loyal Jones of Berea, Kentucky, finds these mixed emotions are well explored in Appalachian song: the nostalgia for home vying with generational tendency to ramble. Some songs in the region trace back to the old country, commending and lamenting the wanderlust in equal measure: "Rake and Rambling Boy," "The Storms Are on the Ocean," "Cumberland Gap," and "Why Did You Wander." In contrast, there is the wrench of home: "Little Log Cabin in the Lane," "Blue Ridge Cabin Home," "Where Is My Father's Family," and "Lamplighting Time in the Valley." The theme is a mainstay of folk music up to the present day, recalled by folk musicians Robin and Linda Williams of the Shenandoah valley in Virginia. Home is a constant pull during their itinerant lives as musicians and a recurrent message in their songs. For Linda, home "means so much. It's about people making something on their own, building a home place with their own hands and time . . . a place you know because you are part of it."[8] In their album *Deepwaters*, they encapsulate these sentiments in the song "Home":

We planted that poplar as a seedling, now it's
    taller than the house,
I've watched it through a hundred seasons, right
    from where I'm sitting now.
We got it through the tender days, until it was
    standing strong,
Now it keeps the side yard shaded all the summer
    long.

[Chorus] Home is that tree outside my window,
Home is this quilt upon my bed,
Home is any place my love goes,
Home is where my heart can rest.

The Scots-Irish

Sheila Kay Adams, American ballad singer, banjo player, storyteller, and author; interviewed in Swannanoa, North Carolina, July 2009, by Fiona Ritchie during Traditional Song Week at the Swannanoa Gathering folk arts workshops.

Now see momma was the only person in her family to be educated. She went on to college on scholarship during the Depression. And so she was college educated, and she said that we were the Scots-Irish, you know, or the Scots that came here. Only she said, they don't like to be called Scots-Irish. But she said that's what we call ourselves, "the Scots-Irish." She said, that's where we got our skin. Anyway, momma said that they were the most genetically programmed-to-violence people on the face of the earth. Yes, living in the border country. She said it was called "country" for a reason. It was their country. Northern England, southern Scotland. They were kin, like east Tennessee and western North Carolina—flowed back and forth across the border.

They came in through Pennsylvania; some of them came in through Charleston. But they all came here. See, I can name all the way back because that was passed down with the songs.

Those who call the mountains home are forever spellbound, according to Appalachian writer Emily Satterwhite: "Appalachia instills in its residents an abiding sense of place that fortifies those who stay and consoles, beckons or haunts those who leave."[9]

APPALACHIAN BALLADRY
From Glen to Grove

They were a man's words, a ballad of an old time
Sung among green blades, whistled atop a hill.
They were words lost to any page, tender and
    fierce,
And quiet and final, and quartered in a rhyme.

This was a man's song, a ballad of ridge and
    hound,
Of love and loss. The words blossomed in the
    throat.
This was a man's singing along behind his plow
With a bird's excellence, a man's shagbark sound.
—*James Still, "Ballad"*[10]

Songs in the southern Appalachian region are characterized by two ballad repertoires: the Child Ballads, songs of Scottish, Irish, and English origins; and the so-called native ballads that originated in the region. The Child Ballads, the 305 ballads assembled and numbered by Harvard professor Francis J. Child, comprise the larger group, which includes "Barbara Allen" (CD track 1), "The Farmer's Curst Wife" or "The Devil and the Farmer's Wife" (CD tracks 11 and 12), "Young Hunting" (CD track 13), and "Willie's Lady" (CD track 18). The native ballads often recalled the older balladry and perhaps borrowed old melodies and ideas here and there, as with "Single Girl, Married Girl" (CD track 16). These ballads show that the mountaineers had found their own Appalachian voices. Even as they reached back to older traditions shipped across the ocean, they were "singing a new song" with their feet firmly planted in the New World.

Ulster Scots, Irish, and English had transported the Old World ballads, that much was clear; but tracing any precise song trail could prove fruitless. As Ulster song collector and writer John Moulden points out,

FRANCIS JAMES CHILD

The monumental ballad classification system developed by Harvard professor Francis James Child (1825–96) became such a standard reference in the American folk music lexicon that it is customary to hear a ballad defined simply as a "Child Ballad," often with the assigned number included. Between the years of 1882 and 1898, Professor Child published five volumes of his signature work, *The English and Scottish Popular Ballads*. The combined book includes written and printed texts known at that time of 305 selected ballads and 1,100 variants. These are contained within some 2,900 pages, along with exhaustive commentary notes. Most of these ballads date to the seventeenth and eighteenth centuries in England and Scotland, although a few can be traced to an era before the seventeenth century. The oldest ballad is thought to be "Judas," dating from the thirteenth century. Some ballads collected by Child were from broadsides; he would generally set apart from the later broadsides the traditional ballads that were of most interest to him. Although a few tunes in his compilation were as old as the words, the melodies for the ballads were of secondary concern; Child saw balladry as a part of literature. His publication included twelve texts from the oral tradition, but Child was an assembler, not a field collector; consequently, he did not seek out material from living ballad singers and believed that the subject of English and Scottish balladry would be closed upon the completion of his exhaustive anthology. The subject matter for Child Ballads covered the spectrum of story and legend: romantic love and chivalry, tragedy and death, supernatural experiences (fairies, witches, goblins), historic events, morality tales, riddles, and humorous (and even a few bawdy) tales.

Francis Child was a New England sailmaker's son. He graduated first in his 1846 Harvard class, studied in Germany for four years, and returned to Harvard, where he was appointed professor of English, a position he held until his death in 1896. During more than forty years at Harvard, Child was a respected and distinguished teacher and scholar and the editor of 130 volumes on the works of British poets. He also edited a five-volume collection of the works of Edmund Spenser and conducted a number of Chaucerian studies.

Child's first popular poetry and ballad publication was entitled *English and Scottish Ballads*, appearing in 1857–59 as part of the British Poets Series. He later said that it was assembled in haste over two years, but it was a precursor to his twenty-two-year magnum opus that set the standard for ballad classification to this day. Child regarded the ballad as a distinct species of poetry, and his objective was to find the roots of English literature in the oral traditions. In the process of his major life's work, Child set the highest standards for his research procedure. He carefully studied rare books and periodicals, collated hundreds of ballad variants, and pursued a vast correspondence with scholars, known and unknown to him, with varying levels of success. It was a labor-intensive, all-consuming process, all the more impressive because this was before mass communication, and even the mail service could be unpredictable. It was critical to his scholarly precision that he secure handwritten copies of manuscript collections from throughout Scotland and England. Child did not assemble works from Ireland, although many of the popular ballads of Ulster originated in Scotland or England. Some of his initiatives bore fruit, while others did not, and he had to educate his contacts about the merit and meaning of his work. One of his meticulous requirements was that he delve as deeply as possible into a ballad's origin to get behind the printed sources. Two Scots were of invaluable assistance to him. Scholar and ballad collector William Macmath copied thousands of lines for Child in spidery handwriting, now archived at Harvard's Child Memorial Library. Anna Gordon in Fife, Scotland, better remembered as "Mrs. Brown of Falkland," was a second significant source. Full of medieval motifs, her ballads dated from an earlier time, having been passed down from her mother, grandmother, and aunts. They are upheld as a superb example of oral transmission at work, moving down the generations through the female line in one family. In his final publication, Child included every one of the nearly thirty ballad texts that Mrs. Brown preserved. He had developed a heightened critical sense, enabling him to sort out the classic popular balladry from the mundane, and Mrs. Brown's repertoire was a rich seam of authenticity.

The organizational task was immense, and Child was aware that Denmark had a long tradition of ballad collection and assemblage. He patterned his classification and numbering system on the Danish model and received helpful advice from Danish ballad scholar Svend Grundtvig, with whom he developed an eleven-year correspondence and friendship, even though they never met. Today, the Child Ballad names and numbering system continue to be used universally. A dry academic manuscript might have been the outcome of Child's enormous accumulation of obscure material. However, the pages radiate with the colorful content of the ballad material itself. Illuminating and witty editorial notes complement each entry, a signature contribution of Child. The collected work includes fifty melody tunes separate from their texts and placed in a section at the end of the final volume. For Child, ballads were narrative poems as much as songs, and it was not until other scholars and collectors came along—Vaughan Williams, Cecil Sharp, and Bertrand Bronson—that Child Ballads finally had tunes to match all the texts. (As a collector, Robert Burns was a noteworthy exception to this approach, always noting or suggesting tunes for the songs he collected.)

Failing health and the relentless pace of Child's work led to his death in 1896 while he was working on a final volume. It is generally assumed that the introduction to this volume would have been his concluding word on the nature of ballads and a commentary on his complex and remarkable formula for ballad selection and classification. He had, however, saved this writing task until last. After more than two decades of work, Child sadly did not have the time

he needed to write the introduction to his extraordinary collection.

The Child Ballads, even if not always termed as such, have been a staple of Appalachian ballad singing. Mountain singers would deliver ballads in the old Scots-Irish way, eschewing any performance drama. They were initially performed without instrumental accompaniment; fiddle, banjo, guitar, or mountain dulcimer often were added later. The litany of Child Ballads in Appalachia is extensive: "Barbara ("Barb'ry") Allen" (Child 84; CD track 1); "Young Hunting" (Child 68; CD track 13); "Gypsy Laddie" (Child 200; CD tracks 7 and 8); "Willie's Lady" (Child 6; CD track 18); and "The Farmer's Curst Wife" (Child 278; CD tracks 11 and 12). Child Ballads have also been widely recorded by artists from diverse backgrounds in the United States, including Joan Baez, Pete Seeger, Judy Collins, the Everly Brothers, Bob Dylan, and Simon and Garfunkel, who learned "Scarborough Fair" (Child 2) from English folksinger and guitarist Martin Carthy. More recently, singer-songwriters Anaïs Mitchell and Jefferson Hamer have recorded a collection of Child Ballads (CD track 18). Child's *English and Scottish Popular Ballads* remains the pinnacle of the ballad canon, although several scholars have added to his work, such as J. Malcolm Laws, with his particular interest in broadside ballads, and Bertrand Bronson, who published *The Traditional Tunes of the Child Ballads*. In John Jacob Niles's *Ballad Book of John Niles*, the author relates Child Ballads to folk songs that he collected in the southern Appalachians and throughout the South during the early twentieth century. In years to come, others undoubtedly will build upon Child's seminal work and examine balladry from different angles, but his life's work has never been surpassed. For anyone interested in engaging with the ballad repertoire, Francis James Child is the "go-to" source.

Music Travels Full Circle

Brian McNeill, Scottish songwriter, singer, multi-instrumentalist, and novelist; interviewed in Swannanoa, North Carolina, July 2013, by Fiona Ritchie during Traditional Song Week at the Swannanoa Gathering folk arts workshops.

I remember particularly meeting a wonderful man called Franklin George—Frank George. It was somewhere in West Virginia. Frank was a fiddler, a traditional fiddler recorded in the Library of Congress. And he and I became great friends, and I would play him a Scottish tune, and he would play me back the American version of it. And very often [it was the] same tune with minimal differences . . . like double-stopped on the fiddle and a slightly different title. For instance, there was one called "Campbell's Farewell to Redcastle," a really well-known Scottish bagpipe tune, and I played that to Frank; and Frank said, "That's not 'Campbell's Farewell to Redcastle.' That's 'Campbell's Farewell to Red Gap'!" And it was great, and you know he taught me a whole load of stuff.

There was a great bunch of ladies from Boone, North Carolina, who came out and accompanied us [Battlefield Band] on tour for about two or three gigs, and they taught us all sorts of things. They taught us a great tune called "June Apple," and we adapted "June Apple" for bagpipes. "June Apple" came from the Appalachian fiddle tradition and came back and became a Scottish bagpipe tune. To the extent that now, if you like, a generation and a half later, the kids in Scotland think that "June Apple" is a traditional Scottish tune because Battlefield Band used to play it, which is very nice.

the ballads had been swept along in the carrying stream of oral tradition from no single source, rarely following any straight line:

> The eras in which, and the methods whereby, orally transmitted materials travel are seldom fathomable. Any one of these reports (of ballads) could have been the end result of an unknown series of passages and re-passages of the Atlantic, the North Channel or the Irish Sea; the passage may have taken days, months or centuries. The reports of a song might be the result of the importation of a single version or of multiple versions. Some versions might have started in Ireland, some in England, some could have been lurking in New England since being imported, on ballad sheets . . . then carried to the mountains. Only the end results are available to us. However, they aggregate to a persuasive argument that the songs . . . were packed by emigrating Ulster Scots . . . and eventually became assimilated in America.[11]

English song collector Cecil Sharp (1859–1924) collected 274 Appalachian songs and ballads and almost 1,000 tunes (some contributed by Olive Dame Campbell) and published them in 1932 in his two-volume set, *English Folk Songs from the Southern Appalachians*, edited by Maud Karpeles. Was this monumental work monumentally misnamed? Professor Tom Burton and his colleagues at East Tennessee State University concluded an exhaustive search into the origins of Child Ballads in the southern Appalachians region and established that 42 percent were actually Scottish (including Ulster). He also determined that of the

"Gypsy Laddie"/"Black Jack Davey"

Jack Beck, Scottish singer and broadcaster; interviewed in Dunkeld, Scotland, June 2012, by Fiona Ritchie as he led a group of American ballad scholars on a tour of Scotland.

When you go into the history, I mean, it's supposedly about a Lady Cassilis, and she did exist. But the gypsy that she's supposed to run away with was the famous Johnny Faa, who was the great legendary king of the Scots gypsies. Now unfortunately, if you then compare when they both lived, she would have been about five years old. So it's, you know, like a lot of these things, probably what we'll have here are two separate incidents, not involving the same people that have been brought together in one song. That frequently happened in ballads, particularly Scots ballads that didn't come from the Continent, but which started in Scotland. So it would be nice to think that it was just simply as it's described in the song, a true story. But I think that it's probably a bit of an amalgam. The interesting thing, too, if you listen to the two versions here—the Scots and the American versions—in the Scots one, if you listen towards the beginning, there's reference to the gypsy laddie "casting the glamour o'er her," in other words, putting a spell on her. There's a kind of magic side to the original ballad, which you do not find in the American ones, they're much more down to earth. He doesn't need to cast any glamour over her, the spell is in the guy's sheer—you know, he's definitely tall, dark, and handsome, and that's all it takes! Well, that was very different in "Black Jack Davey," but you know, you can recognize something of the story in there, the narrative of the song is still in there. But it's much more, I think, down to earth. And I suppose—in fact, there's no supposing about it—clearly these songs, the way they're presented and the way they develop, have a lot to do with the way people are living and, you know, the influences on their lives at that time. Remember that the original version was written hundreds of years earlier when the levels of education and all the rest were different. People's attitude to morals and to the supernatural was very different. Once they got to America, they were dealing with much more down-to-earth matters, I think, and that affected the way they presented things. And of course, other people from other parts of the world and other parts of Europe, in particular the Old World, also all arrived at the same time, and they were all bouncing off each other, so there were all sorts of influences. By the time you get to "Black Jack Davey," there are lots of other cultures that have had a go at it, and I think it's—I wouldn't describe one as being better than the other in any way at all—they are very different.

When I went over to Tennessee, I was shown a video of a wonderful, old, retired coal miner called Nimrod Workman, and he sang a very full version of a ballad called "Lord Bateman"—or as he described him, "Lord Baseman"—which I thought was wonderful, and he sang this ballad straight to camera, and there was hardly a word changed from the versions that you would hear over here [in Scotland]. Sometimes, the songs will be handed on down very preciously, like an old grandfather clock or something, which is looked after and, you know, polished and kept as it was. But sometimes, they are taken apart and rebuilt into something more usable and more relevant to modern times.

eight most commonly sung Child Ballads, five were Scots (including the top three): "The Daemon Lover/ James Harris" (Child 243), "Lord Thompson and Fair Annet" (Child 73), "The Gypsy Laddie" (Child 200; CD track 7), "Lord Randal" (Child 12), and "Young Hunting" (Child 68; CD track 13). In his research, Burton discounted the 205 variants of "Barbara Allen" (Child 84; CD track 1), which is often assigned a Scottish origin, because of its immense popularity and considerable nontraditional influences.[12] The domination of Scottish ballads in the ranking, combined with the disproportionately large number of Scottish ballad variants, leads to but one conclusion: the songs being sung most widely throughout the mountains and transmitted orally through innumerable variations were Scottish songs.

Another gauge of the strong Scottish ballad tradition in the southern Appalachians is the frequency with which the songs' melodic structure is "gapped." In the eighteenth and nineteenth centuries, European musical traditions were largely dependent upon the seven-note heptatonic (Greek for "seven") scale. This is the classic *Sound of Music* configuration of do, re, mi, fa, so, la, ti—seven notes before shifting octaves. Traditional songs, however, including Scottish and Irish ones, more commonly use the five-note pentatonic scale, omitting the two that are only a semitone higher than those preceding—fa and ti (ti is most commonly omitted, in which case it would be a six-note scale, or hexatonic). The pentatonic scale, descriptively termed "gapped," has dominated in Appalachian balladry and music in general, including the southern gospel-hymn tradition. The melody for "Amazing Grace," considered to be Scottish in origin, is pentatonic, with the fourth and seventh notes omitted.

Sheila Kay Adams is a ballad singer, storyteller, and author whose ancestors arrived from Ulster in 1731. She makes her home in Sodom Laurel (now called Reserve), Madison County, within the North Carolina mountains. Seven generations of her storytelling family preceded her in that community, so she notes that her folks "didn't move around much." In 2013 the National Endowment for the Arts bestowed the prestigious National Heritage Fellowship upon Sheila Kay, recognizing her lifelong contributions to enhancing and sustaining the old traditions of her Appalachian heritage. In true mountain fashion, she learned the stories and songs from her kinfolk, including her beloved "Granny Dell," about whom she composed a song. Sheila Kay's knowledge of the old music is encyclopedic in scope, and she often reflects on the Scottish and Ulster lineage of her Madison County repertoire. Her Granny attributed pedigree by declaring, "this one comes from across the big pond" or "this here is one of them 'way back yonder' songs," such as "Black Is the Color" (a reference to Scotland's River Clyde; CD track 14), "Little Margaret" (ghost lover), "My Dearest Dear" (leaving Scotland), "I Never Will Marry" ("My love's gone and left me . . ."), and "True Lover's Farewell" (inspired by Burns's "My Love Is Like a Red, Red Rose"). One of the five most popular Appalachian ballads in Tom Burton's research is a classic murder tale of Scottish origin that reveals the fury of a scorned woman, "Young Hunting" (Child 68; CD track 13):

Come in come in my own true love and spend
    this night with me,
For I have a bed and it's a very fine bed and I'll
    give it up for thee, thee
I'll give it up for thee.

Oh I won't come in I'm not coming in to spend
    the night with thee,
For I've got a wife in old Scotland, this night she
    waits for me, me,
This night she waits for me.

She pulled out her little pen knife and it a' been
    both keen and sharp,
And she stepped it up to her own true love and
    stabbed him through the heart, heart
She stabbed him through the heart.

Woe me woe me Little Margaret he cried woe me
     its undo thee,
For there's no wife in old Scotland that I loved
     any better than thee, thee
That I loved any better than thee.

Lay there lay there my own true love, one hour or
     two or three,
And I will send for a doctor near to save the life of
     thee, thee
To save the life of thee.

And then he said that I won't live from the
     wounds you've given me
No doctors send just Scots' own men could save
     my life for me, me
Could save my life for me.

Sometimes also known as "Henry Lee" and "Love Henry" in the United States, the version sung by Sheila Kay Adams is one that makes a strong connection with Scotland by name throughout:

Lay thee down lay thee down my own false love,
     'til the flesh rots off your frame,
And the little old wife in old Scotland shall mourn
     for your return, 'turn
Shall mourn for your return.

The well-known Appalachian ballad "Shady Grove" originated as "Matty Groves" combined with the melody of "Little Margaret," both from Scotland, describing the true love of a young man's life and his hopes they will wed. Its popularity resulted in the emergence of over 300 stanzas, and the song has been recorded by a striking assortment of artists, including Jean Ritchie, the Kingston Trio, Jerry Garcia, Bill Monroe, Crooked Still, Taj Mahal, and The Chieftains. The refrain of one older version is "Shady Grove my little love I'm going back to Ireland," while a Kentucky rhyming variant substitutes "I'm going back to Harlan." Doc Watson, the flat-pick guitar virtuoso from Deep Gap, North

Carolina, recorded a vintage rendition with his long-time music partner David Holt accompanying on banjo (CD track 17). Doc often recollected singing "Shady Grove" for his wife, Rosa Lee, during their courting days, and the opening verses set the amorous scene:

Cheeks as red as the bloomin' rose eyes of the
     prettiest brown,
You are my darlin' of my heart, sweetest little girl
     in town.

Wish I had a glass of wine and bread and meat for
     two,
I'd set it out on a golden plate and give it all to
     you.

Learning Ballads and Love Songs

Sheila Kay Adams, American ballad singer, banjo player, storyteller, and author; interviewed in Swannanoa, North Carolina, July 2009, by Fiona Ritchie during Traditional Song Week at the Swannanoa Gathering folk arts workshops.

I remembered the very first love song I heard, and I had always connected it with women. It was a man. Sitting on Granny's porch, and it was during tobacco season (now we'd have said "baccar") because there was that smell. You could smell that kind of spicy smell. And I was sitting on Granny's lap. I could also smell her, you know, kinda sweaty, and clean outdoors, and snuffy kinda smell. But it was from behind, because there was a crowd there, her cousins and people, you know, that had come to help her work baccar, and this voice started to sing. And it was Dillard Chandler. And I can remember I was five years old, and the reason I know this is because it was the summer after my grandmother died, and that was in '58, and so that was the first love song I learned.

This is what folks over home called a love song. This was one of Granny's favorite ones. Her sister sang a version of it and called it "The House Carpenter." I found out later when I got old enough and in college and discovered the Child collection of ballads, it was actually called "The Daemon Lover," and I learned it from her when I was about nine years old. Granny's generation's talking about being born 1890–1915: Cas Wallin, Dellie Chandler Norton, her sister Berzilla. They all sang songs that they would refer to as "love songs." It didn't matter how gory or if it was a murder ballad or if three people died, it didn't matter. They would refer to them as love songs. Even if they were dirty, they would refer to them as love songs.

So when I was five, Granny was the singer, and she says she was going to learn these old love songs to me in the old-timey way, which was knee to knee. And that's how I started out at five years old. She'd sing a verse, and I would have to sing it back, and she'd sing the second, and I'd have to sing first and second back . . . so by the end Granny was singing one verse and I was having to start all the way at the beginning and sing straight through using the inflection and the sighs. I would have to sing the whole song back. With telling stories it was about timing, and I think that's what the songs are about too. It's that weird timing of the songs that first gets your attention. 'Cause I mean they're just stories, but God they're great stories.

[Chorus] Shady Grove my little love Shady Grove
   I say,
Shady Grove my little love I'm bound to go away.

Now when I was a little boy I wanted a barlow
   knife,
Now I want little Shady Grove to say she'll be my
   wife.

A kiss from little Shady Grove as sweet as brandy
   wine,
Ain't no girl in this whole world is prettier than
   mine.

The old ballads were traditionally sung in the Appalachians by a solo singer a capella (or "Acapulco" as Sheila Kay Adams's Granny called it[13]). Instrumentation might be added later, but many continued the sean-nós singing style from Ulster and unaccompanied Scottish ballad delivery, performing in a detached manner devoid of drama even though the ballad lyrics might be extremely graphic and emotional. Mountain singers, like their ancestors, had a deep respect for the songs, and while they may have been affected by their stories, they would not tamper with tempo and volume, nor add theatrical gestures. It underscored the communally held philosophy that traditional singing was not about the singer and the performance. The old ballad stories were owned by no one and yet by everyone: generations of singing families and communities. The singer's job was to give the song a voice.

Appalachian ballad lyrics and melodies tended to be mournful in tone, which kept faith with a legacy of toil and struggle, parting and loss. (Modal chords in a minor key were common.) They resonated with the misfortunes and migrations of the centuries, shadows of life from an amalgamation of experiences: repressive rulers, deprivations, families and loves left or lost, perils of oceanic migration, struggles of strangers in a strange land, the fear of foreboding landscapes. Scottish folklorist and ballad singer Margaret Bennett notes that the Scots Gaelic language has expressions

of mournfulness without equivalent in English.[14] Cecil Sharp's collecting colleague Maud Karpeles, who recorded the song words, found Appalachian melodies to be even more "austere" than their Old World counterparts.[15] Little wonder that the eventual merging of the Old World singing and sorrowful Appalachian balladry would produce the "high lonesome sound," a defining characteristic of bluegrass and old-time music. Yet soaring above the soulful nature of many of the ballads is an air of resilience and human perseverance, an essential life spirit filled with love as well as sorrow. Ulster-born singer and guitarist Dáithí Sproule of the Irish group Altan highlights the native Gaelic traditions of Donegal in his repertoire. Introducing them to American audiences, he often remarks that, although most of the songs he sings are sad, they fill him with an abiding feeling of love. Perhaps this is also why Sheila Kay Adams's Granny called them all simply "love songs." Sheila Kay recalls: "Didn't make any difference how much killing, murdering, or . . . you know, the ballads, the old ballads, the story songs, she referred to 'em all as love songs."[16]

The Appalachian ballad singers also preserved another Old World tradition: the intermingling of songs with storytelling. In fact, ballads in the early days were often referred to as "story songs." "Voices from my childhood were just as liable to be singing as talking," Sheila Kay remembers. "As a girl, I would close my eyes and rock back and forth, listening to the words and imagining myself there, being a part of whatever drama was taking place." Sheila Kay is renowned today for reciting stories with vivid imagery, alive with scenarios and incidents that seem stranger than fiction. They stretch the imagination and challenge the notion of credibility, yet she stands by her belief that "if there is a kernel of truth, it is a true story."[17] It recalls the old axiom that many old stories, even if not entirely factual, do convey an essence of truth—Sheila Kay's "kernel."

The storytelling disposition of the Appalachian Scots-Irish, exemplified by the family of Sheila Kay

The High Lonesome Sound

John Cohen, American string-band musician, song collector, photographer, and filmmaker; interviewed in Swannanoa, North Carolina, July 2008, by Fiona Ritchie and Doug Orr during Traditional Song Week at the Swannanoa Gathering folk arts workshops.

Well, there's a lot of lonesome in the Carter Family songs, and many, many ballads and songs, "The Trail of the Lonesome Pine," or . . . in one of the songs, "I went out one morning to share to view the fields, and I thought I heard a mournful sound. I thought I heard a lonesome sound." I mean, a lonesome sound, what's that? Everybody knew. But only if you went to English class in New York! How can you justify a lonesome sound? A sound is not lonesome! Yeah, the longing [of the immigrant] or the acceptance of the fact that life didn't work out, or it didn't work out the way as described, as it was supposed to work out. But even as they settled into the mountains and the coves and hollows, it became a lonesome life for parts of the year. For example, in the last church service at the Primitive Baptist churches before winter set in, they would sing songs like "Farewell My Friends," and they knew that the winter was coming in and they may not get together again. And in many cases, 'cause of the high mortality rate, particularly infant mortality, many didn't see each other ever again. So it was . . . they were singing really for their lonesome life in many cases.

"And if I never see you any more, I'll love you in my heart . . ." Oh, I hear Dillard Chandler singing that in full voice . . . that's how the churches were full, everybody singing that together. I think it's wonderful and very curious that modern people, once they get into that sound, can love it when their voices all join, like in an old Baptist church, when they all can bellow out their lungs; and yet Pete Seeger teaches them to sing the harmony parts. But you don't even need the harmony. Just that big, big, big voice, which is quite moving.

Adams, is an inherent trait passed down through the generations by the immigrants from across the sea, and it continues on both sides of the Atlantic. The idea of sharing stories and anecdotes often falls under the category of "craic" in Ireland, Scotland, and England. The old English word "crack" was imported into Ireland, revised there as "craic," and, with the popularity of Irish music culture, has been imported back into English. The meanings have remained unchanged, however, and news, gossip, fun, and lively conversation are all "good craic." The nineteenth-century Scottish song "Work o' the Weavers" sums up the ambience: "We're a' met thegither here tae sit and tae crack, wi' oor glasses in oor hands and oor work upon oor back."

The ballads "native to America" evolved from the established ballad tradition, but now they reflected day-to-day life in the mountains—all grist for the songwriter's mill. It has been remarked that "mountain folks produced far more stories than could be consumed," so there was never any lack of raw material for the native ballads. Many of the ballads originating in the mountains were patterned after the ones in Francis Child's collection, and stock phrases such as "lily white hand," "the rose and the briar," "shoe your pretty little feet," and "ramblin' boy" are used

STORYTELLING

In practicing what is arguably the world's oldest art form, many Appalachian storytellers had inherited techniques and tales from their Scots-Irish forebears. In Ireland and Scotland, the "seannachie" was a skilled storyteller, carrying fairy tales, legends, and old Gaelic and Nordic sagas. Revered historians, these storytellers held in trust ancestral memories, embroidered with the magical storytellers' art. From the French word *raconter* (to relate), a "raconteur" in Scotland, Ireland, and England is a master weaver of folktales, fables, and funny anecdotes. The Scots and the Irish absolutely love a good raconteur—holding forth at the hearth, leaning on the bar at the local pub, amusing his fellow drinkers in the cattle fair or Highland Games beer tent, performing at the heart of a laughing throng. Many literary giants honed their craft by observing great tale spinners in the community, and the ballad repertoire fed into the raw material of storytelling. In fact, many of the early ballad lyrics—self-contained short stories —were composed as broadsides and posted publicly, either without music or with a note of suggested melodies. It has been a tradition in the folk music scene to intersperse music selections with stories by way of song context or general embellishment and stagecraft. Scots comedian and actor Billy Connolly began his career singing and playing banjo (in the duo the Humblebums with Gerry Rafferty) until, famously, the riotous stories between his songs lasted longer and longer and eventually became his act. David Holt is a Grammy Award–winning storyteller. As music partner to the late Doc Watson for twenty-two years, David dipped into his storyteller's toolbox to draw anecdotes from Doc and weave these through their song and tune sets (CD track 17).

Throughout the Appalachians, skillful storytellers like Sheila Kay Adams and Bobby McMillan can recite countless Celtic or Old English stories and their variants from memory. The late Ray Hicks of Beech Mountain, North Carolina, was especially known for telling traditional stories from British Isles roots known as "Jack Tales." These legends, nursery rhymes, and fairy tales (including "Jack and the Beanstalk") all feature a central Jack character, and, like the ballads, they journeyed into the Appalachian oral tradition. In Scotland, Jack Tales are still widely told in the Scottish Travelling community. Travellers are as mesmerizing spinning tales as they are singing ballads. The Scottish Storytelling Centre in the heart of Edinburgh's old town promotes Traveller and other storytelling traditions, providing a gathering place for cross-generational audiences from around the world to share in an ancient art.

From Orkney to Edinburgh, York to Somerset, and Kerry to Cork, storytelling festivals flourish in the United Kingdom and Ireland. They are just as widespread across the United States, especially in the Appalachian region; Tennessee alone hosts at least five such festivals, including the annual National Storytelling Festival in Franklin. Meanwhile, professional storytellers, including Connie Regan-Blake and Donald Davis, take their tales into the community. They visit schools to remind youngsters that everyone has stories to tell and to help them discover their inner "seannachie."

Ballads and Work

Jean Ritchie, American traditional singer, Appalachian dulcimer player, songwriter, and author; interviewed in Swannanoa, North Carolina, July 2008, by Fiona Ritchie during Traditional Song Week at the Swannanoa Gathering folk arts workshops.

"Ballads are stories, you know. . . . Well, I guess most any song is a story if you stretch your imagination a little bit. But the ballads especially have the good guy and the bad guy or lady, and they have triangles and all kinds of things happen. People get killed, people get away—it's all something that is telling a story. So in the wintertime, we told our stories aloud, all the Jack Tales and things like that, "Tigs and Tags and Long Leather Bags and All My Gold and Silver," that was a good one. [These traditional tales are also told in Ireland and Scotland as "The Old Hag's Long Leather Bag" and "Gallymander."] And then in the summertime, we didn't want to sit around telling stories, we got out on the porch and sang them, and sang all the old ballads, lovely ones.

Well I got thinking about that, and I tried to write down some notes about where I had learned songs very early, and the earliest one I can remember is my mother's sweeping song. She would be sweeping the floor in the front room. We had rough boards for the floor, little narrow ones. They looked very well, but they were all pretty rough, so when she swept, it made a good scratchy noise and accompanied the song! And she'd be singing this song. It mentions Old George's Square, which I think is in Scotland, maybe in Glasgow. So this is what she'd be singing. I didn't think of it as "Old George's Square," I thought of it as "Mama's Sweeping Song" [singing]:

> My parents raised me tenderly they had no child but me,
> But my mind was set on rambling around and with this we couldn't agree.
> There was a girl in this same town she was so wondrous fair,
> There was no other girl in the country 'round that with her I could compare.

liberally. The native ballads tend to be more topical, based on dramatic events in living memory, such as murders, battles, explorations, adventurous occupations, and colorful local incidents. They are more subjective, sentimental, and personal than the older Child ballads and frequently have a first-person narrative, concluding with a moral to the story.[18] There are many well-known examples: "John Henry," "Good Old Bowling Green," "Tom Dula (Dooley)," "Banks of the Ohio," "Wildwood Flower," and "On Top of Old Smoky."

The twentieth century has produced notable ballad composers whose singing continues an older tradition but whose story lines are sketched through more recent times. Perhaps no one epitomizes this trend better than eastern Kentucky's Jean Ritchie. Her compositions exhibit the tone and phrasing of Old World ballads, many of which she has also performed and recorded, but her songs depict Appalachian life through the twentieth century, with tales of courtin', love, hardscrabble mountain life, taking to the road, environmental degradation, and spirituality. Some of her

I asked her if she would agree for me to cross over the main.
She said she would prove true to me 'til I return again.
I got my things went to the dock her tears flowed down like wine.
We kissed, shook hands and parted, I left my girl behind.

As I walked out one morning to view old George's Square,
The mail post boat had just arose and the post boy met me there.
He handed me a letter which gave me to understand,
That the girl I left behind me had married another man.

I turned myself all around and about I knew not what to do.
I read on a few lines farther and I found the news was true.
I'll follow the old train, but company I'll resign.
I'll ramble around from town to town for the girl I left behind. (CD TRACK 15)

Well, we got work done, and at the end of the day, we sat down out on the porch and sang our favorite songs, sort of went 'round the circle and chose what we wanted to sing. And we enjoyed the songs, we enjoyed the stories, but we never thought of them in an intellectual sort of way. We never thought that we were learning something precious. We never felt that they were worth anything, except to us. So no, we didn't have a teaching approach to them at all. It's just if you heard a song and liked it, you learned it, that's all.

compositions draw upon connections across the sea, such as "Killy Kranky Is My Song," harking back to the Perthshire village of Killiecrankie and its eponymous folk song commemorating a battle. Many Appalachian ballads are thus hybrids, fusing musical legacy and Old Country place names with their counterparts in the Appalachian tradition. A song Jean learned from her mother, "Old George's Square," mingles mention of Glasgow's famous landmark with the sorrow of false love across the sea:

As I walked out one morning to view old
     George's Square,
The mail post boat had just arose and the post
     boy met me there.
He handed me a letter which gave me to
     understand,
That the girl I left behind me had married another
     man. (CD TRACK 15)

JEAN RITCHIE: THE MOTHER OF FOLK

Few narratives reflect the saga of Appalachian balladry more completely than the life story of eastern
Kentucky's Jean Ritchie. Balis Ritchie, a subsistence
farmer in Viper, Kentucky, and his wife, Abigail,
raised a family of fourteen children. Jean was the
youngest and grew up singing with her older brothers and sisters and their burgeoning extended family,
sometimes performing at local dances and county
fairs. Her father played the mountain dulcimer, in-
stilling in Jean the connection to the instrument that
became her hallmark. In *Singing Family of the Cumberlands*, Jean's 1955 autobiography, she reflected on a
daily life accompanied by singing ballads ("ballits," in
her dialect) during work and play, in the cornfields,
over the dishes, while walking, or just while idling.
Despite the cramped conditions of a family of sixteen
living within four rooms (she and her nine sisters
slept in a single dormitory-style room), there was
a steady stream of visitors—"peddlers of rugs, herb
cures, spices, dulcimers, and tintypes; travelers over
the mountains, asking to take the night; and once or
twice folks from far away over the ocean in England,
wanting to hear Mom and Dad and the girls sing
the old ballads." She was the first of her family to go
to college, and after graduating with honors from
the University of Kentucky, Jean taught elementary
school during the latter years of World War II.

It was when Jean traveled to New York City in
1947 to work in the Henry Street Settlement, a
center for social and health-care services and arts
programs, that she met a cast of kindred musical
spirits, including Pete Seeger, Woody Guthrie, Oscar
Brand, and Huddie William Ledbetter (Lead Belly).
She shared her Appalachian ballads with the young
people who attended the Henry Street Settlement
and met folklorist and ethnomusicologist Alan
Lomax. The renowned song collector recorded Jean
for the Library of Congress and introduced her to
others in the Greenwich Village music scene. There,
she met her future husband, photographer George
Pickow, who would accrue a remarkable catalog
of images capturing Jean's professional life, major
folk music events of the era, and the Ritchie family
homestead and community in Viper, Kentucky. Jean
produced and hosted concerts at Manhattan's Cherry
Lane Theater with Pete Seeger, Woody Guthrie, and
other prominent singers of the day, helping Ireland's
Clancy Brothers launch their careers in the United
States. Jean also introduced a young Doc Watson
to the Greenwich Village music community, which
in time included Bob Dylan, Jean Redpath, Tom
Paxton, and Ramblin' Jack Elliott. Doc never forgot
Jean's kindness to him when he came to the city,
and in 1963 they recorded an album of ballads and
tunes at Gerdes Folk City music venue, released on
the Smithsonian Folkways label. In 1952 Jean was
awarded a Fulbright Fellowship for travel in Ireland,
Scotland, and England to trace the roots of her family's ballad heritage. She spent eighteen months interviewing and recording local singers. Her visit is still
a childhood memory for some who recall a young
American woman visiting older local singers. Jean

expressed a deep reverence for the tradition bearers she met and, coming from a similar environment, instinctively grasped the importance of their musical communities. She was always warmly welcomed; her collecting process was essentially a song exchange. Jean performed and recorded many of her collected ballads after she returned to the United States, sharing her insight into the music's origins. She brought authenticity and substance to the folk music scene as an embodiment of the resilient, centuries-old ballad tradition.

Jean Ritchie has been rightly recognized as a gifted and important songwriter with many classics to her name, including "Now Is the Cool of the Day," "My Dear Companion," "Sorrow in the Wind," "Black Waters," "The L & N Don't Stop Here Anymore," "None but One," and "Blue Diamond Mines." Dolly Parton, Linda Ronstadt, Emmylou Harris, Judy Collins, Kathy Mattea, Ginny Hawker, Alice Gerrard, John Doyle, and many others have recorded her songs. Jean became known in the traditional music community as "The Mother of Folk," an accolade richly deserved as a leader of the folk music revival of the 1950s and 1960s. She would always demur, however, saying: "I have actively sought not to be famous." Most likely, she was expressing the sentiment that extended through the Appalachians and back to the Old Country: singers in these mountains also placed an emphasis on the timeless, shared community of song rather than on any individual singer.

Apart from her songwriting and ballad-collecting legacy, Jean is also credited with bringing the mountain dulcimer to an international audience. In a career spanning more than six decades, she has recorded forty albums and authored ten books, including several songbooks. Her extensive collection of music, field recordings, letters, and George Pickow's photographs are now housed at the American Folklife Center of the Library of Congress. At heart, Jean Ritchie is a poet who has breathed a gentle life philosophy through all her music, whether ballads of her Scottish forebears or her own songwriting. The sense of place is tangible throughout her work as she turns, always, for inspiration to her beloved "high hills and mountains."

I celebrate life! I tangle my fingers in its long-
    haired grasses with gladness.
I beat upon its breast with futility. I lie across its
    loins with joy. I give to it and
take from it sweet juices of abundance with pain
    and pleasure. I replenish
it with my tears and the vibrations of my laughter.
    Until it sweeps me off,
I will not leave it, this World, this Earth! This
    Universe, this Time and Space!
This chance of finding God!
This Life!

Jean Ritchie playing dulcimer around a cottage hearth with Elizabeth "Bess" Cronin and others, Macroom, County Cork, Ireland, 1952. (Photograph by George Pickow; courtesy of the National University of Ireland, Galway)

THE SONGCATCHERS

The collectors of songs, such as Jean Ritchie and Sheila Kay Adams—"songcatchers" in the Appalachian colloquialism—sustained a collecting legacy from the old countries. It was a tradition upheld by Scotland's Mrs. Brown (Anna Gordon), Sir Walter Scott, and Robert Burns; Ulster's Sam Henry; and Francis O'Neill in Chicago, among many others. Their approaches to song collecting might vary, but they no doubt all stood by Jean Ritchie's truism: "Living is collecting." Jeff Warner, traditional ballad collector and singer and the son of the highly regarded song pair Anne and Frank Warner, recalled that his parents collected people first and songs second.

The icon of twentieth-century song collecting was Cecil Sharp (1859–1924). He was a music teacher and composer who would go on to be venerated as the founding father of the twentieth-century folklore revival in England. During World War I, Sharp struggled to support himself through writing and lecturing and decided to make an extended trip to the United States, working as a dance adviser for a production of *A Midsummer Night's Dream*. By the time of his visit, he was the foremost song collector active in England and had already published collected works of traditional English folk songs and dances. Sharp attracted sizable audiences for his lectures. Indeed, his work in promoting English folk-dance traditions in the United States continues today through the Country Dance and Song Society, founded in 1915 by enthusiastic Americans whom Sharp had inspired. His collaborator was Maud Karpeles (1885–1976), a Londoner whose background interest was English folk dance. She met Sharp during one of his lectures and became as interested as he was in both the songs and the dances. Sharp was also intent on pursuing a line of inquiry pioneered by Olive Dame Campbell (1882–1954). She had conducted fieldwork on old folk songs surviving in the more remote regions of the southern Appalachians, collecting over 200 songs in Kentucky and publishing her *Songs and Ballads of the Appalachians* in 1915. Sharp and Karpeles traveled through the mountains of North Carolina, Tennessee, Virginia, and Kentucky during the summers of 1916–18 and discovered a treasure trove of song conserved by the mountain singers they encountered. They collected from anyone willing to meet with them and share an old song or two from across the sea. Sharp kept meticulous notes, including the date, place, and name of the singer for each ballad they collected. He recorded the melodies and Karpeles the words. They realized they had located, largely undisturbed, a rich seam of ballad history. Like other songcatchers who followed them, they appreciated that the songs were fundamental to the fabric of daily life for those residing in the isolated mountain cabins, every bit as ordinary yet no less vital than the very air they breathed. They learned that performance was not

the intended function of the songs, especially when it came to strangers. Sharp and Karpeles first had to foster the trust of the people they visited. Their interest was respectful and genuine; they maintained lengthy correspondences with many of their source singers, sending gifts and photographs from England. Sharp observed that the isolation of the Scots-Irish settlers, ensconced deep in the hills, had created a sanctuary where the music was better preserved than back in the old countries. Contained within was a unique culture with a special reverence for the old ballads, which Sharp wanted to preserve from outside interference: "These missionaries and their schools! I'd like to build a wall around these mountains and let these mountain people alone. The only distinctive culture in America is here. These people live. They sustain themselves on the meanest food. They are not interested in eating but they have time to sing ballads."[19]

Sharp was scathing about the well-intentioned Presbyterian missionaries. Though their benevolent work had helped mountain communities in many ways, including the establishment of mission schools and homes, missionaries sometimes felt duty bound to reform what they saw as the crude and primitive ways of a rustic world. Yet they eventually came to appreciate that the so-called hillbilly expressions came from Ulster and Scottish extraction as well as Old English, and that the ballads represented a rich heritage that the people cherished—a point Sharp made repeatedly. The songs and their multiple variants were alive and well

Advice for Collectors

David Holt, American multi-instrumentalist, singer, and collector; interviewed in Swannanoa, North Carolina, July 2009, by Fiona Ritchie and Doug Orr at the Swannanoa Gathering folk arts workshops.

I think I made every mistake you could make. I think the first thing is to go get to know the people. Have a relationship with them so that when you go back with your tape recorder or whatever you're recording them with, it's not an uncomfortable situation for them, and they're used to you talking, and you do care about them; and so, next thing would be to get a good tape recorder, a good disc player, whatever is the good technology at the time, because I recorded a lot of my best stuff on cheap cassettes because I had no money and aw, I just, I hated that I did that. But anyways, get [a] good . . . mic and recording unit. The other thing is, photograph them. This has been so important to me later on. I was just doing it because I love photography and I was an art major, but now, that may be the most valuable thing I've done, is these pictures. It's the only pictures that exist of some of these folks. And so definitely photograph them. Try to keep some kind of a catalog of what you're doing so that you don't just end up with a computer file that says the person's name, but try to break it down so you know what's on there so you can go back and listen to it, and somebody else can go back and access it. Those would be the main things I would say.

Yeah, and if there's any money to be made, the person who's collecting should definitely include that person—they don't own that. I think you do have to care about those people. Or try to get the money if you're doing a TV show about them, you need to try and get money from the producers to pay those people, because a lot of times, people don't want to pay anything. But it's just a free-flowing information society. It's going to be very difficult to do. Everything's out there. For better or for worse.

in the southern Appalachians. Their removal from the crosscurrent of influences shaping ballad traditions in Scotland, Ireland, and England had preserved them in an old, less-altered form. The remote coves and hollows were places where, in a mountain expression, "you have to lie down and look up to see out." Perhaps, with a stock of old songs in your heart, you could also sing out, oblivious to the cultural undercurrents of the outside world.

Sharp was invited to be a guest essayist for the Asheville "Pen & Plate Club" on June 13, 1917, and his piece was entitled "Folk Songs of Western North Carolina." According to an account appearing the next day in the *Asheville Citizen*, "Mr. Sharp delighted his audience by singing (accompanied by Maud Karpeles) a number of old ballads collected in Madison County and other counties . . . and among the songs were 'The False Knight on the Road,' 'The Cruel Mother,' and 'Edward Edwards,' the last song found in Tennessee." He was further quoted from his essay: "North Carolina is amazingly rich in folk songs, and I must say without exaggeration that in these sections I heard some of the most beautiful music I ever heard in my life. In these mountains I made the richest collections of ballads that have ever been preserved through the centuries. Here is a collector's heaven. I found everybody singing ballads of rare antiquity. Altogether I collected 400 ballads and hope to collect that many more when I return next summer."

Had he encountered the Gypsy Travellers of Scotland, Ireland, England, and Wales, he may have changed this opinion, but Sharp believed that the old ballads, especially in his native England, were moribund; whereas in Appalachia, they were integral to the everyday life of these descendants of British Isles emigrants. There, he observed, songs grew organically around ways and means of living, and music and dance occurred as a natural complement to family and neighborhood events: cabin raising, corn shucking, bean stringing, and the like. In Appalachia, Sharp had found a "nest of singing birds," a living tradition.[20] His exhaustive collecting and research work contributed a missing link to Francis Child's definitive *English and Scottish Popular Ballads*.

Cecil Sharp's fieldwork and publications benefited from the considerable assistance of three women. Maud Karpeles worked with Sharp until his death in 1924, and thereafter she wrote material for new editions of Sharp's *English Folk Songs: Some Conclusions*. Karpeles continued to collect English country dances through the 1920s and 1930s, and she followed up on Sharp's proposal to trace British Isles songs to Newfoundland, resulting in the publication of her well-received *Folk Songs of Newfoundland* in 1934. When building began for the Cecil Sharp House on Regent's Park Road in London, Karpeles helped lay the foundation stone. Open since 1930, the library and archive of Sharp's work is also the headquarters of the English Folk Dance and Song Society.

Olive Dame Campbell, whose collecting had first inspired Sharp to visit the southern Appalachians, was

Where the Songs Came From

David Holt, American multi-instrumentalist, singer, and collector; interviewed in Swannanoa, North Carolina, July 2009, by Fiona Ritchie and Doug Orr at the Swannanoa Gathering folk arts workshops.

They knew which ones came from "across the waters," as they would say. And which ones were made up here, pretty much. They knew that something like "The House Carpenter" was from Europe, and "Pretty Polly" and those things—even though it could have been from here—that it was a "ballot," as she called it, Dellie [Norton, (1898–1993)] would call it, "from across the waters." But I gotta tell you a little sideline on that. I took Dellie Norton at eighty-six years old to the beach for the very first time. "Across the pond" or "across the waters" is what they called England, Scotland, [Wales,] and Ireland. So she stood on the beach for the very first time, and she looked out across the ocean, and she said, "Where are the trees?" She was thinking it was a pond, you know, a small pond, or just a thing. Not a continent away, and I mean, not an ocean away. And so that changed my mind about what they were thinking and where they were from. But they knew they were from old family members, mostly. Some came in other ways. There was an old guy who used to come to Sodom, this is a little community, very rural community that Sheila Kay [Adams] and different folks are from, Sodom, North Carolina. There was a guy who used to come through and work for people in certain parts of the year, in the spring, in the fall. And he would bring in songs and they would learn new songs from him. But mostly it was from their family.

model of the Danish Folk School. Returning to the North Carolina mountains in 1925, she founded the John C. Campbell Folk School in Brasstown, applying lessons from the Danish example. Today, the folk school attracts participants of all ages from throughout the world, with a curriculum of Appalachian cultural studies, crafts, arts, storytelling, and music. The 2000 film *Songcatcher* was loosely based upon Olive Dame Campbell's song collecting and includes scenes with a fellow collector supposed to represent Cecil Sharp. Many western North Carolina folk musicians played roles in the movie, and Sheila Kay Adams tutored a young actress, whose musical background was opera, so effectively that her voice captured the Appalachian sound with perfect intonation.

The third woman who made a major contribution to Sharp's work was the singer and collector Jane Hicks Gentry (1863–1925). Although she supplied seventy ballads to Sharp's collection, she received no significant credit in his publication. Sharp and Maud Karpeles met Gentry when they visited her hometown of Hot Springs in Madison County, North Carolina, in 1916. Ballad singer and collector Betty Smith has written the biography *Jane Hicks Gentry: A Singer Among Singers*. Smith writes that Jane was a good neighbor and friend to all in Hot Springs, where she collected and made good use of her songs, and that "Jane Gentry was not only a tradition-bearer in her own family, she kept the songs and stories alive by singing them wherever she was."[21] Gentry was also a dedicated storyteller with a repertoire of Jack Tales, a British-American storytelling tradition perpetuated today in the Scottish Travelling community. She also loved collecting and reciting riddles. A Hicks family relative, song collector Frank Profitt, was responsible for uncovering an old mountain ballad and true story of a man by the name of Tom Dula, pronounced by the mountaineers as "Dooley." He was caught in a lover's triangle, accused of murdering Laurie Foster, and hanged in nearby Iredell County in the late 1800s. The Kingston Trio turned Profitt's collected ballad into a best-selling folk song

a native of Massachusetts and Tufts College graduate who married schoolteacher John Campbell. John was awarded a grant to study local culture and conditions of the southern Appalachians with the hope of improving the school systems, and they journeyed together into the mountains. During their time there, Olive observed that the local ballads seemed to have a strong connection to the folk songs of Scotland, Ireland, and England. She collected many, sharing them with Cecil Sharp for inclusion in Sharp's *English Folk Songs of the Southern Appalachians*. Olive was credited on the title page as "Contributing Thirty-Nine Tunes." After her husband's death in 1919, she gathered his notes and published *The Southern Highlander and His Homeland* under his name. Olive Campbell traveled to Denmark on a fellowship to study the educational

in the late 1950s. As for Tom Dula, local controversy lingers to this day about his culpability. There is no argument, however, about the contribution of Jane Gentry to the legacy of balladry. She is commemorated by a Hot Springs historical marker placed outside her house (now an inn), noting her connection with Cecil Sharp. The marker reads:

BALLADRY. English folklorist Cecil Sharp in 1916 collected ballads in the "Laurel Country." Jane Gentry, who supplied many of the songs, lived here.

Sheila Kay Adams recalls that her Granny Dell did not have the opportunity to make such an impression:

Granny was not that fond of Cecil Sharp, and the reason she was not that fond of him is because she went to sing for him, and he refused to listen to her, because she was eighteen. And at that time, see, he was only collecting from the older generation, people over forty, and so he missed a lot of the younger people because he assumed that what had happened in the British Isles had happened here, meaning that folks under forty didn't know the old love songs. He thought he was going to get "Red River Valley," you know, and the American folk songs, when in actuality, the younger folks were still learning 'em, they were being sung within the family here, unlike they were in England. So, indeed, he did come to Madison County and wound up collecting from several of my ancestors. But then it was in Hot Springs when he found the jewel. When he went into Hot Springs, he found Jane Gentry. And of course, Jane Gentry was one of the ones that supplied him with more of the Scottish and English folk songs than any other informant he found in all of America. At that point, the ballads here were in danger of dying out, just like they had started to do in England. But what Cecil Sharp did, I think,

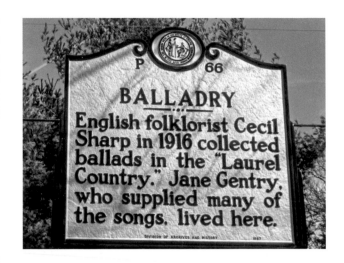

more than anything, was to encourage the older folks to continue singing so the younger folks learned them.[22]

So, notwithstanding Cecil Sharp's apparent blind eye to younger singers, overlooking the widespread influence of African Americans, and even disregarding the continuity of song traditions in parts of his own country, it may be that his visits to the mountains had a motivating effect on his song sources. He may also have inspired a local young man to take seriously the great cultural reservoir of his home. Bascom Lamar Lunsford (1882–1973), the "Minstrel of the Appalachians," wore many hats in his full life: lawyer, public schoolteacher, political party official, justice department agent, fruit-tree salesman, music festival organizer, banjo player, fiddler, singer, and song collector. If the spread of ballads can be likened to the art of plant propagation, it seems only appropriate that it was his role as a fruit-tree salesman that allowed Lunsford to roam the back roads of his North Carolina mountains and collect songs and tunes. He was so accomplished at this that by the end of his life, he had made a memory collection of over 325 ballads, tunes, and tales. His paper collection contained more than 3,000 songs, tunes, square-dance calls, and stories. He was also well versed on the Old Country origins of

Dorothy Scarborough, Song Collector. (Woodcut by
Paul Laune; collection of Darcy and Doug Orr)

the music, making frequent mention of its historic underpinnings. Lunsford was a man of the age: in addition to publishing a song collection, he made cylinder and 78-rpm sound recordings of his many folk song memories for Columbia University and the Library of Congress in the hope that the rising generation would value them as he did. Today, Lunsford's immense collection is housed at Mars Hill College in his native Madison County, North Carolina. His recorded collection of songs, by Lunsford and others, make up the largest oral archive at the American Folklife Center of the Library of Congress.

Lunsford grew up near South Turkey Creek in the Sandy Mush area near Asheville. His father gave him a fiddle, and he and his brother constructed a cigar-box banjo that they played together at dances and parties. The banjo became his favorite instrument for his singing, recording, and performing. As he grew up, he attended college, taught school for a while, and then studied law at Duke University. For the rest of his life, he was torn between making a living by practicing law and pursuing his abiding love of music. His biographer, Loyal Jones, recalls that Bascom lived something of a divided life, dabbling in several professions but always returning to music. Selling fruit trees was a typical example of how he juggled his priorities, as therein lay the possibility of veering off on a backwoods pathway toward another song or tune just waiting to be collected. A born performer, Bascom was ever eager to share a story and described himself, according to Jones, as "always standing outside of myself to see how I'm doing."[23]

Old-timers in Asheville fondly recall that Bascom would show up in the city's Pack Square. His preferred outfit of white linen suit and tie made him easy to spot, and someone would invariably shout: "Hey Bascom, sing one for us." Without missing a beat, he would launch into one of his favorites, such as "I Wish I Were a Mole in the Ground," all the while buck dancing and strumming an imaginary banjo. In popularizing this

old song, he likely inspired later versions or fragments by many others, from Doc Watson to David Holt, John McCutcheon, and Bob Dylan.

I wish I was a mole in the ground,
Yes I wish I was a mole in the ground.
If I was a mole in the ground, I'd root that
    mountain down,
And I wish I was a mole in the ground.

O' I wish I was a lizard in the spring,
Yes I wish I was a lizard in the spring.
If I's a lizard in the spring, I'd hear my darlin' sing,
I wish I was a lizard in the spring.

In the field, Lunsford did not make use of any re-cording devices of his day but took pride in his ability to commit ballads, tunes, stories, and square-dance calls to memory. He enjoyed the company of kindred-spirit song collectors such as Columbia University's Dorothy Scarborough (1878–1935). She was a Texas native who had worked on collecting African American songs and cowboy songs. Scarborough arrived in Asheville in the summer of 1930 to research her book, *A Songcatcher in the Southern Mountains*. She tracked down Lunsford and, armed with her Dicta-phone wax-cylinder dictation machine, announced her intention to "hunt songs." They headed out together, trekking the old back roads in a perpetual song hunt. Scarborough died shortly before her manuscript was published; in the posthumous edition, she reminisced fondly about her song-hunting partner.[24]

Bascom's music took him to Europe, and he was invited by President Franklin D. Roosevelt to perform for Britain's King George VI and Queen Elizabeth (the Queen Mother) at the White House. He was relentless in his promotion of the music as well as his collecting and performing. In 1928 he founded the Mountain Dance and Folk Festival in Asheville, and it has taken place annually every year since, making it the oldest continuing folk festival in the nation. During an inter-view at his home above the Hudson River, Pete Seeger recalled attending the Mountain Dance and Folk Fes-tival when he was in his early twenties. "I remember it well," Pete said, "Bascom had it so well organized that a performer would appear in the spotlight on one side of the stage and immediately upon that performer's exit, the spotlight would shift seamlessly to the next performer or band on the other side. It was my early exposure to the Appalachian music, and afterward Bascom was gracious enough to show me a few banjo licks."[25] Pete Seeger included a dedication in his 1948 music manual, *How to Play the 5-String Banjo*, now considered a classic introduction to the instrument. Alongside Uncle Dave Macon, Rufus Crisp, Samantha Bumgarner, Lilly Mae Ledford, and Earl Scruggs, he named Bascom Lamar Lunsford as having helped him get started and eventually develop his signature long-neck five-string banjo style.

Another contemporary of Bascom Lamar Lun-sford was Kentucky's John Jacob Niles (1892–1980). A composer, singer, and collector, Niles uncovered song material from residents in his native Kentucky mountains. His sources included African Americans and veterans of World War I. Niles followed the prac-tice of earlier collectors and composers going back to the time of Robert Burns, reworking and reinterpret-ing old song fragments. It was an approach that at-tracted some criticism. With his own version of the traditional verses of "Black Is the Color" (CD track 14), for example, he took an old Scottish song, revised its lyrics, and set it to a new modal melody. The song traveled to a worldwide audience in the 1950s when jazz pianist, singer, and songwriter Nina Simone, from Tryon in the North Carolina mountains, embraced it in her repertoire. Niles made several excursions into

Collectors: Bascom Lamar Lunsford

Pete Seeger (1919–2014), singer, songwriter, campaigner, and activist; interviewed in Beacon, New York, November 2008, by Fiona Ritchie and Doug Orr at the artist's home.

I played in the school jazz band. I wanted to be like my teenage peers, so I went clunk, clunk, clunk on a tenor banjo, playing the chords, which were written down in the sheet music. But I really didn't enjoy it that much. It put me in touch with my peers for a while, but at age seventeen, my father took me to a festival in Asheville, North Carolina, and I heard ordinary working people making fantastically good music. They didn't play many kinds of music; they just played the kind they knew. And I'll never forget a woman in her fifties named Samantha Bumgarner, from a small town in eastern Tennessee, and she'd come over the mountains to sing at this festival. The man in charge of the festival was a lawyer, but he actually became a very good showman. He would have only one mic on stage right and another mic on stage left, maybe thirty feet away, it was a broad stage. And he'd have spotlights on stage right, and there, a band would be playing. While they were playing, he would go over to stage left and get another band out and group them around the mic. He'd say, "Now, you know what you're going to play? You know what key you're in? You're all in tune? Now the moment the spotlight hits you, you start playing. But don't play until the spotlight hits you." Now he walks back to stage right, and the band there is finishing up, and he leads the audience in the applause. "Give a hand to the Coon Creek Boys, and aren't they wonderful?" And then he would walk across the stage thirty feet, and the spotlight would follow him. "Now here is the Smith Hollow Gang! And they're going to take over!" So he had a fast-moving show, back and forth from stage right to stage left.

[The man was] Bascom Lamar Lunsford. He gave me my first lesson in playing a five-string banjo. Instead of going and just playing chords, clunk, clunk, clunk, you'd pick up on maybe the middle string and then pick up on the first string, five notes higher. And then come down with your thumb on the fifth string. Gradually—I didn't learn this all at once—I learned you picked one of the strings with your left hand. So now I could get four beats there. Up on the middle string, plucked the first string with your left hand—my mother says that on the violin, that's called left-hand pizzicato. I just call it pulling off, but you know my phrase has been picked up by the whole music world now. Guitar pickers all around the world, it's pulling off when you play a note with your left hand. And sometimes you can, instead of pulling off, you can hammer down on one of the strings, usually a lower string. You pick it with your right hand and then come down strongly on the fretboard with your left hand, and the string is still vibrating in the new pitch. And of course, a man named Earl Scruggs invented a way to divide up eight short notes into three, three, and two—that adds up to eight. And if you analyze it, that's basically the rumba rhythm [makes rhythm noises].

So, I just hit upon something that sounded nice and tried to imitate it. Bascom Lamar Lunsford was a very conservative man. He said, this folk music, it was all right until Seeger got connected with it.

He did not approve of me. Even though he gave me my first lesson on the instrument.

the Appalachians with photographer Doris Ulmann, collecting songs and photographs. Of his 100 song compositions, the best known are the evocative Christmas song "I Wonder as I Wander" and "Go Away from My Window," which Niles wrote at the age of sixteen. Bob Dylan quoted its title line in his song "It Ain't Me Babe." As a performer, Niles liked to accompany himself on a homemade dulcimer-like construction and other stringed instruments, including a lute. The John Jacob Niles Center for American Music at the University of Kentucky exhibits some of the traditional instruments built by Niles.

Alan Lomax (1915–2002) wandered farther afield than any of his predecessors; he was, for some, "the man who recorded the world." The son of folklorist and pioneering song collector John, Lomax rose to prominence as one of the twentieth century's significant American folk music field collectors. The career of Alan Lomax encompassed roles as ethnomusicologist, oral historian, author, filmmaker, political activist, musician, and folklorist. His travels took him from New York to the Mississippi Delta, Texas, the southern Appalachians, and Europe. Lomax worked for the Library of Congress for many years, where he hired a young Pete Seeger as his assistant, collecting and recording blues, zydeco, western, Appalachian, and British Isles folk music. Undaunted by the toils of material gathering in the age before portable recording devices, Lomax was known to carry a heavy load of equipment wherever the song hunt might take him. Since Lomax cast such a wide net in his collecting, he could not spend his career focused on the Appalachian wellspring in the manner of Bascom Lamar Lunsford. He did undertake a 1937 field trip to Clay County, Kentucky, that resulted in fifty recordings for the Library of Congress archives, including ballads, camp-meeting songs, and fiddle and banjo tunes. Unlike most song collectors, he had no scruples about offering his sources cash or even plying them with alcohol, although he shared Lunsford's fondness for

exchanging a song or two to build trust with traditional singers.

Lomax loved to sing and accompany himself on the guitar and made a solo appearance at Lunsford's annual Mountain Dance and Folk Festival in Asheville. A significant Lomax contribution to American music was his discovery of Jean Ritchie, whom he met in New York City. He recorded her 1948 Columbia University concert for the Library of Congress sessions and also her song-collecting travels through Ireland. As a social activist and folk music crusader, Lomax had a special interest in songs of poverty and protest. In the climate of the 1950s McCarthy era, this drew the attention of the FBI, which began to track Lomax. As the House Un-American Activities Committee drew ever closer

Collecting Songs and Memories

Jean Ritchie, American traditional singer, Appalachian dulcimer player, songwriter, and author; interviewed in Swannanoa, North Carolina, July 2008, by Fiona Ritchie during Traditional Song Week at the Swannanoa Gathering folk arts workshops.

Well we got to realize some of the value of the songs through this way because the ladies, as they were called, or the "quare" women—from far off, they came from New England in the beginning and then from Lexington, and the churches would send women down to teach. Very seldom would men come, it was mostly women. And we began to realize that the songs meant something extra special to them, and so we began to learn about it then. And we began to recognize the ones that maybe came from Scotland and the ones that maybe came from Ireland and England, and those three countries were the three backgrounds for our part of Appalachia. So we sort of learned that about the songs. My father came from Knott County, and he came all the way over to Perry County to court my mother, and to the day he died—he lived to be eighty-nine years old, he married my mother when he was twenty-six or so—he was always called "that man from Knott County"!

It was 1952 and '53, yeah. I had applied for a grant to go to England, Scotland, and Ireland and look for the sources of my family songs, because we had quite a few ballads and old songs that referred to the old countries and so on. So, I mean, the people on the board were having their meeting, and I was late in taking my record up to have them hear it. We stopped in one of these places that made records on the street, and they made an actual vinyl record, and you could see all the stuff flying off the record and the needle going round and everything, making the record. And I grabbed that in my hand and ran up there, George and I did. And they were all in the meeting room. She said I better check this record first; sometimes those things don't work so well. And she played something like "Loving Hannah," and my voice was all squeaky and high, and I said, "Oh this is awful," and I started to almost cry. And she said, why don't you just go in there and sing for them. They all started talking about the songs. They kept me going for about six songs, you know, so I knew I was going to get it then. That's how I got my scholarship.

I used a song that we have in our family because it's a well-known song throughout the world, parts of the world—that's "Barbara Allen" (CD track 1). So I used "Barbara Allen" as a collecting technique, and I would say, "Do you know Barbara Allen?" And most everybody would. So I've got many, many verses of "Barbara Allen," all throughout the countries. One from Bess Cronin and one from Jeannie Robertson; all over the islands, people knew that song. The way I would do it: I would sit down with my dulcimer and play "Barbara Allen" for them, and they couldn't wait till I got through so they could sing theirs for me. So that would break the ice, then we'd go on to other songs, and they would sing whatever they felt was popular in their family or whatever they especially loved; they'd pass it on to us. We would sing for them, and they would sing for us. And that was a good way, because you give something and you get something.

Many of them had seen collectors before, like Seamus Ennis and Peter Kennedy, who had been the year before us—no, two years before us. Alan Lomax had been the year before us with some of them, not all of them. Hamish [Henderson] took us all around Scotland. He would say, "See yon pub, there's a lot of good singing in there!" So we'd fall for it every time, we would go into the pub. There'd be nobody there singing. Hamish said, "Oh well, as long as we're here let's have—!" But we had a wonderful time, and we met great people and had a lot of good times singing. A lot of good parties and ceilidhs. A wonderful one in the Makem Cottage in County Armagh, where we met a young boy of the house, Sarah Makem's youngest son, Tommy Makem, and he didn't know any songs. He knew one song. He played the tin whistle, and he knew one song, "Nell Flaherty's Drake," and he sang that for us. Then after we left, his mother told me later that he went all around town and knocked on all the doors and said to the ladies when they came to the door, sing me all your old songs. And they did, and he learned all the love songs and became a folk singer, a singer of traditional songs. So I patted myself, we patted ourselves a little on the back for that, because we had inspired in him the fact that people cherished these songs, and that they were something besides their own enjoyment—the rest of the world was interested also. And he got busy.

I found a lot of wonderful people. When you collect songs, you collect more than songs: you collect friends, people, you collect places, you collect memories. Every time I sing certain songs, I think of the place it was where I learned it. Not every time, maybe. But once, when I was a tiny child, we went out on the school ground, and there was a new girl who had just come into school. She was a little tiny thing, and she had blond hair that came way down. And she was very pale. And it turned out that her name was Blanche White! I didn't know what Blanche meant then, so the name didn't mean anything, but later on, I got a joke out of it. But she wanted to sing a song for us. Her father was working on the railroad, he was a switchman or something. He didn't stay in the neighbourhood long, but he stayed a few months, and we all got to like Blanche White. She sang this song for me, for a bunch of us. We were all huddled up round, like you do in the school ground when you're listening to something. [Jean sings "Oh where are you going, little bird?"] We started dancing around then, and they would say, "Peep Peep," and throwing their arms up, and we had the best time. And I remember that every time I hear anything like that song. I remember that few minutes on the school ground at recess when we learned that song. And so you collect memories like that, and you collect, as I say, a sense of place where the song comes from. It's just wonderful.

Collectors: John and Alan Lomax

Pete Seeger (1919–2014), singer, songwriter, campaigner, and activist; interviewed in Beacon, New York, November 2008, by Fiona Ritchie and Doug Orr at the artist's home.

The man who should be remembered was the son of old John Lomax, who collected cowboy songs. I think that the word "folk" music was invented about 150 years ago in Europe; it meant the music of the peasant class, ancient and anonymous. Well, around the year 1900, [John, as] a young man studying at the University of Texas, on his vacations liked to sit around the campfire with a pencil and paper, writing down the words that the cowboys were singing. His professor said, "Oh just throw this away, you're wasting your time." But a year later, up at Harvard, Professor [George Lyman] Kittredge said, "Oh this is very interesting, this is American folk music." So John Lomax picked up the term. These were not ancient songs, they were not all anonymous—some of them were, but not all—and in 1907 he brought out a book, *Cowboy Songs*, and got President Theodore Roosevelt to write a short forward saying these are good songs, people ought to sing 'em. Whereas in Europe, they would say, oh you're not authentic, this has only to be sung by a peasant! But here in democratic America, John now encouraged people to sing these songs, and although he made a living working in a bank, whenever he could take a week or two off, he would pile his family into a car, and they would visit a singing family wherever they could find one. The Ritchie family is a singing family in Kentucky, and he found other similar families in Texas, or wherever. Sometimes, he reached out through the newspapers. And when his younger son [Alan] said, "Father, I'd like to carry on your work," during the New Deal, the Library of Congress got some money to pay somebody for the archives of folk song. Before that, it was just a junk heap. Poor Robert Gordon didn't have time to catalog them all, there were just piles of disks and papers mounting up in a small room in the very top floor of the library. Well, Alan took over this at age twenty-two. His father called him "the Acting Curator." His father was "the Curator," the man with the reputation, but his twenty-two-year-old son, with the confidence of youth and energy, did in six years what most men would have taken a lifetime to do. Way back in the year 1939–40, he paid me all of $15 a week to listen to hundreds, thousands of old records. Back in the twenties, they found that records would sell in the South if they were local southern songs, and often these were old ballads.

to his circle of colleagues and friends, Lomax departed for Europe. While this allowed him to avoid the threat of entertainment-industry blacklisting, it also enabled him to pursue song-collecting activities in the British Isles. Lomax based himself in London, working with the BBC and folklorists that included the poet and writer Hamish Henderson. He recorded ballad singer and Scottish Traveller Jeannie Robertson and others for his Scottish, Irish, and English folk music archives. Shying away from neither controversy nor adversity, Lomax forged ahead with his song-collecting passion for the next fifty years. He is credited with being a catalyst for Hamish Henderson's founding (with Calum MacLean) of the School of Scottish Studies at the University of Edinburgh (now the Department of Celtic and Scottish Studies).

The time that Alan Lomax spent in 1950s Britain and Ireland inspired another folksinger, playwright, and activist to collect and perform traditional ballads. James Henry Miller was the only surviving child of Scots who, during the Great Depression, migrated to the iron foundries of Salford in the north of England. He launched his musical career as a street singer, and when he began working in the theater, he changed his name to Ewan MacColl. Through the 1960s, MacColl

collaborated with English song collector and singer A. L. Lloyd to record eight albums of the Child Ballads and also volumes of broadside ballads from the seventeenth century. In 1956 he met and fell in love with American Peggy Seeger of the Seeger family of folksingers.

The pair became a prolific recording, performing, and script-writing duo and also vigorous advocates for folk song traditions. They developed a special interest in collecting the music of the Scottish Travellers and produced a profile of the Stewarts of Blair, a singing family of Travellers from Perthshire in Scotland from whom MacColl collected songs. Beyond the folk music world, MacColl will always be best remembered as the author of the song "The First Time Ever I Saw Your Face," which was written for Peggy Seeger and taken to worldwide audiences by jazz and soul singer, songwriter, and humanitarian Roberta Flack, who came from the Appalachian town of Black Mountain, North Carolina. MacColl's daughter, singer-songwriter Kirsty MacColl, was one of the defining voices of 1980s and 1990s British pop music. Like her father, she is especially remembered as a gifted songwriter.

By inspiring Hamish Henderson and Ewan Mac-Coll, Alan Lomax's example had helped fuel the folk

Sustaining the Tradition

David Holt, American multi-instrumentalist, singer, and collector; interviewed in Swannanoa, North Carolina, July 2009, by Fiona Ritchie and Doug Orr at the Swannanoa Gathering folk arts workshops.

I was so lucky, when I got here in Asheville [North Carolina], Sam Scoville at Warren Wilson College [Swannanoa, North Carolina] asked me if I would consider starting an Appalachian Music Program. There really wasn't anything like this in the country where people could come on campus and learn the instruments from the old-timers in the mountains. I mean, I was fairly new here, really, but the thing that I had was that I had gone to meet all the different groups of people around the mountains here. The ballad singers, the bluegrass guys, the old-time people, and there was no animosity to me, but there was animosity between all those groups, so I was like the connecting person.

I think that these old tunes are a bit of old-timey wisdom that we cannot even put into words. If we could've put them into words, we would have made a story or a saying or something. You take a tune like "Ducks on the Pond" or "Frosty Morning" or some kind of modal tune, that's very easy to hear [that] there's a lot of spirit in it. There's a power in that, I think, that just goes to people's hearts; so that's easy to hear, the modal music. But take something like "Soldier's Joy," or something like that, well, that's the same thing. There's wisdom in that, but it's a wisdom about fun and just enjoyment of life and sort of the joy of being alive. You need that wisdom, too, as well as the dark kind of wisdom, and I think that's the powerful part of the music. And then there's the cultural part that we all are attracted to. But to me, I think the deepest thing is that the tunes and the songs themselves have a power that reaches deep inside us. We don't even know what it is.

I learned it because people were so gracious to me and taught me, or didn't teach me, but allowed me to be in their presence watching what they did. And I feel like this music isn't alive unless people are playing it. You can record it and tape it and write it in books and everything, but people have to be playing it to make it really alive, and you have to have people of all levels . . . playing it. People sitting at home that you never heard of that are great, people that do it professionally and push it to the limits. So I think you need all those things, and I really try to help young people in any way I can because I think it's very important that it continues. Just because of the thing I said earlier: this is soul music in a certain part of our soul. It maybe doesn't get our entire soul, but it gets a lot of our soul and can express a lot of our soul as humans.

song revival in Britain; it also served as a stimulus for the 1950s urban folk revival of the United States. Mike Seeger, brother of Peggy, performed old Appalachian songs and tunes learned from some of Lomax's Library of Congress recordings with his New Lost City Ramblers. Mike and Peggy Seeger's mother, Ruth Crawford Seeger, had worked for John and Alan Lomax at the Library of Congress and had encouraged her children to explore folk song traditions. The Ramblers were collectors themselves as well as performers, and they brought the Appalachian repertoire to a new wave of folk musicians, including Joan Baez, Judy Collins, and Bob Dylan. Other songcatchers, such as the Ramblers' John Cohen and the Smithsonian Institution's Ralph Rinzler, Betty Smith, Sheila Kay Adams, and David Holt, would increase the flow of tradition into the mainstream. Bascom Lamar Lunsford spoke for these men and women and their tireless efforts to nurture the musical tree of life in his song "In the Spirit of the Poet," the first two lines of which are from Henry Wadsworth Longfellow:

I shot an arrow into the air, it fell to earth I know
    not where;
But years after still unbroken I found that arrow
    in the heart of an oak.

I breathed a song into the air, it fell to earth I
    know not where;
But long years after from beginning to end,
I found that song in the heart of a friend.

SACRED SONGS AND SHAPE-NOTE SINGING

In addition to balladry and fiddle tunes, the Scots-Irish immigrants imported a third traditional music genre: sacred and religious music derived from the early Presbyterian churches. Along with their elegiac ballads, immigrants to Pennsylvania had hymns to sing. Their voices rose together in songs of praise along the course of the Great Philadelphia Wagon Road and into the Piedmont and southern Appalachians. Over time,

the two song threads were woven into a folk hymn tradition.

Religious or sacred singing drew upon two fundamental traditions: "psalmody," which was the singing of an established set of psalms prevalent in the eighteenth-century Protestant church and dating to the 1560s Geneva Psalter; and "hymnody," modeled on the psalms but branching into a wider variety of music. With psalmody, the Church of Scotland employed the 1650 metrical Psalter, whereby Presbyterian congregations sang biblical psalms to a restricted set of twelve tunes—the "Auld Twelve." Congregations remained seated while they sang, led by a "precentor," who was positioned on a small platform in front of the pulpit and would "give out the line." It was an old custom carried over to America as "lining out" and persisting today in a few churches in the southern United States and on Lewis in Outer Hebrides among the congregations of the Free Church of Scotland, a distinct Presbyterian denomination (the "Free Kirk" in Scots and "An Eaglais Shaor" in Gaelic). This plain ensemble singing of an exclusive psalmody consistent with Calvinism was devoid of harmonies or instrumental accompaniment. Since the Auld Twelve psalm melodies were predetermined, rhyming lyrics had to be invented at the singing schools held in homes or schoolhouses. Individuals would be called upon, in turn, to offer an original couplet. These would draw upon familiar narratives, such as journeys, dangerous exploits, or storms at sea. The relationship between psalm singing and balladry was a natural consequence that most likely led to a loosening of the constraints of psalmody and a move toward more varied hymn-singing styles.[26] Many of the Ulster Presbyterian immigrants and their churches did, nevertheless, make the Scottish Metrical Psalter their main songbook for many years in the Presbyterian Reformed tradition and took particular exception to the popular eighteenth-century hymns written by Anglican clergy.

Hymn singing, sometimes described as epic poems, represented a tradition harking back to me-

An Old Connection

Julee Glaub and Mark Weems, American singers, musicians, and tutors; interviewed in Dunkeld, Scotland, September 2008, by Fiona Ritchie during their visit to Ireland and Scotland.

Julee: It's wonderful to make the connection between Ireland, Scotland, and Appalachia, and I'm more familiar with the Irish side of things, so it's been great to see the connection between the dance, the music, [and] the traditional singing, especially because Mark and I love traditional singing in Scotland. Of course, we make the connection through Margaret Bennett's wonderful CD *Salm and Soul*, that for me was the first eye-opener when I listened to that and connected that with Primitive Baptist singing from areas where Mark and I have grown up. And deep connections of the music and singing, especially unaccompanied singing.

Mark: Coming up in Alabama, you hear a lot of country music, and as you get older and you start exploring, of course, then you find the roots, which are the old-time music and mountain music, and back to North Carolina in particular. The connections: a lot of our mountain ballads and Virginia-area ballads are coming, of course, from Scotland and Ireland—two-or-three-hundred-year-old ballads that are the same in all the traditions. They might have known that it came from across the pond somewhere, but they weren't sure any more than that. But I think now they're aware that it all has Celtic roots. Definitely.

Julee: Singers and musicians would [be aware of the music's roots]. The general person is not, and in a concert, I love seeing a light go on in people's eyes; it's amazing the connection between these two worlds. And often people say, "I have Scottish roots, I have Irish roots," and then they make the connection between North Carolina or Virginia; it's been wonderful for us to watch.

---

dieval times, where harps or lutes might provide accompaniment. The practice came to England with the Norman invasion and was established in sixteenth-century Scotland. During the Wesleyan Revival of mid-eighteenth-century England—the "First Great Awakening"—hymn writers Charles Wesley and Isaac Watts contributed singable hymns to the Anglicans but also to the Presbyterians and Quakers. The early nineteenth century saw a "Second Great Awakening" in the United States, and Wesleyan hymns added to an upsurge of sacred-music writing. This was especially marked through the Methodist and Baptist Churches, which at the time were more likely to adopt new hymns and instrumental accompaniment. However,

a fundamentalist movement found favor within many Baptist churches that sought to avoid any semblance of the Anglican "High Church" in worship rituals. They sought a return to the primitive worship of early Christianity and forbade both hymnbooks and instrumental accompaniment. Singing by ear alone was considered the purer way, not unlike the practice of some of the earlier Ulster Scots and Scottish Presbyterians.

So as settlers headed down the Great Philadelphia Wagon Road, collective sacred music traditions traveled alongside them. Colloquial hymns penetrated deeper into the countryside on their Wagon Road expedition. Methodist revivals, especially after the

American Revolution, contributed more sacred material. Some were published back in Pennsylvania in both German- and English-language hymnbooks.[27]

With each mile of the Wagon Road, the Presbyterian Scots-Irish moved a little farther from Pennsylvania's Presbyterian churches and seminaries. They soon became estranged from the Presbyterian hymnbook. In the remote mountain settings, provision of any formal schooling was problematic to say the least; if a person could read at all, he or she likely could not read music. The conditions were ripe for a new kind of unaccompanied religious harmony singing. Surfacing in the late eighteenth century, this new form emerged as "shape-note singing," also later named "sacred harp" (signifying the God-given human voice). Shape-note singing allowed people to sight-read sacred music without the support of instrumental accompaniment.

It originated in a four-shape system credited to John Connelly, a Philadelphia merchant of Scots-Irish ancestry. Rather than the standard round notes on a musical staff, each of the major scale's seven notes was converted to a geometric shape to represent the four "fa-sol-la-mi" notes on the scale. The notes were sung from the lowest pitch to the highest: "fa, sol, la, fa, sol, la, mi." The four shapes were a right-angled triangle, representing fa; a circle, sol; a square, la; and a diamond, mi. Whatever the key of a song, fa was always the tonic, or root, note. When congregations were learning a new song, they would first sing the shape names rather than the song lyrics. Shape-note singing has a distinctive harmony and rhythmic quality, producing an otherworldly, haunting sound, much in keeping with the modal feel of so many of the old Appalachian ballads.

A significant repertoire for the shape-note songs came from New England psalmody or the music of eighteenth-century composers who predated the adoption of a notation system. In 1835, however, South Carolina's William Walker (who became known as "Singin' Billy") published *The Southern Harmony and Musical Companion*, bringing widespread attention to shape-note singing throughout the antebellum South and beyond. Dozens of other songbooks contributed to the canon, but Walker's *Southern Harmony* was remarkable for its sales figures, which topped 600,000 copies.[28] Perhaps even more noteworthy, *Southern Harmony* contained the first printed version of one of the world's most enduring hymns: "Amazing Grace," the beloved anthem written by reformed slave-trading sea captain John Newton. Walker published the melody that is still sung internationally today. Scholars generally agree that this song derives from an old folk tune called "New Britain," which is possibly Scottish in origin.[29] In 1866 Walker published *The Christian Harmony*, a new shape-note hymnbook that now offered seven shapes based on the "do-re-mi-fa-so-la-ti" scale. Building on the four established shapes, it introduced an inverted keystone shape for do, a quarter moon for re, and an isosceles triangle shape for ti. To the present day, shape-note devotees are divided between those who favor the four-shape "fasola" system and those who prefer the "doremi" seven-shape method. Either way, shape-note singing has been a significant part of the Appalachian music tradition for the past two centuries, with a current resurgence of interest in its tune books, especially *The Sacred Harp* and *The Christian Harmony*. Workshops, camps, and other shape-note singing gatherings attract growing numbers of dedicated participants. In the north Georgia mountains near the Chattahoochee River and the Cherokee Trail, devotees of *The Sacred Harp* meet in Alpharetta City Hall, as they have done annually each June since 1869. A leader stands in the center of their groups, beating time while singers establish and interweave six har-

mony parts. This is not a performance; the singers meet to sing for enjoyment, worship, and the joy of singing for each other. The Alpharetta "June Singing of the Sacred Harp" welcomes newcomers, regardless of their religious affiliation or musical ability, to join in or simply enjoy listening to the powerful old songs.

A circuitous path must be followed to discover the true migratory routes of ballad and fiddle traditions, and so it is with the movement of sacred songs. From their early origins in the Presbyterian Church, they navigated the Atlantic with immigrants and were scattered along assorted pathways according to where people settled and how they chose to worship. Scots-Irish migrants conveyed the psalmody tradition, with its exclusive adherence to the Scottish Metrical Psalter, through western Pennsylvania and down the Great Philadelphia Wagon Road. An unimaginable expanse of wilderness and broad cultural spectrum lay before them, however, so it was inevitable that other influences would intervene: more singable music from the hymnody influences of the Methodist, Anglican, and Lutheran traditions; New England singing-school music migrating into the South; adapted old folk melodies such as Scotland's "Barbara Allen" (CD track 1); harmony singing; instrumental accompaniment; and—when they were obtainable—hymnbooks. In many ways, the evolutions of sacred song began to recapture much older traditions from medieval times, when stringed instruments such as the lute, harp, and lyre were used and harmony singing was not uncommon. In the pews of the humble churches that proliferated throughout the Appalachians and other backcountry areas, change was in the air. More than simply places of worship, these rural churches were social and cultural centers for the surrounding area. In post–Revolutionary War times, the more-progressive Presbyterian ministers introduced newer hymns and encouraged instrumental accompaniment, musical traditions that persist today as part of the larger Presbyterian Church U.S.A. Guarding the old rituals, a

Spirit of the Song

Julee Glaub, American singer, flute player, and tutor; interviewed in Dunkeld, Scotland, September 2008, by Fiona Ritchie during her visit (with Mark Weems) to Ireland and Scotland.

I think, for me, it's all about phrasing. When I lived in Ireland, as much as listening to a singer, I would listen to an air [melody] player on the pipes or the fiddle or flute. How you hold a note, how you hold a word. Ornamentation, especially specifically Irish ornamentation, would be similar to the pipes, similar to the grace notes on a flute, and that would be very similar in a singing voice. And in Appalachian styles, says Jean Ritchie—and I spoke with her this summer about this—what's the main difference between an Irish song and an Appalachian song? And she said, well you go up at the end! And that would be very common, but also maybe the notes would go, you know, a swing up three notes, rather than an Irish ornament, which would be more of a grace note.

That's what traditional music that I know is about, in the mountains of North Carolina, sitting on front porches, watching the John Cohen films that have been so invaluable to learning about all the ballad singers. When you look at what the cultures were about, they were about getting together and singing a song, and that's what I learned in Ireland, sort of stepping away from the song and letting the song flow through me to people as a gift, rather than a time to say that it's about me; it's about a song and it's about a history. It's about a culture, it's about a place, especially in Ireland and Scotland, where the songs are about a connection to the land or a connection to your family.

We don't want the art of traditional singing to be lost, and the habit of it, the culture of it, because when people come together to sing, I believe powerful things happen, young and old gathering together. And it's about being together, about community, about singing, and when all those are in line, that is a beautiful thing.

more-conservative branch, the Associated Reformed Presbyterian Church, located primarily in the South, excluded nonbiblical hymns, adhering to the old Scottish Psalter.

The currents of America's sacred music stream began intermingling—old spirituals, black gospel, jubilee songs, southern gospel (which included northern influences), shape-note singing, and Anglo-American hymnody in general. These rich musical flavors, individually strong and frequently brewed together, helped give birth to the new musical forms of blues, rhythm and blues, rock and roll, and country music as the twentieth century unfolded.

APPALACHIAN MUSIC
A Tapestry

Songs and fiddle tunes of the Scots-Irish emigrants undoubtedly formed the bedrock of Appalachian music. Auxiliary influences were numerous, however, creating a sound tapestry of varied textures and tones. When the nineteenth century dawned, Appalachian music was already woven from a rich repertoire of a capella ballads, sacred music, fiddle tunes, banjo playing, and dances. Each element itself represented a comingling of influences and styles. The people who had emigrated from Scotland to Ulster and onward to America had already

demonstrated a readiness to negotiate boundaries, and so it was with their music. The growing circle of songs and tunes was unrestricted; other styles were always able to breach the circumference and nudge the circle this way and that. It is true that remote communities and traditional cultures do not always welcome change, but the perpetual movement of the Scots-Irish wayfarers allowed them to "gather up everything in their path," in the words of *Ballad Tree* author Evelyn Kendrick Wells.[30] Perhaps that is Pete Seeger's message when he said that "songs are sneaky things, they pay no attention to borders."[31] Scots songwriter, singer, and multi-instrumentalist Brian McNeill makes a similar point: "I've never seen a good tune that bothered with boundaries. . . . I will take my influences wherever I can find them."[32]

To the questions of where and when fusions were forged along music's migratory trail, there is but one simple answer: everywhere. It occurred around the cottage hearths of Aberdeenshire; in the ceili houses of Ulster; below deck on the Atlantic swell; in port town taverns and backcountry farmsteads of Pennsylvania; on the long and winding Great Wagon and Wilderness Roads; and amid the coves and cabins of the southern Appalachians. New varieties proliferated

How the Music Changed in America

David Holt, American multi-instrumentalist, singer, and collector; interviewed in Swannanoa, North Carolina, July 2009, by Fiona Ritchie and Doug Orr at the Swannanoa Gathering folk arts workshops.

It changed to a breakdown: it's less of a lilt and more of a breakdown, and that drives it along harder, and the dancing [has] more emphasis on the 2 and the 4 beat. I think the fiddle and the banjo together added a lot more of the bluesy sounds that were not from Europe. You know, just the flatted third is so important around here, on just about any tune, like "Cotton Eyed Joe," or any of these old tunes—you hear that all the time in these tunes. And that was definitely an American kind of a thing. You know, the influence of black people had a huge impact on the dancing and the music—on the rhythm of the music.

Tapestry woven by Barbara Grinnell. (Photograph by Darcy Orr; collection of Darcy and Doug Orr)

Detail of tapestry woven by Barbara Grinnell. (Photograph by Darcy Orr; collection of Darcy and Doug Orr)

from hill to hollow, and it has been said that "there are as many banjo styles as hollers." The music evolved through an egalitarian process of inclusion. The core Scots-Irish tradition from the glens of Ulster cross-pollinated with cultural gleanings from the English, Scottish, Irish, German, Welsh, Scandinavian, native Cherokee, and, of particular note, the African American community, many members of which contributed richly while suffering a life of bondage. The examples of comingling were many: the banjo, imported and adapted from Africa, injecting a syncopated and rhythmic drive to fiddle playing; the German scheitholt as an antecedent to the Appalachian dulcimer; English, Welsh, and Scandinavian influences entering the song tradition along a much older branch of the ballad tree; Cherokee flutes, whistles, percussion instruments, and Cherokee fiddle playing—learned from the white settlers—which turned around to influence white fiddling styles. This was recorded in the early nineteenth century by British army officer Major John Norton, who visited Cherokee towns in western North Carolina and found many young fiddlers in the tribal communities who were also dancing reels. So the traditions began to merge and flow in both directions.[33]

Graham County, North Carolina, sits up near the Tennessee border. In the community of Snowbird are the descendants of Cherokee who managed to evade the 1838 forced removal of their people on the notorious Trail of Tears. The tribal members of Snowbird have quietly maintained unique mountain song and dance styles, where two Old World traditions have met and mingled. In the ceremonial Cherokee songs, sung in wide circles with traditional drums and percussion, it is easy to see where some of the big-circle dances of the mountain square-dance tradition may have originated.[34] Alfred and Maybelle Welch teach the language of their ancestors and continue a Cherokee hymn-singing tradition, dating from the nineteenth century, when *The Sacred Harp* and *The Christian Harmony* were embraced by their community.[35] In Snowbird's Fading Voices Festival, shape-note and gospel Chero-

kee song ring around the hillsides, giving no indication that they ever intend to fade.[36]

Meanwhile, the Appalachian fiddle repertoire avidly absorbed such tunes as Scotland's "Lord MacDonald's Reel," becoming "Leather Britches" and "Cotton Eyed Joe" from the Irish tune "The Mountain Top." The most popular Appalachian ballads reached down into the deepest Ulster Scots roots: "Pretty Polly," "Gypsy Davy," and "Jack Went A-Sailing." Others, such as

FOREST FOLK AND SCOTO-INDIANS

During the time of the Highland Clearances, from 1762 and continuing through the nineteenth century, many thousands of Highland Scots were forcibly driven from their homes, resulting in mass emigration. There are some parallels with the brutality of the Indian removal policies in the United States, which culminated in the 1830s. Both eras created dispossessed and disenfranchised people on each side of the Atlantic. However, there are also cultural similarities between Native Americans and Gaelic-speaking Highland Scots: both lived in clan groups accustomed to tribal warfare and a long struggle to repel English-speaking aggressors; the heads of both tribal societies were chiefs, traditionally appointed through family lineage, although later by election in Native American societies; land was a commonly held resource with a sense also of communal well-being; lives were lived by the turn of the seasons; and bards were important in both societies, whose traditions were passed down orally through families. In the turbulent times of the nineteenth century, Gaels and Native Americans shared another unwelcome distinction: they were both considered cultures on the edge of extinction.

Highland Scots felt attuned to Native Americans when they interacted in colonial America, and the Gaels called the native people of the Appalachians the "Coilltich" or the "Forest Folk." In 1733 British general James Oglethorpe, founder of the colony of Georgia, encouraged a group of around 100 Scots Highlanders from the Inverness area to settle in Georgia. His motivation was identical to that of King James with the Ulster plantations: Oglethorpe wanted to create a Presbyterian buffer against the Catholic influence of Spanish Florida. In 1742 Captain John Mohr Mackintosh of this group, a direct descendant of his clan chief, raised and commanded a volunteer contingent of Highlanders and Muscogee (Creek) and Tsalagi (Cherokee) men to defeat a Spanish invasion at the Battles of Gully Hole Creek and Bloody Marsh. The clansmen thrived, and within a few years, they were heavily involved in trade among the Creek Nation. Cloth for kilts was especially sought after, and the traditional Highland wear closely resembled the breechcloth garments worn by Creek men. The Scots traders influenced the attire of Creeks and Seminoles, selling turban-like headgear to Muscogulge warriors, who added feathers to complete their look.

Following the 1715 Jacobite Rising, two MacGillivray brothers were among many Scots banished to the Carolinas. Lachlan MacGillivray married a Creek woman, and their son, Alexander MacGillivray, became an influential Creek leader, negotiating with the British, Spanish, and Americans on behalf of his Creek homelands. He visited George Washington to lobby for the Creek Nation to join the new American Union as a discrete ethnic state. MacGillivray managed to forge an alliance between the tribes of the Southeast that lasted until his death, in an attempt to hold off continued American infiltration into their lands. The names McGillivray, McPherson, and McIntosh remained prominent through Creek history; all are Scottish names connected with the geographical region of Inverness in Scotland that fed Oglethorpe's "plantation." Today, many Cherokee and Creek surnames hark back to Scottish ancestry. Waldo Emerson "Dode" McIntosh (1893–1991), chief of the Creek Nation from 1961 to 1971, was descended from Creek and Clan Mackintosh tribal chiefs. He often attended Highland Games wearing a combination of full Creek and Highland regalia, and in 1964 he was welcomed to the Clan Mackintosh gathering in Scotland.

The collision of European incomers with southern tribes set in motion a protracted and distressing chronicle of warfare, smallpox epidemics, and broken treaties, changing forever the fate of indigenous people. Some of the incomers were targets for attack; however, many early settlers in the southern Appalachians were involved in cultural exchange with Cherokee people. They hatched a vibrant Native American fiddle tradition and swapped dance styles. Intermarriage was common and trade enthusiastically pursued.

The most active traders with southern tribes were predominantly Scottish, and many married into indigenous families. The most famous Scoto-Indian was John Ross (1790–1866), principal chief of the Cherokee nation of the southern Appalachian Mountains from 1828 to 1866. Ross's father was Scots and his mother was of mixed Scots-Cherokee ancestry, so he grew up bilingual and bicultural: Scottish and Cherokee Bird Clan. He was also known as "Guwisguwi," or "rare migratory bird" in Cherokee. John Ross traveled to Washington, D.C., as part of a delegation concerned with Cherokee land rights. With his fluent English, he emerged as spokesman for the group. In 1824 he petitioned Congress to address the mounting grievances of the Cherokee Nation and began to build political support in the Capitol. It was the beginning of a long battle to halt the momentum behind Cherokee displacement. Following the Indian Removal Act of 1830, however, it was decreed that the Native peoples of the Southeast would have to leave their lands in a tragic episode known as "Nvna Daula Tsvyi," or the Trail of Tears. The Choctaw were the first to be removed in 1831, followed by the Seminole in 1832, the Creek in 1834, the Chickasaw in 1837, and finally the Cherokee in 1838. The U.S. Army was dispatched to evict forcibly those Cherokees who did not depart from their Appalachian homelands for eastern areas of present-day Oklahoma. A quarter of those forced to migrate, including Ross's full-blood wife, Quatie, died along the trail of exposure, disease, and starvation. (A minority managed to stay in western North Carolina, southeastern Tennessee, and north Georgia by hiding, through their mixed-race ethnicity, or by marriage to white men.) Ross was the first elected leader of the Cherokee and was repeatedly reelected as principal chief until his death in 1866, remaining popular among both full- and mixed-blood Cherokee. Through all the turmoil of his life and his passionate advocacy for Native Americans, he never forgot his Scottish roots. When, in 1847, he learned of an appeal in Philadelphia to send aid to the famine-afflicted Highlands, he wrote a letter to the *Cherokee Advocate* urging the tribe to assist. As a result, the Cherokee of Oklahoma sent $190 to Scotland for famine relief.

As for the Scots-Irish—themselves displaced and migratory over generations—they, in turn, encroached into native lands in the southern Appalachians. They also gained sustenance skills from the Cherokee, circle dance moves and other steps to blend with their own musical traditions, and sometimes life partners. Whether they felt empathy as the Cherokee were deported from their ancestral homelands, we can only imagine. Meanwhile, all around them, the eternal tale of the Tsalagi flowed on through the waters of the Tuckasegee, Chattahoochee, and Nantahala Rivers and through the veins of many of their descendants.

The African Influence

John Cohen, American string-band musician, song collector, photographer, and filmmaker; interviewed in Swannanoa, North Carolina, July 2008, by Fiona Ritchie and Doug Orr during Traditional Song Week at the Swannanoa Gathering folk arts workshops.

A wonderful woman named Joyce Cauthen, from Alabama, gave a talk at a folklore meeting about the disappearance of black fiddlers. At first, you have to say, were there black fiddlers? And apparently from the Civil War on, there were hundreds of black string bands. And there's some photographs of them, no recordings, obviously, of banjo, fiddle, guitar—mostly banjo and fiddle—black musicians. And they were going until the 1920s, and when the record companies suddenly realized there's a hillbilly market, and a blues market, they made two different catalogues for marketing purposes: Race Records and Hillbilly Records. If you didn't fit into one, then there was no place for you. So all the black musicians, who played what we call "banjo fiddle music," didn't get recorded. There was no reinforcement—end of a tradition. And the point that I'm making here is that the commercial tradition of marketing is what made the separation.

In 1952 . . . suddenly you're hearing on commercial records what would be considered, you know, traditional songs. And that was the vehicle that allowed me to really get into it, to perform it. Why did this music hit me so hard? Where did this song come from? How did he play it? How did the banjo get to be played that way? And it's been . . . just fifty years of continually asking . . . more than fifty years, sixty years now actually, just finding out more. And it's wonderful, at this stage of the game, there's still more to find out.

In recent years, they've been finding more and more that the source of the banjo was in Africa,

---

"Rain and Snow," were patched together from a scattering of ballad fragments from both sides of the Atlantic.

Migrating ballads and tunes usually maintained some sense of their basic form; however, the oral tradition, by its very nature, was impartial to the forces of change. Ulster fiddler and author David Cooper notes the outcome of a "conjoining principle" whereby "related tunes and songs may have both common and differing sections."[37] So the musical forms were not static; they migrated with the settlers and had a great capacity for reinterpretation and adaptation. Traditional fiddlers might not play a tune exactly the same way twice. In fact, it was often said of the late east Ten-

nessee long-bow fiddler Ralph Blizard, known for his improvisations with slide and blues notes, that "Ralph never played the same tune the same way *once!*"

THE AFRICAN AMERICAN INFLUENCES

The tapestry that became Appalachian music had incorporated multiple strands since the Scots-Irish immigrants first arrived. Arguably, none has been more underestimated and misunderstood than the contributions of African Americans. Their achievements in the creation of blues and jazz are rightly acclaimed and have been far more often emphasized. Today's West African nations of Guinea, Ghana, Senegal, Gambia,

and places in Africa where people still play the banjo today (or whatever they call it), using that down stroke, frailing style. And it's really a thrill. Like in Mali, they had some of the Malian musicians come over to the [Smithsonian Folklife Festival in 2003]. Well, I couldn't believe it. I'm seeing this guy singing, wonderful singing, but his hand is moving just like my hand. And that's a great communication. So now I'm totally convinced the idea of a thumb string and the hand moving down is definitely accurate. And yet I first heard of it, you know, as an Appalachian style. . . . I know also there's a whole body of northern tunes, they're closer to Scots and Scots-Irish, but then I imagined, you know, or I conceived of, somebody with that tradition playing a fiddle tune and maybe the wealthy people would like to hear it played that way. But then maybe somebody who played the banjo would try to do what the fiddle was doing, but he only had this tool, which was, you know, thumb and a hooked hand, and so he'd have to have a different kind of rhythm to catch, to describe the melody that the fiddler was doing. The fiddler was moving his arm long, back and forth, and doing a lot of little finger work, but this . . . the banjo player had his right hand jumping around playing this boom-tiddy-boom-tiddy rhythm. And so then you could take the fiddle tunes and work them out on the banjo. Now this is a kind of exciting sound. But the fiddler, if he wanted to play with it, couldn't do those long bow things any more, he'd have to start jiggling the bow. Playing with your wrist loose . . . each changes the other. And so that's how that sounded: boom-chicka-boom-chicka-boom. It's that rhythm which is strangely the unique American thing which is a combination of that Irish, Scots, and English tradition meeting the African tradition. African tradition is so underestimated, I think, in this music, including the dance. There's significant influences from African Americans on square dancing. They were often the band for the dances in these mountains, came up from Charleston, [South Carolina].

and Mali were the primary homelands of the slaves whose musical traditions could not be silenced, even by the trauma of their transatlantic crossings. It is generally known that the prototype of the American banjo was a gourd-shaped West African instrument called the "ngoni" among other names. It had a long pole neck attached to a gourd and three or four strings of horsehair, hemp, or catgut.[38] Thomas Jefferson's essay on the state of Virginia included his frequently quoted observation of newly arrived slaves: "The instrument proper to them is the banjar, which they brought hither from Africa."[39] As the banjo, this instrument would shape the sound of Appalachia. Paired with the fiddle, it became a mainstay of old-time music.

Other West African musical influences arrived early and endure to this day. Slaves depended upon group singing for secular restitution and spiritual expression, as well as for call and response, field holler, and work songs. These traditions poured into a rich reservoir of spirituals and their descendants, creating today's African American gospel songs. Drumming came over from the tribal communities of West Africa, as did storytellers—called "griots"—whose role was to reinforce the history, traditions, and stories of village members.

By the middle of the eighteenth century, African American musical influences, including the banjo, were commonplace east of the Appalachians. Blacks

played their "banjars," incorporating a flat-necked gourd shape, a skin head, a short thumb string, and, in time, tuning pegs. Banjo players would play melody and rhythm and also accompany songs. The plantations of the coastal areas, where slave labor was concentrated, were fertile ground for African American musical traditions. Banjo, fiddle playing, work songs, and spirituals all thrived there. By the early nineteenth century, there was a black banjo presence on the Appalachian frontier, and white fiddlers encountered African American banjo players. A reciprocal "short loop" saw influences working in both directions between blacks and whites. African Americans would hear white fiddlers play at the plantation house, imitate what they learned on their own instruments, and return the tunes, now more syncopated and rhythmic, back to whites. The sharing circuit was complete. Black fiddling also developed a bluesy and improvisational edge that had lasting impact on Appalachian fiddle styles. African Americans learned fiddle techniques from the white musicians, but they also had their own take on the music. Plantation owners were known to enter black slave fiddlers into contests, and they were much in demand for white dances. It has been estimated that by the time George Washington was elected as the first president of the United States in 1789, over half of the fiddlers in the South were African American.[40]

The same cycle of influence occurred with the banjo. The Scots-Irish musicians who had adopted the instrument were, by the mid-nineteenth century, working with the African American strumming style known as thumping. Thus was born the iconic Appalachian clawhammer banjo technique. Meanwhile, the banjo structure had evolved from its gourd-bodied beginnings into the wood-rimmed, open-back, five-string instrument used today. By the end of the century, there were both black and white fiddle-banjo duos, though none was integrated. Entire black string bands had formed, usually to perform for white dances but also for African American dance gatherings called

Music for the Dance; photogravure by A. B. Frost, 1891.
(Courtesy of Marshall Wyatt at Old Hat Records)

"frolics." It was not uncommon for black string bands from Charleston, South Carolina, to be invited to the mountains to play for square dances, usually accompanied by a black dance caller. In addition to the indispensible fiddle and banjo, bands were rounded out with tambourines, bones, and other percussive instruments, such as pots and pans. Drums were even included in the mix. This was something of a breakthrough; drums were strictly forbidden during the plantation era for fear the drumming might provoke slave uprisings.

The impact of African American singing on American music has been universal. In the Appalachian example, the mountain song tradition absorbed and adapted African American spirituals and jubilee songs. Czech composer Antonín Dvořák observed the African American cultural connection with the Scots-Irish while studying American folk music and its roots during a late nineteenth-century visit to the United States: "The so-called plantation melodies of the South, with their unusual and subtle harmonies, bore a striking resemblance to the indigenous music of Scotland and Ireland."[41] When African American spiritual singing spilled over from plantations, it flowed throughout other regions, including the Appalachians. The plantation owners were intent on "de-Africanizing" their slaves, prohibiting any religious practice except Christianity. For their part, the slaves identified with biblical stories of other exiled peoples held in bondage, such as the Jews in Babylon. They did manage to conduct clandestine services, or camp meetings, in which they could reconnect with their tribal birthrights of drum-

African and European Roots of Old-Time Music

Mike Seeger (1933–2009), American folklorist, multi-instrumentalist, and traditional roots-music preservationist, Lexington, Virginia; recorded on June 5, 2009, in conversation with Banning Eyre for BBC Radio 3's World Routes, *produced by Peter Meanwell. "An Appalachian Road Trip" was first broadcast on October 17, 2009.*

I think it's really the mixture of African and European cultures that have made American music "American." A lot of the tunes that are played as old-time fiddle tunes—there's no predecessor that has been documented in the Old Country, and so they survive here, or they were created here. And if they are new tunes based on older ones, then they are the continuation of traditions that did exist, and that kind of sound existed.

I've learned most of what I know about the history of the banjo in the past fifteen or twenty years—coming over from Africa as a gourd instrument with a skin stretched across the top of it and whatever you could find for strings, and then being developed probably in the early nineteenth century as a drum-type instrument with a neck on it. And then becoming a popular instrument because people wanted to teach it, people wanted to manufacture it. The entrepreneurial end of things definitely changed the banjo in the late nineteenth century. It's commonly thought that today's clawhammer banjo playing has its roots in African playing. In fact, people even into the mid-twentieth century called that the "African style"—if they were being polite—and it's knocking down on the string rather than picking up—as you pick up on a guitar, for instance, to strike a note.

To go back to "what is old-time music?" [and] trying to figure out how the string band developed: the fiddle [coming] from Europe and the banjo, as we have learned to think about it, coming from Africa (and there may have been African fiddles too) . . . to this country and being played for the entertainment of whomever. Eventually, you have those two traditions influencing one another—sometimes—and staying the same at other times, depending on who was doing the playing. So you had fiddle and banjo music, and you had the vocal music from both sides, and you had the cultural ideas from both sides; and those were mixing in some cases and not mixing in some cases. And by the mid-nineteenth century, it entered in with the theatrical traditions through the minstrel music, and that complicated the mix. And after emancipation, there was a different kind of mixing, because no longer was it a strictly slave situation that most black people found themselves in. And eventually, in about 1900 and after, depending on where you lived in the South, the guitar joined in, and other instruments. Actually, there are photos of fiddle, banjo, bones, string bass, or a cello—there are all kinds of mixtures in the mid-nineteenth century of instruments. But what we think of as "old-time music" now in the mountains is banjo, fiddle, and guitar, but that's really a combination that didn't exist much until the early twentieth century.

ming and dancing. Yet in creating spirituals expressing their sorrows and aspirations—songs of hope echoing their African spirituality—they drew upon Christian ideals from biblical teachings. The African American spiritual leaders and ministers would convey passionate emotions in leading their services, drawing answers from the congregation in the call-and-response tradition of their African ancestry. Evolving into a verse and refrain style, the pattern translated naturally into the outdoor settings of plantation fields. Work songs with rhythmic cadences and resonant refrains eased the drudgery of grueling and repetitive labor and engendered a spirit of shared toil and triumph. Hand clapping and foot stomping worked well in the absence of drumming. An offbeat syncopated rhythm was a hallmark of the style, and this eased its way into the fiddle playing. As spirituals evoked a mournful, modal sound, blues notes slid into the vocal music, lowering the pitch on selected notes on the scale.

What did their spirituals call for if not a release from enslavement and a flight to freedom? Yet these were the very pleas that could not be cried aloud from the depths of exertion on the plantation. So code words were embedded in the songs, especially those relating to the Underground Railroad, which could guide their brothers and sisters to freedom in the north. The language of song was rich with symbols: "Canaan's Land" (Ohio and Canada), "Swing Low Sweet Chariot" (the railroad train to freedom), "River of Jordan" (the Ohio River), and "Follow the Drinking Gourd" (the constellation of the Big Dipper, pointing toward the North Star and freedom). The plantation owners and their foremen were generally oblivious to these double meanings, which must have made singing the songs all the more satisfying.

While slaveholding in the mountains was much less common than in the eastern coastal plantation areas of the South, the Appalachians provided a pathway in the slave's escape to freedom. One of the major Underground Railroad routes was the New River, with its headwaters in the northwest mountains of North Carolina and its meandering northward course through Virginia and West Virginia toward eventual confluence with the Ohio River. Mount Jefferson, in North Carolina's Ashe County, has a distinctive profile that rises sharply above the New River. This landmark was a strategic beacon, guiding runaway slaves to their freedom.

The slaves also heard songs from the slave owners and applied their own rhythm, syncopation, and wording. When they heard "Cotton Eyed Joe," a popular old-time song with melodic roots in Ireland still played today at Appalachian fiddlers' conventions, they gave it a lyric adaptation of their own:

> She was the prettiest gal to be found, anywhar in
>   th' country round;
> Her lips was red an' eyes was bright, her skin was
>   black but her teeth was white.
> I'd been married forty year ago, if it hadn'ta been
>   for Cotton Eyed Joe.
> Whar d'you come from whar d'you go, whar
>   d'you come from Cotton Eyed Joe.

The African American lullabies or "hush songs" also migrated from the plantations and became popular among families, both black and white, from the coastal plain to the mountains. One of these is the sweet but poignant "All the Pretty Little Horses," written and sung by a slave woman who had to leave her own baby in the field while she cared for the white children in the Big House. Collected by songcatchers such as the Lomaxes and Dorothy Scarborough, it entered the American folk music repertoire to be recorded by many artists through the years, including Odetta, Joan Baez, and Peter, Paul and Mary, even crossing over into the Celtic harp repertoire with Kim Robertson:

> In the meadow far away,
> Lies my poor little baby.
> Bees and butterflies are picking at his eyes,
> My poor little baby's crying "mammy."

LIBBA
COTTON
CHAPEL HILL, NORTH CARO

Hush-a-by, don't you cry,
Go to sleep little baby.
When you wake, you shall have cake,
And all the pretty little horses.

Before and after the Civil War, African Americans also participated in shape-note singing, often at camp meetings. Many African Americans in the Appalachians have used a version of *The Sacred Harp* and have been drawn especially to the "New Book" (seven-shape method), forming singing sessions to support their interest.[42]

Spiritual and shape-note singing inspired gospel music, and this entered both black and white singing traditions during the twentieth century. Appalachian regions such as Jefferson County, Alabama, and upstate South Carolina produced prominent black gospel singing groups such as the Blind Boys of Alabama, the Famous Blue Jay Singers, and the Dixie Hummingbirds. The Swan Silvertones spent their earlier years in Coalwood, West Virginia. Many of the black gospel groups in the Appalachians and elsewhere were affiliated with individual or multiple churches rooted in the African American spiritual tradition.

The 1830s and 1840s marked a turning point in the African American connection to Appalachian music, specifically in their historic identification with the banjo. This decade saw the emergence of the era of blackface minstrelsy in the United States—music shows featuring white performers in blackface makeup pretending to be black, performing their version of black music, and speaking in exaggerated black dialect. Blackface minstrelsy became outrageously popular in America and Britain during subsequent decades and was a standard act in the average vaudeville program. At the same time, it created and perpetuated a caricature of African Americans. They distanced themselves from the minstrel-show format and disowned the banjo, the very instrument they had bequeathed to the Appalachians and America at large. When guitars became accessible and affordable through mail order in the early twentieth century, blacks adopted the instrument with ease. A profound black blues tradition was born, initially delivered by solo artists exhibiting their own guitar virtuosity and later grouped with other instrumentalists in acoustic and, eventually, electric blues. White banjo makers in the twentieth century deemphasized the black banjo heritage as they sought to market their wares to a more-affluent white market.

The Fisk Jubilee Singers provided a stark and refreshing contrast to minstrels of the blackface genre. Formed in 1871, this African American a capella group involved students from Fisk University of Nashville, Tennessee. Many of the parents of Fisk singers were recently freed slaves, so the name "jubilee" was fitting. Their early repertoire consisted of the old black spirituals, but they later added a variety of folk songs, including those of Stephen Foster, whose great-grandfather had sailed from the Ulster port of Derry-Londonderry to America around 1728. Tours by the Fisk Jubilee Singers have included following the route of the old Underground Railroad and European appearances. They maintain their proud heritage today, and in 2008 they were the recipients of the National Medal of Arts.

In recent years, the banjo has experienced a revival within the African American community, facilitated by the creation of the Black Banjo Gathering. The original concept was born in an Internet discussion group of black and white banjo enthusiasts. The idea soon evolved into a symposium celebrating the banjo's African origins and customs, and a broad discussion progressed to consider the banjo's future role in traditional and folk music communities. Professor Cecelia Conway and her colleagues in the Appalachian Studies Department at Appalachian State University helped launch the program in 2005 with a series of Black Banjo Gathering reunion concerts. Momentum has gathered in the years since and has involved black banjo and string musicians such as the Ebony Hillbillies, Tony Thomas (founder of the online group

An African American Tapestry

Rhiannon Giddens and Dom Flemons, founding members of traditional African American string band the Carolina Chocolate Drops; interviewed in Asheville, North Carolina, December 2013, by Doug Orr before a performance of the Carolina Chocolate Drops.

Rhiannon: Well, we had a very musical family, singing with my sisters and my dad. My mom exposed me to a lot of other music, and I've always been interested in Celtic history. I didn't get into music so much when I was a kid, but pursued the history because of my name, which my mom selected when reading a book on Welsh mythology. When I was going to college to study opera, I wanted to take a little break and figure out my directions. I auditioned and joined a Celtic band Gaelwynd, which stimulated my interest in learning more about Irish and Scottish music, especially more Scottish stuff because of the Scots-oriented fiddler in the band. That eventually led to my involvement in Gaelic singing when I attended the Grandfather Mountain Highland Games for the fiddle competition. The music is gorgeous, and while still in the band, I went to the Black Banjo Gathering in 2005—that's where I met Dom—and I had already met fiddler Joe Thompson. And you know, life sometimes takes over, so I was with them again at the Swannanoa Gathering, and also met Justin Robinson there. Justin was living in Chapel Hill, I had moved to Durham from Richmond, and Dom [had moved] from Arizona to the Triangle area [in North Carolina], and the three of us started going to see Joe every Thursday night because he always needed a banjo player. It was just learning his music, kinda getting to know him, and he was always open and welcoming to anyone to join him, and willing to learn. I already was learning the old-time clawhammer style, at the Swannanoa Gathering especially, which developed for me during those Thursday night sessions of the four of us. And that eventually led to the formation of our band the Carolina Chocolate Drops. But Joe was always an inspiration, even during those evenings when we were dead tired and didn't know if we were up to making music.

Dom: Growing up, I became interested in the protest songs of the '60s and many of the artists from that time—Jean Ritchie, Tom Paxton, Doc Watson, Mississippi John Hurt, Muddy Waters, Howlin' Wolf—and from there it got me into people like Jimmie Rodgers and Hank Williams. All of that led me to the guitar, harmonica, and banjo. I listened to the Newport Folk Festival recordings and pretty soon discovered the old-time music sounds of Uncle Dave Macon and Charlie Poole. When I heard Mike Seeger's album *Old Time Country Music*, it really opened my eyes for taking different pieces of traditional music and putting them together. And then the Black Banjo Gathering happened, where I happened to meet Mike, and he was one of those to knock me over the edge as to where I wanted to go . . . yeah, he was over there. And he inspired me to pick up the jug instrument, so I would go around to festivals with my jug, harmonica, banjo, and guitar. The funny thing, there were so-called jug bands around at the time, but no jugs. They were doing the jug band repertoire but without jugs, so that was one of the things I was trying to bring in, with Mike Seeger as encouragement.

Rhiannon: Yes, there was a time when the banjo was rejected in the black community as a result of the black-faced minstrelsy era, but then there is the passage of time. Only it's not just the element of time, it is also experience and what you go through in life. We're one of the first generations in the black community—not all of us, but a large percentage of us—that have not had to deal with the horrible things of previous generations. And to be able to look back to the past without a visceral, emotional reaction I think is pretty important. Those generations were fighting for so much. Then we could come along and have the ability to look back and to draw upon those things from our heritage, and say this stuff is really important, and yet we could look at it in sort of a detached and objective way. That you guys went through so much and we owe it to you to preserve the legacy.

Dom: And I think it is important for people to be educated to understand that American music is a complicated tapestry, to realize that they can work on top of other people's work, and make connections that those earlier folks didn't make. So much of our work with the Carolina Chocolate Drops has been in drawing upon scholarly research, the hard work of collectors and field recordings, and to connect things that have been running in parallels. For me, it is all about connecting early country, blues, and jazz with the early songsters that were pre-blues with the string-band music. Then Rhiannon brought in some of the Celtic sounds and traditions that connect as well.

Rhiannon: I do want to say something that is super important in this kind of work, when you are making connections from the Celtic to old-time and all the rest. It takes everybody doing their job. It takes people undertaking the research. We are kind of amateur researchers, but it takes people working at this all the time, who track down the primary sources, make sure it is all right and publish the books. There are the people who are interpreting the historic connections, and we are interpreting music in a certain way when we put it onstage. And there are those who are consuming the music, supporting it and sometimes passing it on. It takes cooperation within an entire population, and so our albums are simply one piece of the whole and no more or less important than your and Fiona's book and the works of so many others.

Black Banjo Then and Now), Cheick Hamala Diabate (from Mali and renowned for playing the ngoni or stringed lute, the ancestor of the banjo), and others.

It was at the Black Banjo Gathering that the Carolina Chocolate Drops were born, possibly the first new black string-band lineup in eighty years. The three young African American musicians met each other and their mentor, the late black fiddler Joe Thompson, at the gathering and formed their sound around his Carolina Piedmont repertoire. The original trio of Rhiannon Giddens, Dom Flemons, and Justin Robinson formed essentially as an old-time jug band, but their performances—which feature the band members swapping their banjo, fiddle, guitar, harmonica, snare drum, bones, jug, and kazoo back and forth—have been described as a medicine show, a vaudeville act, and a contemporary folk performance all rolled into one. They frequently perform with guest roots and acoustic artists, and, most significantly, they have helped revive an old African American banjo tradition that was fast disappearing. Rhiannon Giddens, a graduate of the Berklee College of Music, traveled to Gambia to unearth the roots of the banjo. The Carolina Chocolate Drops have become enormously popular on the festival circuit and developed an ardent following on both sides of the Atlantic, and in 2011 they won a Grammy for Best Traditional Folk Album. They have awakened an interest in the old traditions among young audiences, both black and white. Along with the musicians of the Black Banjo Gatherings and bands like the Ebony Hillbillies, they have bestowed a gift of special importance: the restoration of the legitimacy and dignity of the banjo among many in the African American community. Scars can heal in the passing of generations, and the Chocolate Drops made the point that they share an ability to remain "emotionally detached" from the old blackface minstrelsy parodies. Their disinterest in revisiting the uncomfortable aspects of that era has not diluted a passionate involvement in its music, and their vintage jug-band sound has vigorously advanced its cause.

African American String Bands

Joe Thompson, African American fiddler, Mebane, North Carolina; recorded on June 5, 2009, in conversation with Banning Eyre for BBC Radio 3's World Routes, *produced by Peter Meanwell. "An Appalachian Road Trip" was first broadcast on October 17, 2009.*

My daddy—I picked up a whole lot of tunes [from him]. They come from way back in the olden days. He did same as I did . . . he [played for] a whole lot of white folks dancing. That's how he got started, him and Uncle Jake. Playin' for the white folks: "Georgia Buck," "John Henry." They [the tunes] come from around here, and the most thing I would like to tell you: Roxboro, Person County [in North Carolina], all back down in that area. That's where my daddy and his brother came from. It's local music from way back like when my daddy was young. 1879, that's when my daddy was born, and his daddy, Bob Thompson, was born before the Civil War. That man could play that fiddle.

My older brother [Nate]—fiddle and banjo was all they needed. You can get that power! Folk out [dancing], they got their girl, want to cut up a little bit, and he done had a drink or two, and he's jumping up and a girl . . . and they going the way around, cut up, promenading all the way around, and he [Nate] want to jump up. And I seen him do it too, yessiree! Nate, he was picking [banjo] like he pick a guitar, and my daddy said, "Boy you aint gonna get to do that!," he said, "These folk [Nate and cousin Odell] are dancing too much, and these folks are cutting up!" We were playin' for the white folks a lot then, too, y'know. You gotta play that stuff when your playin' for them, y'know. White folk called it square dancing, black folk called it frolicking—only difference.

Somebody said to me, "You're ninety year old, you've been here a long time." I've been hearing this stuff all my life, but you see, "Jesus got a cross, goin' let the world go free, there is a cross for everyone, and there is a cross for me"; he said; "There is a cross for Jesus, and there is a cross for me." So you might want to get ready. Got to go home one day. Got to be ready.

Unsullied by the mockeries of blackface, the black fiddle tradition was sustained through the last century. The 1920s Kentucky fiddler Jim Booker learned to play the instrument from his father, a former slave. He recorded with Taylor's Kentucky Boys and formed his own string band, Booker Orchestra. Among his recordings were old Appalachian standards "Salty Dog" and "Camp Nelson Blues" and his own composition "Midnight," which was a montage of blues, jazz, and Celtic influences. When fiddler Joe Thompson died in 2012 at the age of ninety-three, the North Carolina native left behind a lifetime of performances, including appearances at Carnegie Hall, the Smithsonian Folklife Festival, and the Kennedy Center and an Australian tour. The black string band sound could have been extinguished during the twentieth century when its musicians dispersed, but Joe and his cousin Odell Thompson persisted. After their string music performance at Carnegie Hall, the *New York Times* reviewer reported that Joe was in fine fettle: "Holding his bow about five inches from the end, Joe Thompson draws a scratchy, rakish tone from his fiddle, full of higher overtones. He breaks melodies into short phrases and often adds double stops that suggest modal harmo-

All in the Family I; pencil drawing by Willard Gayheart showing noted musicians and their African American mentors. (From *Willard Gayheart: Appalachian Artist* [© 2003 Willard Gayheart and Donia S. Eley], by permission of McFarland & Company, Inc., Box 611, Jefferson, North Carolina, 28640, www.mcfarlandpub.com)

nies."[43] Joe almost quit after the death of his cousin Odell in the early 1990s, but he went on to record the solo album *Family Tradition* (Rounder, 1999). In 2007 the National Endowment for the Arts honored him with a National Fellowship Award for "keeping alive an African American musical tradition—the black string band—that predates blues and jazz and influenced country and bluegrass music," and he performed at the Kennedy Center that year. As he reached his ninetieth birthday, Joe said his end would come "when the good Lord sends the morning train." The train fi-

nally arrived on a February morning in 2012 as Joe quietly passed away in Burlington, North Carolina.

Not only did African American musicians generally influence traditional and folk music styles from banjo and fiddle to vocals, but some also were mentors to noted twentieth-century white musicians. This list includes Leslie Riddle, singer and guitar player for A. P. Carter of the Carter Family; Alabama's "Tee Tot" Payne, mentor to Hank Williams; Arnold Shultz, blues guitarist for Bill Monroe; and Louis Armstrong, an important influence on Jimmie Rodgers, as "Satchmo" performed with Rodgers on some of his recordings. Elvis Presley was influenced by guitar player Arthur "Big Boy" Crudup as well as black gospel groups. All acknowledged their musical indebtedness. Tommy Jarrell, the celebrated North Carolina "Round Peak" style fiddler, recalled learning from black fiddlers such as Joe Thompson. As Doc Watson first came to grips with the rigors of touring in 1963, he struggled with homesickness and, as a blind man, with negotiating his way through unfamiliar cities. Accommodation and travel expenses soaked up his performance fees, leaving only a paltry sum to take back home to his wife, Rosa Lee. During this time, he contemplated coming off the road and heading home. After playing at a small venue, the Second Fret, in Philadelphia, the cook at the restaurant offered Doc a room at his home free of charge, provided they share the grocery bill. The cook was Jerry Ricks, an African American blues singer. The pair struck up a friendship and for the next two weeks traded blues guitar licks. Doc would later recall that Ricks was a "friend in need" at a critical time, allowing him to persevere with his budding music career. As rockabilly and early rock and roll emerged through the 1950s, Sun Recording artists Carl Perkins, Jerry Lee Lewis, and Johnny Cash, as well as Elvis Presley, recalled drawing inspiration from black gospel musicians and blues chord progressions. American music had married black and white genres to create new sounds from old traditions. Sun Records recording pioneer Sam Phillips found in Elvis "a white

Music Is a Bridge

Doc Watson (1923–2012), American guitarist, songwriter, and singer; interviewed in Wilkesboro, North Carolina, April 2009, and Asheville, North Carolina, October 2010, by Doug Orr during Merlefest and at the Diana Wortham Theater, respectively.

I got into the music business and took to the road for paying performances simply because I had a family to support, and it seemed like the best opportunity for me to make a living. My dad, who started me playing on the banjo and guitar, said, "Son, just pick out the tune real good, and it will take you through life." New York was a faraway and strange place to me, but Ralph Rinzler [a folklorist with the Smithsonian Institute] lined me up some gigs, and music friends gave me a place to stay. Jean Ritchie had come to the city from Kentucky and was powerful friendly and helpful, introducing me to the Greenwich Village music scene. She also taught me not to use dairy products before performing because it builds up mucous in your mouth and makes it hard to sing. I knew she had traced the ballads back to the Old Country, and she shared with me a few. I always loved the old-time fiddle tunes and, with a lot of hard work, was able to pick them out on the guitar—nothin' prettier, and they always take me back to the old places and fiddlers. But I never wanted to be placed in a box with my repertoire. Good music is good music, and I loved it all: bluegrass, blues, old-time, the ballads, even some rock-and-roll stuff. It's why music brings different folks and cultures together like a bridge. It has been a privilege for me to stand on the shoulders of so many giants in these mountains and elsewhere, many of them long gone; people who willingly shared the tunes, taught me, and extended a hand to this old mountain boy who could have been lost. That's why I want to share as well, to pass it on.

kid who could sing black," permitting the music to break down racial and cultural barriers that had once seemed insurmountable. Music was at the forefront of change, confronting intransigent racial divides. While society caught up, it was often said that "when the music stopped, segregation reappeared."

Whether rooted in African or Scots-Irish traditions, the music had traveled a long distance through time to merge in the cultural maelstrom of the 1950s. Two centuries earlier, in 1745, immigrant Andrew Presley had arrived in North Carolina. His people were from the Aberdeenshire village of Lonmay, in the heart of Scottish ballad country. Perhaps that ancient musical essence still flickered somewhere deep within the incandescent global impact of his illustrious descendant—American cultural icon Elvis Aaron Presley, who grew up playing "hillbilly" music at home with his Scots-Irish mother.

THE MUSICAL INSTRUMENTS

Appalachian music has steadily added a variety of instruments to the tapestry of influences. The contributions of fiddle, banjo, guitar, mandolin, mountain dulcimer, and bass are all well documented. Others also have been of historic significance: jaw harp, bones, harmonica, dobro, psaltry, and mouth bow. The fiddlers' conventions and festivals dotted through the

APPALACHIAN DANCE

Visit the Mount Airy Fiddler's Convention in Surry County, North Carolina, and you will be entertained by an assortment of enchantingly named string bands, including the Iron Mountain Ridge Runners, the New Southern Ramblers, the Sugar Loaf Mountain Band, and the Snow Creek Old Time Band. On one side of the main performance stage, you will notice a special wooden platform reserved for dancers. While bands play in contest, dancers dance in squares or get up onto the platform and mark rhythm by shuffling their feet in time to the music. These free-form dance styles have several different names. In Tennessee, it might be called "buck dancing"; in North Carolina, it is "flatfooting"; and if you go to Kentucky, you may hear it called "hoe-downing." In fiddle festival campsites away from the competition stage, boards are placed on the ground to encourage dancers where music circles are likely to gather. Music at informal jam sessions is not amplified, and there are no drums in old-time music or bluegrass, so the feet are charged with the task of providing a percussive element.

Much like the music, Appalachian dance is a hybrid style, drawing upon British Isles, Irish, African, and Native American cultures. More specifically, the roots of Appalachian square dancing and buckdancing can be traced to Scottish country dancing, Irish set and step dancing, English country and stage step dances, Welsh clogging, French cotillions and quadrilles, African American ring dances, and Native American ceremonial dances. Scots-Irish emigrants' background in Ulster included a significant dance tradition within the cottages, at the crossroads, and in the ceili houses. It followed them to the New World: emigrants danced solo to fiddle accompaniment on the pitching decks of emigration ships; new arrivals kept their dance traditions alive in couples and sets on the Pennsylvania frontier; migrants danced during evenings on the trail, following the Great Philadelphia Wagon Road; and settlers gathered to dance together in their southern Appalachian homesteads. The sparse log-cabin furniture was pushed aside, and friends gathered for song, stories, tunes, and dances. With hard-soled shoes on boards and wooden floors, their percussive steps are a key component of Appalachian dance styles today.

To the sound of the fiddle, Scots-Irish dancing took place at many other venues, such as holiday celebrations, barn raisings, corn shuckings, and bean stringings. Similar "frolics" were widespread, too, in African American and Native American communities, and those cultures contributed different steps to the Appalachian dance mix. Back at the fiddle festivals' dance boards, watch for the steps where the dancers slide their feet backward. This is not a move seen in British or Irish step dancing but is highly characteristic of buckdancing and clogging. African and Native American dances were traditionally practiced on dirt floors and in the open air, so they were not designed to provide rhythmic accompaniment or percussion to the music; feet did not tap so much as slip and slide across the ground.

The enslaved West Africans brought their sliding steps and ring dances to the plantations on the low-country coastal plains. Before the end of the eighteenth century, the African and European dance traditions were comingling at plantation frolics, eventually evolving into the square dance form popular today. African Americans danced to Scottish sets and to English country dances, sometimes with slaves from neighboring plantations. Meanwhile, whites would dance to the strains of an African American fiddler. There was even more trading of steps, along with the music, when minstrel shows emerged in the mid-nineteenth century. White people imitated—and sometimes cruelly caricatured—the dancing of African Americans.

Evolving Appalachian dance styles benefited

from two important African American contributions: the dance caller and, on the instrumental side, the banjo. By the late eighteenth century, banjos were joining fiddles as the core music accompaniment for dances. Guitar, mandolin, and bass joined the string-band lineup in the twentieth century. These instruments helped to strengthen the sound as community venues became larger. African American bands and callers were recruited to perform for square dances throughout the Carolina Piedmont and Appalachian Mountains.

Appalachian dance music up until the twentieth century embraced a number of European traditions that included reels, jigs, hornpipes, cotillion, schottisches, polkas, marches, and waltzes. While many of these persist in the northern Appalachians, reels are the prevailing southern Appalachian group dance form, followed by marches and waltzes. Recent decades have seen the migration of New England contra dance traditions to the southern Appalachian dance culture. Some communities have weekly contra dances, complementing or supplanting the square dances. The contra, descended mostly from English country-dance practices, features a long line of dancers in hypnotic movement not unlike the gavotte line dances of Brittany. The contra is danced at a slower tempo, whereas traditional squares are more spirited affairs where callers take an active role in directing the figures and variations. Solo dancing, meanwhile, continues to evolve and grow in popularity. Today, dancers refer to solo styles with feet moving close to the ground as flatfooting or buckdancing; clogging is characterized by a higher stepping style.

Team clogging arose from square-dance groups performing at Bascom Lamar Lunsford's first Mountain Dance and Folk Festival in Asheville, North Carolina, in 1927. In the 1930s, the Soco Gap Dancers from Maggie Valley, North Carolina, won the team dance competition at the folk festival. They performed freestyle buckdancing steps as they moved through square-dance figures directed by a dancer/caller. In 1939 Eleanor Roosevelt invited the dancers to perform at the White House for visiting British royals King George VI and Queen Elizabeth. The queen was heard to remark that the dance style resembled the clogging she had seen in Wales and the North of England, and the label was set.

Clogging teams began to grow in popularity beginning in the 1950s and 1960s, when many elementary and high schools launched clogging and smooth-dance teams. Cloggers emphasize the downbeat of the music for their percussive footwork, an approach to rhythm shared with African and Cherokee tribal music. Loose-limbed, often with bent knees and drag/slide footwork, the dancers propel themselves across the floor to bluegrass and old-time fiddle tunes. Along the way, two distinct styles of teams have evolved. One, "smooth style," features an even flow through the dance figures. The other is an exuberant, highly syncopated method popularized by many clogging teams in the southern Appalachians, such as the Green Grass Cloggers, who toured Latin America under a U.S. State Department grant. Some teams perform "free style," with each dancer free to express individual steps; others favor "precision" clogging, with choreographed steps danced in unison. Many dancers are virtuoso solo performers, successful competitors, and stage performers. Others develop the traditional art form by teaching the next generation of dancers. Step by step, clogging has grown in popularity, and it is now the official state dance of North Carolina and Kentucky. Like the ceili/ceilidh dancing in Ireland and Scotland, there are few dance styles more fun to watch, and fewer still are more fun to try.

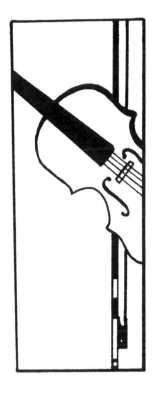

mountains and beyond are good places to observe instrument combinations, tried and tested by today's string bands. Both onstage and in nonstop jam sessions around the festival grounds, the younger generation of old-time musicians are more likely to experiment with any variety of permutations.

Standing at the center of it all is the fiddle, a constant bowed hum reaching from the Appalachians back along the Great Wagon Road to Pennsylvania and across the Atlantic. Such a portable instrument, perfect for driving dances, was always going to have a front seat on the migration trail. Scots-Irish fiddlers reflected a style of playing that recalled the Donegal flavor of northwest Ulster, a hybrid from Scotland and Ireland. It emphasized alternative or cross-tunings, frequent mixolydian modal sounds, and a technique of holding a note and bowing one or more of the open strings to reproduce the drone of the bagpipe. So although the pipes did not make the eighteenth-century Atlantic crossing and subsequent migration into the southern Appalachians, the fiddle and mountain dulcimer rep-

licated its modal and mournful tones. Ballads, if not sung a capella, might be bolstered by fiddle accompaniment, and the instrument was indispensible for up-tempo dance tunes, infused with African American–influenced syncopation and rhythms. Virginia fiddler Henry Reed was particularly known for driving his bow with syncopated techniques.

Alan Jabbour is the founding director of the American Folklife Center at the Library of Congress and fiddler for the Hollow Rock String Band. He describes the Ulster Scots' arrival from across the sea, with their strong fiddle tradition, as a "pilgrimage" to which he has felt deeply connected throughout his life as a musician: "They all went through this kind of pilgrimage, and that meant they transformed their whole world view . . . this world is not my home, I'm only a traveler here. . . . [T]hey carried in their heads what was most important because you may lose everything else. My whole repertory is a fabric of human connections with other people. I believe there's a deep potency in human connections, and if you know the people it illuminates the meaning of the music."[44]

In fiddle-tune migrations, Jabbour observes, tunes are more often subjected to a stripping down, only occasionally becoming more complex. The whole rhythm might change: the 6/8-time Scottish dance tune "The New Rigged Ship" was adapted in the Appalachians to a 4/4 breakdown in reel time. Fiddle tunes were frequently renamed for features in the settlers' wilderness—creeks, coves, mountaintops, or passes—so that the Scottish ballad "Bonnie George Campbell" became a dance tune "Cumberland Gap." Some fiddle compositions became "crooked tunes," where the melody line takes unexpected twists and turns, making the note sequence difficult to anticipate. There is a theory, perhaps apocryphal, among musicians that crooked tunes originated in "crooked places," steep-sided valleys and coves where culture is isolated and landscape features impose their power on the music. It is a hypothesis that can be proved only by much additional fieldwork, involving treks into clefts and crevices deep in the hills.

Collecting Fiddle Tunes

Alan Jabbour, American musician, folklorist, and tune collector; interviewed in Swannanoa, North Carolina, July 2008, by Fiona Ritchie and Doug Orr during Fiddle Week at the Swannanoa Gathering folk arts workshops.

The South was kind of at a spiritual crossroads in the early sixties, and in a funny way, getting interested in folk music was part of my sorting out who I am, you know, growing up as a lad in the South, identifying as a southerner and as an American, but also conscious of problems, really huge problems. So I think a lot of our generation spent a lot of energy sorting through culturally, who are we? And what do we preserve for the future, and also what do we discard and set aside? The cultural arena maybe was one of the places where these kinds of issues got worked out without our quite knowing how it's working it out. In addition, actually, I never knew my grandparents, as chance would have it. Neither set of grandparents was close to me, so I've sometimes felt [that] maybe studying folklore was a way of sort of connecting symbolically with my grandparents. Anyway, for whatever reason, I fell in love with folk music, and I felt, well, if these collectors collected ballads and folk songs and folk tales, I played the violin, I could collect fiddle tunes, and probably they hadn't done a very good job on that, which was true. They hadn't. And so in fact, Cecil Sharp remarked somewhere in the introduction to English Folk Songs from the Southern Appalachians that it seems that the tradition of instrumental music doesn't seem to be active here. It was a great lesson in how you find what you look for.

Henry Reed, for example, who lived right along the border of Virginia and West Virginia up in the Appalachians . . . was in his eighties in the 1960s when I hung out with him; he was the source of dozens of tunes for which he was the sole source. No other person alive anywhere knew these tunes. And these tunes have now sort of gone back into tradition, not just in the Appalachians. I mean tunes like "Over the Waterfall." This is a Henry Reed tune. Well, one of the things that you learn by hanging out with real people is that tradition, despite all the talk of father to son and all that stuff . . . often it skips a generation, and you right away find out, hanging out with fiddlers—which was in that generation mostly a men's thing—that most fiddlers didn't learn from their father. They actually learned from a grandfather, an uncle, a neighbor, and very often what they learned skipped a generation, because, you know, very often fiddlers would have a sort of a period of middle life where they didn't actively practice.

So there's a sort of ancient grandparent education pattern going on there in the cultural transmission. I think that the very fact that a lot of the people in the Appalachians were, you know, not that far from migration from somewhere else, and that there was actually a history of migration—in this case, Scotland to Northern Ireland to, let's say, Pennsylvania or Piedmont North Carolina, and then to the mountains, and then maybe to the Alleghenies west. It creates a kind of a cultural pattern where—and there's a lot of gospel songs that "this world is not my home," "I'm only a traveller here"—this almost religious view of life as a pilgrimage, as a migration, actually matched their life experiences. And as a result, what you carried in your head was all-important, because chances are, you had to periodically lose everything else. But if you carry things in your head, you can always reassemble the rest.

FIDDLE STYLE OUTLIERS: CAPE BRETON AND THE OZARKS

"Don't forget the Ozarks!" said old-time fiddler Betse Ellis when this book was in development. Indeed, there are two areas on the Appalachian periphery that should be remembered for their distinctive fiddle styles: the Ozarks of upland Missouri and Arkansas and Cape Breton, Nova Scotia. The fiddle, dance, and singing styles of Cape Breton sit squarely within the Scottish sphere of influence. They were ferried across the Atlantic by Scottish immigrants during the nineteenth century, emigrating primarily as a result of the notorious Highland Clearances. So they arrived mostly from Gaelic-speaking areas in the Scottish Highlands and Islands. While traditional fiddle music continued to evolve in Scotland, it remained largely unchanged in the remote setting of the Canadian maritime island. Cape Breton fiddling is closely connected with the dance music of the area: step, square, and Highland dancing. The fiddle style is best described as having a "driven bow"—a strong downbeat and a highly accentuated, driven

up-bowing method. The fiddler's heel beating on the floor further invigorates the dancing. Cape Breton ornamentation echoes the grace notes of the Highland bagpipes, reinforced further by the distinctive drone sound. In fact, many tunes are drawn from the Scottish pipes and fiddle repertoire, including reels, jigs, strathspeys, hornpipes, marches, and slow airs. For such a small island, Cape Breton has produced a remarkable number of internationally renowned fiddle players, a group that includes Buddy MacMaster and his niece Natalie, J. P. Cormier, Dan R. and Howie MacDonald, Ashley and Wendy MacIsaac, Kimberly Fraser, John Morris Rankin, Jerry Holland, and many others. The French-speaking Acadia area on Cape Breton's west coast is a keystone of the Cajun fiddle music of southwest Louisiana and southeast Texas, as the Acadians were evicted from Nova Scotia by the British in the eighteenth century and migrated to the French-speaking colony in the South.

A review of the long-standing old-time fiddle lineage quickly confirms the sheer range of regional variations it represents. Alan Jabbour has written about Henry Reed, who memorized rare pieces that might otherwise have died with him had he not shared and played them. Jabbour propagates these old treasures by incorporating many of Reed's tunes in his own repertoire. Tommy Jarrell lived near Round Peak in North Carolina, and his fiddle playing was so distinctive that it became identified as the "Round Peak Fiddle Style." Other notable old-time fiddlers include Benton Flippen (CD track 4) of Surry County, North Carolina; Clyde Davenport of Monticello, Kentucky; Ralph Blizard from Blountville, Tennessee; Fiddlin' John Carson of Fannin County, Georgia; J. P. Fraley

from Rush, Kentucky; and Bruce Green of Madison County, North Carolina. Together, these musicians and others have established the southeastern United States as a world fiddling hotspot.

The rise of the banjo after its introduction by African Americans was rapid. Some instruments had four strings, and others added a fifth to establish the drone sound. In the 1830s, Joel (Joe) Walker Sweeney, of Scots-Irish descent, became the first outside the African American community to achieve fame for his banjo talent and enjoyed immense popularity on his performance tours. He had learned his style from slaves in Virginia. By the mid-nineteenth century, the banjo was being mass-produced, and, as mentioned earlier, it was a fixture in the minstrel shows. Its thumping claw-

Ozark fiddle styles, or Missouri fiddling, are related to the old-time fiddle traditions of the Appalachians. Some of the Scots-Irish settlers who made their way across Pennsylvania and traveled down the Great Wagon Road through the Shenandoah valley opted to turn west through the Cumberland Gap and settle in the Ozarks area. Geologically separate from the Appalachians, it is an upland plateau region that covers the southern half of Missouri, a large portion of northwest and north-central Arkansas, and slivers of Oklahoma and Kansas. The fiddle style that evolved there largely drew upon the Scots-Irish and Appalachian traditions, later adding elements of Midwest fiddling, western swing, and even a bit of rag and pop. Earlier French settlers in the region had imported Franco fiddle styles, but these did not fully integrate with the more-dominant Scots-Irish repertoire, and their influence eventually faded. Likewise, Ozark fiddlers of German descent essentially merged with the Scots-Irish fiddle playing.

The sound of the Ozark fiddle varies regionally, but the style is generally fiery, with energetic bowing driving very slightly ahead of the beat. It is a clear, crisp sound, as opposed to the laid-back bowing style and the modal tone of Scots-Irish and Appalachian fiddle playing. Indeed, modal tunes were sometimes converted from a minor key to a major key in the Ozark tradition, even to the point of altering the melody. Universally appealing, waltzes are popular there, along with many of the old Appalachian standards—such as "Soldiers Joy," "Old Joe Clark," and "Bile Them Cabbage Down"—and homegrown Ozark tunes like "Finley Creek Blues." Bluegrass is popular, too, but it seldom mixes with the old-time fiddling. Classically trained violinist Betse Ellis, fiddler with the Wilders, is passionate about old-time fiddle styles. The fiddling traditions of her home region are in good hands, as the Arkansas-born player has devoted her musical life to learning, performing, teaching, and promoting Ozark fiddle.

hammer right-hand style, when paired with the fiddle, formed the unassailable foundation of the Appalachian string-band sound. "Scruggs style" fingerpicking became a predominant force in twentieth-century bluegrass bands. Earl Scruggs is another Appalachian area musician, hailing from Rutherford County, North Carolina. The original Scots-Irish music tradition was thus enriched yet again, cross-pollinated by a different cultural influence in its North American hub.

At the beginning of the twentieth century, traditional music expanded its limitless boundaries to include the guitar, today's ubiquitous instrument of popular music. The guitar's origins can be traced to a long line of instruments that lead back through prehistoric civilizations in ancient India and central Asia.

The modern instrument was in use in Spain by the year 1200 as the "guitarra" and spread through Italy and France from the late sixteenth century. Renaissance and baroque guitars became popular throughout the continent well before the eighteenth century; the Dutch painter Johannes Vermeer's portrait *The Guitar Player* (ca. 1672) shows one such instrument in fine detail. The first guitars came to the Americas with the earliest Spanish explorers and missionaries, arriving in the Spanish settlement of St. Augustine in Florida by the mid-sixteenth century. To the north, the French colonists taught the instrument to French settlers and Native Canadians in the province of Quebec.

The rise of mail-order merchandising through the early twentieth century allowed guitars gradually to

How Tunes Have Changed

Alan Jabbour, American musician, folklorist, and tune collector; interviewed in Swannanoa, North Caro-lina, July 2008, by Fiona Ritchie and Doug Orr during Fiddle Week at the Swannanoa Gathering folk arts workshops.

Sometimes they were changed in the direction of stripping down, sometimes in the direction of complexity. Sometimes the rhythm of it was changed. I played—you heard the example I gave the other night of a Scottish tune, called "The New Rigged Ship," which is a 6/8-time tune—it was a dance tune, then it got adapted as a martial tune in the United States, and then it gets converted to 4/4 breakdown to reel time, and goes back into dancing again, and so in a funny way, there's the same continuity of the tunes and the same change, the same sense of transition from world to world that you get in the human beings themselves. They all went through this kind of pilgrimage, and that meant they transformed their whole worldview. Old Maggie Hammons Parker from the Hammons family used to say, those old men, you know, talking about the old people in the old days when she was young—she'd say, "You know, they named the fiddle tunes, they named the forests, you know, and the creeks."

Somebody had to name this wilderness and in effect make it a cultural domain, as well as a natural wilderness. That's who she evoked. Now those people may have come from across the ocean, but when I talked to the Hammons about "across the ocean," they didn't resist the idea, but it didn't inter-est them that much. In a way, they thought of themselves as springing from the wilderness in America, you know. But all the same, they were still deeply respectful of tradition, and so the tradition ends up carrying over Scottish tunes, or Irish tunes, or English tunes, whether or not they know it, and sometimes their idea of what's old is different from my own knowledge as a scholar. But their respect for the old is still important, and in a way, maybe it's the respect for the old that's the key cultural element, because that again is what is your barricade against pitching everything out and reinventing culture, because you're pitching so much out already, you've got to have something that you preserve; and that becomes your thread of continuity.

There's a lot of Scottish tunes, for example, in the Appalachian repertory, but most of them don't have Scottish names anymore. The lords-and-ladies tunes that got names attached, well that wasn't part of the American way of looking at things, so without any ceremony, the lords and ladies got pitched overboard! And they got new names. So "Lord MacDonald's Reel" in the upland South is "Leather Britches"! And "Leather Britches" connects to their lives.

Culture is a process, a dynamic process, you know, as I sometimes say to people. Culture is what you cultivate, and sometimes people say to me, "I've got to learn more about my culture." It's not your culture until you've learned it, and it's an active part of you. And therefore, talking about it is talking about process, you know, and how that process, that chemistry, proceeds over time, and different circumstances for different people. So I think it's wonderful to show connections, but you also have to be careful not to assume that everything started in one place and then was passed down. It's more complicated than that. I play "George Booker," which is a great tune that was originally a Scottish strathspey. Well nowadays . . . I play it for Scottish people, and they say, "That doesn't sound like the tune that I know that it came from," so it's changed some. But the main thing is that it's sped up. The original strathspey is called "The Marquis of Huntly's Farewell." Another one of those lords and ladies that got pitched overboard! But by the early nineteenth century or even the late eighteenth century, it was already being played in Virginia as a Virginia tune. Booker's a Virginia name. Right? So "The Marquis of Huntly" is lost completely. But the tune is the tune, but it's sped up.

But how much has it sped up? I think it's also the case that the strathspey that it was from has been slowed down some. It was always slower than the fast reels, but at a certain point in Scotland, there was an exaggeration of that slow quality of the strathspeys, in my opinion, and so it's changing over there while it's changing [here]. The version I play of what I call "Chapel Hill Serenade" that's related to that 6/8 tune from Scotland that we were talking about earlier, "The New Rigged Ship"—the version I play is different from the version that is played by Angus Grant, the fiddler from the Highlands of Scotland. Angus and I sat down and played it together, and he does a lovely little twist to it that's somehow crept into his version of it. But that's not the original. Actually, the original way of playing it is the way I learned it in North Carolina, and the way you hear it in Scotland now has changed. So all of these wonderful complexities are, in a way, a part of the magic of the process of culture.

infiltrate the mountains. Appalachian music evolved again, in this form with fiddle playing lead melody, clawhammer banjo providing rock-solid rhythm or occasional melody, and the guitar introducing full rhythm and bass runs. In time, guitar gurus like Doc Watson, raised in the remote Appalachian hollow of Deep Gap, North Carolina, took folk guitar to a new level, picking out the old fiddle-tune melodies in his hallmark "flat pick" style as well as supplying sophisticated back-up for vocal accompaniment.

Montgomery Ward in 1872, then Sears, Roebuck & Company in 1893, founded mail-order catalogs that offered increased retail prospects for mountaineers. Both companies sold and shipped musical instruments, including the mandolin. Evolving in Italy from the lute family in the seventeenth and eighteenth centuries, the mandolin is tuned like a fiddle but has a fretted fingerboard and four pairs of strings. The string-band combos, as well as harmony duos, soon embraced the mandolin, and its versatility facilitated an easy passage into a wide variety of other music forms, including bluegrass (led by Bill Monroe), country, classical music, jazz, blues, and, reaching back across the sea again, Celtic music.

The twentieth-century mail-order trend also boosted sales of the autoharp, a relatively new instrument. The construction was essentially a modified zither, developed in the late nineteenth century and consisting of movable chord bars pressing down upon thirty-six or thirty-seven strings. The autoharp was intended to be played across the lap or on a table, but all that changed in the 1920s, when Maybelle Carter of the Carter Family of Maces Spring, Virginia, popularized the instrument. She held it upright against her chest while playing the strings above the chord bars. This abiding image of "Mother" Maybelle launched the autoharp as an accessible, popular instrument for vocal accompaniment. The Carter Family's repertoire of Appalachian ballads, old hymns, and Victorian popular songs, backed up by autoharp and guitar, redefined the Appalachian sound in the public consciousness. The Appalachian and folk songs of Mike Seeger, Brian Bowers, Mike Fenton, and John McCutcheon, accompanied on autoharp, carried the instrument and the music into the twenty-first century. In the arms of Dolly Parton, it is shared today with an international audience.

With its introduction during the era of the Great Philadelphia Wagon Road and the Wilderness Road, where it was used for pioneer dances, the mountain dulcimer was entrenched as an archetypal Appalachian instrument. Jean Ritchie popularized it for ballad accompaniment, where its drone strings harked back to the roots of balladry. Others reconnected with its dance-music roots; this group includes Don Pedi of Madison County, North Carolina, who plays string-band-style dulcimer, often in tandem with fiddle players. Like other instruments in the Appalachian genre, the dulcimer has demonstrated versatility with many music forms, including Celtic music. Billy Ross and Billy Jackson formed the Scottish music group Ossian in the 1970s. Ross sang in Scots and Gaelic, adding Appalachian dulcimer to the band's mix of harp, pipes, whistle, and fiddle. It is one of many contemporary examples where the shared heritage expresses itself in an Appalachian-Celtic fusion as the music travels back to its root and reinvigorates a connection sounding as old as the hollows and Highlands themselves.

The upright bass rounds out the primary Appalachian string-band ensemble with its steady grounding beat, sometimes accentuated with the percussive slap-style technique. Many old-time and bluegrass bands include a bass player to drive the music along and keep up a steady tempo for dancers. In string-band jam sessions on back porches, at tailgate parties, in festival sites, and around the summer music-camp scene, many players are drawn toward the hive of music activity. With the potential for a runaway rhythm, the thrumming pulse of a bass player is always a much-sought-after addition.

DOC WATSON FROM DEEP GAP

Doc Watson traced his Appalachian and ancestral roots to the late eighteenth century, when Scottish immigrant Tom Watson settled in the North Carolina mountains. The son of Edinburgh shoemaker John Watson, Tom had served his apprentice as a saddle maker. By the 1770s, he had saved enough money to emigrate to America with his new wife. Tom Watson fought the British as a cavalryman in the Revolutionary War, and when hostilities ended, he was rewarded with land in the Watauga Wilderness region of western North Carolina. The Watsons never left the area, and Doc continued to make his home in Watauga County's Deep Gap until his death in 2012 at the age of eighty-nine. From his self-described humble beginnings as the sixth of nine children on a "little dirt farm," he became a virtuoso guitarist, singer, and songwriter of old-time, bluegrass, folk, country, blues, and gospel music—in short, an American music icon.

Arthel Lane "Doc" Watson (the nickname was suggested by an audience member during a live radio broadcast after the announcer complained that "Arthel" was too unusual) reflected his surrounding environment in every sense. Doc was not only from the mountains but was "of" his beloved mountains. "Doc from Deep Gap" seemed almost, at times, a figure drawn from fiction, and yet it was his very authenticity that added to his great appeal. His mother, Annie Watson, sang the old ballads around the house, and his father, General Dixon Watson, played the banjo and also led the singing at church with his store of old gospel songs. From his grandmother came a storehouse of old story songs, such as "Tom Dula" and "Shady Grove" (CD track 17). Before he was a year old, Doc had lost his sight as a result of an infection. A heightened sense of hearing soon began to compensate for his blindness, enabling him to become finely attuned to the most subtle music intonation. Doc received his first musical instrument, a harmonica, as a Christmas present when he was five. When Doc turned eleven, his father skinned

a recently departed household cat to provide the raw material for the head of a fretless banjo, which he built for Doc.

Then came the guitar. Inspired by hearing its tuneful tone, Doc saved his allowance and bought a $10 Stella guitar from the Sears, Roebuck & Company catalog. His first song on the instrument was the Carter Family's "When the Roses Bloom in Dixieland." Initially, he played a thumb and finger pick style, influenced by picking pioneer Merle Travis. When he tuned in to music programs on the family's first radio—a four-tube model purchased in 1936—Doc was captivated by the singing and flatpicking of Jimmie Rodgers. From then on, he was determined to emulate Rodgers's style as a more harmonious approach to working with the Carter Family songs. More influences poured in from a collection of 78-rpm records: blues from Mississippi John Hurt, Memphis jug-band sounds, Dixieland, Bill Monroe's bluegrass, and the old-time string-band tunes of Gid Tanner and the Skillet Lickers. From just across the mountain, Doc heard the well-known fiddler Gaither Carlton and met his daughter Rosa Lee, who became Doc's wife. A few years later, when Doc was playing electric guitar in a rockabilly band whose fiddler was notorious for not showing up, Doc learned to improvise, transposing the lead fiddle parts to guitar. When Gaither Carlton introduced Doc to an extensive old-time fiddle repertoire, Doc found that the process worked just as well for old-time tunes. Doc Watson had the self-discipline to practice his guitar technique relentlessly; with repeated listenings, he learned every note of melody lines, a regimen he called "wood sheddin." It was a work ethic he would later recommend to aspiring guitar players seeking advice from the master.

Doc Watson was discovered by Smithsonian folklorist Ralph Rinzler in 1960 at the Union Grove Fiddlers Convention in North Carolina. Rinzler visited Doc at home and recorded him playing with family members, including his father-in-law, Gaither

Carlton. On a mission to discover tradition bearers and announce them to the world, Rinzler convinced Doc to come to New York City, where he promised to arrange opportunities at music venues. Doc embarked on the first of what would be many lonely excursions from Deep Gap, taking the bus first to Bristol, Tennessee, and then onward New York City. In his resonant baritone, he loved to sing the old ballads, hymns, and country blues he had learned while growing up. He first performed these at a Greenwich Village concert sponsored by Friends of Old Time Music, leading to more appearances at clubs, colleges, and folk festivals, including his breakthrough at the 1963 and 1964 Newport Folk Festivals. Rinzler also introduced Doc to fellow musicians in the city who all played their part in the 1960s folk music revival, including Jean Ritchie, Tom Paxton, Joan Baez, and Bob Dylan. In 1964 Doc recorded his first solo album and began performing with his son Merle, a father-son partnership that alleviated some of the challenges and loneliness that Doc had faced on the road. Commercial interest in folk music declined somewhat after the 1960s boom, and this affected Doc's ability to work. Then in 1972 he contributed to the highly praised album *Will the Circle Be Unbroken* that brought the Nitty Gritty Dirt Band together with artists such as Maybelle Carter, Earl Scruggs, Chet Atkins, and Merle Travis (his son's namesake). The album sold over a million copies and won new audiences for Doc. The father-son pair became a trio with bassist T. Michael Coleman, and together they toured extensively throughout the United States, Europe, Africa, and Japan until Merle's tragic death in a tractor accident in 1985. The grieving Doc's first reaction was to stop performing altogether, but he later revealed that Merle spoke to him in a dream, urging him to go back out on the road. Guitarist Jack Lawrence was the first to join him, and then Merle's son Richard. For the last fourteen years of his life, multi-instrumentalist and Grammy-winning storyteller David Holt partnered with Doc. Onstage, Holt had a particular knack for drawing stories from Doc, and the result was captured in a biographical recording project, a three-CD set entitled *Legacy* that won the pair a Grammy in 2002 (CD track 17).

Doc Watson's lifelong legacy has many dimensions—unmatched fiddle-tune flatpicking; an authentic voice of mountain music, rare in the folk-revival years; banjo and harmonica playing to add warmth to his musical mix; fostering of the oral song and story tradition so deeply rooted in the southern Appalachians, Scotland, and Ireland; and a source of inspiration to countless guitar players. As David Holt has observed, Doc could take newer material and give it a traditional feel. And yet he would not be categorized and did not consider himself a niche performer. He firmly believed all good music has merit and considered himself a bridge across various strains, such as blues, bluegrass, gospel, old-time, rhythm and blues, and jazz. At the annual Merlefest event, created in honor of his late son and music partner, Doc would make several stage appearances and might spontaneously break into an Elvis song with a rockabilly beat. His achievements and accolades are numerous: more than fifty recorded albums; eight Grammys; the National Endowment for the Arts Heritage Award; and the National Medal of Arts, presented by President Bill Clinton. And yet if there is a thread that runs through this remarkable life, it is one of humility, in keeping with his mountain upbringing and values. Doc never needed to dominate when performing. Belying his years of hard work "wood sheddin" and honing his craft, not to mention overcoming his lifetime disability, he would offer an understated introduction to a tune by saying: "If you got any good notes you're liable to find 'em." In Boone, not far from his Deep Gap home, there is a life-sized statue of Doc Watson. It is situated where he once played for tips as an unknown guitar picker from a nearby "little dirt farm." The inscription reads: "Just One of the People."

Americana Scots

Archie Fisher, Scottish singer, songwriter, guitarist, and broadcaster; interviewed in Dunkeld, Scotland, November 2011, by Fiona Ritchie during his visit to the Perthshire Amber Festival.

Looking back to the sixties and before the sixties, it was Americana and Appalachian music that actually inspired most of the young Scottish musicians of the time. We loved the instrumentalism of it; we didn't pay much attention to the content of the words, they were just nice little bits and pieces of ballads, mostly murder ballads. It's almost going full circle in a way because I'm using a mandolin and fiddle on my new album that sounds more American than Scottish, and I'll be using mountain dulcimer and other American textures because these were the things that first attracted me to music. I wasn't going to be a singer, I was just going to be a musician, because I had all these talented sisters to accompany.

In many ways, we in Scotland and Britain in general seemed to be more aware of the Americana culture before America became aware because it went through quite a manicured folk revival there—Peter, Paul and Mary close-harmony stuff, while we were listening to people like Buell Kazee and Aunt Samantha Bumgarner on obscure folk labels and trying to pick up their instrumental techniques on guitar and banjo. Now, if there was some kind of subliminal identity with it, I wasn't quite sure at the time. But we also had quite a few Americans in Scotland, because we had the protests and the nuclear submarine base down at the [River] Clyde, and there were quite a few American musicians around. Hamish Imlach knew quite a few of them for some reason, I don't know why; I think they drank at the same pubs as he did. And, quite often, they'd go back to Hamish's, and there would be a guy from Tennessee singing "John Hardy" or something like that.

I think the first real legend that arrived on our doorstep was—well, Woody Guthrie had appar-

OLD-TIME MUSIC

Thousands of bows, picks, and strums had joined over time to create another richly layered tapestry of cultural and regional influences. The old-time sound had filled out considerably from the fiddle and banjo duos; the music's essence remained "old-time," however, honoring its origins and values. Mike Seeger called it "music from the true vine," remaining faithful to its roots yet winding its way through generations of musicians who have nourished it along the way. Mike Seeger's mother, modernist composer Ruth Crawford Seeger, said that "old-time music is the folk term for folk music."[45]

The traditional folk style of old-time music has always been place based, thriving in the southern Appalachian regions of western North Carolina, east Tennessee, southeastern Kentucky, southwest Virginia, northern Georgia, and West Virginia. Ginny Hawker, a West Virginia old-time ballad singer, advised: "When singing traditional music, take it to the place from which it comes."[46] So old-time music has always been rooted in a home place, most recently Appalachia, with ancestral roots reaching back to Ulster and Scotland. Yet the interest in old-time is now multinational. At a recent Swannanoa Gathering music camp on the Warren Wilson College campus near Asheville, North Carolina,

ently been in Glasgow, but that was well before our time, in the 1950's or some time—but Cisco Houston came over and did a series of concerts in Britain, very shortly before he passed on. And that was just unbelievable to see somebody of that era. And then Sonny Terry and Brownie McGhee came over, and that was the beginning of the sort of rule of American. Jack Elliott (who was, if you like, not real Americana, but was a sort of clone, but a very talented clone, and still is) and Derroll Adams were the other two Americans that made a big impression on the British folk scene, not just the Scottish one.

We weren't really even slightly academic about what we were doing in these days. It took the scholars to tell us what we were doing sometimes. It was more an intuitive thing, because when you sing a song, you indentify with the content in the story line of the song, or even the personality that was narrating the song. There may have been a lot of escapism; there were a few of what they called "clawhammer prophets" walking down dusty roads in these days. The Steinbeck image of what Woody Guthrie was about was much more romantic than singing about places like Auchtermuchty! American place names had a much more, sort of, lyrical element to them than Scottish [ones]; until eventually, as I say, the full circle went around.

It occurs to me also that—and I've found this in Nova Scotia and Cape Breton—that there's certain purity on the periphery. That at home, in Scotland, things become diluted, and they change, but when you take that culture and place it somewhere far away from its origins, the imperative is preserving the purity of it. And I'm sure that's what happened when people carried songs to the New World, that it was important that these were conserved, almost ritually. And that, in a sense, was their identity they were carrying with them. And without that, they had no sense of pride of place or past. I think that was the agent that made the music continue. And the explanation of why there are no bagpipes in Appalachia? They threw them overboard before they reached America [laughs].

the themed Old-Time Week saw thirty participants from other countries complementing the large American core of enrollees; this was by far the largest international contingent of any of the seven theme weeks.

In the 1920s, with the advent of the recording industry, old-time music emerged from its very localized exposure. The dissemination of indigenous Appalachian music through the media has continued apace. For the purposes of music marketing, "Appalachian" became an all-encompassing term that covered a potpourri of elements: fiddle tunes, old and new ballads, parlor songs, sacred and shape-note songs, spirituals, gospel, and work songs—all music embedded in the fabric of day-to-day life in the southern Appalachians. As old-time music gained broader exposure and commercial success, artists began to diversify with new forms and interpretations. String bands reflected this from the 1930s, consciously branching out with their music. Gid Tanner and the Skillet Lickers produced a sound that was especially spontaneous and raucous. Their unrestrained style included an assertive lead fiddle and an unstructured rhythm backup from the guitar and banjo, all supporting high-spirited vocals. Other bands would pattern their style after the Skillet Lickers. At the opposite end of the spectrum was Charlie Poole and the North Carolina Ramblers, delivering a pol-

ished, tightly controlled sound. Future string bands usually set their stylistic course somewhere in between. Old-time musician and scholar Paul Brown notes that the textile-mill era in the South provided a stimulus for playing the old-time music. Individuals were drawn from the farms to the factories, and during breaks from the plant floor, they would play tunes. Mill towns were the scene of many evening and weekend gatherings of like-minded old-time enthusiasts.[47]

In fact, mill owners intent on preserving a nonunion environment would look for ways to add popular leisure activities to the factory community, including music. In Swannanoa, North Carolina, outside Asheville, Charles Owen built the Beacon Blanket Manufacturing Company, a thriving mill, which became the largest blanket producer in the world during World War II. When he heard the masterful Appalachian fiddling of Marcus Martin during the 1920s, he hired him on the spot, providing housing in the mill village and later also employing his musical sons. They were encouraged to play at company events and even during breaks in the work schedule. Company string-band sessions flourished. In their spare time, the Martins also built instruments and eventually developed

to preserve the authenticity of the classic players while
assiduously avoiding simple replication of sounds
and styles. Researching and performing widely over
the years, the band members assembled an extensive
discography. Their mission served the cause of old-
time music well, as the Ramblers rediscovered early
musicians such as Roscoe Holcomb, Dock Boggs, and
Fiddlin' John Carson.

The New Lost City Ramblers inspired a younger
generation of old-time players, and the folk revival
flourished in far-flung places such as Ithaca, New York;
Lexington and Charlottesville, Virginia; and Chapel
Hill and Asheville, North Carolina. Alan Jabbour
and the Hollow Rock String Band helped expand the
fiddle-tune repertoire in the same manner as the New
Lost City Ramblers by going to the living tradition
bearers. For Jabbour, the most important of these was
Henry Reed. Other old-time fiddlers were also sought
out, such as Tommy Jarrell, with his Round Peak style
and repertoire; Ralph Blizard and his long-bow technique patterned after Fiddling Arthur Smith; and the
Hammons family of West Virginia.

It was a bountiful time for traditional and roots
music. Fiddle conventions and festivals blossomed
throughout the Appalachians and the Piedmont, including Fiddlers Grove and Mt. Airy in North Carolina, Galax in Virginia, and Cliff Top in West Virginia.
An intergenerational scene developed, attracting enthusiasts from places all over the map. Competitions
and concert stages may have been the centerpiece, but
the real action was the all-night jam sessions erupt-
ing amid a tangled web of tents and fiddle-wielding
campers. A chorus of strings and voices would fill the
air, sometimes joined by the percussion of a flat-foot
dancer shuffling on a board. Onstage, meanwhile, a
seemingly endless cavalcade of bands made brief appearances, their eccentric names announcing equally
characterful styles of play. The pure old-time band
sound would reign, punctuated occasionally by groups
like the Red Hots and the Highwoods String Band,

a reputation for their fiddle and mountain dulcimer
craftsmanship.

The profile of old-time music would wax and
wane through successive decades, but the post–World
War II generation was part of a significant revival extending into the 1970s and 1980s. Young players in
the Appalachians and beyond actively embraced the
tradition. The New Lost City Ramblers were an influential urban-based group that included musicians
Mike Seeger, John Cohen, and Tom Paley, who was
later replaced by Tracy Schwartz. The Ramblers came
together in New York City in 1958 as part of the folk
revival and diligently studied old 78-rpm recordings of
1920s and 1930s old-time bands. They were determined

The New Lost City Ramblers

John Cohen, American string-band musician, song collector, photographer, and filmmaker; interviewed in Swannanoa, North Carolina, July 2008, by Fiona Ritchie and Doug Orr during Traditional Song Week at the Swannanoa Gathering folk arts workshops.

Well, I've been asked in various ways, mostly as a criticism, "How did John Cohen, living in the sub-urbs of New York, pick up old-time Appalachian music?" You know, a folklorist friend of mine said, "Oh, this is the most incongruous thing." And it was repeated over and over in [a] book. And . . . it caused me to think that I really loved this music, I had feeling for it, even before I was born, because my parents . . . the biggest joy in their life was doing folk dancing. And so, I was . . . I must have been responding to that joy, and I can only refer to it as joy. Life in middle-class America is not always joy-ous. They sang, sometimes it was folk songs, but sometimes it wasn't. And my father played the piano. There was a lot of dance. Dance with good feeling around it. And then, of course, in my adolescent years, I had a fight with them and got away from that. But then when I suddenly heard it in string band music and old hillbilly records, I said, "There it is." I didn't think of it in terms of them. This is not what they did, this is what I'm going to do. And so I found it as a great continuity there. But first, in 1948, when I heard those burly country music records with banjo players and string bands, it just hit me hard. It was wonderful, you know. And then ten years later, when I suddenly found two other guys—Mike Seeger and Tom Paley—who had that same kind of ability, and we came together, then we suddenly made music that I had only heard before.

I had met Tom separately, Tom Paley. He was famous as a guitar player in Washington Square [New York City] before I met him. And then, he was also a mathematics professor at Yale, and I was an art student at Yale, so we got together there. And then a few years later, when he went to Maryland, he met up with Mike. Actually, it was the first time banjo and fiddle players were meeting. Playing banjo and fiddle music was not done. The folk song revival in 1948, and even in '58, it was guitars and banjos and that's it. Of course, there was the Weavers. But fiddles and mandolins, and banjo and fiddle combinations . . . so this was a lot of fun for us, and that excitement is what carried us through our ignorance of what we were stepping into.

When the New Lost City Ramblers starting traveling, I mean, we maybe sold 500 records in a year, but everywhere we went, we'd come back, there'd be another string band. So that people were actually not just listening to it, or not just buying records, but they were doing it. And when we started, there really wasn't that much interest in this kind of music in the South, like country music, modern, national music had replaced all the old-time stuff pretty much. Yeah, there were lots of fiddlers' conventions, where the old fiddlers could emphasize and be rewarded for their excellence of a tradition that wasn't being listened to, but to watch the change, to watch the size of . . . it's not even a revival, but it's a different kind of animal, where people are finding richness in playing music and in singing music. Not even studying it. Everywhere on the map that I could think of, there's people . . . and they weren't imitating us, they were going back to the sources. And what a joyful recognition that was for me to see people using their hands and their voices, rather than their entertainment, you know.

I like the fact that folklore departments all over the country are drying up. They're disappearing. They've become English departments again, or ethnomusicology. The interest is more in, you know, not finding out the footnotes, not reading the academic battles. You know, I've done fifteen films, and I never used the word "folk" in any of them, because none of the people in the films ever used the word anyhow. That's a balancing act that I've been doing. And, you know, to some people . . . I'm looking at this big map of America there . . . the word "folk" rings all kinds of . . . pushes all kinds of buttons. For the years that I was in academia. . . people say, "Oh he's just a folksinger." They could undercut all that I was thinking about and studying.

I think we were very important in getting that idea about it's okay to play traditional music not from your own family, or to listen to other parts of the country, and that the actual playing is challenging enough and entertaining and enriching, so the act of making music is wonderful there. Like my very first experience of hearing the early hillbilly records, I was like, wow this is so rich I can't understand it. And then I pick up a guitar and say, oh there's the run that that guy was playing. Pick up a mandolin, oh there's those notes he was playing. Or here's a banjo, I can hear that lick in there. So that it's a way that you can take what your hands do and relate it to the bigger music. I personally don't have the need to, like they do in the classes, you know, spend all day on one tune. You know the Irish singer, Paul Brady? He told me once that when he was growing up . . . our music was so inspiring to him, not the sounds, but the idea that someone from the city could learn the traditions of their country and actually play it and have a great time with it. And that's what got him going, he said. I really appreciated that.

Fall Festival. (Watercolor; courtesy of Jane Voorhees)

Four Days in August; pencil drawing, Galax, Va., Fiddlers'
Convention. (From *Willard Gayheart: Appalachian Artist* [© 2003
Willard Gayheart and Donia S. Eley], by permission of McFarland
& Company, Inc., Box 611, Jefferson, North Carolina, 28640,
www.mcfarlandpub.com)

who brought a driving rock-and-roll-flavored energy. By the 1980s, the Horse Flies were fusing alternative rock and world music influences with the old-time sound. For the Chicken Chokers, it was a reggae-rap-old-time hybrid. The music reached new audiences with adventurous interpretations and crossovers. By the 1990s, the members of the Chicken Chokers had gone back to the more-traditional roots of the old-time sound in the fiddle-band lineup of the Primitive Characters. The strength of the tradition was always in its ability to embrace all comers, who were, sooner or later, infused with the deep essence of old-time.

OLD-TIME MUSIC GIVES BIRTH TO COUNTRY AND BLUEGRASS

By the turn of the twentieth century, an invention was being refined that has more to do with the widespread popularity of Appalachian music than any particular instrument: Thomas Edison's recording machine. Columbia and Victor made Edison wax cylinders and Berliner flat discs commercially available for the first time. By the 1920s, the recording industry was in full swing. The 1922 Victor recordings of Henry Gilliland and Alexander "Eck" Robertson in New York, and Fiddlin' John Carson on Okeh Records the following year, encouraged other national record labels—such as Columbia, Decca, ARC, Sears, and Paramount—to sign string-band musicians, ushering in a golden age of recorded old-time music. In a matter of a few years, the music of the Appalachian fiddle and banjo would travel from the remote mountain hollows to audiences who might never have seen these instruments being played. Radio was the partner needed to complete this journey. It is difficult for most of us now to imagine the revolution that radio technology ushered in during the early twentieth century. In 1920 the "wireless" was being declared the new object of home-based entertainment. People had to purchase kits at first that used razor blades and crystals as the main components for building their own wirelesses. By 1930, people were

able to purchase ready-built units, and 12 million homes were equipped with radio sets in the United States (although this was not a luxury everyone could afford; in 1930 only 1 percent of African American families owned a radio). Sales grew during the Great Depression, and by 1935, the number of homes with radios had grown to 22 million. Radio was the original mass media outlet for entertainment, information, and advertising, drawing even larger audiences than cinema. For the first time, Appalachian music reached out over the airwaves from the hills and into homes all across America.

Regular programs on radio and national live concerts meant that old-time musicians were able to make a living from what may only have been a hobby. High-powered southern radio stations in Atlanta, Georgia; Charlotte, North Carolina; and Nashville, Tennessee, reached audiences far and wide, from the mountain coves to the textile towns. A new label, "hillbilly," was coined to describe the old-time sound crossing the airwaves. The origin of the term is unclear, but it is doubtful that, as some have contended, it came from the "Billy Boys," Ulster Protestant supporters of Ireland's seventeenth-century King William, now dwelling in the hills. More likely, it is simply another example of Scots and Ulster vernacular migrating along with the music: "billie" or "billy" is an old Scots word for "fellow" or "companion." "Hillbilly" first appeared

Doc Watson: Feeling Every Note at 78-rpm

David Holt, American multi-instrumentalist, singer, and collector; interviewed in Swannanoa, North Carolina, July 2009, by Fiona Ritchie and Doug Orr at the Swannanoa Gathering folk arts workshops.

Doc Watson grew up in Deep Gap, North Carolina, among . . . mountain people, deep mountain-roots people, deep mountain roots. His grandmother sang ballads, and different people in his family played, but he didn't have a lot of musicians to listen to, and when he was young, his father bought a crank 78, I mean, he bought a hand-cranked 78-rpm record player, and that was a revelation to Doc because he could hear these great people like the Delmore brothers and, you know, a lot of blues guys like Mississippi John Hurt, Bill Monroe, and Merle Travis, all these guys. He could hear these guys in his home and sit there and learn it off the records. So he was one of the first guys, you know, to be super influenced by the mass media. Not one of the first, but certainly, it was a big part of his life, because he was blind, and he had access to the record player and he could listen to that as much as he wanted.

And he had an unbelievably quick ear, and he's, I would say, he's the most musical person I've ever met, and . . . I've met some really musical people, but I think, at the heart of things, he's the most musical person I've ever met. Very smart, intelligent person, you know; realize that he was trying to make a living performing and figuring out how to do that pretty quickly and make it natural and not make it phony, and make it real, and people really connected to that and he's still that way. He's eighty-six now,* we've been playing together for twelve years, and his picking is slowing down just a little bit, but I mean, he still does things that blow my mind every time that I play with him. He's really something, because he's so musical, he hasn't learned something rote, he really feels every note. And I think because he's blind, he can put all of his feeling into that note. He's not looking out into the audience and seeing how people are reacting, he's just like thinking about that and totally involved in what he's playing. It's powerful. [*Doc Watson passed away on May 29, 2012.]

in print in a 1900 *New York Journal* article and was used in 1925 when a group of old-time musicians recorded at Okeh Studios in New York and then in a Washington, D.C., radio broadcast the following year.[48] "Hillbilly" then entered the American vernacular, often used sneeringly to refer to hill folks and their music. Jean Ritchie recalls in her autobiography, *Singing Family of the Cumberlands*, that "they were getting to be all the fashion, those radio songs, the young folks went around singing 'Pale Wildwood Flower' and 'Sweet Fern.' 'Hillbilly Songs' the radio called this music, and it claimed that these songs were sung all through the mountains, but we never heard anything just like them before. I guess if it hadn't been for radio, it's no telling how long it would have taken us to find out that we were supposed to be 'hillbillies,' or what kind of songs we were supposed to sing."[49] No matter how clichéd and inaccurate it was, the hillbilly label stuck. It recalls, to some extent, the lampooning endured by the African Americans during the blackface minstrelsy era and beyond, albeit without the more-serious racist undertones.

Impact of Radio and the Recording Industry

Mike Seeger (1933–2009), American folklorist, multi-instrumentalist, and traditional roots-music preservationist, Lexington, Virginia; Recorded on June 5, 2009, in conversation with Banning Eyre for BBC Radio 3's World Routes, *produced by Peter Meanwell. "An Appalachian Road Trip" was first broadcast on October 17, 2009.*

Imagine a time before there was radio and recordings, and during that time, you got all your information by somebody that you could see face to face, or hear face to ear. And all of a sudden, there is this possibility of hearing somebody you've never seen before and who's been elevated to the place of this new gadget that can reproduce that voice from somebody somewhere else. And it gives you a different idea towards the music that you make. The recording companies would come into a place where there was a circle of musicians around, and they'd advertise in the papers: "Wanted—Old Time Musicians," or they'd do it by word of mouth sometimes. And then the record people who came in [would] sell that music back to the people of that surrounding community and actually all over the United States.

In the 1920s, the new thing was a banjo, fiddle, and guitar group. About 1930 (and not necessarily to do with the Depression) record companies needed to move on; they couldn't continue recording the same things over and over again. So as rural music became more of a commodity through recordings and radio, things had to move along more quickly to create new sounds. So people were trying to figure out new ways of playing traditional music. Those new ways dominated to such an extent that people at home would rather turn the radio on than try to play the banjo themselves because they thought that music was better—and it probably was in some cases, more in tune and so forth, because these were played by professional musicians. So the effect was for the new commercial musics to kill homemade music, and that reached its bottom point sometime in the fifties. Then there was a revival in the urban areas (as there had been from time to time), and then our group started [The New Lost City Ramblers], and then a few of us in the urban areas started documenting the music and then started playing it, going to fiddlers conventions or just celebrating the older forms of music. And people in the South began saying: "Well you know what was back then . . . maybe it is good, maybe it is interesting." And I think that we are now in a reflowering or revitalization of the concept of making music for yourself amongst people—in the South, too, not just from the urban areas. We should always remember that most of the people living in the city need only go back one or two generations to find people who were rural people, and so you're not that far from it always.

Carter Family Influences

Jack Beck, Scottish singer and broadcaster; interviewed in Dunkeld, Scotland, June 2012, by Fiona Ritchie as he led a group of American ballad scholars on a tour of Scotland.

If I hear someone like older people singing a song which has a verse in it, for instance, which goes, "Who's gonna shoe your pretty little foot? Who's gonna glove your hand?," I know that comes straight from "Lord Gregory," you know, "The Lass of Roch Royal." I know the Scottish ballad where that comes from. I love the idea that it's still there, and it's still being sung. It isn't that big a deal if these people don't know where it comes from. But I can see it in front of me with my own eyes, carrying on. And it's all still there.

Oh, there's a shiver goes down my spine, every time. Sometimes it's much more subtle than that. I'm sure you're aware, there's a Carter Family song, one of the first ones they recorded, one that they had in their family for quite a while before they were ever discovered. It's called "The Storms Are on the Ocean." And the first verse could have been written by Robert Burns: "I'm going away to leave you, love. / I'm going away for awhile, / But I'll return to see you sometime, / Though I go ten thousand miles." You know, very familiar stuff. And then it has the two verses: "Who will dress your pretty little feet? / Who will glove your hand?" Obviously, these two verses were straight out of "Lord Gregory," so that is a very good example of that much subtler connection, that first verse which has the timeless folk phraseology in it that Burns so connected to. So the connections can be a lot subtler than the same tune with a different title or verses in a song. It can be much more subliminal, more of a character, cultural, subtle connection. And I find that fascinating as well

A significant watershed in the music's evolution was the fabled "Bristol Sessions" in 1927, sometimes referred to as the "Big Bang" of country music. There had been southern field sessions before at the historic Okeh Studio in Atlanta and in Asheville in 1925. The Victor Talking Machine Company brought a field unit to Bristol, Tennessee/Virginia, in order to record the region's musicians on State Street, Bristol's main thoroughfare. The sessions took place between July 25 and August 5, and string bands, sacred-song singers, harmonica soloists, and other musicians were all recorded. Most of the performers did not achieve any commercial success from this exposure, but two certainly did: Jimmie Rodgers and the Carter Family. A. P. Carter; his wife, Sara; and her first cousin, Maybelle Addington, were from nearby Maces Spring, Virginia. Upon hearing their distinctive mountain harmonies, Victor's Ralph Peer knew he had struck gold. Their family voices blended perfectly, accompanied by guitar and autoharp. Some consider this encounter, including the Bristol Sessions recording of Jimmie Rodgers, as the birth of country music. The Carters were drawing upon the old ballad and hymn traditions of the mountains. Their repertoire encompassed A. P. Carter's collection of hundreds of Scots-Irish and Appalachian folk songs in the vicinity of their Virginia and Tennessee homes.

Regardless of origin, most of their songs were simply referred to as "Carter Family songs." Some were composed by others, such as "Wildwood Flower," a

THE CARTER FAMILY

The members of the original Carter Family were Alvin Pleasant (A. P.) Delaney Carter; his wife, Sara Dougherty; and her younger cousin, Maybelle. They grew up in southwestern Virginia surrounded by the music traditions of the mountains: old ballads, gospel songs, and shape-note and close-harmony singing. A. P. and Sarah were married in 1915, settling in Maces Springs, where A. P. worked at various jobs. Through the first decade of their marriage, A. P. and Sara performed regularly at local events and gatherings. In 1926 Maybelle, who was married to A. P.'s brother Ezra ("Eck"), joined the couple, and they began auditioning at newly established recording companies. During the legendary Bristol Sessions of 1927 in Tennessee, Ralph Peer of the Victor Talking Machine Company, soon to become RCA Victor Records, recorded the Carters on several tracks: the eighteenth-century parlor song "Bury Me under the Weeping Willow," the old Scots-sourced ballad "Storms Are on the Ocean," and a gospel song found by A. P. called "Poor Orphan Child." These records sold well, and RCA Victor signed the trio to a long-term contract. A mere three years after they were recorded at the Bristol Sessions, the Carter Family had sold 300,000 records and were well on their way to becoming an American music institution.

The Carters' hallmark blend of voices and instruments, whether recorded or in live performance, swiftly struck a chord with their audiences. Sara sang lead and played autoharp and guitar. A. P. produced a haunting baritone with a "tear drop" in his voice, a distinctive regional style from the heart of his native Clinch Mountains. Maybelle contributed alto harmony and played a bass-string lead on a large L-5 Gibson guitar, while strumming a rhythm on the treble strings. This innovative approach to guitar accompaniment became a signature of the Carter sound. "Maybelle-style leads" soon influenced other players who had previously strummed rhythm guitar in the background of string bands. The Carter Family's recordings opened people's ears to the potential for guitar accompaniment offering a solo melody line.

The Carter Family repertoire reflected the values and concerns of traditional mountain communities: a longing for home and a strong sense of locality, lost and unrequited love, the hardships of life and work, hopes for a better tomorrow, church and religion, faraway places, family ties, and fond returns to the beloved coves and hills of home. A. P was the song collector, arranger, and occasional composer of the group's material. Once the Carters had exhausted their own family repertoires, A. P. embarked upon song-hunting expeditions, primarily through the Tri-Cities region of Johnson City, Kingsport, and Bristol, Tennessee (and Bristol, Virginia). Lesley "Esley" Riddle proved to be a valuable resource. The African American singer and guitarist would accompany A. P. on his song hunts and had a gift for retaining melodies to share later with Sara and Maybelle. With verses, song fragments, and expressions picked up from the locals they encountered, they would then build complete songs. In this way, they continued in the tradition of song collecting and restoring dating back to Ulster and Scotland, most famously practiced there by Robert Burns. In the quest for fresh material to refurbish, they would also peruse old songbooks and pamphlets. As the Carters' fame grew, yet more material would arrive by mail, with admirers sending them songs, sayings, and poems. A. P. did sporadically compose songs from scratch, although he was primarily a collector and arranger of old songs and verses gleaned from the public domain. For example, three of the titles most commonly identified as "Carter Family songs" were actually composed much earlier by others: "Wildwood Flower," originally "I'll Twine 'Mid the Ringlets" (1860), composed by Joseph Webster to a Maud Irving poem; "Will the Circle Be Unbroken" (1907), a Christian hymn written by Ada Habershon and Charles Gabriel; and "Keep on the Sunnyside" (1899), written by Ada Blenkhorn and Howard Entwisle. The Carter Family song "Single Girl, Married Girl" (CD track 16), recorded by Atwater Donnelly, was an early frontier favorite drawing upon many variants, including "Still I Love Him," collected by Ewan MacColl and Peggy Seeger for their anthology *Travellers' Songs from England and Scotland*.

The Carter Family's radio following became so widespread that in 1938 they moved to Texas to perform on the Mexican high-wattage "Border Radio." Charlotte, North Carolina, where radio station WBT transmitted a powerful 100,000-watt signal covering the South and beyond, was their destination in 1942. In early December 1941, with *Life* magazine ready to run a Carter Family cover story, they had been primed for high-profile national exposure. World events, however, ensured that the *Life* story never went to print. December 7, 1941, is forever recorded as President Franklin D. Roosevelt's "date which will live in infamy." Pearl Harbor was attacked, and the following day, the United States declared war on Japan. Understandably, all other news took a backseat.

The Carters continued to record, perform, and ride a wave of popularity throughout the 1930s, despite the collapse of A. P. and Sara's marriage. The couple divorced in 1939, and the group disbanded in 1943 when Sara and her new husband, A. P.'s first cousin Coy Bayes, moved west to California. A. P. headed back to Maces Springs to run his country store. Maybelle began to record and tour with her daughters June, Anita, and Helen as "Mother Maybelle and the Carter Sisters." In 1949 and 1950, a promising young guitarist, Chet Atkins, joined them. The year 1970 saw the original members of the Carter Family honored as the inaugural inductees into the Country Music Hall of Fame.

Today, the Carter Family Memorial Music Center is located in the Poor Valley region of southwest Virginia at the foot of Clinch Mountain. The complex includes the Carter Family Museum, the Carter Store, and the Carter Fold concert center, which has an 842-seat auditorium and a dance floor. The weekly concerts held there are dedicated to preserving the mountain music tradition advanced by the Carter Family. Johnny Cash, who married Maybelle's daughter, June Carter, performed his last concert there in July 2003, shortly before his death. Folk revivalists of the 1960s, including Joan Baez, the Kingston Trio, and Bob Dylan, ensured the Carter Family legacy would endure, and it docs still today. From back-porch song circles to festival stages, a "Carter song" will almost always find its way onto the bill. There is a "folktale" character to the family's rise from humble beginnings to a musical career that has had a lasting impact upon bluegrass, country, pop, gospel, and folk music in the United States and beyond. The story has even been revisited in a graphic novel, the 2013 Eisner Award–winning illustrated biography *The Carter Family: Don't Forget This Song* by Frank M. Young and David Lasky.

variant of lyricist Maud Irving's and composer Joseph Webster's 1860 song "I'll Twine 'Mid the Ringlets." Others had been brought across the sea on the emigration ships, such the old Scots ballad "The Lass of Roch Royal," adapted for the Carter Family standard "The Storms Are on the Ocean":

> I'm going away to leave you love I'm going away
> or a while,
> But I'll return to see you sometime, if I go ten
> thousand miles.
>
> [Chorus] The storms are on the ocean, the
> heavens may cease to be,
> This world may lose its motion love, if I prove
> false to thee.
>
> Have you seen that mournful dove, flying from
> pine to pine,
> Mournin' for his own true love, just like I mourn
> for mine.

> I'll never go back on the ocean love, I'll never go
> back on the sea,
> I'll never go back on my blue-eyed girl, though
> she goes back on me.

William Cash, who emigrated from Scotland to the American colonies in the mid-seventeenth century, would likely have known some of the songs collected by A. P. Carter. The next generation of William's family migrated into the Virginia area, and his descendant, Johnny Cash, married Maybelle Carter's daughter June. The carrying stream had found yet another tributary that flows onward today through the music of Rosanne Cash.

From their first recordings on Victor 78-rpm records and early radio broadcasts, the Carter Family attracted a loyal audience across many parts of the country. Also in 1927, Jimmie Rodgers, the "Singing Brakeman," made his first radio appearance on WWNC in his adopted hometown of Asheville. Despite his untimely death from tuberculosis just five years later, Rodgers went on to sell more records for Victor than possibly any artist until Elvis Presley. The Carter Family, meanwhile, performed over high-wattage radio outlets from the Mexican border stations to WBT in Charlotte. By 1943, the year the original band-member configuration stopped performing together, they had created a remarkable song legacy: over 300 master recordings.

In launching the careers of the Carter Family and Jimmie Rodgers, the Bristol Sessions marked an important watershed in American cultural history. Their discovery and widespread transmission was seminal. The popularity of these artists helped the so-called hillbilly music gather momentum and then diverge, some ethnomusicologists believe, along two paths: Rodgers provided the basis for modern country music, with its emphasis on individual singing, songwriting, and acoustic guitar accompaniment; and the Carter Family, with their use of traditional songs, melodies, and high-nasal harmony vocals, was the foundation for bluegrass and folk music.[50] The real foundation

THE SEEGER FAMILY

There are few families more strongly linked with the cultural heritage of the United States than the Seegers. For well over half a century, Pete, Mike, and Peggy Seeger each made an indelible impression on the American folk scene, including music of the Appalachians and transatlantic traditions. The Seegers' home setting was one in which music always thrived. Their father, Charles, was an ethnomusicologist. Mike and Peggy's mother was modernist composer Ruth Crawford Seeger; Pete's mother, Charles' first wife, was Constance de Clyver Edson, a classical violinist and music teacher at the Juilliard School. A partial list of steady visitors to the Seeger home reads as a roll call of the American folk-music revival's inspirational forces: Woody Guthrie, Lead Belly, John and Alan Lomax, John Jacob Niles, Lee Hays, and Beth Lomax Hawes. As Pete was the older half sibling, he, too, was a warmly anticipated guest on visits home, especially with his long neck banjo slung across his shoulder.

Mike Seeger (1933–2009) was the sibling most deeply involved with the traditional music of the Appalachians and the southern United States. A performer, collector, researcher, and writer, he would become a highly influential figure in the traditional music revival of the late twentieth century. At age five, Mike was already singing "Barbara Allen," Appalachia's ubiquitous old Scottish ballad (CD track 1). Distinguished musical guests were regularly passing through the Seeger household, but there was a more permanent fixture in the home that had long since retired from music. Ruth Seeger had hired Elizabeth "Libba" Cotten as a housekeeper. While working at the Seegers' instrument-filled home, Libba was inspired to revisit her own guitar playing. After a break of four decades, she retaught herself her own unique style, turning the guitar upside down for left-handed play without reversing the strings. In this position, she created a melody and bass finger style now known as "Cotten picking." She rediscovered her own songs, including her signature "Freight Train," which she had written at the age of eleven.

Peggy and Mike soon realized that Libba had an extensive repertoire of secular and gospel songs in addition to the songs she had written. In the late 1950s, Mike made home recordings of Libba's songs, later released on Smithsonian Folkways Records. The impact of this work demonstrated to Mike the importance of discovering and preserving tradition and helped set his life's course as a collector and torch bearer of the music for over fifty years. Mike was intent upon divining and sharing the "story behind the music," tracing the migration of the songs and tunes to their European and African origins. He was dedicated to valuing authenticity in what he called "music from the true vine" and was a persistent researcher, eventually securing several grants from the National Endowment for the Arts for his work. As a performer, he was skilled on a remarkable assortment of traditional instruments, including banjo, fiddle, autoharp, guitar, mandolin, mountain dulcimer, jaw harp, quills, and even the Andean pan pipes. Banjo was his favorite, however, and in 1956 Mike produced his first documentary recording *American Banjo: Three Finger and Scruggs Style*. The following year, he cofounded revivalist string band the New Lost City Ramblers, a group that became an integral part of the urban folk revival. He performed with the band for the next twenty-one years, as the Ramblers drew upon traditional playing styles they picked up from 78-rpm records in the Library of Congress collection. He applied himself to extensive fieldwork, covering the spectrum of Appalachian and southern music. As a direct result, a new generation was soon rediscovering long overlooked musicians. One of those was Moran Lee "Dock" Boggs, an old-time singer and banjo player from Virginia who combined Appalachian traditional music with African American blues. Mike invited Boggs to the 1963 Mountain Dance and Folk Festival in Asheville and uncovered many more musical gems. Mike's career eventually included six Grammy nominations, thirty documentary recordings, and performances in forty more recordings. There has not been a more faithful and valued steward of the music of the mountains than this Seeger family member, born and raised in the cities of the Northeast.

After leaving the Seeger home, Peggy Seeger embarked upon a life of music and travel, living for periods in Washington, D.C.; the Netherlands; London; Asheville, North Carolina; and Boston. She is now settled in England to be close to her children. Twenty-two solo recordings of Peggy singing with guitar and banjo, as well as her dozens of collaborations, feature traditional ballads, songs of social and political commentary, love songs, children's songs, and self-penned anthems for the women's movement. While staying in London in 1956, Peggy met British folksinger, songwriter, social activist, and playwright Ewan MacColl. MacColl's 1957 ode to their first meeting, "The First Time Ever I Saw Your Face," became a major international hit for Roberta Flack in 1972. The Seeger-MacColl love match resulted in a fruitful musical partnership—and eventually a marriage that lasted until MacColl's death in 1989. MacColl and Seeger performed in folk clubs all over Britain. During their travels, they were avid collectors of little-known traditional songs, including songs of the Scottish and English Traveller communities, through their field recordings of the Stewarts of Blair, "Queen" Caroline Hughes of Dorset, and Maggie McPhee of Banffshire. Their commercial recordings included two multivolume projects of Child Ballads. Peggy would later reflect that she and Ewan were particularly enthralled with finding songs on each side of the Atlantic that shared similar themes and origins. Uniquely positioned to appreciate the transatlantic flow of traditions, Peggy Seeger performs today with her children, recording the old ballads, savoring the unaccompanied songs, and still working on her own songwriting. At London's Royal Albert Hall in 2014, Peggy Seeger led an international array of guest musicians, as well as a national television audience, in the singing of Pete Seeger's "Quite Early Morning" in tribute to her late brother. Pete Seeger himself had performed at the hall on four occasions between 1961 and 1978.

Pete Seeger (1919–2014) was already immersed in a life of music while Mike and Peggy were growing up. He was a regular on U.S. radio stations in the 1940s and, with the Weavers, enjoyed many chart hits in the 1950s. From his early days with the

Almanac Singers and Woody Guthrie to more-recent performances with grandson Tao Rodriguez Seeger seven decades later, Pete's journey has been devoted to harnessing the power of music to unite, enlighten, and change hearts and minds. There are so many chapters to the Pete Seeger story that it can read like a chronicle of twentieth-century American sociopolitical movements: the McCarthy hearings and the blacklisting that followed; the civil rights movement, in which he popularized the anthem "We Shall Overcome"; the protest movement of the Vietnam War era; and the raising of environmental consciousness through his Hudson River Sloop Clearwater Foundation to highlight and resolve the polluting of the river. Through the decades, Pete Seeger's chosen music accompaniment was his long neck banjo, central to his influential 1948 manual *How to Play the Five-String Banjo*. During July 1936, seventeen-year-old Pete traveled through the Blue Ridge Mountains with his father and stepmother, attending Bascom Lamar Lunsford's Mountain Dance and Folk Festival in western North Carolina. There, Pete watched square-dance teams, heard family string bands, and had his formative exposure to five-string banjo, played by Samantha Bumgarner. In an interview with the authors (excerpted elsewhere in this book), he described the experience as life changing. Seeing Lunsford stage the event and announce a steady parade of solo performers and bands left a lasting impression of "ordinary working people making fantastically good music." Most of all, Pete said that Lunsford patiently showed him basic banjo licks that he practiced for the next several years, grounding his

playing technique. Pete Seeger, at an impressionable age, had looked firsthand into the deep well of tradition, and the moment stayed with him for life. He went on to invent the long neck, or Seeger, banjo, taking the five-string instrument, until then largely limited to the Appalachian region, out to an international audience. He thus helped embed the image of the archetypal American folk instrument. It is but one of Seeger's indelible impressions on popular and folk culture, as marked by his lifetime achievement Grammy Award in 1993 and his National Medal of Arts in 1994. He nurtured the transatlantic musical dialogue through recordings and tours in the United Kingdom and by embracing social-justice singers and songwriters, including Scotland's Dick Gaughan and Northern Ireland's Tommy Sands, both of whom have recorded Pete Seeger songs. His dedication to the power of song and his commitment to his causes were unshakable. In August 2013, one month after the death of Toshi, his wife of sixty years, Pete Seeger traveled to attend a 400-year commemoration in New York City of a treaty between the Iroquois and the Dutch. Interviewed that day by Democracy Now!, he sang "I Come and Stand at Every Door" to commemorate the sixty-eighth anniversary of the nuclear bombings of Hiroshima and Nagasaki. His full life ended at age ninety-four on January 27, 2014. Across the world, people remembered Pete Seeger and celebrated his unique contributions by singing his songs. No doubt they always will.

Dolly Parton playing her dulcimer, 2005.
(Courtesy of Duane Gordon)

ring source of inspiration. Their music traveled back across the sea to the British Isles and Ireland to replenish the old musical wellspring once again. The Beatles freely acknowledged their debt to the close harmonies of the Everly Brothers, who had polished their sound growing up in Knoxville, Tennessee, initially singing with parents Ike and Margaret as the Everly Family. Their Appalachian harmonies also had a profound impact on some of the most successful American recording artists of the 1960s and 1970s, including the Beach Boys and Simon and Garfunkel.

Radio broadcasts continued to extend this rural, mountain-based music to an expanding audience across the United States. The Barn Dance format was launched in the 1920s in Fort Worth, Texas, and radio stations in other cities followed that successful formula over the years, such as Shreveport's KWKH *Louisiana Hayride* (which helped introduce Hank Williams, Kitty Wells, and Elvis Presley) and the WSM *Grand Ole Opry* out of Nashville, which first broadcast on various stations in 1925, being picked up for national broadcast by NBC in 1941. Nashville and the Opry soon became the hub of American country music, and today's Opry general manager Pete Fisher could be speaking on behalf of more traditional musical styles when he says: "The key to the Opry's longevity can be attributed to its ability to evolve with the ever-changing musical landscape of the times." Musicians and Nashville music-industry representatives dropped the term "hillbilly music" in favor of "country" some time ago. In recent years, musicians with Appalachian roots—Ricky Skaggs, Doc Watson, Dwight Yoakam, Kathy Mattea, and Dolly Parton (with her trilogy of folk- and bluegrass-flavored albums released between 1999 and 2002)—have helped reconnect country music with its heritage.

Bluegrass music sprang from the Appalachian tradition, going back to the Scots-Irish forebears. In the bluegrass trademark "high lonesome sound," it is easy to detect the a capella or sean-nós singing of the old balladeers, and likewise the earlier fiddle playing

stones were, of course, located at a much deeper level, in soil that nourished the roots of traditions stretching back through the Appalachians and across the sea. The Carters' legacy of pure mountain harmonies would inspire other family music groups in the 1930s and 1940s, leading to the continued development of folk song and the beginnings of bluegrass, while also providing a key ingredient in the birth of rock and roll. Many artists followed in their path: Woody Guthrie, the Seegers, Bill Monroe, the Kingston Trio, the Everly Brothers, Doc Watson, Joan Baez, Judy Collins, Emmylou Harris, Peter Paul and Mary, Bob Dylan, and Dolly Parton, for whom traditional Appalachian songs are a recur-

DOLLY PARTON: A LIFE OF MANY COLORS

Dolly Rebecca Parton was born in Locust Ridge near Sevierville, Tennessee, where the foothills of the Great Smoky Mountains give way to the Tennessee valley. Her parents, tobacco sharecropper Robert Lee Parton and Avie Lee Owens, could never have imagined that their fourth-born child would become one of the most successful songwriters—in any genre—of her generation.

Dolly Parton's ancestors settled in Sevier County in the eighteenth century, some having migrated there via Pennsylvania. Family names reveal a classic southern Appalachian blend of English, Scots-Irish, and German ancestry. Although the Partons were relatively poor, Dolly's childhood was musically rich; her mother played guitar, and her maternal grandfather was a fiddler. Dolly was one of twelve children, and her siblings and extended family commonly played mandolins, guitars, and fiddles. As a child, it was the banjo that enchanted Dolly, and she learned to play traditional clawhammer style. As it did in so many families in Appalachia, singing played a significant role in the Parton home, and Dolly learned traditional ballads and love songs, writing her own songs beginning at age seven. Through the years, her lyrics have often echoed the rhythms and narrative craft of the ballads that filled her childhood. On one of her earliest recordings in 1963, *Hits Made Famous by Country Queens*, Dolly arranged two Appalachian ballads—"Two Little Orphans" and "Little Blossoms"—in addition to her own "Letter to Heaven," which sensitively recalls the ballad form. Remarkably, Dolly has composed in excess of 3,000 songs, scoring major international hits with "Jolene," "9 to 5," and "Coat of Many Colors," an ode to her mother's determined efforts to provide for her children during times of scarcity. For all of Dolly's success, her pride in these humble roots remains undiminished; Dolly's original coat of many colors, fashioned by her mother from scraps of material, is still on display at the Dollywood Museum in her family vacation park in Pigeon Forge, Tennessee.

Dolly Parton is one of country music's true superstars, and her album sales have gone gold, platinum, or double platinum more than two dozen times. She has eight Grammy Awards and countless Country Music Awards to her name. Her cherished movie appearances have attracted an Academy Award nomination. As a songwriter, she achieved the rare feat of topping the U.S. country charts twice with "I Will Always Love You," as well as seeing the song become one of the best-selling singles of all time when Whitney Houston recorded it for the 1992 film *The Bodyguard*.

With Dolly's substantial successes in both the commercial music industry and the wider business world, it is easy to overlook the current of Appalachian musical traditions that flows gently through her musical life. In the 1990s, she explored these roots in a trilogy of recordings inspired by folk, bluegrass, and country gospel music; released between 1999 and 2002, the resultant albums were *The Grass Is Blue*, *Little Sparrow*, and *Halos & Horns*. The works were critically acclaimed and credited with winning new devotees for bluegrass and music from Appalachian roots. On her 1994 album *Heartsongs: Live from Home*, she blended original and traditional songs, including "Wayfaring Stranger" and "Barbara Allen" (CD track 1).

Dolly Parton's musical career is shaded with many colors. Her more-mainstream country albums often resonate with the sounds of her early traditional music making and the spirituals she heard in church as a child. The early country music radio of her youth and her years in Nashville have bestowed yet more influences: gospel, honky-tonk, bluegrass, blues, and country pop. She has managed to stitch it all together in a uniquely fulfilling career with a lilting soprano voice widely celebrated as one of the most expressive in country music.

While other parts of the southern United States saw significant growth in the second half of the twentieth century, many areas of Appalachia continued to struggle economically. Dolly Parton met local concerns head-on, taking the initiative of investing in business ventures in the heart of her native eastern Tennessee. With over 3 million visitors annually, her Dollywood amusement park at Pigeon Forge has been a major boon in revitalizing the region. Through the Dollywood Foundation, she supports many charitable efforts, and "Dolly Parton's Imagination Library" has made childhood literacy a major focus of her efforts. Beginning in Sevier County, Tennessee, the program is now distributing millions of books to children across the United States, Canada, and the United Kingdom.

Dolly Parton continues to record albums into the fifth decade of her career, and her live show is as popular as ever across North America, Europe, and Australia. Among all her international acclaim, however, she is most proud of the statue on the lawn of the Sevierville courthouse, a touching local tribute that keeps her close to the heart of the community in which she sang her earliest songs.

We Were Waltzing That Night: Blue Grass Boy. (Pencil drawing; from *New Art of Willard Gayheart* [© 2014 Willard Gayheart and Donia S. Eley], by permission of McFarland & Company, Inc., Box 611, Jefferson North Carolina, 28640, www.mcfarlandpub.com)

styles. Bill Monroe, the "Father of Bluegrass," came from the outskirts of the Appalachians. Born in 1911 in Rosine in the western Kentucky lowland country north of Nashville, he readily attributed his music's roots to Appalachia and the Scots-Irish connection and in turn helped revive post–World War II interest in the music of the mountains. An important Monroe family member was Uncle Pendleton Vandiver, who played the fiddle and "got a wonderful Scots-Irish sound."[51] Monroe remembered him in his composition "Uncle Pen."

Oh the people would come from far away,
To dance all night to the break of day.
When the caller would holler "Do Si Do,"
They knew Uncle Pen was ready to go.

Well, he played an old tune they called "Soldiers Joy,"
And he played the one they called the "Boston Boy."
Greatest of all was the "Jenny Lynn,"
To me, that's where the fiddlin' begins.

OLD-TIME AND BLUEGRASS: THE DIFFERENCES

Most people who hear fiddles, banjos, guitars, and mandolins think they are listening to "bluegrass" music. The shared array of instruments, interspersed with songs of the mountains, does blur the distinction between old-time music and bluegrass. And there is, indeed, overlap: the repertoires share some fiddle tunes, a few bands have carved out a hybrid position, and they are each branches of the same musical family tree. Both are nominally acoustic genres. Most of the dissimilarities, once highlighted, are easy to hear, and they start with an appreciation of the old-time and bluegrass positions in the musical timeline. Old-time is the immediate descendant of the music ferried across the Atlantic to America and the Appalachians in the eighteenth century by the Scots-Irish immigrants. They played, sang, re-interpreted, and retitled pieces brought from home, and they fashioned original music to suit their new environment. Bluegrass evolved largely out of the old-time tradition in the late 1930s with Bill Monroe and the Blue Grass Boys. The following characteristics, based on the work of folklorist and old-time musician Ron Pen, are some of the things to listen for when differentiating between the two American music genres.

Tempo. Bluegrass is simply much more up-tempo than old-time music, which is more restrained. Strict dance tempo is still the basis for much fiddle playing back to the old countries, and old-time is likewise often set to dance tempos. Old-time fiddlers are well versed in the style and tempo of various kinds of dances, including squares, contras, ceilis, balances, and waltzes.

Instrumentation. Old-time music emphasizes the fiddle as its lead instrument with a distinctive clawhammer banjo accompaniment, supported by acoustic guitar, upright or double bass, and sometimes mandolin. Bluegrass highlights the fingerpicked banjo, with frequent guitar riffs and strums as well as the acoustic bass. In bluegrass, the mandolin will often replace the fiddle, and the dobro, or resonator guitar, has become a popular part of these ensembles. There is more emphasis on harmony singing within bluegrass circles, a sound that was not so established in the timeworn singing styles of the immigrants.

Musical style. The emphasis in old-time music is generally on rhythm, while bluegrass is more note dense. Many old-time tunes are conceived with fiddle cross tunings, with the pitch of the strings altered to resonate and drone. Double stops are frequent. Bluegrass is jazzier, with long bow strokes, a swing feel, and bluesy slides. Old-time banjo is usually frailed, clawhammer style, or played in a two-finger method to accompany the fiddle, whereas bluegrass banjo is picked with three-finger rolls, and the player wears metal or plastic fingerpicks.

Arrangements. The old-time sound stresses continuous melody in a full instrumental flow, with sung couplets overlaid for contrast. Like jazz, bluegrass tunes are arranged around a lead (head) instrument, with other instruments showcased in turn, performing break-out melody solos (leads). Others sit back in accompaniment before each solo comes back, in turn, to the head.

Context. Old-time music reflects its origins. It is dance music, back-porch music, festival music. It is enjoyed by concert audiences but not usually consciously designed for performance stages. Playing old-time is a communal activity. From the beginning, bluegrass has been largely intended as a commercial form for concert and festival stages and for recordings. A significant bluegrass-music industry has developed, whereas old-time defines itself in contrast to that marketable commodity. As a result, there are many successful bluegrass bands touring full-time, while old-time music may be a recreational pursuit for most players—albeit a passionate one. There are a number of exceptions, of course, including old-time fiddle virtuoso Bruce Molsky, who has traveled the world performing and teaching.

Repertoire. The tune roster straddles both genres; "Soldier's Joy," "Blackberry Blossom," "Whiskey Before Breakfast," and "Sally Goodin" are widely popular. Ralph Stanley and the Clinch Mountain Boys, and Ralph Blizard and the New Southern Ramblers, are two examples of bands that spanned both old-time and bluegrass. Bluegrass has extended well beyond the early fiddle repertoire, however, to embrace new songs with trademark high vocal harmonies; "Fox on the Run," "Orange Blossom Special," and "Rocky Top" are classic examples. Bluegrass bands like the Seldom Scene, founded in 1971, incorporated other influences, including gospel quartet singing and bluegrass versions of country music, rock, and classical pop. Banjo innovator Béla Fleck's New Grass Revival and Béla Fleck and the Flecktones further stretched the genre, as Fleck explored the possibilities of bluegrass-based crossover music and collaborations with many other artists. He has also moved beyond the bluegrass world in his passion for tracing the African roots of banjo, visiting Uganda, Tanzania, Gambia, and Mali (captured in the documentary *Throw Down Your Heart*) and playing the Malian ngoni (a banjo ancestor instrument). Old-time is also in touch with the roots of tradition, holding a place for earlier threads, including ballads, lyric folk songs, and hymns.

Learning Styles. Old-time music is generally an example of the oral tradition at work. Instruments and repertoires are often learned from family members, from sought-after veteran players, and, especially today, through the perpetual tune trades in festival campgrounds, where the red recording lights of compact digital devices illuminate the evening jam sessions. Method books, DVDs, and transcriptions in publications such as *Old Time Herald* have taken the music further. While individuals often develop their old-time and bluegrass repertoires by being immersed in sessions, bluegrass is also often learned through publications, such as Earl Scruggs's popular method book, tablature, and professional lessons. Both styles are taught at colleges and universities, where the curriculum includes bluegrass and old-time band classes; Appalachian State University, Belmont University, Berea College, East Tennessee State, and Warren Wilson College are all centers of learning in the heartlands of the music. Instrumentalist Happy Traum began Homespun Tapes to offer lessons on video and then DVD. Now his company offers thousands of lessons as direct downloads via Homespun Music Instruction. Other artists offer streaming lessons on video, sharing them on websites such as YouTube. Old-time and bluegrass instruction has never been more widely accessible to would-be players.

Improvisation. Old-time improvisation is narrowly focused. Players hone their performances over time, refining the tunes in subtle, nuanced ways. Bluegrass is based more on chorus improvisation, with solos taken, by arrangement, at the culmination of a chord progression. Bluegrass banjo, fiddle, mandolin, and guitar stylists deliver an abundance of notes at a rapid tempo.

Performer positioning and the "microphone bob." Bluegrass performers showcase the "bob and weave" around the microphone as they take turns with their instrumental breaks, leaning into the microphone for the characteristic three- and four-part harmonies. Old-time musicians, echoing the Scots-Irish dance roots of the music, prefer a stationary, simple semicircle that faces the dancers or an audience. Some old-time bands of many decades ago arranged performances and radio broadcasts as comedy sketches, with snippets of music interspersed, perhaps to help promote recordings. Today's old-time musicians share in the culture of performance restraint also respected by traditional ballad singers. In this way, they carry on a time-honored tradition that harks back to Scotland and Ireland, where, even in the company of the finest players, "it's not the singer, it's the song."

Bill Monroe also credited the itinerant African American blues guitarist Arnold Shultz as a key influence. Monroe had started performing professionally with his brother Charlie in the early 1930s as the Monroe Brothers, and his skill with the mandolin and emblematic high tenor voice contributed to their success. In the late 1930s, Monroe started his band the Blue Grass Boys, which gave a name to their distinctive sound. With fiddler Chubby Wise, bassist Cedric Rainwater, and the addition of Earl Scruggs and Lester Flatt in 1945, this lineup is generally considered the first bluegrass-band configuration. As it evolved, the style is noted for several key characteristics: string instruments with mandolin often in place of the fiddle as lead (especially in the Monroe band); a rolling, finger-picked banjo (the Earl Scruggs influence); guitar backup with instrumental breaks; dobro and bass; a high male lead vocal with close harmonies, the highest part providing a falsetto descant; some song selections from the gospel tradition; and a driving, fast-paced tempo, which Alan Lomax called "folk music in overdrive."

When listenership for live radio began to decline from its dizzy heights in the 1950s, bluegrass performers reached new audiences through up-and-coming syndicated television programs, recordings, and live concerts. The emergence of bluegrass festivals, numbering in the hundreds today in the United States and internationally, established this American art form on the global concert stage.

SUSTAINING THE MUSIC AND THE MOUNTAINS

Economic and social change descended on Appalachia in the first two decades of the twentieth century. To feed the burgeoning lumber industry, railroads were constructed, sawmills were built throughout the mountains, and new towns materialized. Landscapes and lifestyles altered substantially as mountain people were employed to cut trees, saw timber, and

Southern Appalachian Mountains.
(Courtesy of Amy White and Al Petteway)

Sustaining Song Traditions

Sheila Kay Adams, American ballad singer, banjo player, storyteller, and author; interviewed in Swannanoa, North Carolina, July 2009, by Fiona Ritchie during Traditional Song Week at the Swannanoa Gathering folk arts workshops.

World War II really came close to obliterating it, because that was when all those boys left, even if it was to work. See, daddy was deaf in one ear, and they wouldn't take him. He tried to volunteer three times. They wouldn't take him. And so he wound up going down from the mountains with momma, and they worked in the shipyards. And daddy said that that just about did away with the culture. Momma said that they just threw it away with both hands. . . . It was connected with poverty. Because they saw then how poor they were. Daddy said, he was on the same boat before, everybody bailing just as hard as they could until we got out.

That music . . . still reaches in there and touches something. And it comes from your heart. Because Granny said, if it don't, don't sing it. Yeah, if it ain't from your heart, don't sing it. I've had people come up to me from all over the place and say, "I remember my grandmother singing. I can just remember a little bit of it, have you ever heard?"—and they'll start asking about "The Two Sisters" or one about this cloven-hoofed thing ("The Daemon Lover"), or, you know, any number of 'em. Most of 'em have heard and remembered "Barbara Allen" (CD track 1) or some of those that Joan Baez did. But it's those old, old ones that they'll come and ask about that . . . it was all over the place at one time. The music will go on, you know, it always will. But the songs I worry about, because you really do have to have somebody sing it. Granny said looking at it in a book, and even Cecil Sharp himself says there's no way that I can put on there the ornamentation that these people do. They'll hold the weak spot, and slough over the spot that should be held. You know, it's an unusual style of singing, and you really do have to hear somebody. And Granny said it can't be on no record, 'cause you have to watch it.

---

build roads. Forests that had stood largely untouched for millennia were leveled, often causing heavy erosion, and fires ravaged the mountain slopes. In some regions, notably West Virginia and eastern Kentucky, another natural resource was coveted: coal. Coal mining became the mainstay of local economies, who paid a heavy price in denuded hillsides, coal-company exploitation, and poor health conditions from the effects of coal dust.

Next came improved roads, rural electrification in the 1930s, and the Tennessee Valley Authority (TVA), a government agency created in 1933 to modernize the region. The TVA built dams to provide cheap electricity across much of Tennessee and also parts of Kentucky, Georgia, North Carolina, Virginia, Alabama, and Mississippi. Electricity drew industry into the region and improved the farms, yet 15,000 families had to be relocated for the hydroelectric dam construction projects. Even as the outside world slowly arrived in the southern Appalachians, the younger generation began to hear of improved economic prospects in the textile mills of the Piedmont and the factories of the North. In some cases, company agents recruited whole families of "millbillies" who migrated to the mill towns in wagons containing all of their worldly goods. Catherine Marshall refers to this in her book *Christy*, based on her mother's experiences as a young schoolteacher in early twentieth-century Appalachia. In the prologue, she writes of visiting the area with her mother after World War II. The floor of the deserted mountain cabin where her mother had lived was littered with pieces of paper—receipts of many weeks of pay from a South Carolina textile mill. She looked at the dates and thought, "They're so many years back. The children must have left the mountains to work in a mill. And they sent most of their pay home."[52]

The outflow of young people and families from the mountains and rural areas continued after World

The Next Generation

Len Graham, Irish traditional singer and song collector; interviewed in Swannanoa, North Carolina, July 2012, by Fiona Ritchie and Doug Orr during Traditional Song Week at the Swannanoa Gathering folk arts workshops.

This is a big event that Sheila Kay Adams has been given the National Endowment of the Arts Award [National Heritage Fellowship]. That'll bring the profile up a bit. All of these things contribute to people becoming more aware that all these things are important; they're all part of the tradition. Reels, jigs, and hornpipes, all these dances that are danced all over the world now, a lot of them have common origins that we have to look [for] even beyond the isles of Ireland and Scotland and over here [in the United States] to mazurkas and polkas and all those dances coming in from eastern Europe. So those are all elements that we have to include in the big "traditional Celtic music," you know? So there's all sorts of other elements as well, and we should celebrate them all and make it all-embracing and not make it exclusive—make it inclusive that everybody can play this music and sing these songs and feel part of it. That's the important thing.

I hope they learn the "grá," which is the Irish [word] for a love of this music. But if they've never encountered this tradition of songs and music and dance that we love so much and we celebrate, this will give them a flavor of it, and they'll take it from there. Especially the younger people, they're the hope that will carry this baton to another generation and the next generation and the like to start to study it more thoroughly, and the next thing you know . . . well, like when I was starting out, there were very few books available on the traditions, you had to really delve deeply; but nowadays there's all sorts of access to collections up on the Internet, you've got all sorts of opportunities now for people to take it into third-level education. A lot of universities over in Scotland, in Ireland, and over here [in the United States] include traditional music and traditional song and folklore as part of their curriculum. So there is hope, and hopefully the people that come here to the Swannanoa Gathering will take away a little seed that will carry on, [and they will] pass it on to another generation.

War II. They left behind a culture that was one of America's oldest and richest, although one that was largely undervalued through the old hillbilly stereotypes perpetuated in the media. Some mountain counties looked destined to plummet to critically low population levels, with intractable pockets of poverty. Tourism began to surge in subsequent years, however, aided by the renowned scenery of the national parks and wilderness areas and the provision of outdoor sporting and leisure activities, such as skiing, kayaking, hiking, mountain biking, whitewater rafting, fishing, and golf. Although jobs were modestly paid, the tourist industry supported a growing service economy. A combination of retirement communities, colleges and universities, and a rapidly growing culture of traditional arts, crafts, and music began to attract people to visit and live in the mountains. Small- and medium-sized towns were revitalized, reclaiming their historic character and architecture. Asheville and Boone, North Carolina; Berea and Lexington, Kentucky; Johnson City and Bristol, Tennessee; and Roanoke and Charlottesville (also Bristol), Virginia, have all benefited from people reconnecting with the landscape and heritage. Visitors and residents are helping to reverse decades of decline, at least in some parts of the mountains.

Traditional music has played a major role in the cultural and economic resurgence of the southern Appalachians. Every Saturday night throughout the summer in Asheville's city plaza, "Shindig on the Green" attracts thousands who enjoy bluegrass and old-time music and dance. Tight circles of bands jam together all through the park, while locals lounge in lawn chairs and families spread blankets and share picnics. It is a scene recurring in other mountain villages and towns from West Virginia to Tennessee. A number of organizations offer programs in Appalachian music and crafts, including the John C. Campbell Folk School and Whitesburg Kentucky's Appalshop Center. Students can pursue Appalachian studies and music at several colleges and universities, including East Ten-

nessee State University, the University of Kentucky, Appalachian State University, Western Carolina University, Berea College, Mars Hill College, and Warren Wilson College. The Blue Ridge Music Center near Galax, Virginia, on the Blue Ridge Parkway features displays of Appalachian music history and a regular concert series.

The Swannanoa Gathering and Augusta Heritage Center summer music camps attract attendees from throughout the world and include popular Appalachian Old-Time and Celtic theme weeks. The legacy of the Carter Family endures at the Carter Family Fold near Hiltons, Virginia, dedicated to the preservation and performance of old-time and bluegrass music. With each of these initiatives distributed throughout the mountains, the economic well-being of communities is enhanced, while an old and valued musical tradition is sustained. It may be that the traditional arts are more important than ever in the southern Appalachians.

Folk and Appalachian musicians have a long history of using their voices to draw attention to social causes and campaigns. It is a tradition passed down from Woody Guthrie and Pete Seeger through the 1960s civil rights era to the present, joining hands across the water in solidarity with Dick Gaughan, Tommy Sands, and many other contemporary voices of peace and protest in the British Isles and Ireland. In 1992 Woody Guthrie's daughter Nora approached British singer-songwriter Billy Bragg to arrange and record some of her late father's previously unheard lyrics; these songs, performed by Bragg with the backing of the American alternative rock band Wilco, were released in 1998 on the album *Mermaid Avenue*. Today, voices speak and sing about threats to the environmental sustainability of the Appalachian Mountains. The local news is inundated with eco issues: acid rain devastating fir trees on the mountain ridges, mountaintop removal and strip mining of coal, poor air quality related to power-plant carbon emissions, clear-cutting of forests and destruction of pristine countryside for new

Protests and Poems: Writing New Songs

Jean Ritchie, American traditional singer, Appalachian dulcimer player, songwriter, and author; interviewed in Swannanoa, North Carolina, July 2008, by Fiona Ritchie during Traditional Song Week at the Swannanoa Gathering folk arts workshops.

Well, I didn't think of it so much as political, as protesting, you know, because I didn't like what was going on. When they started strip-mining the mountains, that's when I started writing songs about it. And now they'[ve] even gone farther, they're taking the tops off the mountains, and that's even more worrisome to me, so the songs are in protest against that. And I used a pseudonym. . . . I wanted to use John Hall, which was my grandfather's name, but they said, "Oh, John Hall, that's the president of BMI, and he wouldn't like it if you took his name." So I took the end of the name, which sometimes people called him anyways. . . . So, instead of John, I took 'than, so I was Than Hall for a while. And [for] two reasons: one was, my mother was still alive, she was very old (she was almost as old as I am now), and I didn't want people bothering her, saying, "Your daughter's up there in New York and writing protest songs and she's a communist." So I just didn't want that to happen, so I went under the pseudonym. And the other thing is that if it was a man that wrote the song, then it would be listened to. But if a woman wrote the song, people would say, "What is she doing, what does she think she's doing?" In those days, it was really hard to do anything that—I mean it was like, boys playing with trucks and girls playing with dolls. That was the way it was then. It went on like that for years, but I really was protesting. I did "Black Waters" and "The L&N Don't Stop Here Anymore" and "Blue Diamond Mines" and, what else did I do? "West Virginia Mine Disaster" about then, I guess.

The latest one to record them is Kathy Mattea on her album called *Coal*. She leads off the album with "The L&N"—beautifully sung—and "Blue Diamond Mines" follows that. And I've written other kinds of songs, I mean, it sort of got me into writing songs. Most of my songs, people think are folk songs. Flatt and Scruggs recorded one of my songs, "My Dear Companion." And later on, it was done on the trio album: Dolly Parton, Linda Ronstadt, and Emmylou Harris. Emmylou Harris also recorded "Sorrow in the Wind," which I also wrote. So all of the songs are not protest songs, some of them are love songs.

I don't write a song just to write a song, or to make money. If something comes into my mind that I think ought to be said, I do a poem, and I want to set it to music. Then it becomes a song. "None but One" was one of those. I did a little poem, and I think I said, "I think that ought to be [a song]." I don't think I can get across things when I'm speaking as much as I can when I'm singing [sings]:

Across the plain, there moves a sway, it moves with human sound.
Some do walk and some do run, some move upon the ground.
And some do stop to help the weak, some trample on the others.
And some do laugh and some do weep, and all of them are brothers.

And then the second verse is [singing]:

I saw four travelers in a dream, all in the wind and weather.
The chain they carry in their hands, it bound them all together.
And one was yellow, one was red and older than the others, one was black and one was white
    and all of them were brothers.

So that was my poem, and I put it to "Nonesuch," the tune for "Nonesuch," and added a chorus to it, and that's how that tune got built [singing]:

And sounding all around us sound, sounding everywhere
And none but one can understand, and none but one can hear
I mine and I thine—father, mother, son—
I'm me and I'm thee, and all of us are one.

So that's a very intellectual song, and it doesn't have much to do with folk songs, but it was a just poem that was set to music, so in some ways, that's the way a song gets written.

housing developments. The songs of West Virginia native Billy Edd Wheeler have been recorded by 200 artists, from Johnny Cash to Judy Collins, Glen Campbell, and Elvis, selling over 60 million records. Kathy Mattea, Wheeler's fellow member of the West Virginia Music Hall of Fame, sings his "Coming of the Roads," a modern ballad that grieves for a love moved on and a long-lost way of life, all gone by way of the relentless pace of change.

> Now that our mountain is growing with people
>   hungry for wealth,
> How come it's you that's a going, and I'm left
>   alone by myself?
>
> We used to hunt the cool caverns, deep in our
>   forest of green,
> Then came the roads and the taverns, and you
>   found a new love it seems.
>
> Once I had you and the wild woods, now its just
>   dusty roads,
> And I can't help but blamin' your goin', on the
>   coming, coming of the roads.
>
> Look how they've cut all to pieces, our ancient
>   redwood and oak,
> And the hillsides are stained with the greases that
>   burned up the heavens with smoke.
>
> You used to curse the bold crewmen, who
>   stripped our earth of its ore,
> Now you've changed and gone over to them, and
>   you've learned to love what you hated before.
>
> Once I thanked God for our treasure, now like
>   dust it corrodes,
> And I can't help but blamin' your going, on the
>   coming, coming of the roads.

In "A Prayer for Slowness," Fred Davis Chappell, poet laureate of North Carolina (1997–2002), suggests that we will only connect with the spiritual power of the mountains when we stop to rediscover, on a personal level, an older, slower pace of life.

> Let the deep valley take me over
> with its sundown shadow a little at a time,
> by little and little, as if the hourglass
> lay on its side and the grains leaked through
> one by one into the cloud of infinite separate
> moments.[53]

Jean Ritchie had long confronted environmental challenges such as coal mining and its double-edged threats to health and the land, as she laments in her "Farewell to the Mountains":

> Their railroads found your valleys, they tunneled
>   you with mines,
> But still my branch runs sweet and clear and
>   greener grew my pines.
> And then the coal so hard to get, they came one
>   awful day,
> Drove their machinery up your sides and they tore
>   your crown away.

Amid life's trials and transformations, an unshakable love for her hallowed mountains has always sustained Jean. Among her high hills lies the fountain of hope deep within her Appalachian spirit. So in "Farewell to the Mountains," the chorus turns from their destruction back to their beauty.

> How I love you, lovely mountains,
> In the summer or in snow.
> For the sweetest song I know is here,
> Where your little branch waters flow.

For Jean Ritchie, the future of the mountains depends upon our joining together in a sacred pact: we must tend the great landscape as a garden, we must keep its waters pure, as she urges in "Now Is the Cool of the Day."

Living Is Collecting

Jean Ritchie, American traditional singer, Appalachian dulcimer player, songwriter, and author; interviewed in Swannanoa, North Carolina, July 2008, by Fiona Ritchie during Traditional Song Week at the Swannanoa Gathering folk arts workshops.

I once did an article for the retirement of Cratis Williams . . . he was a wonderful man. And I did an article and went and read it, that's the only time I ever did anything with footnotes, and . . . I called it, "Living Is Collecting," and so I just wanted to pass that on to you, so just think about that as you live, that all your life is collecting wonderful things, bad things, good things. And you are becoming what you are because of all the experiences you have, and many things that I've done have been because of music and because of songs that I know.

People ask that a lot. They say, "Why do you keep on singing these old songs, there is so much new stuff now you could be learning." And I was raised on the songs, and partly it's the memories they bring back, and partly it's that they're good songs. They wouldn't have lasted all these years if they hadn't been good, you know. And they also have advice, and they have things happen in the songs that still happen today, unfortunately sometimes. Many murder ballads we shouldn't emulate, but still, it does happen. And you get people's feelings about it, you get sometimes to know what to do about it, and they're not only still beautiful, but they're still meaningful, and I think that's the reason they last so long.

There was a time in my career of singing when I sort of got burned out and I decided to just stop singing for a while because I didn't want to lose my love of the music by overdoing it. And I stopped and took care of my kids and things for several months and maybe over a year before I went back to it. And then, when I went back, it was wonderful again. So keep that in mind: don't overdo it. Music should be not your whole life, but a wonderful accompaniment to your life. So I'm glad to pass that along to you.

Then my Lord said unto me,
Do you like my garden so green?
You may live in this garden if you keep the waters
    clean,
And I'll return in the cool of the day.

[Chorus] Now is the cool of the day, now is the
    cool of the day.
O this earth is a garden, a garden of my Lord,
And I'll return in the cool of the day.

Here lies our land: every airt
Beneath swift clouds,
glad glints of sun,
Belonging to none but itself.

We are mere transients, who sing
Its westlin' winds and fernie braes,
Northern lights and siller tides,

Small folk, playing our part.
"Come all ye," the country says
You win me, who take me most
to heart.

—Kathleen Jamie, poem (2012)
inscribed in 2014 on the timber ring
crowning the Battle of Bannockburn
rotunda monument

Epilogue

A GREAT TAPESTRY

In September 2013 the Great Tapestry of Scotland was unveiled in the Main Hall of the Scottish Parliament in Edinburgh. Stitched by thousands of hands with 300 miles of wool, this is the longest tapestry in the world a hugely ambitious project that traces the history of Scotland from the end of the last Ice Age to modern times. One hundred and sixty panels provide a colorful illustrated chronicle of the history of an ancient nation. One depicts the Highland and Lowland Clearances and evictions, and another illustrates the nineteenth-century Scots emigration to America. People who remain in their native country, and immigrants who settle there, are compelled to join together in shaping their national story as it unfolds over time. So it is for others to pick up the threads and depict the saga of all the ones who left—Ulster Scots or Scots-Irish and the rest. It is easy to imagine, for example, four sister panels of the Great Tapestry stitched to illustrate a sea crossing and settlement in Ulster, an ocean passage, an arrival and relocation, and finally a journey onward to resettle in a new Appalachian homeland. With fibers from other realms woven into the fabric, the embroidered cloth would surely also be decorated with musical motifs: fiddles, dulcimers, and banjos; quotations from old ballads; and perhaps a line from a contemporary song to represent the living tradition of music in the southern mountains. The refrain of the Tim O'Brien–Pierce Pettis songwriting collaboration "A Mountaineer Is Always Free" would create a fitting banner: "No more a wanderer, no more a refugee."

We need only scan the panels of the Great Tapestry of Scotland to remind ourselves that every journey must start somewhere, as each wayfarer looks to the

(*opposite*)
Twisted heather echoes the Celtic knot work. (Photograph by Doug Orr)

horizon to take the first step forward. How the path may meander beyond this brief, unmarked moment, or what might be picked up and put down along the way, is unknowable, but one thing is clear: most journeys from Scotland soon lead onto the rolling deck of a boat. In 1540 an unnamed vessel brought adventurer Thomas Blake across the Atlantic as part of a Spanish expedition into present-day Arizona and New Mexico.[1] History records that Blake was the first Scot officially to land in North America, but the names and faces of hordes of other very real people are long forgotten; the mists of time have obscured their identities and draped a veil of anonymity across their personal treasures and artifacts. Yet in their great migrations, forced and chosen, across seas and frontiers, innumerable wayfaring travelers from Scotland's Highlands and Lowlands and from Ulster's fertile fields together seeded a precious legacy and left it to grow in their wake. It was an inspirational, tenacious musical spirit, holding fast against tidal waves of change and adversity. To discover it, all we ever needed to do was to follow the song routes and trails of melody.

Early twentieth-century songcatchers had to navigate the hills and hollows of Appalachia to unearth the musical legacy of the Scots-Irish. Today, a few clicks on a computer keyboard can open the door to a world of musical resources, an overwhelming range of choice from across time and place. Musicians with the skill and curiosity can quite literally learn to play anything from anywhere now, reaching international audiences via digital and social media. The origins of regional music can easily be blurred as strong local styles and subtle dialects are mixed and fused. By the same token, information and research on the roots and branches of traditional and folk music is also more widely available than ever. There is no need to be confused about its lineage. Even so, engaging with tradition is less about being knowledgeable than it is about telling a collective story that must be retold by each generation if it is to survive. It is this communal act of narration that fortifies a feeling of belonging and a sense of identity, renewing and evolving but also reconnecting with ethnic roots. Contemporary media offers almost unlimited opportunities for self-expression. Young people on cultural borderlands in Scotland, Ireland, and Appalachia can, through their traditional arts, be empowered to discover their native voices and define themselves on their own terms, while also appreciating what they hold in common with other cultures and places. In doing so, perhaps they will establish more transatlantic dialogs to explore the connections between their landscapes and shared cultural heritage. Plans are afoot to create at least one "sister city" arrangement between communities in Scotland and western North Carolina.

People have poured across the Atlantic overwhelmingly from east to west, but the cultural conversation flows in both directions. It took centuries for a ballad like "Barbara Allen" (CD track 1) to work its way through the British Isles and across the Atlantic, but its appearance in print on an early nineteenth-century broadside was what really boosted its popularity in the United States. Oral transmission may have kept everything going for generations, but with Thomas Edison's invention of the recording machine at the turn of the twentieth century, the means of circulation would forever after be more aural than oral. When Columbia and Victor made their Edison wax cylinders and Berliner flat discs commercially available, it was a turning point for all music and changed forever how traditions were disseminated. Where folk music had been a natural, unremarkable part of local life, now it could travel out of remote areas to reach homesick exiles or musicians from other ethnic backgrounds. It could find its way into the heart of communities depleted by generations of emigration. It could provide a direct route to the sound of "source" singers who were by then long gone, and to instrumentalists who might guide a new generation toward the true origins of their music. With radio as partner to a burgeoning recording industry, traditional music could spread even further from its rural roots.

Woody Guthrie had been a well-known figure in the British Isles, and then, in the 1950s and 1960s, American roots music, including blues and Appalachian styles, rolled across the ocean to a growing band of enthusiasts. Artists like North Carolina fiddler and banjo picker Samantha Bumgarner, the Coon Creek Girls, Cisco Houston, Sonny Terry and Brownie McGhee, and Pete Seeger were all heard on the radio and seen performing in person in the United Kingdom by young Scottish and English artists like Archie Fisher and Martin Carthy. Along with his band the Weavers, Pete Seeger inspired a transatlantic folk scene. His book *How to Play the 5-String Banjo* was highly prized by budding pickers on both sides of the ocean and has never been out of print since 1948. The music migration came full circle when Seeger toured the United Kingdom, from the Royal Albert Hall to the tiniest folk clubs, and Bob Dylan embraced British Isles folk song. What had taken centuries to relocate and take root overseas had now come back home as a not-so-distant cousin to replenish and also to influence the source. Today in the United States, indie folk and rock musicians such as Anaïs Mitchell and Jefferson Hamer,

the Decemberists, Sam Amidon, and Fleet Foxes have all been reworking some of the ballad canon as Bob Dylan did before them. Inspired by the field recordings of Alan Lomax, Valerie June brings blues into the mix, also tapping the rural roots of Appalachian folk, gospel, soul, and country. In Britain and Ireland, Bellowhead, the Chair, and Pauline Scanlon each explore and fuse flavors from Celtic, Appalachian, and old-time music roots on each side of the Atlantic, and this cast of characters will grow and change with every reading of this book. Meanwhile, in the towns and glens of Scotland and Ireland and in the shady groves of Appalachia, large numbers of learned and accomplished young performers are immersed in their native traditional repertories with raw energy and fire, demonstrating that they, as Hugh MacDiarmid said, "have no use for emotions, let alone sentiments, but are solely concerned with passions."[2] And this is the essence of the living tradition, the hues and textures of the great tapestry.

Hamish Henderson, the founding father of the Scottish folk song revival of the twentieth century, concluded his own elegy: "Tomorrow, songs will flow free again, and new voices be borne on the carrying stream."[3] He reminded us that folk tradition neither stands still nor exists in isolation. It is the same with identity—Scottish, Irish, or American. Culture becomes a platform upon which we construct our concept of identity. As people move and ideas are shared, so their identities become more fluid, overlapping and blurring around the edges. Openness to new ideas and cultural exchange are at the heart and soul of social music. That is, after all, the way culture works; repertoires evolve and thrive by flowing among the rituals of life, writing a score that is far from linear. So anyone who opened the front cover of this book with an old ballad or fiddle tune in mind and hoped to speed-read through to the back, arriving at the threshold of country music or rock and roll, has misunderstood the process. There is no one stream

and no one source; rather, there is a merging of many tributaries trickling from springs through place and time and coursing together onward across fresh terrain. Cajun musician Dewey Balfa's assertion that "a culture is preserved one generation at a time" reminds us that the stream must be replenished, refreshed, and cared for.[4]

> Because I want my children to share my memories, I pass on to them the songs of my life, and they may listen when they are ready to hear. I call them the songs of all time, and in time my children will find them to have been their own all along—therein lies the secret of their everlasting truth and beauty.
> —*Jean Ritchie*[5]

Compiling this book has brought us into the company of remarkable people, pearl fishers in the carrying stream and chroniclers of living traditions. These individuals are our reminder that each eighteenth- and nineteenth-century wayfarer was also an individual whose experience feeds into a much larger migration narrative that continues to this day. Against the per-

petual tide of migration, piper Gary West detects an innate crosscurrent, driven by our need for "an appreciation of where things have come from, where we stand within the stream . . . and to embrace the future with the confidence that comes from knowing where we've been."[6] If music marks the wayfaring strangers' footfall, it may also help explain why hearing its echo, a verse for every mile, makes us yearn to find a way back home ourselves.

> *A Verse for Every Mile (a new ballad)*
> Come all ye gentle Southern hearts,
> Combine and lend an ear,
> I'll tell to you a story,
> If you've a mind to hear,
> I grew among the old ones,
> In a land of sea and stone
> Watched them till the hillsides,
> Work fingers to the bone.
>
> They gathered meagre harvests,
> For masters just as mean,
> Who made them fight their battles,
> Crushed their simple dreams,
> They fished along the shoreline,
> Nets deep beneath the foam,
> Saw the far horizon,
> And felt the urge to roam.
>
> [Chorus] We graft and go: in for the long haul,
> Graft and go: no effort too small,
> We graft and go, then settle for a while,
> Mark the ballad footfall, a verse for every mile.
>
> Huddled round the hearth at e'en,
> Warmed by the glowing light,
> I brought them tears and laughter,
> As tales and tunes took flight,
> They sang and shushed the bairns to sleep,
> In prayer they clasped their hands,
> For safe return of wayfarers,
> With word of better lands.

Some sang a song of parting,
Lived stories yet to tell,
And others, broken hearted,
Fled a cruel, burning hell,
Some sailed for closer coastlines,
Tried to make the best,
In time their sons and daughters,
Crossed wild oceans with the rest.

[Chorus] We graft and go: in for the long haul,
Graft and go: no effort too small,
We graft and go, then settle for a while,
Mark the ballad footfall, a verse for every mile.

I am the spirit of the song,
That traveled on the tide,
With brave hearts and kind faces,
Sharing stories far and wide,
Rocking bows on fiddles,
Driving dancers 'round the floor,
Weaving verse so I could touch,
Their souls and see them soar.

Tho' many years have passed, my friend,
And times have changed, it's true,
I live on in the hollows,
Of those distant ridges blue,
So raise your voice and dream a dream,
Where strangers once did roam,
'Neath smoky peaks that tower above,
Your mountain laurel home.
(Copyright © 2007 Fiona Ritchie.
All rights reserved.)

"Voices of Tradition" Profiles

Many voices speak through the pages of this book. Several were interviewed for radio and are quoted directly. Some interviewees contributed insights and advice that helped shape particular sections of the narrative; others made themselves available for ongoing exchange and helpful banter as the book progressed. They are all our "Voices of Tradition."

SHEILA KAY ADAMS, Appalachian storyteller, ballad singer, banjo player, and author from a small mountain community in Madison County, North Carolina. Her family handed down Scottish and Irish ballads and stories through seven generations since her ancestors immigrated in 1731. A 2013 recipient of the National Heritage Fellowship from the National Endowment for the Arts.

JACK BECK, from Dunfermline, Scotland, singer, ballad scholar, teacher, and host of a weekly Celtic music program on public radio station WETS-FM in Johnson City, Tennessee. Toured and performed with many of Scotland's foremost traditional singers. Co-owner, with Wendy Welch, of the Tales of the Lonesome Pines Bookstore in Big Stone Gap, Virginia, where he directs the annual Big Stone Celtic Festival.

MARGARET BENNETT, Scottish singer, folklorist, and writer brought up on the Hebridean Isles of Skye and Lewis in a family of Gaelic-speaking tradition bearers. Has taught workshops throughout Scotland, Ireland, England, the United States, and Canada and is a former lecturer in the School of Scottish Studies at the University of Edinburgh (now the Department of Celtic and Scottish Studies). A protégé of the late Scottish folklorist Hamish Henderson, who inherited his mantle as "Scotland's foremost folklorist." Resides in Perthshire, Scotland.

TYLER BLETHEN, retired professor of history at Western Carolina University. Served as director of the university's Mountain Heritage Center. Coauthor, with Curtis W. Wood Jr., of *From Ulster to Carolina: The Migration of the Scotch-Irish to Southwestern North Carolina* (1998); and coeditor, with Wood, of *Ulster and North America: Transatlantic Perspectives on the Scotch-Irish* (2001).

PAUL BROWN, journalist, broadcaster, and musician. Played and sought out the sources of traditional southern music in the United States over a lifetime, especially many of the fiddle masters in North Carolina and Virginia, such as Benton Flippen. Recorded and produced highly regarded traditional music albums; also worked in public radio as an NPR® newscaster/reporter, including presenting features on iconic traditional musicians, such as his old friend Mike Seeger.

JOHN COHEN, founding member of the New Lost City Ramblers and musicologist, photographer, and filmmaker. Films include *End of an Old Song* and *High Lonesome Sound*. "Discovered" and recorded a number of traditional musicians, including Roscoe Holcomb and Dillard Chandler; his archives were recently acquired by the Library of Congress. The Smithsonian Network's film *Play On, John: A Life in Music* explores his lifelong involvement with traditional music.

CECELIA CONWAY, professor of Appalachian studies at Appalachian State University. Conducted extensive research on the history of the banjo; author of *African Banjo Echoes in Appalachia: A Study of Folk Tradition* (1995). Instrumental in launching the Black Banjo Reunion, which helped bring black banjo players together and revitalize the African American banjo heritage.

CARA DILLON, Northern Irish singer and songwriter from Dungiven, County Derry-Londonderry. Formed, at age fourteen, the traditional Irish band Óige and later joined the acclaimed folk group Equation, when she began collaborating with husband Sam Lakeman on piano and guitar. Dillon and Lakeman have won recognition for their traditional and original song arrangements, including "Hill of Thieves," voted by BBC Radio Ulster listeners as one of the ten best original songs to come out of Northern Ireland. The song was performed in 2012 with the Ulster Orchestra.

JOHN DOYLE, guitarist, singer, songwriter, producer. Originally from Dublin and son of Irish sean-nós singer Sean Doyle. One of Ireland's most prolific accompanists, playing a distinctive hard-driving guitar style that has influenced a generation of players. As instrumentalist and producer has collaborated on over 100 recordings by a variety of artists and is a founding member of the Irish American band Solas. Resides in Asheville, North Carolina.

ARCHIE FISHER, Scottish singer, songwriter, guitarist, and broadcaster born in Glasgow. An influential force in the Scottish folk scene for over five decades. Recorded in the 1960s with sisters Ray and Cilla as the Fisher Family; released his classic solo album in 1968 and began writing original songs for, and appearing on, radio and television. Directed, in the 1980s, the Edinburgh Folk Festival and began a two-and-a-half-decade stint as host of the long-running radio program *Travelling Folk* on BBC Radio Scotland. Has produced albums by Irish music legends Tommy Makem and Liam Clancy and the Scots band Silly Wizard.

PADDY FITZGERALD, with the Centre for Migration Studies in Omagh, Northern Ireland, where he has served as lecturer, curator, and development officer. Teaches Irish migration studies at Queens University in Belfast; coauthored, with Brian Lambkin, *Migration in Irish History, 1607–2007* (2008). A leader of the biennial Ulster-American Heritage Symposium.

DOM FLEMONS, founding member of the Grammy Award–winning Carolina Chocolate Drops old-time string band. Performs with the four-string banjo, guitar, jug, harmonica, snare drums, bones, and quills. A dedicated student and researcher of traditional music origins, now embarking upon a solo career and international tours.

RHIANNON GIDDENS, singer, instrumentalist, songwriter, and founding member of the Grammy Award–winning Carolina Chocolate Drops. Performs on five-string banjo, fiddle, and kazoo; pursued her longtime interest in Celtic music with her former band, Gaelwynd. Along with Dom Flemons, was mentored and inspired by the late African American fiddler Joe Thompson. Studied at Oberlin Conservatory of Music as a versatile vocalist across many genres, including blues, rhythm and blues, gospel, opera, and Gaelic song. A native of Greensboro, North Carolina.

JULEE GLAUB AND MARK WEEMS, teachers and performers, partners in music and life, blending Appalachian, Celtic, old-time, and gospel as the band Little Windows. Mark is steeped in southern musical traditions, having played with Alice Gerrard, Tony Ellis, and Carl Jones. Julee absorbed Irish musical traditions during seven years as a social worker in Dublin. The duo leads singing and harmony workshops and music camps throughout the United States and beyond, including the Swannanoa Gathering, where Julee serves as coordinator of Traditional Song Week, while Mark teaches in the program. North Carolina natives based in Durham.

LEN GRAHAM, one of Northern Ireland's foremost traditional singers, folklorists, and song collectors. Previous winner of the All-Ireland Traditional Singing Competition and author of *Joe Holmes: Here I Am Amongst You* (2010), profiling the songs, dance music, and traditions of fiddler Joe Holmes. Known among his peers as "Mr. Ulster Music" for his decades of research, field recordings, and performances of the music of the area. Resides in Newry, Northern Ireland.

SARA GREY, American singer of traditional songs from Scotland, Ireland, and the United States, banjo player, and song collector. With son Kieron Means, combines balladry, cowboy songs, and hymns with clawhammer banjo and acoustic blues-style guitar. Has been involved with traditional music for several decades in the U.S. Northeast, Midwest, and southern states and also as a resident of Scotland for many years. A specialist in transatlantic song connections from years of research and collecting.

NANCY GROCE, folklorist, musicologist, and senior folklife specialist with the American Folklife Center of the Library of Congress. Previously, curator at the Smithsonian Center for Folklife and Cultural Heritage, where she devised and coordinated the annual Smithsonian Folklife Festival on the National Mall. Author of *New York: Songs of the City* (1999).

GINNY HAWKER, singer of gospel harmony, early bluegrass, unaccompanied hymns of the Primitive Baptist Church, and songs of the Carter Family. Grew up in southern Virginia surrounded by song. A genuine voice of the southern Appalachians who performs—with husband Tracy Schwartz, a fiddler and onetime member of the New Lost City Ramblers—across North America and the United Kingdom. Resides in West Virginia.

DAVID HOLT, four-time Grammy Award–winning musician, storyteller, historian, and host on radio and television. Collected traditional songs and stories of the southern Appalachians over a period of years. A former Appalachian music faculty member at Warren Wilson College. Toured and performed for fourteen years with the late Doc Watson. A specialist on such diverse instruments as banjo, dobro, guitar, bones, paper bag, and hambone.

ALAN JABBOUR, founding director of the American Folklife Center of the Library of Congress and highly respected fiddler known for his knowledge and performance of the music of renowned Virginia fiddler Henry Reed. Founded the Hollow Rock String Band, which became the core of the old-time music scene

in the Chapel Hill, North Carolina, area in the 1960s and 1970s. Published widely on traditional music and folklore subjects.

PHIL JAMISON, nationally known dance caller, musician, and dancer performing throughout the United States and internationally. Professor of Appalachian music at Warren Wilson College and founding coordinator of the Swannanoa Gathering's Old Time Music and Dance Week. Former member of the Green Grass Cloggers. Author of *Hoedowns, Reels, and Frolics*, a book on Appalachian dance. Toured with Ralph Blizard and the New Southern Ramblers.

LOYAL JONES, former director of the Appalachian Center at Berea College that now bears his name. Often referred to as "Mr. Appalachia" for his many years of writing and teaching Appalachian folklore, music, and culture. Author of a biography of the legendary songcatcher and musician Bascom Lamar Lunsford; also author of many more books about the Appalachians, including several titles on humor with songwriter Billy Edd Wheeler.

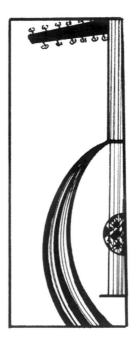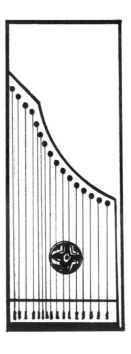

KEVIN KEHRBERG, professor of music at Warren Wilson College with a particular focus on the music of the Appalachians, including the history and performance of shape-note singing. Performs on bass, fiddle, and guitar, playing on tours with his old-time string band, the Red State Ramblers. Also teaches and researches the music of other world cultures.

NUALA KENNEDY, Irish singer, songwriter, and flute and whistle player. Grew up in Dundalk, County Louth, an area with historical links to Scotland. Studied classical piano at the Royal Academy of Music in Dublin and relocated to Edinburgh, where she deepened her knowledge of traditional music and passion for Gaelic song. With her partner, A. J. Roach of Virginia, performs in a duo exploring the crossover between Scottish, Irish, and Appalachian musical traditions both old and new.

JAMES LEVA, active in the old-time music scene since the 1970s. Learned firsthand from masters of the older generation, such as Doug Wallin, Tommy Jarrell, Art Stamper, and Melvin Wine. Researched the African American role in shaping old-time and bluegrass music. Has won scores of fiddle competitions and also is acclaimed for his singing and songwriting.

KATHY MATTEA, Grammy Award winner and twice Country Music Association Female Vocalist of the Year. A West Virginia native who has embraced Celtic, gospel, bluegrass, and folk influences in her contemporary song arrangements. Also a presenter of educational programs on environmental themes who has extended her Grammy-nominated album *Coal* by creating the multimedia presentation "My Coal Journey."

BRIAN MCNEILL, named by *The Scotsman* newspaper as "Scotland's most meaningful contemporary songwriter," reflecting his work and influence as a composer, multi- instrumentalist, teacher, novelist, and folklorist. A founder of Scotland's Battlefield Band and former head of Scottish Music at the Royal Conservatoire of Scotland. Produced an audiovisual presentation entitled *Back o' the North Wind* about Scottish emigration to America.

JOHN MOULDEN, one of Ireland's leading authorities on traditional song, including the interconnected traditions of Scotland, England, Ireland, and the Appalachians. Researched the printed ballad in Ireland and its impact on the oral tradition. Did major work with the Sam Henry Collection, the largest compilation of Irish songs, and published *Thousands Are Sailing: A Brief Song History of Irish Emigration* (1994). Also a well-regarded singer.

AIDAN O'HARA, writer, broadcaster, and part-time singer, with wife Joyce, of Irish traditional music. Worked with Irish and Canadian national broadcasting, including documentary programs on the traditional music of Ireland and Newfoundland. Frequent contributor to *Irish Music* magazine and in 2013 published *Atlantic Gaels: Links between Donegal and the Hebrides*. Originally from County Donegal and now residing in County Longford.

RON PEN, professor of music and director of the John Jacob Niles Center for American Music at the University of Kentucky and author of *I Wonder as I Wander: The Life of John Jacob Niles* (2010). Founding member of the Appalachian Association of Sacred Harp Singers and shape-note singer and scholar. Plays fiddle and teaches in many area workshops and festivals. Recently performed in China, Kyrgyzstan, and Ecuador with the Red State Ramblers.

JOHN PURSER, Scottish composer, musicologist, poet, playwright, researcher, and presenter of award-winning radio since the 1970s on stations in the United Kingdom, Ireland, New Zealand, and Iceland. Born in Glasgow of Irish parents and studied at the Royal Scottish Academy of Music and Drama (now the Royal Conservatoire of Scotland). Lectured on classical music at the University of Glasgow and on Scottish music internationally. In 1993 named McVitie's Scottish Writer of the Year for his widely acclaimed book, *Scotland's Music*, accompanying his eponymous radio series; an expanded edition was published in 2007 to accompany a second series for BBC Scotland. Lives on the Isle of Skye.

JEAN REDPATH, Scottish singer and educator, born in Edinburgh and raised in the Kingdom of Fife. Encountered Hamish Henderson at the School of Scottish Studies, inspiring her to embrace traditional and folk song. Has encyclopedic knowledge of British Isles ballads, Scottish and American folk songs, and art songs and is considered the leading interpreter of the songs of Robert Burns, having recorded 180 of them. Shared lodgings in Greenwich Village with Ramblin' Jack Elliott and Bob Dylan, becoming immersed in the 1960s folk revival. Has toured the world performing and teaching for over five decades, recording over forty albums and attracting a faithful audience across the United States through her many public radio appearances on *A Prairie Home Companion*. Was artist-in-residence in Celtic and Scottish studies at the University of Edinburgh in 2011.

ALAN REID, singer, songwriter, and pioneer of keyboard use in folk music. Recorded thirty albums with Scotland's Battlefield Band and was the band's principal songwriter beginning in 1990, composing songs with storytelling grounded in Scottish history. Nominated as Scots Traditional Composer of the Year. Contributed to the Linn Records series of the complete works of Robert Burns and recently composed an album of songs about the Scots-born Revolutionary War hero John Paul Jones.

JEAN RITCHIE, from the mountains of Kentucky, American traditional singer, dulcimer player, songwriter, author, song collector, and 2002 National Endowment for the Arts National Heritage Fellowship honoree. A key figure in traditional American music for her generations-old Ritchie family song heritage, for her influential songwriting, and for bringing the Appalachian dulcimer to an international audience. Her album *None but One* received the Rolling Stone Critics' Award in 1977 and influenced other singers

to explore their musical roots. Important spokesperson for the challenges and environmental concerns affecting the Appalachian region. In 1950 married photographer George Pickow (1922–2010), who captured her career and traditional Appalachian folkways in his photographs.

MIKE SEEGER, player of a variety of styles on the banjo, fiddle, guitar, autoharp, jaw harp, mountain dulcimer, harmonica, and other instruments. Dedicated his life to singing and playing southern traditional mountain music and producing documentaries and concert presentations of traditional musicians, singers, and dancers. Founded and toured with the vanguard old-time string band the New Lost City Ramblers and discovered and assisted many old-time musicians. Died in 2009 at age seventy-five.

PEGGY SEEGER, solo concert artist and leader of numerous musical workshops. Life partner with the late Ewan McColl, who wrote "The First Time Ever I Saw Your Face" for Peggy, which became an international hit. Together they researched songs of Scottish and English gypsy Travellers and revealed connections between Appalachian and British ballads. Peggy has released two dozen solo recordings and is featured in over 100 recordings, including performances with brothers Mike and Pete.

PETE SEEGER, eldest of the Seeger siblings whose musical journey over seven decades reads like a chronicle of American social and political movements. At age seventeen, traveled through the North Carolina mountains with his parents and attended Bascom Lamar Lunsford's Mountain Dance and Folk Festival, exposing Pete to a new world of old-time music that would shape his musical journey. Learned some basic banjo licks from Lunsford, and the five-string banjo became his signature instrument. A compatriot of Woody Guthrie, who was a fellow member of the Almanac Singers. A founding member of the hugely popular band the Weavers. As a singer, songwriter, campaigner, and activist, led 1960s protests with

"We Shall Overcome," "Where Have All the Flowers Gone?," and "Turn, Turn, Turn." Died in 2014 at age ninety-four.

BETTY SMITH, performer, teacher, and ambassador for the traditional music of the South on mountain dulcimer and psaltery for over forty years, sharing songs in classrooms, concert halls, workshops, and festivals. Sings, in her clear mountain voice, the old Scottish and Irish ballads she learned from her father and grandmother. Author of *Jane Hicks Gentry: A Singer among Singers* (1998), a book about the noted Appalachian ballad singer and collector.

DÁITHÍ SPROULE, a native of Derry-Londonderry, Irish guitarist, traditional singer, accompanist, and composer. One of the first guitarists to develop the D-A-D-G-A-D tuning, now common in Celtic-rooted guitar accompaniment. Performs internationally with Irish group Altan and has also collaborated with Liz Carroll, James Keane, Peter Ostroushko, and many others. In demand as a teacher and lecturer on guitar stylings and accompaniment, Irish language, literature, and songs. Has lived for many years in Minnesota.

JOE THOMPSON, North Carolina fiddler who, with his brother Odell in "The Thompsons," is credited with keeping alive an African American tradition of the black string-band music that predates blues, country, and bluegrass. A mentor and inspiration to members of the Carolina Chocolate Drops. Performed at the Kennedy Center and Carnegie Hall and recipient of the National Endowment for the Arts National Heritage Fellowship. Died in 2012 at age ninety-three.

DOC WATSON, guitar virtuoso from Deep Gap in the North Carolina mountains, whose ancestors immigrated from Scotland in the 1770s; lost his sight from an infection at age one and developed an acute sense of hearing; perfected a remarkably fast flat-picking style that emulated the fiddle lead for old time bands; part of the 1960s Greenwich Village music scene with Jean Ritchie and others; recorded over fifty albums, awarded eight Grammys, recipient of the NEA National Heritage Fellowship and the National Medal of Arts; died in 2012 at age 89.

ROBIN AND LINDA WILLIAMS, husband and wife musical team residing in Middlebrook, Virginia, in the heart of the Shenandoah valley. Songwriters as well as performers, blending folk, bluegrass, and gospel harmonies. Have been regulars since 1976 on public radio's *A Prairie Home Companion*. Recorded twenty-one albums, featuring many of their own compositions that often reflect their deep-felt Appalachian roots and connections.

CURTIS W. WOOD, retired professor of history at Western Carolina University, where he served as department head for many years. Coauthor, with Tyler Blethen, of *From Ulster to Carolina: The Migration of the Scotch-Irish to Southwestern North Carolina* (1998); and coeditor, with Blethen, of *Ulster and North America: Transatlantic Perspectives on the Scotch-Irish* (2001).

Glossary of Less-Familiar Musical Terms

Ballad. Narrative poem.

Bard. Older term for a musician or poet, often itinerant or retained by nobility, who may compose songs and music in honor of patrons. Clan chiefs' bards had particularly high status and were expected to memorize hundreds of stories, songs, poems, and melodies.

Bellows-blown pipes. Any set of bagpipes in which the sound is created by air pumped from a set of bellows strapped to the elbow.

Border pipes. See **Lowland bagpipes**.

Bothy ballad. Humorous, earthy songs written by male agricultural workers to describe farm life in the North East of Scotland. Workers (unmarried men) gathered at "feeing" or hiring markets and traveled to farms for the season, where they were housed in small huts and cottages called bothies.

Broadside ballad. These were the newspapers of the day, an early product of the printing press. Also known as broadsheets, street ballads, stall ballads, and slip songs, they were printed on sheets the size of handbills and often included a rough woodcut illustration.

Cauld wind pipes. Another name for Scottish bellows-blown bagpipes.

Ceilidh/ceili. Gaelic word meaning "a visiting," originally used to describe an informal gathering in someone's home where music and storytelling might take place. Now the word is more commonly used to describe a community dance and music party, as well as a style of traditional group dancing.

Clarsach. A small Scottish harp.

Craic. A word used in Ireland and Scotland loosely meaning "good fun" and particularly associated with the music scene.

Cross tuning. An alternative fiddle tuning that changes the pitch of the string's resonance and drones, altering the sound. Commonly used in the southern Appalachians, the wider U.S. South, and Scandinavia.

Double-stop. A technique wherein two separate fiddle strings are stopped by the fingering and bowed simultaneously, producing a fuller sound for a variety of textures, harmony, and color. Triple and quadruple stops exist but are less common.

Drone. A sustained note, usually low in pitch, providing a constant foundation beneath a higher pitch melody. The term may also be used to describe an instrumental string as found on a hurdy-gurdy, or a pipe that sustains a tone such as the three drones in a set of Highland bagpipes (see below).

Frailing. A right-hand banjo style popularized by Pete Seeger. The index finger is used for up-picking and the middle finger for rhythmic downward brushing of the strings. In the related clawhammer style, only down strokes are used by the thumb and fingers, all held within a claw-like hand position.

Hardanger fiddle. A Norwegian instrument originating in the area around the Hardanger fjord, known there as the "hardingfele." It has four strings played in the standard way plus four or five "understrings" below the fingerboard. These resonate freely when the main strings are bowed, creating eerie drones and harmony. Instrument makers often decorate hardanger fiddles with carved wooden adornments and mother-of-pearl inlays.

Highland. A version of the Scottish strathspey developed in Donegal, Ireland.

Highland bagpipes. The most recognizable of the bagpipes and the variety seen played in pipe bands the world over. Highland pipes comprise a bag made of animal hide, a blowpipe, two tenor and one bass drones, and the fingered pipe or chanter.

Hornpipe. Especially popular with sailors, this is a traditional dance tune of English origin played in 2/4 or 4/4 time.

Hymnody. The practice of singing hymns. Also describes the collective hymns of a particular religious denomination.

Jaw harp (Jew's harp). A lyre-shaped metal frame held between the teeth and played by plucking a bent piece with the finger, producing a twanging tone. Popular in the southern Appalachians with the Scots-Irish settlers, it went by many names dating to the early seventeenth century, including the "trump" in Scotland and "Jew's harp" in England.

Jig. A traditional dance tune, most commonly played in 6/8 time, older than all other Irish-style dance tunes.

Literary ballad. Intellectuals and a growing upper class fostered interest in the literary or lyrical ballad beginning in the latter part of the eighteenth century.

Lowland bagpipes. Similar in sound to the Highland bagpipes but with less volume, these sets of bagpipes (also known as Borders pipes) are small, three droned, and bellows blown.

Mixolydian mode. Commonly used in the music of the medieval church, this is the fifth mode of the major scale. Although it differs by only one note (the 7th) from the standard major scale, it creates a very different overall sound, with a sense of the melody being unresolved. This produces a feeling of musical tension, and some describe mixolydian mode as sounding like a starker or grittier version of the major scale.

Muckle sangs (songs). Long narrative Scottish ballads covering a wide variety of themes. Particularly prevalent in the repertoire of ballad singers from the Scots Travelling tradition, such as Jeannie Robertson.

Ngoni. An ancient West African stringed instrument that evolved into the American banjo, imported through the transportation of slaves to southern plantations. It is still played in parts of West Africa.

Pipe bands. Massed bands of pipers and drummers, first established by Scottish regiments and then by civilian groups in the nineteenth century. The conventional setup uses one bass drum, two tenor drums, four to six side drums, and at least six pipers.

Planxty. An Irish tune written in praise of someone, often a patron. Planxties are associated with the compositions of Irish harper Turlough O'Carolan.

Psalmody. Based on the biblical psalms for congregation singing in the early Protestant Church. The Protestant Reformation broadened the music to include many hymns, some of which were drawn from old folk melodies.

Reel. A traditional dance tune in 4/4 time, originating in Scotland and most popular in set and step dancing.

Scheitholt. Forerunner of the Appalachian dulcimer imported into Pennsylvania by German settlers. Also called the "Hummel" in northern Germany for the humming sound of its drone strings, a tone reminiscent of the bagpipes.

Scots snap. A distinctive feature of Scottish music in which a short, heavily accented note, followed by a longer one, creates a rhythmic skip in the music. In the case of Scottish fiddling, this is created by a sudden upstroke of the bow and is most pronounced in a strathspey.

Sean-nós. Literally translated, it means "old style," the ancient unaccompanied style of singing in Irish.

Session (also seisuin). An informal music gathering, most often held in a pub or private home.

Set. A traditional group dance; also a grouping of dance tunes played on any instrument.

Singing schools. Popular in late eighteenth-century New England for teaching sacred music, eventually dwindling and thereafter spreading into the South and the southern Appalachians. Travelling "song masters" taught the rudiments of the music, including sight-reading, often using shape-note notation.

Slide. A traditional Irish dance tune in 6/8 time.

Slip jig. A traditional dance tune in 9/8 time.

Small pipes. Another type of Scottish bagpipe, quieter still than the Lowland or Border pipes and played with the distinctive fingering heard in Highland piping.

Songcatchers. A name for the song collectors of the southern Appalachians. The label was popularized by the 2000 movie *Songcatcher* that depicted musicologists Olive Dame Campbell and Cecil Sharp, who visited the area in the early twentieth century.

Step dancing. A traditional dance form, performed solo or in a group, in which the feet tap out the dance rhythms of hornpipes, jigs, and reels.

Strathspey. A slow dance tune thought to have originated in the Spey valley, this is a dance rhythm unique to Scottish music. Most often heard on fiddle, it is recognizable for its built-in rhythmic skip.

Traditional folk ballad. The earliest ballad form. The author was usually anonymous, and the ballads were passed on in an oral tradition.

Travellers. Song and story tradition bearers, the indigenous itinerant families of Scotland and Ireland, known in earlier times as "tinkers" (now pejorative), toured the country performing seasonal farm labor and at one time, repair work for the settled community. As they camped across the land, they would pick up songs and stories and became great sources of traditional balladry and storytelling.

Troubadours. Emerging as lyric poets in the Occitania region of southern France, troubadour repertoire became a significant foundation in the development of balladry. Their golden age spanned 1100 to 1350.

Uilleann pipes. The most complicated of all the bagpipes, these Irish bellows-blown pipes have a two-octave range. There are three different drones (bass, baritone, and tenor) and also thirteen regulators (closed pipes), allowing the piper to create harmonies and chords over the melody.

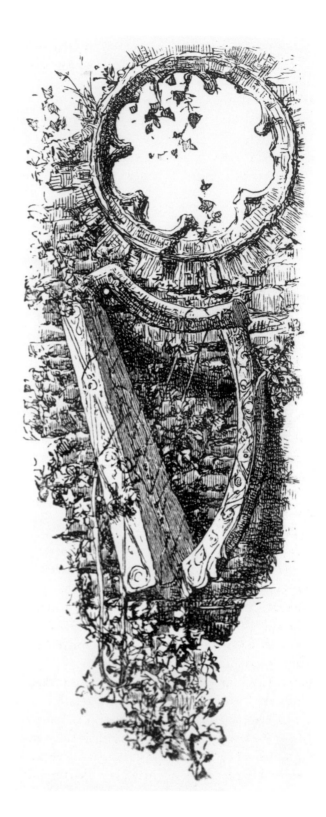

A Contextual Timeline

8000 B.C. First inhabitants arrive in Ireland, crossing from Scotland after the end of glaciation.

300 B.C. First Celtic migrations from France to Great Britain and Ireland. Celtic languages (Q-C and B-C) spread easily among the disparate communities.

96. Picts first mentioned in Roman literature.

350. Tribe known as "Scotti" (or "Scoti") begin to arrive on the west coast of today's Scotland, crossing from Ireland.

432. Saint Patrick, a Roman British missionary, is taken as a slave in Ireland. Goes on to convert the Celts to Christianity.

489. Saint Brendan born in southwest Ireland. According to legend, he is the first to make a voyage all the way across the North Atlantic.

535. Columba travels from Ireland to Scotland with twelve companions to establish a monastery on the island of Iona in the Inner Hebrides and convert the Picts to Christianity.

793. Vikings destroy the abbey of Lindisfarne on the Northumbrian coast of northeast England, and the age of Viking influence in Britain and Ireland begins.

794. Vikings attack Iona, center of Celtic monasticism.

843. Scots and Picts unite under Kenneth MacAlpin, marking Scotland's birth as a nation.

980–982. Norse explorer Eric the Red discovers Greenland, geographically considered part of North America.

1000. Icelander Leif Ericson establishes settlements in Newfoundland, Canada, the first European known to have set foot in North America.

Ca. 1010. Thorfinnr Karlsefni attempts to establish Viking settlement in North America but is driven away by Native Americans.

1100–1300. Golden age of the Troubadours in southern France sees balladry and lyric poetry flourish.

1263. Battle of Largs finally sees Vikings retreat from Scotland.

1266. Treaty of Perth establishes formal trade links between Scotland and Norway.

1295. Auld Alliance signed between Scotland and France, now the world's oldest mutual defense treaty.

1314. The Scottish army, under King Robert the Bruce, defeats Edward II's English forces near Stirling in the Scottish Wars of Independence. The decisive victory is one of the most significant battles in Scottish history.

1320. Declaration of Arbroath urges the pope to recognize Scottish independence from England. The document is considered an inspiration to drafters of the American Declaration of Independence.

1398. Henry Sinclair from Orkney believed by some to have sailed to Nova Scotia and back.

1450. Peak of the age of minstrelsy in England. Minstrels later outlawed by Elizabeth I.

1492. Christopher Columbus makes landfall on the island of San Salvador in the Bahamas.

1507. The word "America" is first applied to the New World, named after Italian explorer Amerigo Vespucci.

1530. Kingdom of Dalraida spans the North Channel between Scotland and Ireland, creating a cross-channel cultural domain.

1542. Mary, Queen of Scots, born.

1550s to early 1700s. Primary era of the broadside ballads.

1580s. Beginning of the slave trade. Millions of Africans will be forcibly shipped to the Americas.

1587. Elizabeth I signs death warrant for execution of Mary, Queen of Scots.

1588. Spanish Armada shipwrecked off the west coast of Ireland, a flotilla of more than seventeen galleons. Survivors possibly introduced Spanish song and dance traditions, remnants of which may survive within Irish music.

1590. The English colony of Roanoke vanishes.

1603. Union of the Crowns. King James VI of Scotland, son of Mary, Queen of Scots, inherits the thrones of England and Ireland from his double first cousin twice removed, Queen Elizabeth I.

1604. French settlers begin to establish colonies in Canada.

1606. Dawn of the Ulster Scots. James Hamilton and Hugh Montgomery receive land in Counties Down and Antrim as a reward for rescuing local chieftain Con O'Neill. They settle over 10,000 Scots to work the land in these areas, bringing their language, customs, and religious beliefs.

1607. Flight of the Earls. Hugh Ó Neill and Rory Ó Donnell leave Ireland for mainland Europe, taking ninety followers. The departure of these Irish lords, descended from Gaelic clan dynasties, marked the end of the centuries-old Gaelic order in Ulster and the beginnings of the Irish diaspora.

1607. The English establish a settlement in Jamestown, Virginia.

1608. Bushmills distillery, today the oldest licensed whiskey distillery in the world, founded in County Antrim.

1610. Plantation of the west of Ulster—King James I and VI establishes first plantations for English and Scottish Protestants.

1620. Carrying English pilgrims, the *Mayflower* arrives in what is now Massachusetts.

1622. Scots settler community in Ulster grows to 7,700.

1624. The Dutch settle in New Amsterdam, now New York.

1630. Adult male settler population in Ulster swells to 20,000.

1636. Excommunicated Presbyterian ministers and 140 followers set sail for America but are driven back by storms.

1638. The National Covenant is signed in Scotland, asserting Presbyterian doctrine as the true church.

1638–1688. Persecution of Presbyterian Covenanters known as "The Killing Times."

1641. Irish stage a rebellion against Ulster planters in an attempt to regain confiscated lands. Many planters are killed.

1649. Rebellion ends after much loss of life on both sides.

1665. English diarist Samuel Pepys records hearing the "little Scotch song of Barbary Allen."

1682. Scots colony founded in South Carolina.

1682. Port of Philadelphia founded.

1688. The "Glorious Revolution" sees Roman Catholic James II (King of England, Wales, Ireland, and Scotland) deposed by his Protestant daughter, Mary, and her husband "William of Orange."

1689. Siege of Derry. The city, a Williamite stronghold, is besieged by the Jacobites, loyal to King James, as they gather support to regain his kingdoms. After 105 days, Royal Navy ships relieve Derry-Londonderry.

1690. The Church of Scotland (Presbyterian) is officially recognized.

1690. Battle of the Boyne fought between the two rival claimants of the English, Scottish, and Irish thrones, James and William. The battle is won by William, bolstering the Protestant position in the north of Ireland.

1696. Outbreak of famine in Scotland starts new wave of emigration to Ulster.

1698. Scots attempt to establish settlement in Panama. This "Darien Project" is a failure, bankrupting Scotland.

1699. The French create the colony of Louisiana.

1700. Scots now represent the majority of settlers in Ulster.

1707. Acts of Union passed. The Kingdom of England and the Kingdom of Scotland are formally united politically into a single United Kingdom named Great Britain. The Scottish parliament is adjourned.

1713. Andrew Presley, ancestor of Elvis, marries Elspeth Leg in the Scottish village of Lonmay, Aberdeenshire.

1715. Jacobite Rising fails. Many Scots are transported to the Americas.

1717. Large-scale migration of Ulster Scots to America begins when five ships carrying 700 Ulster Scots set sail for Boston. Others begin arriving on a regular basis at the Philadelphia docks.

1726. Scots immigrants established the philanthropic St. Andrew's Society of Charleston, South Carolina.

1729. First Highland Scots arrive in eastern North Carolina to settle Cape Fear River backcountry.

1731. Charleston's historic First Scots Presbyterian Church founded.

1733. British colonies in America now number thirteen.

1733. General James Oglethorpe settles a group of Scottish Highlanders in the colony of Georgia.

1736. Hanover County, Virginia, hosts the first fiddling contest of colonial times on November 30 in honor of the holiday of Saint Andrew, patron saint of Scotland.

1745. Final Jacobite Rising led by Charles Edward Stuart, or "Bonnie Prince Charlie," grandson of James II.

1745. Andrew Presley, son of Andrew and Elspeth from Lonmay in Aberdeenshire, Scotland, arrives in North Carolina. He is the first Presley ancestor of Elvis to come to America.

1746. The Battle of Culloden is a resounding defeat for the Jacobite army, comprised mostly of Scottish clans and troops loyal to the line of King James. It is the final attempt to restore the House of Stuart to the British throne and the last land battle fought on British soil.

1746. Act of Proscription and Dress Act introduced to assimilate the Scottish Highlands, dismantle the clan system, and weaken Gaelic culture. Wearing of tartan is banned in Scotland except as a uniform in the British army.

1746. More Scotsmen transported to American Colonies after the Jacobite defeat at Culloden.

1747. The St. Andrews Society of Philadelphia founded to aid newly arrived Scots.

1747. Ballad source Anna Gordon, "Mrs. Brown of Falkland," born in Aberdeen, Scotland.

1751. Peter Jefferson (Thomas Jefferson's father) and Joshua Fry draft map depicting "The Great Road from the Yadkin River thro Virginia to Philadelphia distant 455 Miles," the route that came to be known as the Great Philadelphia Wagon Road.

1759. Robert Burns born in Ayrshire, southwest Scotland.

1760. North Carolina General Assembly establishes a permanent community in Cape Fear region of North Carolina named Campbelltown.

1762. Clearances begin as crofters in Highlands and Islands of Scotland are forced to leave their smallholdings to make way for sheep farming and agriculture.

1768. James Ritchie, ancestor of musician Jean Ritchie, sets sail from Liverpool docks with five brothers. They settle in Virginia, east Tennessee, North Carolina, and Texas.

1769. James Watt of Greenock on the River Clyde patents an improved version of the steam engine. The innovation of using steam to propel boats would soon follow.

1770. The Clyde Trust was created to convert the River Clyde, until then a shallow river, into a maritime thoroughfare for Atlantic trade through excavation and dredging.

1770s. Doc Watson's Scottish ancestor Tom Watson emigrates from Edinburgh to America with his new wife, eventually settling in the North Carolina mountains.

1771. Sir Walter Scott born in Edinburgh.

1773. Boston Tea Party. Colonists protest taxation by dumping English tea into Boston Harbor.

1773. Four thousand Highland Scots have by now arrived to settle along the Cape Fear River, bringing the total Scottish population in the colony to 20,000, according to the North Carolina Museum of History.

1775. Daniel Boone, with thirty axmen, clears and marks a trail through the Cumberland Gap to today's Boonesboro, Kentucky.

1775–1783. American Revolution.

July 1776. The thirteen British colonies sign the Declaration of Independence.

1776. Battle of Moore's Creek Bridge, North Carolina. Loyalist Highlanders defeated by Patriots.

1781–1782. Thomas Jefferson's State of Virginia review refers to the "banjar," brought by slaves from Africa and played on the plantations.

1782. Acts of Proscription repealed.

1786. Only encounter between Robert Burns and Sir Walter Scott, in Edinburgh.

1786. Robert Burns becomes a published poet in Scotland.

1787. Robert Burns song collection *The Scots Musical Museum, 1787–1803* first published by James Johnson.

1787. U.S. Constitution drafted.

1787. John Fitch makes first successful trial of a steamboat on the Delaware River.

1787. Robert Burns sees his poems published in Belfast, Ulster.

1789. George Washington is chosen to serve as the first president of the United States of America.

1792. Belfast Harp Festival. Edward Bunting collects many ancient Irish airs.

1801. Political Union of Great Britain and Ireland. The Irish Parliament is abolished, and the United Kingdom of Great Britain and Ireland is created.

1802. Sir Walter Scott's song collection *Minstrelsy of the Scottish Border, 1802–1803* first published.

1804. U.S. northern states make slavery illegal.

1807. Meriwether Lewis and William Clark explore the Missouri valley.

1812. Britain and America go to war.

1813. Thomas Mellon born in County Tyrone, Ulster.

1818. Mellon family emigrates from Derry-Londonderry to Philadelphia.

1820–1860. Thousands of slaves are led to freedom via the Underground Railroad.

1824. John Ross petitions Congress on behalf of the Cherokee Nation.

1830. Indian Removal Act passed by Congress.

1831–1838. Many Native Americans in the southern states are forcibly removed from their homelands on the "Trail of Tears," culminating in the relocation of the Cherokee from the Appalachian Mountains to Oklahoma. A quarter of the refugees die on the trail.

1838. First crossing of the Atlantic by steamship.

1845. The Great Hunger—An Gorta Mór—begins in Ireland with the first cases of blight in the potato crop.

1846. Scottish Highland potato famine begins, eventually causing over 1.7 million people to leave Scotland.

1848–1849. Most devastating years of the Irish famine. Over 1 million die, and a further 1 million emigrate.

1861. The American Civil War breaks out.

1862. U.S. Western Territories are opened for settlement through the Homestead Act.

1863. Emancipation Proclamation. Slavery outlawed throughout the United States.

1865. General Lee surrenders and the Civil War ends.

1869. Completion of the transcontinental railroad.

1876. Scotsman Alexander Graham Bell invents the telephone in Canada.

1882. Bascom Lamar Lunsford, the "Minstrel of the Mountains," born.

1882–1889. Harvard professor Francis James Child publishes his monumental five-volume compilation and classification of Scottish and English popular ballads.

1889. The Scotch-Irish Society of the United States of America founded, evolving from the Pennsylvania Scotch-Irish Society.

1890. Native Americans are defeated at the Battle of Wounded Knee.

1892. Ellis Island is established as the main U.S. immigration-processing center and receives more than 12 million people from across the globe.

1901. First wireless broadcast by Guglielmo Marconi.

1903. The Wright brothers make a successful flight in their flying machine and invent the first engine-powered airplane.

1911. Bill Monroe, "Father of Bluegrass," born.

1912. Proposals for Home Rule in Ireland are approved by Parliament but suspended for the duration of World War I.

1912. RMS *Titanic* ocean liner, constructed at the Harland and Wolff shipyard in Belfast, sinks in the North Atlantic after colliding with an iceberg. More than 1,500 lives are lost.

1916–1918. English folklorist Cecil Sharp travels through southern Appalachian Mountains, accompanied by Maud Karpeles, collecting ballads and tunes shared by descendants of early settlers. His informants include Jane Hicks Gentry and members of the Wallin family of Madison County, North Carolina, kin to present-day singer Sheila Kay Adams.

1918. Descendants of Highland Scots in eastern North Carolina dispersed to make way for U.S. Army camp at Fort Bragg.

1919. John Alcock and Arthur Whitten Brown pilot a British airplane from Newfoundland to Ireland, the first nonstop transatlantic flight.

1919. Pete Seeger, folk musician and songwriter, born.

1920. Irish Partition creates two separate jurisdictions, Northern Ireland and Southern Ireland, both part of the United Kingdom.

1920. The first radio stations are set up in the United States.

1922. BBC begins daily wireless transmissions in Britain.

1922. Jean Ritchie, singer and mountain dulcimer player, born in Kentucky.

1923. Doc Watson, singer and flatpick-style guitarist, born in North Carolina.

1925. Olive Dame Campbell founds the John C. Campbell Folk School in Brasstown, North Carolina, with a curriculum of Appalachian cultural studies, crafts, art, storytelling, and music.

1925. The Grand Ole Opry is launched on radio, taking the sound of Appalachian music across the United States for the first time.

1927. Charles Lindbergh makes first solo nonstop transatlantic flight from New York City to Paris.

1927. The "Big Bang" of Country Music traced to the "Bristol Sessions," which introduce the Carter Family and Jimmie Rodgers.

1928. Bascom Lamar Lunsford founds the Mountain Dance and Folk Festival in Asheville, North Carolina, still running annually.

1930. Twelve million U.S. homes are now equipped with radio sets, although only 1 percent of African American families own a radio.

1930s. BBC pioneers range of radio broadcasts, and experiments with the world's first regular TV service under John Logie Baird.

1932. Amelia Earhart is first female to make a solo trans-Atlantic flight.

1935. Twenty-two million homes now own radio sets as sales grow through the Great Depression.

1949. Republic of Ireland established and granted full independence from Britain, with Northern Ireland's six counties remaining within the United Kingdom.

1950s. Poverty and a lack of economic opportunity forces approximately 2 million Appalachian residents to leave their homes for other regions.

1952–1953. Jean Ritchie awarded a Fulbright Fellowship to travel in Ireland, Scotland, and England to trace the lineage of her family's Appalachian ballads. She spends eighteen months interviewing and recording local singers.

1953. "Crazy Man Crazy" by Bill Haley is the first hit record by a rock and roll artist.

1954. Elvis Presley records Arthur "Big Boy" Crudup's old blues song "That's Alright Mama" at Memphis's Sun Records studio. The song became a hit, transforming the American music scene. The flip side is Bill Monroe's bluegrass composition "Blue Moon of Kentucky."

1955–1956. Following the success with Elvis, Sun Studio's Sam Phillips records Johnny Cash, Carl Perkins, Jerry Lee Lewis, and Roy Orbison.

1957. Mike Seeger cofounds the revivalist string band the New Lost City Ramblers.

1958. The Kingston Trio records the old Appalachian murder ballad "Tom Dooley," which sells over 3 million copies and launches the pop-folk boom of the 1960s.

1962. First TV image across the Atlantic via the satellite Telstar.

1962. Bob Dylan records "Barbara Allen" on his album *Live at the Gaslight* and travels to the United Kingdom, where he meets English folksinger and guitarist Martin Carthy. Dylan's albums subsequently show the influence of traditional ballads.

1963. President John Kennedy, struck by the poverty he witnessed in West Virginia, creates the Appalachian Regional Commission. It develops a blueprint for relieving rural poverty and creating sustainability for livelihood and culture in the mountains.

1963. The March on Washington draws 300,000 to the National Mall and is a signature event in the civil rights movement. Highlighted by Martin Luther King's "I Have a Dream" speech, the march attracts the support of singers Marion Anderson, Joan Baez, Bob Dylan, and Mahalia Jackson and the group Peter, Paul and Mary.

1964. The Beatles land in America.

1969. Woodstock Music Festival attracts over 500,000.

1969. Moon landing of Apollo 11, the first of six manned missions to land on the lunar surface.

1980. Fiona Ritchie makes her first Atlantic crossing

to study for a semester at the University of North
Carolina at Charlotte.

1981. Doug Orr first travels to Scotland to study new
town planning and developments.

1981. Debut of Music Television (MTV), offering
round-the-clock music videos.

1983. First national broadcast of *The Thistle & Shamrock*
on public radio across the United States.

1990s. Dawn of broadcasting's digital age.

1992. Launch of the first Swannanoa Gathering folk arts
workshops in the Blue Ridge Mountains of North
Carolina.

1998. Good Friday Agreement significantly reduces
sectarian violence and eases political tension between
Nationalists (Catholic) and Unionists (Protestant) in
Northern Ireland.

1999. Scottish Parliament reconvened after 292 years,
following the devolution of powers from London
through the Scotland Act (1997).

2000. Jean Ritchie receives a National Endowment for
the Arts National Heritage Fellowship, the highest
honor in the United States for folk and traditional arts.

2000. Release of *Songcatcher* movie loosely based on the
Appalachian song-collecting work of Olive Dame
Campbell in the early twentieth century.

2003. NPR® offers first mp3 free music download—
"This Love Will Carry" by Scottish singer-songwriter
Dougie MacLean.

2004. St. Andrews University, Scotland's oldest, confers
the degree of Doctor of Music on Bob Dylan,
recognizing the inspirational role Scottish traditional
songs had played in his music.

2008. Presidential proclamation designating April 6
as "National Tartan Day" in the United States is a
culmination of events that started with a New York
City celebration in 1982.

2010. Recognizing the ancient geological connection,
the International Appalachian Trail officially extends
the eastern U.S. hiking trail with a course through
Scotland.

2012. Swannanoa Gathering celebrates its twentieth
anniversary. Music enthusiasts travel from across the
United States and Europe to western North Carolina
to learn and celebrate Appalachian and Celtic musical
traditions.

2013. Sheila Kay Adams receives the National
Endowment for the Arts Heritage Fellowship for her
contributions to preserving and fostering Appalachian
folk song and story traditions.

2013. The Great Tapestry of Scotland is unveiled. Panels
trace Scottish history from the end of the last Ice
Age to the twenty-first century, including depictions
of Highland and Lowland Clearances and Scots
emigration to America.

Resource Centers

UNITED STATES

American Folklife Center, Library of Congress, Washington, D.C.

Appalachian, Scottish and Irish Studies Program, East Tennessee State University, Johnson City, Tenn.

Appalshop, Whitesburg, Ky.

Blue Ridge Institute and Museum, Ferrum College, Ferrum, Va.

Blue Ridge Music Center, Blue Ridge Parkway, Galax, Va.

Center for Appalachian Studies, Appalachian State University, Boone, N.C.

Center for Scotch-Irish Studies, McCelvey Center, York, S.C.

Cumberland Gap National Historical Park and Visitors Center, Middlesboro, Tenn.

Digital Collections and Service and Prints and Photographs Reading Room, Library of Congress, Washington, D.C.

Frontier Culture Museum, Staunton, Va.

Loyal Jones Appalachian Center, Hutchins Library Southern Appalachian Collection, Berea College, Berea, Ky.

Mountain Heritage Center, Western Carolina University, Cullowhee, N.C.

North Carolina Collection and Southern Folklife Collection, Wilson Library, University of North Carolina at Chapel Hill, Chapel Hill, N.C.

Pew Learning Center and Ellison Library, Warren Wilson College, Swannanoa, N.C.

Renfro Library, Southern Appalachian Archives and Bascom Lamar Lunsford Folk Music Collection, Mars Hill College, Mars Hill, N.C.

Scotch-Irish Association of America, Media, Pa.

SCOTLAND

Aberdeen Maritime Museum, Aberdeen

Centre for Scottish and Celtic Studies, University of Glasgow, Glasgow

Department of Celtic and Scottish Studies, University of Edinburgh, Edinburgh

Highland Folk Museum, Newtonmore

Inverness Museum and Art Gallery, Inverness

McLean Museum and Art Gallery, Greenock

Mitchell Library, Glasgow

National Archives of Scotland, Edinburgh

National Library of Scotland, Edinburgh

National Museum of Scotland, Edinburgh

Research Institute of Irish and Scottish Studies, University of Aberdeen, Aberdeen

Scotland's People Centre, Edinburgh

Scottish Centre for Diaspora Studies, University of Edinburgh, Edinburgh

Scottish Storytelling Centre, Edinburgh

Stirling Centre for Scottish Studies, University of Stirling, Stirling

NORTHERN IRELAND

Belfast Public Library, Belfast

Centre for Irish and Scottish Studies, University of Ulster, Coleraine

Institute of Ulster Scots Studies, University of Ulster, Derry-Londonderry

Linen Hall Library, Belfast

Mellon Centre for Migration Studies, Omagh

Monreagh Heritage and Education Centre, Carrigans

Monreagh Ulster Scots/Scots Irish Heritage Centre, Belfast

Public Records of Northern Ireland (PRONI), Belfast
Ulster-American Folk Park and Centre for Migration
    Studies, Omagh

REPUBLIC OF IRELAND

Centre for Irish-Scottish Comparative Studies,
    Trinity College Dublin
National Library of Ireland, Dublin
Ritchie-Pickow Collection, James Hardiman Library,
    National University of Ireland, Galway

BALLADS ONLINE

www.ed.ac.uk/celtic-scottish-studies/greig-duncan.
    Filmed performances of acclaimed Scottish ballad
    singers via the Department of Celtic and Scottish
    Studies at the University of Edinburgh.
www.tobarandualchais.co.uk. The "Tobar an Dualchais"
    (Kist o' Riches, or Chest of Riches) offers thousands
    of hours of Scots and Gaelic recordings. These
    include songs, folklore, music, and poetry gathered by
    collectors working from the 1930s to the present time,
    including Hamish Henderson's field recordings of
    Scottish Travelling People.

Note on Illustrations

The broad scope of this story, covering 500 years or more of history, presented the challenge of finding images for each era that added visual meaning. But the selection of illustrations gathered here, from the earliest woodcuts and drawings to contemporary paintings and photographs, testifies to the enduring passion evoked by the musical migration that inspired this book. The earliest included images date from the sixteenth century, still near the beginning of what we think of as modern print culture. Jump forward to our present day—to the most-photographed of generations, a time when practically every smile, word, activity, and experience is recorded and revisited many times over. We capture our moments electronically, often so quickly that we can view a picture of an event even before the event itself has ended. In their own way, the images in this book are a chronicle that parallels the journey of ballads and songs from oral to print to recorded sound. We invite our readers to join us in appreciating the juxtaposition of illustrations produced by old and newer technologies—lithograph next to photograph next to hand-drawn and painted art—and in seeing the beauty of each, with the visual and the aural tying together the threads of this musical tapestry.

As recently as twenty-five years ago, most of the images included here could not have been acquired without bulky recording and printing devices and thousands of miles of travel. In our far-flung search for illustrations, visits to great libraries—such as the National Library of Scotland in Edinburgh; the Library of Congress in Washington, D.C.; and the University of North Carolina at Chapel Hill Library—certainly proved fruitful, as did trips to the archives of the Ulster American Folk Park in Northern Ireland, the American Folklife Center at the Library of Congress, and the Museum of Frontier Culture in Virginia. And yet over half of our images were found online by searching the contents of library catalogs, historical societies, music blogs, and personal websites. One might say we have "pen pals"

in all of these places, people who helped track down the obscure print, the ownership of a particular painting, or the source of a needed photograph merely by responding to our e-mail request for help. From Inverness and Edinburgh in Scotland to Omagh and Donegal in Ireland; from Eugene, Oregon, to Albany, California; from Ithaca, New York, and Berea, Kentucky, to just up the road in West Jefferson, North Carolina—we have benefited from a network of acquaintances who shared their talents, knowledge, and resources to further this project.

Thank you to all who contributed; because of you, this book is a more-vibrant portrait of the wayfarers' epic story.

Darcy Orr

Discography

If *Wayfaring Strangers* has stirred your curiosity, then it is time for you to explore the musical links for yourself. Where do you begin? The fifty recordings offered here, rooted on both shores of the Atlantic, will set you on your way. Like Barbara Allen's rose and briar, many works on this list reach back and forth across the ocean to weave the strands of tradition together. Some tap the deepest roots; others, inspired by the old tales and melodies, course onward along the carrying stream. Delve into this discography and you will soon be navigating your own musical voyage from Scotland and Ulster to Appalachia. (*denotes that a track from the album is included on the accompanying *Wayfaring Strangers* CD.)

OLD WORLD

Seán Donnelly. *Cut a Long Story Short . . .* Ulster folk song. Seandonnellyfolkmusic.com, 2012.

Fiddlers Five. *Fiddle Music from Scotland*. Temple, 1991.

Len Graham and Brian O'hAirt. *In Two Minds*. Ulster traditional song. Storyandsong.com, 2012.*

Colum Sands and Maggie MacInnes. *The Seedboat (Bàta an tSìl)*. Musical bridges between Ireland and Scotland. Spring, 2010.*

Various artists. *The Complete Songs of Robert Burns*. Linn, 1997.

———. *Fiddle Music of Donegal*. Cairdeas, 1995.

———. *Heat the Hoose*. Celtic fiddle. Foot Stompin', 1998.

———. *The Scottish Diaspora: The Music and the Song*. Greentrax, 2013.

———. *Scottish Tradition 1: Bothy Ballads*. Greentrax, 1993.

———. *Scottish Tradition 5: Muckle Sangs*. Greentrax, 1992.

———. *Scottish Tradition 24: Songs and Ballads from Perthshire (Field Recordings of the 1950s)*. Greentrax, 2011.

———. *Thousands Are Sailing: Irish Songs of Immigration*. Shanachie, 1999.

NEW WORLD

Sheila Kay Adams. *All the Other Fine Things*. Granny Dell, 2004.*

Duck Baker and Molly Andrews. *American Traditional*. Day Job, 1993.

Norman and Nancy Blake. *Just Gimme Somethin' I'm Used To*. Shanachie, 1991.

Laura Boosinger. *Down the Road*. Laura's Label, 1998.

James Bryan and Carl Jones. *Two Pictures—Fiddle Tunes and Songs in a New Southern Tradition*. Martin, 1995.*

Carolina Chocolate Drops. *Genuine Negro Jig*. Nonesuch, 2010.

Sara Grey. *Sandy Boys*. Fellside, 2009.*

Hesperus. *Early American Roots*. Maggie's Music, 1997.

David Holt. *Grandfather's Greatest Hits*. High Windy Audio, 1991.

Yo Yo Ma, Edgar Meyer, and Mark O'Connor. *Appalachia Waltz*. Sony Classical, 1996.

Talitha MacKenzie. *Indian Summer*. Sonas, 2007.

Kathy Mattea. *Calling Me Home*. Sugar Hill, 2012.

Sarah McQuaid. *I Won't Go Home 'til Morning*. Saramcquaid.com, 2008.

Kieron Means. *Far as My Eyes Can See*. Fellside, 2005.

Dirk Powell, Tim O'Brien, and John Herrmann. *Songs from the Mountain*. Howdy Skies, 1998.

Jean Ritchie. *High Hills and Mountains/ None but One*. Greenhays, 1998.*

Jean Ritchie and Doc Watson. *Jean Ritchie and Doc Watson at Folk City*. Smithsonian/Folkways, 1990.

Pete Seeger. *American Favorite Ballads, Vol. 2*. Smithsonian/Folkways, 2003.*

Various artists. *Anthology of American Folk Music*. Smithsonian/Folkways, 1997.

———. *Dear Jean—Artists Celebrate Jean Ritchie*. Compass, 2014.

——. *Songcatcher: Music from and Inspired by the Motion Picture*. Vanguard, 2001.

Doc Watson and David Holt. *Legacy*. High Windy Audio, 2002.*

Doc Watson and Merle Watson. *Remembering Merle*. Sugar Hill, 1992.

BRIDGING THE ATLANTIC

Timothy Cummings. *The Piper in the Holler*. Birchenmusic.com, 2012.*

Atwater Donnelly. *The Blackest Crow*. Rabbit Island Music, 2004.*

John Doyle. *Evening Comes Early*. Shanachie, 2001.*

David Ferrard. *Across the Troubled Wave*. Alter Road, 2009.

Julee Glaub. *Blue Waltz*. Juleeglaub.com, 2004.*

Ian Hardie. *Westringing: Scotland Meets Appalachia*. Musicscotland.com, 2007.

Brian McNeill. *The Back o' the North Wind: Tales of the Scots in America*. Greentrax, 1991.

Anaïs Mitchell and Jefferson Hamer. *Child Ballads*. Wilderland Records, 2013.*

Tim O'Brien. *The Crossing*. Alula, 1999.

Dolly Parton. *Heartsongs: Live from Home*. Sony Music, 1994.*

Al Petteway and Amy White. *High in the Blue Ridge*. Fairewood Studios, 2011.*

Jean Redpath. Leaving the Land: A Collection of Songs, Scottish and Western. Rounder, 1990.

Kim Robertson. *Shady Grove*. Traditional music of North America performed on Celtic harp. Gourd, 2009.

Touchstone. *The New Land*. Green Linnet, 1982.

Various artists. *Bringing It All Back Home: Music from the BBC TV Series*. BBC Enterprises, 1991.

Notes

LETTERS FROM HOME

Fiona Ritchie:

1. Winchester, *Atlantic*, 15.

2. The 1947 film *Paddy's Milestone* documents the Ailsa Craig's role in the manufacture of blue hone granite curling stones, used to slide across the ice in the winter sport of curling.

3. The Dress Act of 1746 made the wearing of any "Highland Dress," including kilts and tartan, illegal in Scotland.

Doug Orr:

1. Kenneally, *Living Ghosts*.

2. Hettinger, *Springs of Music*, 8.

3. Shakespeare, *Twelfth Night*.

4. Pen, "A Cursory Glance at Old Time Music," 22.

5. Brian McNeil, "The Rovin' Dies Hard." McNeil's original composition refers to "Alaska's wild mountains." This has been revised with his permission to fit the *Wayfaring Strangers* story, a modification he sometimes also makes, depending on the performance venue.

PROLOGUE

1. Lunsford, *Asheville Citizen*, May 22, 1948.

2. Moulden, "The Printed Ballad in Ireland," 390.

3. Stewart, *Appalachian Heritage*, 3.

4. Ritchie, *Singing Family of the Cumberlands*, 254.

BEGINNINGS

1. Wells, *The Ballad Tree*, 180.

2. Ibid., 193.

3. Bogin, *The Women Troubadours*.

4. Aubrey, *The Music of the Troubadours*, 254–62.

5. Ibid., xvii.

6. Ibid., 272–73.

7. Buchan, *The Ballad and the Folk*, 271.

8. Wells, *The Ballad Tree*, 6.

9. Buchan, *The Ballad and the Folk*, 313.

10. Wells, *The Ballad Tree*, 208.

11. Ibid., 211.

12. Ibid.

13. Ibid., 214.

14. Laws, *American Balladry*, 55.

15. Wells, *The Ballad Tree*, 214.

16. John Purser interview.*

17. Bronson, *The Ballad as Song*.

18. Ibid.

19. Pepys, *Diary of Samuel Pepys, Vol. 41*.

20. Jack Beck interview.*

21. Quinn, *The Atlantean Irish*, 42.

22. Ibid., 42.

23. Williamson, Joan of Arc Archive, 1.

24. Talbott, "Beyond 'the Antiseptic Realm of Theoretical Economic Models.'"

25. Fraser, *Mary, Queen of Scots*, 182.

26. Ibid., 131.

27. Annie Lennox, South Bank show, ITV, 2007.

28. *A Welcome to Aberdeen*, 1.

29. Buchan, *The Ballad and the Folk*, 6–7.

30. Ibid., 7.

31. Bronson, *Traditional Tunes of the Child Ballads*, 265.

32. Buchan, *The Ballad and the Folk*, 59.

33. Ibid., 16.

34. Ibid., 28.

35. Ritchie, *The NPR Curious Listener's Guide to Celtic Music*, 39.

36. Fischer, *Albion's Seed*, 621.

37. Wells, *The Ballad Tree*, 56.

38. Ibid., 57.

39. Fischer, *Albion's Seed*, 621.

40. Wells, *The Ballad Tree*, 74.

41. Ibid., 68

42. Leyburn, *The Scotch-Irish*, 27–29.

43. Buchan, *The Ballad and the Folk*, 62.

44. Jack Beck interview.*

45. Wells, *The Ballad Tree*, 248–49.

46. Ibid., 249.

47. *The Meeting of Robert Burns and Sir Walter Scott at Sciennes Hill House*, painted by Charles Martin Hardie, 1893.

48. Munro, *The Poetry of Neil Munro*, 28.

VOYAGE

1. McHardy, *A New History of the Picts*, 89.

2. Ibid., 95.

3. Ibid., 186.

4. Vann, *In Search of Ulster-Scots Land*, 42

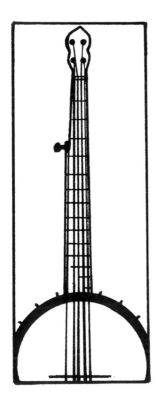

5. Ibid., 44–45.

6. Hugh MacDiarmid, "The Little White Rose" (verse inscribed on the Canongait Wall, Edinburgh, as part of the Scottish Parliament complex).

7. Blethen and Wood, *From Ulster to Carolina*, 12.

8. Ulster Historical Foundation, *The Plantation of Ulster, 1610–1630*.

9. Leyburn, *The Scotch-Irish*, 133.

10. Ibid., 136.

11. Ibid.

12. Ibid., 139.

13. Len Graham interview.*

14. Graham, *Joe Holmes*, 15.

15. Aidan O'Hara interview.

16. Graham, *Joe Holmes*, 102.

17. Moloney, *Far from the Shamrock Shore*, 4.

18. Len Graham interview.*

19. Cooper, *The Musical Traditions of Northern Ireland and Its Diaspora*, 36–39.

20. Breathnach, *Folk Music and Dances of Ireland*, 57–62.

21. Graham, *Joe Holmes*, 233.

22. O'Hara, *Atlantic Gaels*, 17.

23. Sir Alexander Gray, "Scotland" (verse inscribed on the Canongait Wall, Edinburgh, as part of the Scottish Parliament complex).

24. Lunney, "Home and Leaving Home in Eighteenth-Century Ulster," 6–7.

25. Heaney, *Preoccupations*.

26. Fischer, *Albion's Seed*, 632.

27. Ulster-American Folk Park exhibit.

28. Fitzgerald and Lambkin, *Migration in Irish History, 1607–2007*, 23.

29. Eileen Ivers, *Immigrant Soul*, liner notes, Koch Records, 2003

30. Miller, *Emigrants and Exiles*, 557.

31. Moulden, "The Printed Ballad in Ireland," 390.

32. Miller, *Emigrants and Exiles*, 560

33. Eileen Ivers, *Immigrant Soul*, liner notes.

34. John Doyle interview.*

35. Moulden, "The Printed Ballad in Ireland," 389–90.

36. Heaney, *Poems, 1965–1975*, 81–82.

37. Winchester, *Atlantic*, 154.

38. Hewitson, *Tam Blake & Co.*, 11.

39. Ibid., 11.

40. Ibid.

41. Winchester, *Atlantic*, 75.

42. Fitzpatrick and Lambkin, *Migration in Irish History, 1607–2007*, 18.

43. Ibid., 27.

44. Ulster-American Folk Park exhibit.

45. Fitzgerald and Lambkin, *Migration in Irish History, 1607–2007*, 24.

46. Ibid., 27.

47. Blethen and Wood, *From Ulster to Carolina*, 25.

48. Fitzgerald and Lambkin, *Migration in Irish History, 1607–2007*, 27.

49. Len Graham interview.*

50. Rouse, *The Great Wagon Road*, 33.

51. Leyburn, *The Scotch-Irish*, 177–78.

52. Fitzgerald and Lambkin, *Migration in Irish History, 1607–2007*, 31.

53. Blethen and Wood, *From Ulster to Carolina*, 122.

54. Moloney, *Far from the Shamrock Shore*, 7.

55. Blethen and Wood, *From Ulster to Carolina*, 123.

56. Mott, "A History of Homesickness."

57. Fitzgerald and Lambkin, *Migration in Irish History, 1607–2007*, 52.

58. Fischer, *Albion's Seed*, 605–6.

59. Griffin, *The People with No Name*, 2–4.

60. Blethen and Wood, *From Ulster to Carolina*, 35.

61. Dunaway, *The Scotch-Irish of Colonial Pennsylvania*, 192–95.

62. Gilmore, "A Fiddler Was a Great Acquisition to Any Neighborhood," 154.

63. Breathnach, *Folk Music and Dances of Ireland*, 42

64. Dunaway, *The Scotch-Irish of Colonial Pennsylvania*, 199.

65. Gilmore, "A Fiddler Was a Great Acquisition to Any Neighborhood," 156.

66. Dunaway, *The Scotch-Irish of Colonial Pennsylvania*, 199.

67. Gilmore, "A Fiddler Was a Great Acquisition to Any Neighborhood," 156.

68. Ibid., 156.

69. Ibid., 159–60.

SINGING A NEW SONG

1. Pen, "A Cursory Glance at Old Time Music," 22.

2. Rouse, *The Great Wagon Road*, 163.

3. Ibid., 162.

4. Smith and MacNeil, *Songs and Tunes of the Wilderness Road*, 17.

5. Ibid., 18.

6. Hulme, *Mountain Measure*, 84.

7. Dykeman, *The French Broad*, 43–44.

8. Alarik, "Robin and Linda Williams: Home, Home on the Road," 37-43.

9. Satterwhite, *Dear Appalachia*, 215.

10. Stewart, *Appalachian Heritage*, 3.

11. Moulden, "Country Music Is Ulster Music," 9.

12. Burton, "The Lion's Share," 5–13.

13. Sheila Kay Adams interview.*

14. Margaret Bennett interview.

15. Karpeles, *Cecil Sharp: His Life and Work*, 169.

16. Sheila Kay Adams interview.*

17. Ibid.

18. Abramson and Haskell, *Encyclopedia of Appalachia*, 1121.

19. Sandburg, *The American Songbook*, 306.

20. Strangeways, *Cecil Sharp*, 142.

21. Smith, *Jane Hicks Gentry*, 75.

22. Sheila Kay Adams interview.*

23. Loyal Jones interview.

24. Scarborough, *A Song Catcher in Southern Mountains*, 53–59.

25. Pete Seeger interview.*

26. Cooper, *The Musical Traditions of Northern Ireland and Its Diaspora*, 36.

27. Rouse, *The Great Wagon Road*, 199.

28. Abramson and Haskell, *Encyclopedia of Appalachia*, 1208.

29. Scoggins, *The Scotch-Irish Influence on Country Music in the Carolinas*, 88–89.

30. Wells, *The Ballad Tree*, 275.

31. Pete Seeger interview.*

32. Brian McNeill interview.*

33. Fussell, *Blue Ridge Music Trails of North Carolina*, 218.

34. Ibid., 34.

35. Ibid., 220.

36. Ibid., 222.

37. Cooper, *The Musical Traditions of Northern Ireland and Its Diaspora*, 138.

38. Abramson and Haskell, *Encyclopedia of Appalachia*, 1122.

39. Carlin, *The Birth of the Banjo*, 3.

40. Cooper, *The Musical Traditions of Northern Ireland and Its Diaspora*, 151.

41. Sawyers, *The Celtic Roots of Southern Music*, 16.

42. Abramson and Haskell, *Encyclopedia of Appalachia*, 1209.

43. Joe Thompson obituary, *New York Times*, March 4, 2012.

44. Alan Jabbour interview.*

45. Pen, "A Cursory Glance at Old Time Music," 4.

46. Ginny Hawker interview.

47. Paul Brown interview.

48. Pen, "A Cursory Glance at Old Time Music," 7.

49. Ritchie, *Singing Family of the Cumberlands*, 248.

50. Scoggins, *The Scotch-Irish Influence on Country Music in the Carolinas*, 105–7.

51. Ibid., 113.

52. Marshall, *Christy*, 16.

53. Garin, *Southern Appalachian Poetry*, 39.

EPILOGUE

1. Hewitson, *Tam Blake & Co.*, viii.

2. Grieve and Scott, *The Hugh MacDiarmid Anthology*.

3. Neat, *Poetry Becomes People*.

4. Ancelet and Gould, *Biography of a Cajun and Creole Music Festival*.

5. Ritchie, *Clear Waters Remembered*, liner notes, Greenhays, 1974.

6. West, *Voicing Scotland*, 13.

* Interview excerpt © Fiona Ritchie Productions/ The Thistle & Shamrock®, as heard on NPR®.

Bibliography

A bibliography of works related to the Scots, Ulster Scots, Scots-Irish, and Appalachian pioneers is potentially huge before even considering the musical directory. The following list therefore includes only works that appear in the notes, as well as others that were of special assistance in researching and inspiring *Wayfaring Strangers*. We hope that these titles will open the library door toward your own journey into this musical diaspora.

Abramson, Rudy, and Jean Haskell, eds. *Encyclopedia of Appalachia*. Knoxville: University of Tennessee Press, 2006.

Adams, Sheila Kay. *My Own True Love*. New York: Ballentine, 2005

Alarik, Scott. "Robin and Linda Williams: Home, Home on the Road." *Sing Out!* (Summer 2004): 37–43.

Ancelet, Barry Jean, and Philip Gould. *One Generation at a Time: Biography of a Cajun and Creole Music Festival*. Lafayette, La.: University of Louisiana at Lafayette Press, 2007.

Ascherson, Neal. *Stone Voices: The Search for Scotland*. London: Granta, 2002.

Aubrey, Elizabeth. *The Music of the Troubadours*. Bloomington: Indiana University Press, 1996.

Bellamy, Martin, and Bill Spalding. *The Golden Years of the Anchor Line*. Catrine, Ayrshire, Scotland: Stenlake Publishing in association with Glasgow Museums, 2011.

Blethen, Tyler H., and Curtis W. Wood Jr. *From Ulster to Carolina: The Migration of the Scotch-Irish to Southwestern North Carolina*. Raleigh: North Carolina Department of Cultural Resources, 1998.

Bogin, Magda. *The Women Troubadors*. New York: Paddington Press, 1976.

Breathnach, Brendan. *Folk Music and Dances of Ireland*. Dublin, Ireland: Mercier Press, 1971.

Bronson, Bertrand Harris. *The Ballad as Song*. Berkeley: University of California Press, 1969.

———. *The Traditional Tunes of the Child Ballads, with Their Texts, According to the Extant Records of Great Britain and North America*. 4 vols. Princeton, N.J., and Berkeley, Calif.: Princeton University and University of California Presses, 1959.

Buchan, David. *The Ballad and the Folk*. London and Boston: Routledge and K. Paul, 1972.

Buchan, John. *The Poetry of Neil Munro*. Edinburgh: William Blackwood, 1931.

Burton, Tom. "The Lion's Share: Scottish Ballads in the Southern Appalachians." File article shared with authors.

Clay, James W., Paul D. Escott, Douglas M. Orr Jr., and Alfred W. Stuart, eds. *Land of the South*. Birmingham, Ala.: Oxford House, 1989.

Cohen, Ronald D., ed. *Alan Lomax: Selected Writings, 1934–1997*. New York: Routledge, 2003.

Conway, Cecelia. *African Banjo Echoes in Appalachia: A Study of Folk Traditions*. Knoxville: University of Tennessee Press, 1995.

Cooper, David. *The Musical Traditions of Northern Ireland and Its Diaspora*. Farnham, England: Ashgate, 2009.

Craig, Carol. *The Scots' Crisis of Confidence*. Glendaruel, Scotland: Argyll, 2011.

Dickens, Charles. *American Notes for General Circulation*. London: Chapman & Hall, 1842.

Dunaway, Wayland F. *The Scotch-Irish of Colonial Pennsylvania*. Baltimore: Genealogical Publishing, 1979.

Dykeman, Wilma. *The French Broad*. Newport, Tenn.: Wakestone Books, 1955.

Erbsen, Wayne. *Old Time Songbook*. Asheville, N.C.: Native Ground, 1981.

——. *Rural Roots of Bluegrass: Songs, Stories, and History.* Asheville, N.C. : Native Ground, 2003.

Evans, Mari-Lynn, Robert Santelli, and Holly George-Warren, eds. *The Appalachians: America's First and Last Frontier.* New York: Random House, 2004.

Fischer, David Hackett. *Albion's Seed: Four British Folkways of America.* New York: Oxford University Press, 1989.

Fitzgerald, Patrick, and Brian Lambkin. *Migration in Irish History, 1607–2007.* New York: Palgrave MacMillan, 2008.

Ford, Henry Jones. *The Scotch-Irish in America.* Princeton, N.J.: Princeton University Press, 1915.

Fraser, Antonia. *Mary, Queen of Scots.* London: Weidenfield & Nicolson, 1969.

Fussell, Fred C. *Blue Ridge Music Trails of North Carolina: A Guide to Music Sites, Artists, and Traditions of the Mountains and Foothills.* Chapel Hill: University of North Carolina Press, 2013.

Garin, Marita, ed. *Southern Appalachian Poetry: An Anthology of Works by Thirty-Seven Poets.* Jefferson, N.C.: McFarland, 2008.

Gilmore, Peter. "A Fiddler Was a Great Acquisition to Any Neighborhood: Tradional Music and Ulster Culture on the Pennsylvania Frontier." *Western Pennsylvania History* 83, no. 3 (Fall 2000): 148–65.

Goring, Rosemary, ed. *Scotland: The Autobiography.* London: Penguin, 2007.

Graham, Len. *Joe Holmes: Here I Am Amongst You.* Dublin, Ireland: Four Courts Press, 2010.

Grieve, Michael, and Alexander Scott, eds. *The Hugh MacDiarmid Anthology: Poems in Scots and English.* London: Routledge & Kegan Paul, 1972.

Griffin, Patrick. *The People with No Name: Ireland, Ulster Scots, America's Scots-Irish, and the Creation of the Atlantic World.* Princeton, N.J.: Princeton University Press, 2001.

Gustavson, Kent. *Blind but Now I See: The Biography of Music Legend Doc Watson.* Boston: Sumach-Red Books, 2010.

Heaney, Seamus. *Preoccupations: Selected Prose, 1968–1978.* New York: Farrar, Straus & Giroux, 1980.

——. *Poems, 1965–1975.* New York: Noonday Press, 1988.

Hettinger, E., ed. *Springs of Music.* London: Search Press Ltd., 1995.

Hewitson, Jim. *Tam Blake & Co.: The Story of the Scots in America.* Edinburgh: Canongate, 1993.

Hofstra, Warren. *Ulster to America: The Scots-Irish Migration Experience, 1680–1830.* Knoxville: University of Tennessee Press, 2012.

Hogg, James, ed. *The Jacobite Relics of Scotland: Being the Songs, Airs, and Legends of the Adherents to the House of Stuart.* Paisley, Renfrewshire, England: Alex Gardner, 1874.

Hulme, Francis Pledger. *Mountain Measure: A Southern Appalachian Verse Notebook.* Boone, N.C.: Appalachian Consortium Press, 1975.

Hunter, James. *Scottish Exodus.* Edinburgh: Mainstream, 2005.

James, Simon. *The Atlantic Celts: Ancient People or Modern Invention?* London: British Museum Press, 1999.

Johnson, David. *Music and Society in Lowland Scotland in the Eighteenth Century.* Oxford: Oxford University Press, 1972.

Jones, Loyal. *Minstrel of the Appalachians: The Story of Bascom Lamar Lunsford*. Lexington: University Press of Kentucky, 1984.

Karpeles, Maud. *Cecil Sharp: His Life and Work*. London: Faber and Faber, 2008.

Kenneally, Brendan. *Living Ghosts: 23 Poems by Brendan Kenneally*. Audio recording. Dublin: Livia Records, 1982.

Kephart, Horace. *Our Southern Highlanders*. Knoxville: University of Tennessee Press, 1976.

Laws, G. Malcolm, Jr. *American Balladry from British Broadsides*. Philadelphia: American Folklife Society, 1957.

Leach, MacEdward, ed. *The Ballad Book*. New York: Barnes, 1975.

Leyburn, James G. *The Scotch-Irish: A Social History*. Chapel Hill: University of North Carolina Press, 1962.

Lunney, Linde. "Home and Leaving Home in Eighteenth-Century Ulster." Ulster-American Heritage Symposium presentation, Omagh, Northern Ireland, June 30, 2012.

Lunsford, Bascom Lamar. *Asheville Citizen*, May 22, 1948.

MacColl, Ewan, and Peggy Seeger. *Travellers' Songs from England and Scotland*. Knoxville: University of Tennessee Press, 1977.

Malone, Bill C. *Music from the True Vine: Mike Seeger's Life and Musical Journey*. Chapel Hill: University of North Carolina Press, 2011.

Marshall, Catherine. *Christy*. New York: Avon Books, 1967.

McHardy, Stuart. *A New History of the Picts*. Edinburgh: Luath Press, 2010.

Meyer, Duane. *The Highland Scots of North Carolina, 1732–1776*. Chapel Hill: University of North Carolina Press, 1961.

Miller, Kirby A. *Emigrants and Exiles: Ireland and the Irish Exodus to America*. New York: Oxford University Press, 1985.

Mitchell, Patricia B. *Mountain Foodways: Flavors of Old Europe on the Southern Frontier*. Chatham, Va.: Mitchell's Publications, 2000.

Moffat, Alistair. *The Great Tapestry of Scotland*. Edinburgh: Birlinn, 2013.

Moffat, Alistair, and James F. Wilson. *The Scots: A Genetic Journey*. Edinburgh: Birlinn, 2011.

Moloney, Mick. *Far from the Shamrock Shore: The Story of Irish-American Immigration through Songs*. New York: Crown Publishers, 2002.

Mott, Susan. "A History of Homesickness." Talk at TEDx, Waterloo, Ontario, 2013.

Moulden, John. "Country Music Is Ulster Music." Ulster-American Heritage Symposium presentation, Omagh, Northern Ireland, June 22, 2002.

———. "The Printed Ballad in Ireland: A Guide to the Popular Printing of Songs in Ireland, 1760–1920." Ph.D. diss. Galway: National University of Ireland, February, 2006.

———. *Thousands Are Sailing: A Brief Song History of Irish Emigration*. Portrush, Northern Ireland: Ulster Songs, 1994.

Munro, Neil. *The Poetry of Neil Munro*. Preface by John Buchan. Edinburgh: William Blackwood and Sons, 1931.

Neat, Timothy. *Poetry Becomes People (1952–2002)*. Vol. 2 of *Hamish Henderson: A Biography*. Edinburgh: Polygon, 2009.

O'Hara, Aidan. *Atlantic Gaels: Links between Donegal and the Hebrides*. Ravensport, Scotland: Islands Book Trust, 2013.

Orr, Douglas M., Jr., and Alfred W. Stuart. *The North Carolina Atlas: Portrait for a New Century*. Chapel Hill: University of North Carolina Press, 2000.

Pen, Ron. "A Cursory Glance at Old Time Music." Swannanoa Gathering essay, Warren Wilson College, July 2013.

———. *I Wonder as I Wander: The Life of John Jacob Niles*. Lexington: University Press of Kentucky, 2010.

Pepys, Samuel. *Diary of Samuel Pepys—Volume 41: 1665*. London: Bell & Hyman, 1970–83.

Quinn, Bob. *The Atlantean Irish: Ireland's Oriental and Maritime Heritage*. Dublin: Lilliput Press, 2005.

Ritchie, Fiona. *The NPR Curious Listener's Guide to Celtic Music*. New York: Berkley Publishing Group, 2004.

Ritchie, Jean. *Celebration of Life: Her Songs . . . Her Poems*. Port Washington, N.Y.: Geordie Music Publishing, 1971.

———. *Folk Songs of the Southern Appalachians*. 2nd ed. Lexington: University Press of Kentucky, 1997.

———. *Singing Family of the Cumberlands*. Lexington: University Press of Kentucky, 1955.

Rouse, Parke. *The Great Wagon Road: From Philadelphia to the South*. Richmond, Va.: Dietz Press, 1915.

Sandburg, Carl. *The American Songbag*. New York: Harcourt Brace Jovanovich, 1927.

Sanger, Keith, and Alison Kinnaird. *Tree of Strings*. Temple, Midlothian, Scotland: Kinmor Music, 1992.

Satterwhite, Emily. *Dear Appalachia: Readers, Identity, and Popular Fiction since 1878*. Lexington: University Press of Kentucky, 2011.

Sawyers, June Skinner. *The Celtic Roots of Southern Music*. Bruceton Mills, W.Va.: Unicorn Limited, 1994.

Scarborough, Dorothy. *A Song Catcher in Southern Mountains: American Folk Songs of British Ancestry*. New York: Columbia University Press, 1937.

Scoggins, Michael C. *The Scotch-Irish Influence on Country Music in the Carolinas*. Charleston, S.C.: 2013.

Sharp, Cecil J. *English Folk Songs from the Southern Appalachians*. 2 vols. Edited by Maud Karpeles. London: Oxford University Press, 1932.

Sharp, Cecil J., and Maud Karpeles. *Eighty Appalachian Folk Songs*. Winchester, Mass.: Faber and Faber, 1968.

Smith, Betty. *Jane Hicks Gentry: A Singer among Singers*. Lexington: University Press of Kentucky, 1998.

Smith, Ralph Lee, and Madeline Macneil. *Songs and Tunes of the Wilderness Road*. Mel Bay, 1999.

Sokolow, Fred. *The Carter Family Collection*. Milwaukee, Wis.: Hal Leonard, 2012.

Stewart, Albert, ed. *Appalachian Heritage: A Magazine of Southern Appalachian Life and Culture*. Hindman, Ky.: Appalachian Heritage, 1983.

Strangeways, A. H. Fox. *Cecil Sharp*. New York: Oxford University Press, 1955.

Talbott, Siobhan. "Beyond 'the Antiseptic Realm of Theoretical Economic Models': New Perspectives on Franco-Scottish Commerce and the Auld Alliance in the Long Seventeenth Century." *Journal of Scottish Historical Studies* 31 (November 2011): 149–68.

Turner, William H., and Edward J. Cabbell, eds. *Blacks in Appalachia*. Lexington: University Press of Kentucky, 1985.

Ulster Historical Foundation. *The Plantation of Ulster, 1610–1630*. Belfast, Northern Ireland, 2005.

Vann, Barry Aron. *In Search of Ulster-Scots Land*. Columbia: University of South Carolina Press, 2008.

Walker, William. *The Christian Harmony*. Philadelphia: J. Fagan & Son, 1873.

Webb, James. *Born Fighting: How the Scots-Irish Shaped America*. New York: Broadway Books, 2004.

A Welcome to Aberdeen. Aberdeen Accommodation Index, 2012.

Wells, Evelyn Kendrick. *The Ballad Tree*. New York: Ronald Press, 1950.

West, Gary. *Voicing Scotland*. Edinburgh: Luath Press, 2012.

Williamson, Allen. Joan of Arc Archive. Http://archive .joan-of-arc.org/joanofarc_Brief_Biography_html. 2006.

Winchester, Simon. *Atlantic: Great Sea Battles, Heroic Discoveries, Titanic Storms, and a Vast Ocean of a Million Stories*. New York: Harper, 2010.

Young, Frank, and David Lasky. *The Carter Family: Don't Forget This Song*. Abrams ComicArts, 2011.

Zwonitzer, Mark, with Charles Hirshberg. *Will You Miss Me When I'm Gone? The Carter Family and Their Legacy in American Music*. New York: Simon & Shuster, 2002.

Acknowledgments

Our aim to invite true "Voices of Tradition" to speak through the pages of *Wayfaring Strangers* has guided us into the company of many extraordinary people. The conversations we shared provide a first-person perspective throughout the unfolding narrative. Each contributor is profiled following the text as a measure of our gratitude. Though some of these voices are now stilled, to all of them we extend our eternal admiration and deepest thanks.

The book's art editor, Darcy Orr, applied herself diligently to the task of accumulating illustrations from both sides of the Atlantic, trawling through the centuries to compile a visual match for this epic story. She provides a review of the process and sources elsewhere in this appendix. She also journeyed with us and assisted with the collecting and research, sitting in on a number of the interviews and contributing countless ideas and valuable text proofing. Darcy joins us in thanking all the artists and photographers for their stunning contributions to this volume.

We could not have accomplished this without our families: Ian Hodgson, always available to illuminate new pathways into the language of the story, offered boundless humor, insight, and cups of tea to Fiona. Their children, Eilidh and Finley, were continually supportive during Mum's many hours at the computer, sitting close by in quiet solidarity with their homework and reading projects. Gordon, Joyce, Stewart and Ella Ritchie backed the venture all along with heartening encouragement and helpful feedback. Other family members Heather and David Abernathy and Holly Orr and Jenn Lindenauer patiently abided by Doug's and Darcy's unceasing time commitments and deadlines. Their offspring are mentioned on the dedication page. Don and Mary Hart Orr lent their ever-present support with reminders of our shared family Scottish heritage.

With ease and good nature, Margaret Kennedy endured many spells when her colleague shifted energy and time from radio to book production. The enclosed CD is a vital and valued accompaniment to *Wayfaring Strangers*. It would not have been compiled without Margaret's dedication, a logistic task she juggled with her many responsibilities managing *The Thistle & Shamrock*® radio program in the United States. Thanks also to all the musicians who made it possible for us to create, with their music, a wonderful sonic accompaniment to the text.

Seven generations of Dolly Parton's family have lived where our story unfolds, and so she is perfectly placed to reflect upon the enduring impact of this music and its tradition bearers. With her foreword, she contributed generously and enthusiastically to our book, highlighting how her family legacy lives on in her own work and musical passions. The warm and sincere support of Dolly and Grammy-winning producer Steve Buckingham reinvigorated us greatly. We are also grateful for Steve's support, along with Teresa Hughes, in assisting us with the completion of our CD project.

The Swannanoa Gathering at Warren Wilson College, now in its twenty-second year, has been a treasure trove of musician friends (many are our "Voices of Tradition") and a vital source of background information, ideas, and inspiration. We thank director Jim Magill, his staff and theme-week coordinators Julee Glaub Weems, Phil Jamison, Al Petteway, David Roth, and Julia Weatherford for their leadership in helping establish the gathering as one of the nation's premier summer music camps, drawing attendees from throughout the world to the Blue Ridge Mountain setting. Also at Warren Wilson, library director Chris Nugent kindly provided us workspace as we reconvened each summer during the Swannanoa Gathering, taking advantage of the opportunity to work shoulder to shoulder on the book.

We were extremely grateful to receive permission to

excerpt interviews with Mike Seeger and Joe Thompson, recorded in conversation with Banning Eyre for BBC Radio 3's *World Routes*, produced by Peter Meanwell. "An Appalachian Road Trip," which first broadcast on October 17, 2009, preserved the insights of these two tradition bearers not long before they passed away. Peter Meanwell was conscious of their importance in our story and kindly supportive in allowing us to add his work to our "Voices of Tradition" passages.

Three individuals tapped their expertise to carefully review particular segments of the book. Through suggestions large and small, Jack Beck (Scotland and France's Occitania), Len Graham (Ulster), and Ron Pen (the southern Appalachians) contributed greatly to the narrative. Ron was also joined by Rosanne Cash, William Ferris, Brian McNeill, Kathy Mattea, and Cerys Matthews in offering honest appraisal of our work on the book's cover. Thank you all.

Our own wayfaring journey in researching this project carried us through the Appalachians to Washington, D.C.; New York; Scotland; and Northern Ireland. Special thanks to Edinburgh's Ian Young for driving us along the back roads of Scotland and Northern Ireland, for the animated conversations en route, and for his artistry with camera and song. Always helpful were Paddy Fitzgerald and Brian Lambkin—noted authors of the emigration story in their own right—at Northern Ireland's Centre for Migration Studies and Ulster-American Folk Park. The Centre's library and the Folk Park's reservoir of "living history" images were invaluable resources. Brian and Paddy have served as hosts and are stalwarts of the biennial Ulster-American Heritage Symposium, which brings together knowledgeable scholars of the many-faceted Scots-Irish story. Nancy Groce at the American Folklife Center of the Library of Congress is a noted researcher, author, and curator. She was so helpful in guiding us through the center's vast collection of materials. Her prior work at the Smithsonian Institute Center for Folklife and Cultural Heritage is likewise much appreciated. The staff and resources at the Frontier Culture Museum in Staunton, Virginia, located along the historic route of the Great Philadelphia Wagon Road, helped us relate the story of the wayfarers' migration as they made their way into the southern Appalachians through the Shenandoah valley.

The Scotch-Irish Society of the United States of America offers a welcome to the descendants of families who followed our migratory path. As with other ancestral organizations, their volunteers help sustain one of the many rich cultural traditions of the American melting pot.

Our shared musical journey began in 1983 at the Charlotte Folk Society. To this day, it draws together devotees of Appalachian musical traditions and their Celtic roots. Our thanks to Folk Society founder Marilyn Price and countless friends who share the music with schools and civic organizations, preserving tradition, passing it on, and enriching the community.

Thanks also to NPR® and its member stations throughout the public radio system for their partnership in bringing authentic music, from a myriad of evolving traditions, to audiences across the United States and the globe. Our readers may be especially grateful for the precious airtime public radio dedicates to music from Appalachian and Celtic roots. Please remember your local stations at fundraising time.

We extend our heartfelt gratitude to special friends and organizations that provided financial and moral support that sustained our work and assisted with production costs: Joel, Marla, and Dot Adams of the Beattie Foundation; Tom Schwartz; and the Susan Marcus Collins Foundation. Warm thanks also to everyone who helped fund the enclosed CD by supporting the online North Carolina Arts Council power2give campaign.

Many friends and kindred spirits lent a hand and created a chorus of encouragement along our way. Elspeth Baillie transcribed some of the earliest interviews as the fledgling book took shape, and Richard Blomgren, a Warren Wilson marketing master, advanced the promotion of *Wayfaring Strangers* with ideas and support. Thanks also to Robin Bullock, Celtic guitar wizard and dedicated student of the music's origins; Wayne Erbsen, author, musician, and public-radio music host for old-time and bluegrass music; Arlin Geyer, whose photography artfully captures the Swannanoa Gathering each year and who contributed images to this book; Joe and Karen Holbert, music companions with a reservoir of information about Appalachian and shape-note songs; Sara James, who offered an author's wisdom, guidance, and encouragement by phone from Australia; television director and author Andrew Johnson, who first suggested our book title; and Eliza Lynn, musician, singer, songwriter, and theology student, who transcribed most of our "Voices of Tradition," tackling their diverse accents with care and enthusiasm. Along the way, she also placed a clawhammer banjo on Fiona's lap and thus provided a fitting musical retreat for writing breaks. Elizabeth Kostova, gifted best-selling author, helped point the way through the maze of the literary world. Christine Kydd and her community vocal group *Just Singin'* affirm the power of shared song each week and offer many insights into the treasure "kist" of tradition. Ever supportive, Dougie and Jenny MacLean carry the torch for Scotland's evolving music and bring it all home to their Perthshire Amber music festival. Enthusiasm for this project radiated from Beth Magill, whose virtuosity with the Celtic flute enhances and sustains the tradition, while she encourages and mentors the next generation of young musicians. Al Petteway and Amy White produce superb photographic images that capture the spirit of the mountains, and Al made excellent recordings of some of our "Voices" interviews for radio. Rowena Pomeroy transcribed interviews and provided many years of thoughtful support. Cathie Ryan's God-given voice inspires us all as she shares the magic and mystery of Irish song and folklore. Elizabeth Sanderson helped keep Fiona's Scottish office and studio running and was always available to exchange ideas on the book. Michael Scoggins, of the Center for Scotch-Irish Studies at the McCelvey Center in York, South Carolina, offers fine scholarship regarding the Scots-Irish music legacy. Peggy Seeger made possible our inspiring visit to Beacon, New York, to interview the late Pete Seeger, an afternoon etched in our minds. Steve Solnick, Warren Wilson College president, advocates and offers unfailing support for sustaining the music traditions. And finally, grateful thanks to Pete Wyrick, lifelong friend, talented book editor, and music buddy spanning the decades.

We have been blessed to work with a highly talented professional staff at the University of North Carolina Press in Chapel Hill. Our senior editor Mark Simpson-Vos possessed a sixth sense in guiding us through what he first called the "braiding and weaving" of a story line that sweeps across time and place. With skill, patience, support, and an eye on the big picture, Mark applied his fine editorial hand to the task of integrating many component parts and gave us confidence to work as coauthors. UNC Press project editor Jay Mazzocchi guided us through the copyediting and production process, and we could not have wished for a more gifted and detail-conscious editor. Kim Bryant, Heidi Perov, and their design and production colleagues brought a sharp eye to the considerable layout issues, seamlessly combining illustrations, interviews, sidebars, and text. The UNC Press marketing team—Dino Battista, Ivis Bohlen, Ellen Bush, Michael Donatelli, Jennifer Hergenroeder, Gina Mahalek, and Joanne Thomas—worked diligently with us in the far-flung promotion of the book. Finally, we appreciate the visionary leadership of UNC Press by director John Sherer and his predecessor, Kate Torrey, whose tenures have spanned the years of our work on *Wayfaring Strangers*.

The swell of a thousand voices carried this book to shore upon the waves of ten thousand tales. So we raise our parting glass to the untold nameless souls, across generations, who lived through this unique migration saga, lifting their hearts with songs, fiddle tunes, and dances. We have savored this chance to dwell among them for a while, all the better to tell their remarkable story.

Index

Page numbers in *italics* refer to illustrations.

40; troubadours' use of, 37; types of, 37–38; in Ulster, 82–84. *See also specific types*

Bain, Aly, 31

Balfa, Dewey, 284

Ballad(s): authorship of (*See* Authorship of ballads); definition of, 15, 295; of minstrels, 12–14; oldest known, 8; origins and evolution of, 7–8; printing of, 13, 14, 15, 282; psalm singing in relation to, 209; repetition in, functions of, 33, 34; scholarship on, history of, 8; subjects and words of (*See* Lyrics); travels and migration of, 16–20, 176–80; of troubadours, 8–12; tunes of (*See* Melodies); types of, 15; variation and versions of, 8, 13, 48. *See also specific types and titles of songs*

"Ballad" (Still), 3, 176

Ballad Book of John Niles (Niles), 179

Ballad Tree, The (Wells), 7, 214

Ballentine, James, 49

Ballycastle, Ireland, *114*

Banjos: in African American music, 218–20, 225–28; African origins of, 215, 218–19, 222, 228, 269; in Appalachian music, 219–20, 233, 236–37; clawhammer, 220, 222, 236–37, 265; dancing to, 233; five-string, 200, 201, 263; in old-time vs. bluegrass, 268; styles of playing, 215

"Banks of the Ohio" (ballad), 188

Bannockburn, Battle of (1314), 37, 281

Baptists: on fiddle music, 29; hymns of, 210

"Barbara Allen" (ballad), 16–20; in Child collection, 176, 179; Dylan's recording of, 16; and evolution of religious music, 212; lyrics of, 16–17; origins of, 182; Parton's recording of, x, 266; Ritchie's (Jean) performance of, 204; Seeger's (Mike) performance of, 261; travels of, 16, 282; versions of, 16, 182

Bards: definition of, 295; value of, 8, 18, 21

Barn Dance format, 264

Barra MacNeils (band), 131

Bashful Brother Oswald (Beecher Ray Kirby), xiii–xiv

Baskets, *5*

Bass, in Appalachian music, 233, 240, 268

Bàta an tSìl (boat), 103

"Báta an tSìl" (Sands and MacInnes), 76

Battlefield Band, 180

"Battle of Harlaw, The" (ballad), 36

Battles: bagpipes in, 38, 57, 82; medieval, in Aberdeenshire, 34–36. *See also specific locations and names of battles*

Bayard, Samuel P.: *Dance to the Fiddle*, 148; *Hill Country Tunes*, 148

Bayes, Coy, 259

BBC, xix, 207, 222, 229, 255

Beach Boys, the, 264

Beacon Blanket Manufacturing Company, 246

Beatles, the, 264

Beck, Jack: on Carter Family, 256; on English vs. Scottish ballads, 44; interviews with, 44, 181, 256; profile of, 289; thanks to, 321; on travels of ballads, 20; on versions of ballads, 181

Bedouins, 20

Beer, in Atlantic crossings, 121

Behan, Dominic, "The Patriot Game," 55, 56

Béla Fleck and the Flecktones, 269

Belfast, Ireland: Atlantic crossings from, 110, 113, 116; as capital of Northern Ireland, 72, 73; ethnonationalistic conflict in, 73; Harp Festival of 1792 in, 83, 100; harps in, 83; Linen Hall Library in, 80; population of, 73

Belfast Newsletter, 80

Bellowhead, 283

Bellows-blown pipes, 37–38, 82, 295

Belmont University, 269

Benandonner (mythic figure), xii

Benfield, Shoner, *275*

Bennett, Margaret: on mournfulness, 185; profile of, 289; *Salm and Soul*, 210

Berea College, 269, 274

"Bidh Clann Ulaidh" (lullaby), 64

Big ballads, 36, 47, 85

"Bile Them Cabbage Down" (song), 237

Billy Boys, 253

"Binnorie" (ballad), 28

Biograph (Dylan), 57

Birch, W.: *High Street from the County Market Place, Philadelphia*, 144; *Second Street, Philadelphia*, 144

Catholicism: in colonial Maryland, 129; in Ireland, 72–73, 74–75; Protestant Reformation challenging, 59–61

Cauld-wind pipes, 37–38, 82, 295

Cauthen, Joyce, 218

Ceilidh/ceili, 78; alternative names for, 78; definition of, 32, 78, 295; locations used for, 76–77, 78; in Pennsylvania frontier, 146–47; in Ulster, 76–79

Ceilidh house, 78

Celtic church, 18

Celtic Harp, The (the Chieftains), 100

Celtic knot, *280, 282*

Celtic languages, 18–19

Celtic nations, definition of, 18

Celts, 18; ancient musical artifacts of, 9; as cultural vs. ethnic identity, 18; origins and migration of, 18, 37; use of term, 18

Ceol mor, 82, 83

Chair, the (band), 283

Chandler, Dillard, 184, 186

Chansonniers, 12

Chapbooks, 14

"Chapel Hill Serenade" (tune), 239

Chapmen, 14

Chappell, Fred Davis, "A Prayer for Slowness," 278

Charles II (king of England, Scotland, Ireland), 129

Charles Edward Stuart (prince), 38

Charleston, S.C., 124

Charlotte, N.C., xii–xiii, xiv–xv

Charlotte Folk Music Society, xviii

Cherokee: on Appalachians as unending, 154; diet of, 170; forced removal of, 215, 217; music of, 215; place names of, 158; Scots-Irish interactions with, 216, 217; treaties with, 168

Chestnut, American, 157

Chicken Chokers, 253

Chieftains, the, 100, 183

Child, Francis James, 178–79; ballads treated as poetry by, 8, 178, 179; song collecting by, 1, 8, 15 (*See also* Child Ballads)

Child Ballads, 178–79; from Aberdeenshire, 25, 27–28, 31, 36; from Appalachians, 176, 179, 180–82; Bronson

on tunes of, 8, 179; classification system for, 178, 179; definition of, 176; in *English and Scottish Ballads*, 178; in *The English and Scottish Popular Ballads*, 8, 15, 16, 44, 178–79; Gordon's (Anna) influence on, 50, 178–79. *See also specific ballads*

Christian Harmony, The (Walker), 212

Christianity: Celtic, 18; Gaels' conversion to, 19. *See also specific denominations*

Christy (Marshall), 273

Chronology, 299–305

Churches: in Appalachians, 212; music in (*See* Religious music); in Pennsylvania frontier, 146

Church of England, 92, 129, 209, 210

Church of Scotland, 59, 92, 209

Citterns, 11

Clachan communities, 71–74

Clairseach (small harp, Ireland), 83

Clancy, Liam, 56

Clancy Brothers, 190

Clannit society, 31

Clans, Scottish: bagpipes associated with, 37, 38; in Borders, 44–45; breakup of system of, 38, 82, 83; harps and, 83, 84; intermarriage among, 69

Clarsach (small harp, Scotland), 82–84, 295

Clawhammer style, 220, 222, 236–37, 265

Clearances, Highland, 126, 127, 130–31, 216, 236

Clinch Mountain Boys, 269

Clinton, Bill, 243

Clogging, 233

Clothing: of Scots, xiii, 38, 82, 216; of Scots-Irish, 141–42

"Clough Water" (ballad), 128, 138

Clyde, Firth of, xii

Clyde, River, xi–xii

Coal (Mattea), 276

Coal mining, 272, 276, 278

"Coat of Many Colors" (Parton), 265

Cohen, John: films of, 213, 251; on "high lonesome sound," 186; interviews with, 161, 186, 218–19, 250–51; in New Lost City Ramblers, 248, 250–51; profile of, 289; as songcatcher, 209

Coilltich, 216

Phillips, Sir Thomas, 86
Phoenicians, 66
Photography, in song collecting, 194
Picking style: clawhammer, 220, 222, 236–37, 265; Cotten, 261; flat, 240, 242; in old-time vs. bluegrass, 268; Scruggs, 237, 270; thumb and finger, 242
Pickow, George, 190, 191
Picts, 18–19; harps of, 19, 83, 84; in Orkney Islands, 28
Pilgrims, emigrants as, 234, 235
Piobaireachd, 36, 38, 82, 83
Piob mor, 82
Pioneers, Scots-Irish as, 149, 168–71
Pipe bands: definition of, 296; modern-day, 38; origins of, 38
Pipes. *See* Bagpipes
"Piping Live!" Festival, 38
Place, sense of: in Appalachians, 174–76, 191; in Ulster, 90–91, 141
Place names: in Appalachians, 158; in Ireland and Scotland, 90–91
Plantation of Ulster, 23, *59*, 61, 69–74, 86
Planxties, 84, 296
Plymouth colony, 110
Poems, ballads treated as, 8, 178, 179
Poland: emigration to U.S. from, 124; Scottish emigration to, 70
Poole, Charlie, 245–46
"Poor Old Woman, The" (tune), 148
"Poor Orphan Child" (song), 258
Portative organs, 11
Portpatrick, Scotland, 64
Portrush, Ireland, Atlantic crossings from, 110
Ports: for Atlantic crossings, *97*, 110–16, 124–25; for North Channel crossings, 70. *See also specific cities*
Potato famine, 94, 121, 124, 126, 130, 143
Poteen, 78, 89
"Prayer for Slowness, A" (Chappell), 278
Presbyterianism: in Appalachians, 160, 171, 193; music of, in U.S., 209–11, 212–13; in North Carolina, 125; in Pennsylvania, 125; in Scots-Irish identity, 144; in Ulster, 61, 70, 74–75, 80–81, 92, 144

Presley, Andrew, xvii, 231
Presley, Elvis, xvii, 230–31, 264
"Pretty Peggy-O" (Dylan), 56
"Pretty Polly" (ballad), 195, 215
"Pretty Saro" (ballad), 134
Primitive Characters, 253
"Printed Ballad in Ireland, The" (Moulden), 101
Printing of ballads: broadsides, 14, 15, 282; as death of ballads, 13
Profiles, 289–94
Profitt, Frank, 196
Promised land, U.S. as, 91, 110, 128
Protestantism, in Ireland, 72–73. *See also specific denominations*
Protestant Reformation, 59–61
Protest songs, 276–77
Psalmody, definition of, 209, 296
Psalms: in Ulster, 80–81; in U.S., 209
Psaltries, 11, *12*
Public Radio International (PRI), xiv
Purser, John: on ancient musical artifacts, 9; interviews with, 9, 33, 66–67, 156–57; on "King Orfeo," 33; profile of, 292–93; on surviving medieval ballads, 16, 33

Quakers: hymns of, 210; in Philadelphia, 92, 128–29, 133, 141–43
Quarantines, after Atlantic crossings, 133–34
Queen, James Fuller, *The Power of Music*, *147*
Quinn, Bob, *The Atlantean Irish*, 20
"Quite Early Morning" (Seeger), 262
Quota Act of 1921 (U.S.), 125

Raconteurs, 187
Radio: Appalachian music on, 253–54, 255, 259, 260, 264; rise and influence of, 253–54, 255
Raeburn, Sir Henry, *31*
"Raggle Taggle Gypsy, The" (ballad), 79
Rainey, Valentine, 81
Rainwater, Cedric, 270
"Rambling Boys of Pleasure, The" (song), 91
"Rambling Irishman, The" (ballad), 75, 94, 102, 117

Second Treble.

CD Notes

The *Wayfaring Strangers* CD offers our living soundtrack for the migration saga chronicled in the book. As our "Voices of Tradition," many of the featured artists have already spoken from earlier pages. Now it is time to listen to their music, a sonic accompaniment well worthy of the story.

1. "Barbara Allen," by Dolly Parton with Mairéad Ní Mhaonaigh and Altan.

In his famous seventeenth-century diary, Samuel Pepys speaks of hearing the actress Elizabeth Knepp singing the "little Scotch song of Barbary Allen." This is the earliest existing reference to the song, still well loved on both sides of the Atlantic. After crossing the ocean, "Barbara Allen" (Child 84) appeared on American broadsides and in songbooks such as the *Forget Me Not Songster* (along with "The Farmer's Curst Wife," track 12). Country music icon and songwriting legend Dolly Parton acknowledged the ballad's transatlantic journey and timeless appeal in her live recording of original and traditional songs. Trading verses in English matched to Irish ones sung by Mairéad Ní Mhaonaigh of the Irish traditional band Altan, Parton creates a magical pairing that encapsulates the *Wayfaring Strangers* music migration.

2. "It Was a' for Our Rightfu' King" by Dougie MacLean.

Beginning in 1610, King James VI (Scotland) and I (England) decided to pacify his kingdom in Ireland by "planting" English-speaking Presbyterians there. Border Scots and northern English, scraping a living from depleted lands, were offered arable farmland. People had been navigating back and forth between Scotland and Ireland for thousands of years, but the Plantation policy created a substantial Scottish presence in Ulster and set off waves of migration. When James II was deposed, Jacobite Scots

rallied in Ulster and Scotland to support his cause. Contemporary Scots songwriter Dougie MacLean sings these verses, set by Robert Burns to a traditional tune he had collected. They tell of yet another farewell to Scotland.

3. "Dh'fhalbh Mo Nighean Chruinn Donn" by Colum Sands and Maggie MacInnes.

The Scots in Ulster began settling into life in their new land, but the memories were still fresh of a home across the sea. For some, the connections were restored by occasional return visits to family and friends. The majority never again set foot on their ancestral land, however, and some were missed evermore by those they left behind. Scots Gaelic singer Maggie MacInnes sings a traditional Hebridean song, "Dh'fhalbh Mo Nighean Chruinn Donn" ("My Lovely Brown-Haired Girl Has Gone"). These verses tell of a man missing his lost sweetheart, who has crossed the sea to live in Newry, near the mountains of Mourne. She may have married for better prospects in Ulster, but sorrow lingers on both shores.

4. "Benton's Jig/Benton's Dream" by Patrick Street.

There had been a modest flow of emigration from Ulster to America before 1718; in that year, it began in earnest. An estimated 250,000 people departed Ulster for America between 1718 and 1800, and 85 percent were Ulster Scots emigrating into Philadelphia and the Delaware valley ports. Onboard the emigrant vessels, music and dance became a mainstay of passengers' lives at sea, and the fiddle accompanied many an emigrant's Atlantic crossing. Irish band Patrick Street, with fiddler Kevin Burke and Jacky Daly on accordion, capture the spirit of the voyage. The music shifts from Irish-jig time to Appalachian old-time as Daly's "Benton's Jig" blends with North Carolina fiddler Benton Flippen's composition "Benton's Dream" in the more-syncopated and rhythmic Appalachian fiddle style, which evolved from New World banjo-fiddle pairings. Along with Tommy Jarrell, Benton Flippen was one of the last of the early twentieth-century fiddlers playing in the venerated "Round Peak" style concentrated in Surry County, North Carolina.

5. "The Rambling Irishman" by Len Graham and Brian ÓhAirt.

An assortment of threads and textures colored the musical fabric of Ulster as smaller ethnic groups were attracted there by the linen industry—Welsh, French Huguenots, and English Plantation settlers among them. So over time, people embraced other forms of singing, including two or more a capella singers joined in unison (without harmony). This became a hallmark of the Ulster singing style that the Scots-Irish carried to the New World. Although homesickness was often the theme in new songs, other verses give the impression of maintaining a brave face as thoughts turned to anticipating the life that lay ahead. Ulsterman Len Graham and Brian ÓhAirt of the Irish American group Bua sing "The Rambling Irishman" in the traditional Ulster unison style. This emigrant's song, also known as "The Banks of Sweet Lough Erne," traveled throughout the United States. In 1961 Ozarks ballad singer Bertha Lauderdale sang it for Max Hunter, who included it in his collection.

6. "The Winding River Roe" by Cara Dillon.

The first arrivals in Pennsylvania held clear images of home in their minds and fond memories of family close to their hearts. Not all Scots-Irish immigrants were able to settle, and their lingering homesickness sometimes found an outlet in sad songs. Especially poignant are the verses avowing that one day, the immigrant would return to the old home place. If they accepted that it would not happen in the physical realm, they might yet hope for return from exile in the spirit world and, until then, in their dreams. Irish vocalist Cara Dillon originally comes from Dungiven, County Derry-Londonderry, near the spot where the Rivers Roe, Owenreagh, and Owenbeg meet at the foot of Benbradagh. The gentle countryside provides the setting for this sad song, arranged by Cara and her husband and musical partner, Sam Lakeman.

7. "The Gypsy Laddie" by Jack Beck (paired with track 8).

Jack Beck notes that of the top ten ballads collected in southern Appalachia, seven were Scottish, and the second most commonly sung was "The Gypsy Laddie." He enjoys examining what happens to songs as they travel, and how the magical elements in this Scottish version are brought back down to earth in Appalachia. Emerging hundreds of years ago in Scotland, the ballad (Child 200) is known throughout the British Isles, Ireland, and North America. It is associated with the Ayrshire house of Cassilis (pronounced "Cassels") and sometimes held to be based on a true elopement incident, although it is probably an amalgamation of historical strands. The story of handsome gypsies enthralling a noble lady with their sweet singing has made it very popular with the Scots Travelling folk. More than a hundred versions have been collected in Britain, Ireland, and North America. Jack Beck, Sara Grey, and Anne Neilson were asked to create a presentation illustrating the Scottish-American ballad connection, which they performed at Glasgow's Celtic Connections Festival and then toured in the United States from New York to South Carolina. This recording, from Jack's private collection, was from the first such event at Auchtermuchty town hall in 1997.

8. "Gypsy Davy" by Julee Glaub (paired with track 7).

The song that originated in Scotland as "The Gypsy Laddie" or "The Earl o' Cassillis Lady" traveled through Ireland as the "Raggle Taggle Gypsy" or "Seven Yellow Gypsies" and settled on American shores as "Black Jack Davy" and "Gypsy Davy." It is undoubtedly one of the most popular and well traveled of the ballads. The song's narrative remains strong across the miles, although by the time it evolved into "Gypsy Davy," it had moved among many cultures from other parts of the world, both old and new. Woody Guthrie recorded "Gypsy Davy," and Bob Dylan included a version of "Blackjack Davey" on *Good As I Been to You* (1992). Julee Glaub (Weems) draws upon her North Carolina roots and Irish travel experiences in her music. Pete Sutherland accompanies Julee's singing and offers a clawhammer banjo welcome to the southern Appalachians for "Gypsy Davy."

9. "Pretty Saro" by John Doyle.

Newfound freedom did not always come with immediate benefits. House and land ownership could be a long time coming to the Scots-Irish. Families struggling to find farmland and newly released indentured servants would dream of gaining the privileged "freeholder" status mentioned in the old ballad "Pretty Saro." The term gives a clue to the British Isles origins of the ballad, originating in early seventeenth-century England. Early twentieth-century songcatchers, including Dorothy Scarborough, rediscovered it in the North Carolina mountains, where it is still widely sung. Bob Dylan had recorded the song in his *Self Portrait* sessions in 1970, but it did not make the final cut for the album. It was eventually released on Dylan's box set *Another Self Portrait* in 2013. Singer and guitarist John Doyle—Irish native and Asheville, North Carolina, resident—bestows a dreamy quality upon his arrangement and notes the similarity between "Pretty Saro" and the Irish song "Bunclody."

10. "Indian Whoop" by James Bryan and Carl Jones.

One of the very earliest American fiddle tunes, this one was included in G. P. Knauff's *Virginia Reels*, an old collection of southern fiddle music with many tunes of Scots-Irish origin. Mississippi string band Hoyt Ming and his Pep Steppers recorded the tune named "Indian War Whoop" in the 1920s with Rozelle Ming flatfoot dancing to the rhythm. Historians of old-time music sometimes point to this tune as an example of "hollering," as fiddlers would often shout along with the high notes at the end of phrases, with each player having a trademark whoop. A version of the tune was recorded by John Hartford for inclusion in the Coen brothers' film *O Brother, Where Art Thou?* From Alabama, James Bryan is held to be the finest southern-style fiddler of his generation and was inducted into the Alabama Music Hall of Fame. He has taught on the staffs of the Augusta Heritage Center and the Swannanoa Gathering Old Time Week. Songwriter-musician Carl Jones, joining on guitar, has also taught at music camps around the United States and internationally. The two played together with Norman and Nancy Blake in the Rising Fawn String Ensemble.

11. "The Devil and the Farmer's Wife" by Alan Burke (paired with track 12).

Versions of this lively ballad (Child 278) have been traced back to the early seventeenth century throughout the British Isles and Ireland. Usually known as "The Farmer's Curst Wife," "Kellyburnbraes" is a Scottish variant collected by Robert Burns for *The Scots Musical Museum, Vol IV*. Many folktales in almost every European country tell of a wife so fierce that she terrorized the devil himself. Seosamh Ó hÉanaí (Joe Heaney), the great Irish traditional singer from Connemara, County Galway, was Alan Burke's source for this version, which features Alan Burke on vocals, guitar, and bodhrán; Tim Potts on bouzouki and tin whistle; Giles Lewin on fiddle; and Kevin Rowsome on uilleann pipes.

12. "The Farmer's Curst Wife" by Pete Seeger (paired with track 11).

The tale of a fearsome wife who terrifies even demons is ancient and widespread, appearing in a sixth-century Hindu fable collection, the *Panchatantra*. It seems to have traveled westward through the Middle East into Europe and onward to America early in the Scots-Irish emigration era. As with "Gypsy Davy" (track 8), the American version of the tale lightens the story up a bit, removing references to the terrifying spouse's more violent acts toward the demons she encounters. Pete Seeger's arrangement locates the ballad firmly within America's folk song canon, his trademark long-neck banjo setting contrasting with the more urgent Irish instrumentation of track 11.

13. "Young Hunting/Elzig's Farewell" by Sheila Kay Adams.

Francis James Child cataloged "Young Hunting" as number 68 in his collection. English variants of the song titled "Earl Richard" and "The Proud Girl" remain closely tied to the original Scottish version, all detailing the violent act of a scorned woman. The song appears in Motherwell's *Minstrelsy of the Scottish Border*, so it would have likely been in the repertoire of Scots who migrated to the Ulster Plantations. In all the Scottish versions, a bird witnesses the murder, but it seems to have flown before the song arrived on U.S. shores, where it is often sung as "Henry Lee" and "Love Henry." Sheila Kay Adams of Sodom, North Carolina, sings the version she learned from her beloved Granny Dell, a version that is true to the lineage of her kinfolk's seven generations of ballad singers. She accompanies herself on banjo, with Josh Goforth on fiddle and John Doyle on guitar. They slip into a West Virginia tune from the Civil War era, "Elzig's (or Elzic's) Farewell," that has sometimes been described as sounding like an old bagpipe tune.

14. "Black Is the Colour" by Sara Grey.

Musicologist and collector Alan Lomax asserted this song's Scottish origins, calling the American versions "re-makes." John Jacob Niles retained a modal setting when he contributed one of its more popular melodies. When African American spiritual singing spilled over from plantations, it flowed throughout other regions, including the Appalachians. Sara Grey identifies this song as a Scottish "parlour ballad" that traveled in and out of the African American tradition. She based her version on the singing of Dellie Norton—"Granny Dell" to Sheila Kay Adams—feeling that her treatment of the song was strongly influenced by the African American singing style. Kieron Means joins Sara on guitar, vocals.

15. "Old George's Square" by Jean Ritchie.

This song is often known as "The Girl I Left Behind" and is found on both sides of the Atlantic. As with other songs, the U.S. versions often downgrade the "wealthy squire" to a "wealthy farmer." Bob Dylan based his version on the singing of Woody Guthrie and recorded it for Oscar Brand's radio show in 1961. Len Graham learned it in Ulster as "My Parents Reared Me Tenderly," and Scottish actress and singer Isla Cameron recorded the song on her eponymous 1966 album as "My Parents Raised Me Tenderly." She learned her version from Kentucky's Jean Ritchie, an example of the song tradition flowing in both directions. Jean has always taken Old George's Square to be the famous landmark in the heart of Glasgow, and she delivers the song here in the classic Appalachian style, with its trademark vocal hook at the end of some lines.

16. "Single Girl, Married Girl" by Atwater Donnelly.

This early frontier favorite has many relatives, including the Irish song "Do You Love and Apple" and "Still I Love Him," collected by Ewan MacColl and Peggy Seeger for their anthology *Travellers' Songs from England and Scotland*. The Carter Family made the song famous as their "Single Girl, Married Girl," released in 1928 on a 78-rpm record. They rerecorded it during the last months of Sara and A. P. Carter's marriage in 1935 at a slow pace, with Sara Carter singing at a much lower pitch. Aubrey Atwater and Elwood Donnelly explore the song in one of several collections of traditional American and Celtic songs and Carter Family favorites, many collected during their performances throughout Appalachia. With Aubrey Atwater on Appalachian dulcimer, the song is very much at home.

17. "Shady Grove" by Doc Watson and David Holt.

The English ballad "Matty Groves," dating from the seventeenth century or even earlier, describes an adulterous tryst that ends in murder. When Francis James Child collected the ballad, he listed it as "Little Musgrave and Lady Barnard" (Child 81). On its transatlantic travels, the melody ended up covering more ground than the ballad narrative; "Shady Grove," based upon the "Matty Groves" melody, arose in the southern Appalachians around the time of the Civil War. The popular American descendant is noteworthy for its many lyric variations, all in a gentler, brighter vein than the root ballad. Doc Watson sang it as a courtship song to his wife, Rosa Lee, in the early 1940s when he was perfecting his signature flat-pick guitar style. This version, with David Holt partnering on clawhammer banjo, was recorded live at the Diana Wortham Theatre in Asheville, North Carolina, in 2001.

18. "Willie's Lady" by Anaïs Mitchell and Jefferson Hamer.

Ballads flowed freely between Sweden, Denmark, and Norway and crossed into Aberdeenshire in Scotland's North East. Scandinavian variants with similar plots to "Willie's Lady" mark this ballad as an example of those music migrations, and it has all the hallmarks of classic North East balladry. James Francis Child collected only one version of this ballad from Scotland (Child 6), but he cites a few other stories in his notes, including tales in "classic mythology" where women are prevented from giving birth. Child's source was Anna Gordon, better known as Mrs. Brown of Falkland, who held one of the most significant and oldest ballad collections drawn from her family's oral tradition. With all their twisting story lines and hypnotic melodies, the Child Ballad canon captivates each generation of musicians in turn. "Willie's Lady" is one of many that are enduringly popular in this way, having been recorded by English folksinger and guitarist Martin Carthy, among others. Attracted by the archetypes and psychological dramas, Anaïs Mitchell and Jefferson Hamer are eager to take the material to new audiences in the United States by reclaiming the songs in their own voices and allowing the stories to build in their vocal/guitar duo.

19. "Wayfaring Stranger/British Field March" by Timothy Cummings.

More than a few sets of bagpipes must have crossed the ocean from Scotland and Ulster, but they never became established on the Pennsylvania frontier or in southern Appalachia. Most theories explaining this settle around the timing of Scots-Irish emigration: in seventeenth-century Ireland, Oliver Cromwell's troops destroyed many sets of pipes, while the instrument was sidelined after the 1745 defeat of the clans in Scotland. However, pioneers would

surely also have found them difficult to maintain in the New World, and pipe makers would have needed access to materials and some community of players to sustain their craft. So in Appalachia, it was left to fiddlers, dulcimer players, and banjo pickers to express the drones and modal moods of pipe music. Timothy Cummings is committed to reconnecting the musical traditions of Appalachia and Scottish piping, recording what may be the first bagpipe album devoted to Appalachian music. He plays our book's signature tune, "Wayfaring Stranger." The ancient melody of "The Dowie Dens of Yarrow" (Child 214) is held to be the source spring of a tune stream that flows through this early nineteenth-century spiritual. Alan Jabbour collected the "British Field March" from Henry Reed. According to folklore, this tune was played as British soldiers retreated from the Battle of New Orleans in 1815. Attuned to the Scottish Lowland heritage of the Scots-Irish, Tim plays Border pipes, with Pete Sutherland on clawhammer banjo and Caleb Elder on fiddle—the sound of old-time piping.

20. "The Parting Glass" by Al Petteway and Amy White.

Still popular today on both sides of the Atlantic, "The Parting Glass" was well known in Scotland and Ireland long before Robert Burns's farewell anthem "Auld Lang Syne" came into the popular repertoire. As an eighteenth-century broadside, it would likely have been distributed among the inns and taverns close to the quays where the immigrant sailing ships were docked. Before new arrivals went their separate ways, they may well have raised a parting glass to this song. The oldest buildings on Philadelphia's Market Street might yet echo with their voices, joined in chorus before they headed out to the Pennsylvania frontier or down the Great Philadelphia Wagon Road. We raise our own glasses, too, dedicating this song to the hardy souls who lived through an epic migration saga and left an enduring legacy in American music. Guitarist Al Petteway and vocalist Amy White capture the bittersweet farewell, recorded high in the heart of North Carolina's Blue Ridge Mountains.

Wayfaring Strangers Track List

A FIONA RITCHIE PRODUCTION FOR THE UNIVERSITY OF NORTH CAROLINA PRESS

1. "Barbara Allen" by Dolly Parton with Mairéad Ní Mhaonaigh and Altan (traditional, arranged by Dolly Parton), from *Heartsongs: Live from Home* ℗ Notice and "Under License from SONY Custom Marketing Group, SONY MUSIC ENTERTAINMENT." 1994. Used by permission.

2. "It Was a' for Our Rightfu' King" by Dougie MacLean (traditional, arranged by Dougie MacLean), from *Craigie Dhu*, courtesy of Dunkeld Records ℗ © 1983. Used by permission.

3. "Dh'fhalbh Mo Nighean Chruinn Donn" by Colum Sands and Maggie MacInnes (traditional, arranged by Maggie MacInnes and Colum Sands), from *The Seedboat (Bàta an tSìl)*, courtesy of Spring Records © Elm Grove Music 2010. Used by permission.

4. "Benton's Jig/Benton's Dream" by Patrick Street (Jacky Daly/Benton Flippen), from *No. 2 Patrick Street*, courtesy of Green Linnet Records ℗ © 1988. Used by permission.

5. "The Rambling Irishman" by Len Graham and Brían ÓhAirt (traditional), from *In Two Minds*, courtesy of Graham & ÓhAirt 2012. Used by permission.

6. "The Winding River Roe" by Cara Dillon (traditional, arranged by Cara Dillon and Sam Lakeman), from *Sweet Liberty*, courtesy of Rough Trade Records ℗ © 2003. Used by permission.

7. "The Gypsy Laddie" by Jack Beck (traditional), from a private recording, courtesy of the artist. Used by permission.

8. "Gypsy Davy" by Julee Glaub (traditional, arranged by Julee Glaub), from *Blue Waltz*, courtesy of Julee Glaub © 2004. Used by permission.

9. "Pretty Saro" by John Doyle (traditional, arranged by John Doyle), from *Evening Comes Early*, courtesy of Shanachie Entertainment Corp. ℗ 2001. Used by permission.

10. "Indian Whoop" by James Bryan and Carl Jones (traditional), from *Two Pictures*, courtesy of Martin Records ℗ © 1995. Used by permission.

11. "The Devil and the Farmer's Wife" by Alan Burke (traditional, arranged by Alan Burke and Tim Potts), from a private recording, courtesy of the artist. Used by permission.

12. "The Farmer's Curst Wife" by Pete Seeger (traditional), from *American Favorite Ballads, Vol. 2*, SFW40151, courtesy of Smithsonian Folkways Recordings ℗ © 2003. Used by permission.

13. "Young Hunting/Elzig's Farewell" by Sheila Kay Adams (traditional, arranged by Sheila Kay Adams), from *All the Other Fine Things*, courtesy of Granny Dell Records © 2004 Sheila Kay Adams. Used by permission.

14. "Black Is the Colour" by Sara Grey (traditional, arranged by Sara Grey, Kieron Means), from *Sandy Boys*, courtesy of Fellside Recordings ℗ © 2009. Used by permission.

15. "Old George's Square" by Jean Ritchie (traditional), from *High Hills and Mountains*, courtesy of Greenhays Recordings ℗ © 1998. Used by permission.

16. "Single Girl, Married Girl" by Atwater Donnelly (traditional) from *The Blackest Crow*, courtesy of Rabbit Island Music ℗ © 2004 Aubrey Atwater and Elwood Donnelly. Used by permission.

17. "Shady Grove" by Doc Watson and David Holt (traditional, arranged by Doc Watson and David Holt), from *Legacy*, courtesy of High Windy Audio ℗ © 2002. Used by permission.

18. "Willie's Lady" by Anaïs Mitchell and Jefferson Hamer (traditional, arranged by Anaïs Mitchell and Jefferson Hamer), from *Child Ballads*, courtesy of Wilderland Records ℗ © 2013. Used by permission.

19. "Wayfaring Stranger/British Field March" by Timothy Cummings (traditional, adapted and arranged by Timothy Cummings, Caleb Elder, and Pete Sutherland), from *The Piper in the Holler*, courtesy of Birchen Music/ Timothy Cummings ℗ © 2012. Used by permission.

20. "The Parting Glass" by Al Petteway and Amy White (traditional, arranged by Al Petteway), from *High in the Blue Ridge*, courtesy of Fairewood Studios ℗ © 2011. Used by permission.